Praise for **Consulting**

"*Consulting That Matters* showcases contributions by prominent scholars who convey their expert knowledge about various kinds of consulting, their appreciation for the critical importance of communication processes, and their personal experiences that illustrate precisely different challenges and answers that they provided. It blends theoretical understanding and personal experiences very well....

Consulting That Matters covers an impressive range of different types of consulting and how consulting practices vary across those types. This book is a 'must' for individuals interested in learning about consulting processes, steps involved in different consulting environments, experiences and stories about consulting, and how to adapt to various problematic situations."

Daniel J. Canary, University of Utah

"*Consulting That Matters* focuses on making a difference with our work whether we are scholars, practitioners, or both. The chapters and cases in this book effectively integrate the scholar's ability to bring theory and research to consulting engagements with the values and frames of the consultant. The discussion of 'making a difference' through transforming practices and engagements is critically important for all of us."

Pam Shockley-Zalabak, Chancellor, University of Colorado, Colorado Springs

"The authors have developed a 'must-have' resource for communication scholars who already apply or wish to apply their rich theoretical scholarship to a broad range of communication consultation opportunities situated in an increasingly complex society. The book offers a strong theoretical basis for communication consulting, rich case examples, theories informing practice and the reverse, and useful 'how-to' sections for those wanting to begin serving as communication consultants and/or those wishing to sharpen their skills. The rich overview of communication consulting featured in Part I is worth the price of the book."

Paul Lakey, Past Chair, Training and Development Division,
National Communication Association; Professor, Abilene Christian University

"At exactly the moment you think you know what you're doing, you need to read something smart to shake you up and challenge what you believe. Even better when the book leads to new ideas and insights worth putting into practice. This is one of those books. You can't borrow my copy. I won't be done with it for several years."

Randall Stutman, Managing Partner, Capitol Reef Advisors

"This fabulous book is written by a who's who of communication scholars. It does an excellent job of integrating the scholarly and the practical."

Peter A. Andersen, Professor Emeritus, San Diego State University

"This book is a 'must-have' for anyone interested in or practicing action research/consulting. It provides the perfect blend of history/context, theory/practice, and serves a comprehensive guide to action research and consulting practice. I can't imagine *not owning* this book! If you have ever considered consulting as a way to augment your scholarship, are a consultant interested in reinforcing your work with what is emerging from the research literature, or are curious about what consulting involves, you'll want to read this work from the top scholars in communication. These scholars are well-known for their contributions to theory *and* their successes in consulting. Each chapter is a gem!"

Terre H. Allen, California State University, Long Beach

"As a communication consultant, coach, and trainer for more than four decades, I found *Consulting That Matters* to both introduce practical communication skills and techniques for use in a variety of environments, then to validate each with a copious review of salient research. This is a must-read for anyone aspiring to strengthen their capabilities as a practitioner of communication consulting."

Dennis Becker, Founder and Senior Coaching Partner,
The Speech Improvement Company, Inc.

"An impressive array of communication scholar/consultants attest to the reciprocal relationship between theory and practice in this exciting contribution to the field. Using both short examples and extended case studies, the contributors explain how theory informed their consulting work in the field, which, in turn, led to new understandings about the theory. *Consulting That Matters: A Handbook for Scholars and Practitioners* will energize your consulting, your teaching, and your research."

Deborah Socha McGee, College of Charleston

Consulting That Matters

This book is part of the Peter Lang Media and Communication list.
Every volume is peer reviewed and meets
the highest quality standards for content and production.

PETER LANG
New York • Bern • Frankfurt • Berlin
Brussels • Vienna • Oxford • Warsaw

Consulting That Matters

A HANDBOOK FOR SCHOLARS & PRACTITIONERS

JENNIFER H. WALDECK
DAVID R. SEIBOLD
EDITORS

PETER LANG
New York • Bern • Frankfurt • Berlin
Brussels • Vienna • Oxford • Warsaw

Library of Congress Cataloging-in-Publication Data

Names: Waldeck, Jennifer H., editor. | Seibold, David R., editor.
Title: Consulting that matters: a reader for scholars and practitioners /
edited by Jennifer H. Waldeck, David R. Seibold.
Description: New York: Peter Lang, 2015. |
Includes bibliographical references and index.
Identifiers: LCCN 2015032073| ISBN 9781433127700 (hardcover: alkaline paper) |
ISBN 9781433127694 (paperback: alkaline paper) | ISBN 9781453917183 (e-book)
Subjects: LCSH: Consulting firms. | Communication—Social aspects. |
Interpersonal communication. | Teams in the workplace.
Classification: LCC HD69.C6 .C65556 2015 | DDC 001—dc23
LC record available at http://lccn.loc.gov/2015032073

Bibliographic information published by **Die Deutsche Nationalbibliothek**.
Die Deutsche Nationalbibliothek lists this publication in the "Deutsche
Nationalbibliografie"; detailed bibliographic data are available
on the Internet at http://dnb.d-nb.de/.

Cover image: ©iStock.com/Candice Cusack

The paper in this book meets the guidelines for permanence and durability
of the Committee on Production Guidelines for Book Longevity
of the Council of Library Resources.

Contents

Preface

Each year, thousands of consulting contracts are awarded by organizations to experts that help them with challenges involving people, processes, technologies, goals, resource allocation, decision making, problem solving, and more. These experts—consultants—diagnose problems, recommend solutions, facilitate interventions, and evaluate outcomes. Many times, these consultants are academics with some special expertise in the area of the organization's concerns; other times, they are employees of large or small professional consulting firms who do this type of work on a full-time basis. Although consulting is often associated with the "corporate world," consultants also provide consulting services to federal, state, and local governments; nonprofit organizations; healthcare facilities; educational institutions; start-up firms; and those enterprises specializing in creative, technical, intellectual, and manufacturing work.

Over the past thirty years, the editors of this volume, who are college professors, have engaged in a variety of consulting activities that have enriched our teaching and scholarship in significant ways. Simultaneously, we have encountered colleagues who resisted consulting because they did not view it as an intellectually enriching activity, and full-time practitioners who sought greater credibility and substance in all they did. The former group failed to realize the potential of the reciprocal relationship between scholarship and action. The latter group wanted to do what they were doing, but better. Whether they were delivering training, writing curriculum, developing leaders, building teams, designing effective systems and processes, mediating conflict, helping organizations facilitate change, or any number of other activities, these professionals expressed a hunger for consulting frameworks that were grounded in some evidence pointing to their appropriateness or potential for positive outcomes. The first editor of this volume, Jennifer Waldeck, for example, has partnered with two professional consulting firms that were interested in a research-based approach to performance improvement. She introduced them to the classic and state-of-the-art findings and theoretical perspectives for better understanding the types of challenges their clients faced, and which guided the generation of solutions and productive plans.

In our view, theory and research are the blueprints for successful action within organizations. Believing strongly in this premise, and facing a scarcity of literature pointing to the value of a scholarly approach to consulting with respect to organizational problems, strategy, and opportunities, the origins of this project took shape. We knew that if we could assemble the right group of scholar/practitioners to write about their work and the issues associated with consulting from a research and theoretically based perspective, we could shed light on the reciprocal relationship between scholarship and the applied practice of consulting. We believed we had an opportunity to influence the thinking of both scholars and full-time practitioners that *consulting can matter* in innumerable ways when this approach is taken. The authors represented in this volume, and the manner in which we have assembled and organized their work, speak to both the ways in which consulting matters. These authors have a vast expanse and depth of both knowledge and experience. They write with conviction and eloquence, using plenty of real examples drawn from their own and others' experiences. They claim the critical importance of using research and theory in one's consulting work, and provide ample evidence with compelling illustrations from a wide variety of organizational types.

Further, the scholar-consultants featured here demonstrate the importance of careful observation and critical analysis of the environments in which they consult, and the constant application of ethical frames for determining how to proceed or whether to continue the consulting relationship at all. Numerous authors in this book share stories of declining or ending (potentially lucrative) consulting engagements based on mismatched values and beliefs or conflicting ethical concerns. The accounts here demonstrate the necessity of a healthy respect for how consulting actions and outcomes impact all stakeholders in a system, from front-line employees to upper management to customers, clients, and vendors (and everyone in between).

The authors' chapters also illuminate how their collaborations with their clients are typically interactive in a classic communicative and sociological sense; the nature of the relationships among consultants and members of their client organizations are the foundations of all they are able to accomplish in their work together. This rigorous and collaborative approach to consulting ensures it addresses actual (rather than superficial or perceived) organizational challenges, increases the likelihood of success, and provides consultants with justification for what they do and why they do it. Working from a solid theoretical framework and thoughtfully allowing empirical knowledge to guide our decisions during consulting makes consultants credible, effective, and valuable to the organizations which seek their help.

Thus, across four parts and 21 chapters, this volume provides both full-time practitioners and scholars interested in exploring the applied implications of their expertise with in-depth exposure to:

- The external consultant's role in analyzing, diagnosing, and addressing organizational challenges
- The importance of using theoretical frameworks and empirical research findings for substantive consulting interventions
- How to identify and make a productive connection with prospective clients
- The range of needs assessment and diagnostic tools that consultants employ
- A variety of methodological designs for consulting interventions
- The skills required for effective consulting, such as persuasion, instructional design, facilitation, coaching, training and pedagogy, research ability, strategic planning, and more
- Specific consulting activities including training, leadership development, organizational development and change, and research
- Why and how new media and communication technologies matter in the consulting process
- How to evaluate consulting outcomes

More specifically, Part I, *Creating a Consulting Identity That Matters,* discusses a range of issues for scholar-consultants to examine:

- What exactly is consulting?
- Why would a client want to hire me?
- What does my background/my degree/my research area have to offer potential clients?
- What is the role of scholarship—theory, research, and data analysis skills—in consulting?
- How can I maximize the chances that my academic colleagues will view my consulting work as legitimate, meaningful, and related to my scholarship?
- Will consulting work distract me from my research?
- Can consulting help me with my research?
- Is it ethical for me to consult?

The chapters in Part I offer an introduction and framework to the importance of developing an epistemological paradigm for consulting work; working from a theoretical perspective; appreciating and using a wide range of methodological approaches and a working knowledge of the scientific method; as well as the ability to read, interpret, and draw upon theory and research at all stages of the consulting process.

Part II, *Creating a Consulting Experience That Matters: The Groundwork,* addresses issues critical to:

- Assessing the consulting context, setting, and situation before taking action
- Understanding clients and building trusting, collaborative relationships with them
- The role of stakeholders in understanding an organization and its challenges and opportunities
- Methods for identifying issues of interest, defining needs and problems, and potential strategies and solutions

Additionally, Chapter 6 offers advice on how to plan consulting based on what the consultant learns through a careful, systematic needs analysis. These chapters encourage readers to consider the importance of designing and making persuasive, action-oriented recommendations to clients. Part II concludes with a chapter that explores the communication skills necessary for credible, professional, ethical consulting that results in measurable impact.

Part III, *Facilitating a Consulting Experience That Matters,* investigates a range of consulting interventions and the challenges and opportunities each presents to facilitators and clients in the areas of:

- Creating shared understanding among stakeholders through facilitated communication
- Conflict resolution among organizational teams through the use of transformative mediation principles and methods
- Team development
- Training
- Using technology appropriately and effectively
- Conducting original research for clients

Finally, Part IV contains a series of brief essays and cases which illustrate the concepts, methods, and issues raised in Parts I–III. Each essay focuses on a highly specialized type of consulting or a specific project, and describes the context or client, the process, intervention, and evaluation methods. Each author gives special attention to unique challenges, theoretical considerations that frame or aid the specific type of consulting in it, and how research findings can help guide what to do and how to do it.

We are indebted to the willing experts—friends and colleagues—who shared their time, talent, and experiences within these pages. The conversation concerning the relevance of theory to practice is not a new one; but we view the voices here as incredibly articulate and important for advancing that conversation. The insights contained in this volume expand the reach and usefulness of what we publish in our academic journals to the action of what happens within organizations. Further, these chapters speak to how our activities within organizations inform scholarship. And most importantly, they illustrate how the reciprocal relationship between scholarship and practice facilitates positive change for organizations and the lives of their members. And when this happens, we have engaged in *consulting that matters.*

Jennifer H. Waldeck
Chapman University
Orange, CA

David R. Seibold
University of California, Santa Barbara
Santa Barbara, CA

Foreword

Consulting That Matters: A Handbook for Scholars and Practitioners

In the title, *Consulting That Matters: A Handbook for Scholars and Practitioners*, the editors clearly identify their audience as both researchers and practitioners. Their premise is that the two roles, being an academic researcher and being a consultant, should be merged. The editors take the approach that using research and theory in consulting practices is critical. They claim that "working from a solid theoretical framework and thoughtfully allowing empirical knowledge to guide our decisions during consulting makes consultants credible, effective, and valuable to the organizations that seek their help." This makes perfect sense and prepares the reader for an examination of theoretical frameworks used by consultants that may not be obvious without the scholar/practitioner revealing them.

Consulting is the application of organizational communication principles and theories to real-world problems. The fact that many of the most published organizational communication researchers also serve as consultants may not be well known. This book has asked a number of authors to describe how their research informs their consulting practices.

In an edited volume the reader looks first at the premise of the book and then at the collection of authors assembled to address that theme to determine if the book will successfully meet one's needs. In this book the theme is clear and the authors are well-known researchers who have years of experience as consultants. The authors are able to deliver what the editors have asked for: writing about the theoretical perspective they use in their consulting work, using a wide range of methodological approaches, and applying these findings to the stages of the consulting process. So from this admittedly superficial review of the book it definitely meets these two criteria for a successful book.

Looking beyond those two initial criteria and reading the chapters the reader will find much more that makes this book useful to both scholars and practitioners. Part I includes the two editors (David Seibold and Jennifer Waldeck) and a third author (Joann Keyton) all of whom write from a personal perspective. The questions they ask are ones they have encountered in their own consulting work. Waldeck makes the argument that theory and research make consulting better. She traces the history of consulting by starting with one of the most widely known scholar/practitioners, Kurt Lewin. She also mentions the National Training Laboratories and acknowledges Charles Redding, the first scholar/practitioner in the field of organizational communication. He led the way for many others in the field of organizational communication and deserves our recognition. I was pleased to see her give even slight reference to some of the historical underpinnings of this field. I would add an additional reference that should be mentioned: the American Society for Training and Development (now the Association for Talent Development), which for many years produced some of the best consulting tools as well as a journal addressing issues in training and consulting.

Waldeck does an excellent job of arguing for the relevance of consulting to conducting research. Academics have often claimed that their research informs and enriches their teaching. Waldeck successfully argues that consulting informs one's research as well as teaching, and makes both processes stronger and more relevant. I absolutely agree with her premise. If the reader is looking for justification for consulting from a theoretical base you will find it here.

Seibold identifies a number of communication theories that are directly relevant to the work of a consultant. His review of these theories, and the use of his own personal cases, convinces the reader that these theories do indeed inform how he practices the art of consulting.

In the last section of Part I, which frames the discussion for subsequent chapters, Keyton provides some basic definitions of consulting which are necessary for the reader to understand exactly what kind of activity is being examined in this book. What Keyton does in this chapter is repeated throughout the book: she cites personal examples of actual cases she was involved with. These actual examples are much more helpful than the typical hypothetical scenes the reader encounters in other books. She gives just enough detail so the reader understands the problem and Keyton's approach to solving it. Her discussion of the paradigms of consulting is especially useful to readers who are trying to identify what their own approach might be. What is particularly refreshing is her honest appraisal of how one's paradigm may not allow the consultant to see the whole organizational problem.

In Part I of the book these three authors clearly establish what the reader should expect to follow: detailed explanations of consulting approaches and a wide variety of consulting challenges. Personal lived experiences in such diverse organizations as media companies, healthcare settings, law enforcement, and higher education are woven throughout.

Once the consultant fully understands the theoretical framework from which she wants to operate then a careful analysis of the organization's needs must follow. Understanding everything about the context of this particular organization is discussed in depth by Pettegrew; conducting a client needs assessment is detailed in Jorgensen's chapter; and collecting rich data through carefully constructed focus groups is proposed by Plax, Waldeck, and Kearney. The last two chapters in the second part of the book are very practical: how to write a proposal (Waldeck, Plax, and Kearney) and what communication skills the consultant needs (Beebe). It is surprising how many times the communication consultant does not practice what he preaches.

In Part III we begin to get actual examples of the use of theories in consulting. Coordinated management of meaning (Sostrin); transformative mediation (Folger); team development interventions (Seibold); and research services (Boster) are chapters which demonstrate to the reader, in very understandable ways, how a theoretical approach informs the consulting activity. Two chapters provide practical techniques for consulting: training techniques (Houser); and technology in consulting (Stephens and Waters).

Finally, Part Four features detailed case studies of consulting projects. These case studies are rich with illustrations of consulting in particular contexts. Each case study identifies challenges in unique settings: healthcare (Kreps, Pettegrew), the corporate environment (Daly), law (Ross and Waldeck), and education (Cody). Two other topics of interest are working with big data (Barbour, Faughn, and Husband) and workplace ageism (McCann).

This is not a book one would read cover to cover. Rather the reader might want to read the overview and then select those chapters that have a particular relevance to situations being faced. I would predict that the reader will return to this book over and over as those situations change.

What I like most about this book is that it gives you a wide variety of perspectives combined with actual consulting cases. These cases reveal a great deal about how each author approaches organizational problems. While the reader's approach may differ there is something to be learned from each author's perspective. And that is what reading this book should do: show the reader how communication theory informs practice and how these authors practice what they preach. I found it to be informative, insightful, and meaningful to my own practices.

When I wrote *The Consultant's Craft* I was trying to open up the field of consulting and provide a detailed explanation for those who wanted to engage in this activity. I wanted to explain how one might go about consulting from a communication perspective. What these authors have done is provide theoretical underpinnings for many of the approaches I described in my own book. Reading these chapters helped me articulate my own consulting approach. I commend this reading to you.

In the foreword to my book, Charles Redding said: "As members of organizations, who among us can honestly report having never endured some sort of damage associated with such phenomena as insensitive supervision, confusing instructions, fruitless meetings, deceptive announcements, vicious defenses of 'turf'… scapegoating memoranda, clumsy explanations, paucity of information, conflicting orders, ambiguity (both intentional and unintentional), worship of inane regulations, refusal to listen to bad news…? (Space limitations prohibit a complete inventory of evils)." The field of communication should be the place where people turn to meet these challenges. If a researcher really wants to test his theory he should go into the field. Try it out with organizational members whose livelihoods depend on how well they communicate instead of testing theories on college sophomores.

The authors in this book have done just that. They have tested their own approaches developed in the privacy of their academic offices. Those tests have occurred in organizations where conflict and tension abounds and where the consequences of action may be quite dramatic. Congratulations to these authors who choose to share with the reader exactly what goes on when a communication consultant is asked to "fix things."

Sue DeWine
President Emeritus
Hanover College
Hanover, Indiana

suedewinenaples@gmail.com

PART ONE

Creating a Consulting
Identity That Matters

CHAPTER ONE

How Communication Theory and Research Make Consulting Matter

JENNIFER H. WALDECK
Chapman University

AN HISTORICAL BACKDROP FOR CONSULTATIONS THAT MATTER

The authors who have contributed to this book celebrate and illustrate the important role that theory and research play in their organizational consulting work. Despite the beliefs of clients who may be interested primarily in things like fewer conflict-ridden days, easier decisions, more productive meetings, higher-profit quarters, more satisfied employees, and greater competitive advantage, the prolific theoretician and social psychologist Kurt Lewin was correct when he famously wrote that "there's nothing so practical as a good theory" (1945, p. 129). In thinking about that soundbyte most of us have heard or read many times, it's easy to forget the original context from which it emerged. Although Lewin developed many theories during his career and advanced the importance of theoretical frameworks for good scholarship, he was not sitting in an ivory tower generating esoteric ideas. He was an *action researcher*, credited by many to be one of the "fathers" of the applied social sciences in the United States. His life's work illustrates the reflexivity of theory, research, and practice which serves as the foundation for this book.

For example, some of Lewin's later work in the mid-1940s involved a series of commissioned experiments designed to test messages for combatting ethnic, racial, and religious prejudice. His research on attitude change and group behavior suggested that people who learn by experience are more likely to change their attitudes and behaviors than those who learn primarily through lecture and reading. This conclusion led to his development of the *T-Groups* methodology, which is the foundation of the kinds of human relations, cultural sensitivity, and group dynamics training programs still used within organizations worldwide (but perhaps known by a different and broader set of names). Although he died suddenly in 1947 before actually working there, Lewin was the co-founder of the National Training Laboratories (NTL) Institute, which continues to be a transformative source of applied behavioral training programs and ideas about organizational development (NTL, 2015).

In our own field, W. Charles Redding, a contemporary of Lewin's, was the first scholar/practitioner of organizational communication that I'm aware of. He is credited as the "father" of organizational communication. Engaged in activities such as communication skills training for military officers from the earliest days of his career, Redding applied the content of the discipline. Much like the field did, Redding's own work moved from a focus on skills to the application of social scientific methods and theory building, and he was instrumental in establishing the Communication Research Center at Purdue University. Redding believed firmly that empirical research produced knowledge that made organizations better places. The "Redding Tradition" influenced numerous luminaries in our field, including Sue DeWine. Redding's student and protégé, DeWine has been an advocate for consulting as a serious, substantive activity for several decades. Her most important contribution to the field was a book entitled *The Consultant's Craft*—the culmination of her many years of scholarly research and practice in service to numerous corporations, educational institutions, and government agencies. *The Consultant's Craft* represents the only existing book to date written from an organizational communication perspective that examines a breadth of consulting activities from needs assessments to strategic planning to communication skills training. Sue was one of my first teachers in the discipline at Ohio University, where I received my bachelor's degree, and she has shaped my thinking in important ways over the years. I am honored that she has provided a foreword for this volume.

This truncated historical account underscores that the earliest consulting work of the last century was performed by some of social science's brightest academic minds. They wore their "scholarly hats" to develop useful theories and conduct rigorous research to support the academic reputation and advancement of their work, and then took it to applied settings to positively impact and transform human behavior and organizational functioning. What they learned in their interactions with practitioners—leaders, managers, laborers, administrators, secretaries—undoubtedly prompted new scholarly questions to ask and hypotheses to test.

OVERCOMING BIASES ABOUT CONSULTING

However, along the way, consulting became somewhat of an academic pejorative, framed less by scholarship and more by popularized, watered-down approaches with little or no science behind them (cf. Van de Ven, 2002; Weick, 2001). As Boster points out in this volume, the prevailing attitude was "serious academics do not consult." Although that hard line might have softened, many do feel obliged to conceal their consulting work from their academic colleagues (Perkmann & Walsh, 2008). Over time, the practice became polluted and often characterized as the sale of "useless best practices for high fees" (McKelvey, 2006, p. 825). Many academics view this type of work largely as opportunity-driven and a distraction from scholarly relevance (Lee, 1996), having little academic value (Boyer & Lewis, 1984), and lacking complementarity with rigorous research (McKelvey, 2006; Perkmann & Walsh, 2008). In this volume, Keyton notes an alternative but related critical view held by some that consulting privileges those in power.

Further, some professors react negatively to the idea of consulting for three reasons. First, their dispositions, skill sets, or research interests may not lend themselves to consulting or action, so they misunderstand, distrust, or resent those who can and do get paid for their efforts. Second, their only experience with it might have been on the (negative) receiving end of distasteful changes imposed by "hired guns" at their institutions, which often result in a more corporate, and less intellectual and academic environment than they prefer (Blumenstyk, 2014). Finally, consulting is stereotypically associated with the purpose of financial gain for the consultant and the client organization (Boyer & Lewis, 1984). Some academics have a biased view toward engagements that promote financial gain as capitalist and simultaneously anti-intellectual (Baumard, 2010; Nozick, 1998). The engaged scholarship community (cf. Van de Ven & Johnson, 2006), for example, prides itself on ethical considerations which suggest that scholars collaborate with organizations "doing good works" and, admirably, does pro bono and service work when appropriate (Simpson & Seibold, 2008, p. 270).

Even among people with neutral or positive attitudes toward consulting, there is confusion about what it really entails. Through conversations with colleagues on both the academic and practitioner sides, I have come to believe that there is a pervasive stereotype supporting the assumption that anyone with some management experience or knowledge, basic observation ability, general familiarity with the industry of interest, and some degree of communication competence can offer consulting advice. Consistent with these assumptions are popular books about consulting that promise "seven-figure salaries" for those with "supreme communication skills" (Weiss, 2011), and that encourage the use of fairly easily facilitated, predesigned cookie-cutter training and consulting activities (Weiss, 2005) similar to what a graduate-level teaching assistant might facilitate in a college classroom. Other popular literature is focused more on the business of consulting, such as marketing (Block, 2011; Katcher & Snyder, 2010), than on its intellectual and practical substance.

The frameworks and specific cases described in this volume, however, return the conversation to the science, rigor, ethics, and depth of good consulting. Pettegrew (in Chapter 4), for instance, emphasizes the importance of *clarifying the consulting context, setting, and situation carefully* before embarking on one's project. And overarching all of the methods, frameworks, and specific examples of consulting in the book is Keyton's reminder that *good consulting, like good scholarship, is undergirded by a set of philosophical and ethical values unique to the epistemology from which the consultant operates.* The consultant's paradigm, which should correspond to that which frames his or her scholarly research agenda, guides the nature and practice of the consultation. When one's scholarly and consulting perspectives are aligned, the consultant-scholar is in a position to see a great deal of reflexivity between the two activities and how they inform one another.

HOW DO THEORY AND RESEARCH MATTER?

Theory and research make consulting matter in many ways, a number of which are elucidated in this volume. Specifically, the chapters here illustrate ways that consultants (a) use theory and research to frame their interventions; (b) support their processes, actions, and recommendations with research findings; (c) translate research and theory for clients in a fashion that is applicable to organizational contexts; and (d) employ relevant methodological skills in their work. Theory and research distinguish truly effective, impactful consulting because it directs, substantiates, and legitimates what consultants do and how we do it.

The authors whose work is included in this book furnish evidence of the good that consulting can do when it is *grounded in theoretical frameworks and driven by research findings.* For example, in Chapter 9, Sostrin guides readers through his sophisticated, rich approach to improving patterns of organizational communication, which is framed by Coordinated Management of Meaning theory. In Chapter 10, Folger illustrates how his transformative mediation perspective can be applied in team situations to improve communicative outcomes. Seibold showcases his broad and deep experience with using empirical research on groups and teams to design teambuilding interventions in Chapter 11.

Among a series of brief essays in Part IV of the book, McCann describes how consulting aimed at bridging intergenerational differences in the workforce can be designed through the lenses of intergroup theories like Social Identity and Communication Accommodation. Kreps explains how he employed the research findings on dissemination of health messages in minority communities to design an effective AIDS/HIV education campaign for African Americans. Based on both his consulting experience and stature as an interpersonal communication scholar, Cody points out how the interpersonal literature—such as Leary's self-presentation framework and the research on self-disclosure—can aid external reviewers in conducting a useful academic program review. The bottom line is that substantive theories and research findings offer useful frames for a wide range of consulting activities which then guide the consultant on what to do and how to do it as the engagement unfolds.

While the previous examples reveal fairly macroscopic ways that consultants think about, plan, facilitate, and evaluate their work, a number of the examples in this book illustrate important "micro" approaches to using theory and research in consulting, as well. *Good consultants make decisions about the processes they use, the content they share, and the behaviors they exhibit during their engagements, based on research and its theoretical underpinnings.* For example, in Chapter 8, Beebe substantiates all of the skills he recommends consultants acquire and develop with evidence from communication and other social science literature. Similarly, successful trainers operate with mindfulness toward the behaviors that instructional communication literature suggests are related to learning, such as clarity (Houser, Chapter 12). Strong, credible proposals for consulting work can motivate organizational representatives to consider the possibilities of meaningful change, but only when they are written according to the principles of effective persuasion and audience analysis, as discussed by Waldeck, Plax, and Kearney. In Chapter 13, Stephens and Waters leverage the empirical findings on information and communication technology use to make recommendations on how consultants might make good choices relative to media use and face-to-face communication in their work. Still other chapters illustrate how consultants actually teach their clients about research conclusions in intervention settings. For instance, Daly describes coaching and training employees at a global oil industry firm about advocacy, leadership, teamwork, and change management; Ross and Waldeck share a case focused on cultural change, front-line empowerment, and leadership development for law enforcement personnel, guided by both research and theory. Taken together, these examples demonstrate how consultants use theory and research in their work. The authors in this volume show, in compelling ways, how their reliance on theory and corresponding research lends credibility to their interventions, and gives them confidence in their recommendations to clients. In some instances the consultations also inform theory and research (Seibold, Chapter 2).

In addition to discussing the utility of the theory and research they draw upon in their work, a number of the authors in this book illustrate the importance of being able to *translate theory and research into working principles that can be applied to problems in the organizational context.* For example, Plax, Waldeck, and Kearney describe "educating" clients, in language they can relate to, about the process of designing theoretically framed applied research (Chapter 6) as critical to successful consulting outcomes. Boster recalls providing advice to law firms through the lenses of social influence theories in an audience-centered fashion and translating important statistical principles in a nontechnical way (Chapter 14). In sum, applying research and theory to consulting in ways that all stakeholders find meaningful and understandable is easier said than done, but is a vital skill.

Chapters in this book also demonstrate how *good consulting requires many of the same sophisticated skills that we use in our scholarship*. The parameters of research conducted for consulting clients in particular contexts and situations are usually different than those put in place by scholars who seek to build generalizable knowledge through basic research. Although we don't seek the same types of results and outcomes from consulting work as we might in our academic research, Boster aptly points out that "the methodological skills obtained while pursuing the Ph.D.... have tremendous value both in the public and private sectors." He goes on to describe a number of engagements in which he conducted original research for clients, including a public utility and firms in the K–12 educational products industry. In his chapter on the value of valid, reliable needs analyses, Jorgensen offers the reader a "research methods for consultants" primer. Pettegrew illuminates the use of ethnographic methods in work he performed within the healthcare industry. Plax et al. describe how they leverage focus group methodology in a number of their consultations, including considerations for sampling and developing interview questions. Waldeck et al. remind consultants of the importance of evaluating their processes, products, and delivery using sound testing methods. And Barbour, Faughn, and Husband share a case in which they relied on their analyses of archived 360-degree data to inform executive decision making at a Fortune 500 firm. When consultants employ strong research methodology and data analysis skills in the design and facilitation of their work and in analyzing its outcomes, their results become credible and legitimated. When they can then communicate the value of their rigorous procedures in understandable ways, they enhance their own credibility and value to clients.

CONCLUSION

To the reader unfamiliar with the rigors of truly impactful consulting—that which really matters—the importance of scholarly theories and research findings in these endeavors may not seem obvious. However, as this chapter foreshadows and the remainder of the book elaborates, strong consulting work is made robust in key ways by both theory and research. Consulting that matters in terms of the goals and needs of consultants, organizational clients, *and* organizational members is characterized by the appropriation of theory and research to design interventions and facilitate useful outcomes. In turn, consulting relationships and activities hold great potential for nourishing the consultant's scholarship in a world where appropriate action matters and is valued.

As an academic who has done quite a bit of consulting, including several years of full-time work with a professional consulting firm, I discovered very quickly how useful my knowledge of social science—theory development, testing, research design, measurement, assessment, statistics, qualitative data analysis, archival data retrieval and analysis, interviewing, writing, and more—was to my work in applied settings. Although clients may not speak the language of science in the same way that scholar-consultants do, they operate from a similar perspective. They rely on evidence to design products, scan and assess their environment, determine performance standards, defend product quality, promote products and services, monitor morale, solve problems, make decisions, and more. They appreciate defensible, objective, and evidence-based approaches to defining and addressing the challenges and opportunities they face. They are impressed by the systematic rigor that a scholarly approach brings to their project, leading to a fruitful relationship and a challenging engagement that raises interesting questions (and answers) for consultants—which we can incorporate into both our scholarship and teaching at the undergraduate and graduate levels. And, despite the bias some might hold against the financial gains attached to consulting work, we cannot ignore the fact that when we bring the credibility of theoretical frames, rigorous methods, and research-based recommendations to our consultations, we tend to elicit profitable, highly valued results for clients, which is more than we can ask or expect of pure research.

So, rather than dismiss consulting as incompatible with scholarship, we need to remember and embrace our applied roots. The landscape of social inquiry and problem solving that we know today began with the work of social scientists like Argyris, Lazarsfeld, Lewin, Lippitt, Merton, and many others who implicitly understood the reflexivity of their theory, research, and practice. They made a significant difference in the social, economic, and political fabrics of the United States with their work; the mutually informative nature of their research and practice was an everyday reality of their scholarly lives. Their work models an important lesson for contemporary academics interested in applied work: Consulting need not be limited to the simplistic, opportunity-focused work that merely yields an extra paycheck for the academic. Indeed, it can be financially rewarding; but it can also be an *intellectually* rewarding activity that stands to enhance the organizations consultants serve, and the lives of organizational stakeholders. In considering the relationship between research and practice in professional settings, Van de Ven (1989, p. 486) echoed Lewin in reminding us that "good theory is practical precisely because it advances knowledge in a scientific discipline, guides research toward crucial questions, and enlightens the profession of management." When consultants utilize sound methods, theory, and corresponding research-based knowledge in their work, organizations, their members, the consultant, and his or her academic discipline stand on the precipice of outcomes that truly matter.

REFERENCES

Baumard, N. (2010, June 14). *Why do academics oppose capitalism?* Retrieved from http://www.cognition andculture.net/home/blog/16-nicolas/658-why-do-academics-oppose-capitalism

Block, P. (2011). *Flawless consulting: Your guide to getting your expertise used* (3rd ed.). San Francisco: Pfeiffer.

Blumenstyk, G. (2014, December 15). 2014 influence list: Hired guns. *The Chronicle of Higher Education.* Retrieved from http://www.chroniclecareers.com/article/Hired-Guns-The-Consultants/150843/

Boyer, C. M., & Lewis, D. R. (1984). Faculty consulting: Responsibility or promiscuity? *The Journal of Higher Education, 55*(5), 637–659.

Katcher, B. L., & Snyder, A. (2010). *An insider's guide to building a successful consulting practice.* New York: AMACON/American Management Association.

Lee, Y. S. (1996). "Technology transfer" and the research university: A search for the boundaries of university-industry collaboration. *Research Policy, 25* (6) 843–863.

Lewin, K. (1945). The Research Center for Group Dynamics at Massachusetts Institute of Technology. *Sociometry, 8*(2), 126–136.

McKelvey, B. (2006). Response: Van de Ven and Johnson's "engaged scholarship": Nice try, but… *Academy of Management Review, 31*(4), 822–829.

Nozick, R. (1998, January 1). *Why do intellectuals oppose capitalism?* Retrieved from http://www. libertarianism.org/publications/essays/why-do-intellectuals-oppose-capitalism

NTL Institute (2015). Over 67 years at the forefront of experiential learning: The vision. Retrived from http://www.ntl.org/?page=History

Perkmann, M., & Walsh, K. (2008). Engaging the scholar: Three types of academic consulting and their impact on universities and industry. *Research Policy, 37*(10), 1884–1891.

Simpson, J. L., & Seibold, D. R. (2008). Practical engagements and co-created research. *Journal of Applied Communication Research, 36,* 266–280.

Van de Ven, A. H. (1989). Nothing is quite so practical as a good theory. *Academy of Management Review, 14* (4), 486–489.

Van de Ven, A. H. (2002). 2011 Presidential address—Strategic directions for the Academy of Management: This Academy is for you! *Academy of Management Review, 27,* 171–184.

Van de Ven, A. H., & Johnson, P. E. (2006). Knowledge for theory and practice. *Academy of Management Review, 31* (4), 802–821.

Weick, K. (2001). Gapping the relevance bridge: Fashions meet fundamentals in management research. *British Journal of Management, 12,* S71-S75.

Weiss, A. (2005). *Million dollar consulting toolkit.* Hoboken, NJ: Wiley.

Weiss, A. (2011). *The consulting bible: Everything you need to know to create and expand a seven figure consulting practice.* Hoboken, NJ: Wiley.

CHAPTER TWO

The Communication Scholar's Unique Perspective on Organizational Consulting

Personal Reflections and a Design Approach

DAVID R. SEIBOLD

University of California, Santa Barbara

Theory and practice are not merely interdependent. They also can be reciprocally enhancing—and should be. Recognition of the interconnections between theory and practice is not new in communication. As Craig (1989) notes, "the history of communication as a practical discipline is a history of communication practices and their cultivation by critical reflection" (p. 116). Craig's efforts to explicate a practical theory of communication (1995; 1999; 2006; Craig & Tracy, 2014) concomitantly have underscored communication as a practical discipline *and* the need for theory that addresses practical problems and creates new opportunities for action.

Drawing on distinctions introduced by Barge (2001), Barge and Craig (2009) identified three principal forms of practical theory. *Mapping* approaches to practical theory offer a map of the communicative terrain of actors' experiences through empirical descriptions of problems, tactics, and outcomes. A wide range of applications of social scientific theories and methods exemplify mapping including, for example, use of the Extended Parallel Process Model to create and assess the utilization of fear appeals in messages in public health campaigns (Witte & Roberto, 2009). *Transformative practice* approaches to practical theory involve the development of theory to be utilized by practical theorists who intervene in communicatively problematic situations. For example, as a social constructionist model of communication, Coordinated Management of Meaning theory provides heuristic concepts that the theorist-practitioner can appropriate to understand communication episodes and patterns in specific situations and direct efforts to intervene (cf. Pearce, 2007). *Engaged reflection* approaches to practical theory seek to develop a reflexive relationship between theory and practice such that "theory emerges out of systematic reflection on communication problems and practices and, in that sense, is grounded in practice" (p. 63). Besides Grounded Practical Theory (Craig & Tracy, 1995), communication as design (CAD) is another form of practical theory as engaged reflection. According to Jackson and Aakhus (2014), the design of communication perspective entails empirically examining communication problems and answers to which extant communication theories can be applied as "design languages" (p. 131) and that may stimulate powerful new theoretical concepts and practical design objects.

Communication consulting to organizations—that is, engagements with organizational members and other stakeholders concerning communication-related challenges—involves partnering relationships in which theory and practice are not merely recursive but should be reciprocally enhancing. Ostensible challenges of employee (or customer) satisfaction, production quality and quantity, planning and intentional organizational change, forming and maintaining effective teams, determining optimal structures for key organizational processes, facilitating coordination and cooperation between and across units, and so forth typically require consultants to address and assist with correlative communication challenges that are at the nexus of theory and practice: "problems of participation and voice, efficacy and influence, inequity and marginalization, performance and productivity, oppression and powerlessness, intergroup conflict, misunderstandings, and quality of work life, among many others" (Seibold & Flanagin, 2000, p. 181). Indeed, the chapters in this book are replete with authors' framing of their consultations in terms of prominent communication theories and concepts—many of which they helped to originate as communication scholars (see especially the chapters by Folger, Sostrin, Boster, Cody, Barbour, Daly, McCann, Stephens & Waters, Seibold, and Kreps). In some instances, those authors describe how their consultations have informed or reformed communication theory and research (e.g., see chapters by Pettegrew; Seibold; Boster; and Plax; Waldeck, & Kearney).

Many of the chapters in this volume also exemplify approaches to practical theory. Mapping approaches are most evident in Sostrin's recommendations concerning use of CMM is an example of the transformative practice approach to practical theory. While there are few explicit examples of engaged reflection approaches in these chapters (for an exception see Seibold's critical praxis method of team development in Chapter 12), most authors implicitly bring a communication as design (CAD) approach to their consulting. For example, Folger addresses the "unique design considerations that have to be taken into account when conducting team building interventions from a transformative perspective" (Chapter 10, p. 169). Cody (Chapter 20) discusses the challenges for external reviewers of designing effective reports to university administrators following evaluations of academic units and program on their campus. Houser (Chapter 12) argues that appropriation of instructional communication principles can guide the design of effective organizational training programs. Waldeck, Plax, and Kearney (Chapter 7) explicate six primary topics that must be attended to in planning and proposing consulting work, and each of these areas can be thought of as challenges to the design of the proposal and the project. Finally, the three methods of team development interventions reviewed by Seibold (Chapter 11) represent three different designs for interacting with those teams and for facilitating members' interactions.

Overview

In this chapter I attempt to illuminate the unique perspective that communication consultants bring to their engagements with organizational members and stakeholders. My thesis is tripartite. First, as representatives of a practical discipline yet steeped in recursive theory-practice relationships, communication consultants also are practical theorists in the main. To greater or lesser degrees, their goals are those of practical theory: "to address practical problems and generate new possibilities for action" (Barge & Craig, 2009, p. 55). Second, and central to my thesis, organizational communication consulting inherently involves "design work" (Jackson & Aakhus, 2014, p. 125) that reflects the application of theory to be sure but, more that that, involves theory building. The authors of chapters in this volume repeatedly demonstrate that effective consultants must employ a wide range of skills and must be credible in enacting their varied roles—and their chapters offer detailed descriptions of those skills and roles. I wish to add to that conversation the importance of managing the theory-practice interface in all its richness and potential, beginning with recognition of the design work that interpenetrates our interactions with clients and their interactions with each other and their stakeholders. Third, for the well-being of society and its institutions (including organizations), for the growth of knowledge, and for the benefit of our discipline, "the academy" should encourage organizational communication consulting that facilitates the mutual enhancement of theory and practice.

Toward those ends, I offer personal reflections on the extent to which my engagements over nearly 40 years have (and have not) met those standards— and opportunities for others in communication to do so. First, I underscore my core commitment to socially relevant communication research, document my organizational consulting experiences as an extension of that commitment, note some applied scholarship that resulted, and reflect on what have become premises and ethics in my approach to organizational consulting partnerships. Second,

I highlight in two major and representative consultations some ways in which I utilized theory/research as a basis for *designing* organizational consultations—including complex design challenges I am now facing (and, I suspect, most communication consultants encounter). Although I ground these discussions in my experiences, I also hope to show how the design choices I have made are at once like those of other organizational communication consultants and (relatively) unique to communication consulting. Third, I conclude with a summary of many of the unique attributes of communication scholars' approaches to organizational consulting.

Although I discuss in some detail my own consulting experiences, those consultations are only a part of my focus here and more complete discussions of them are available in what may be treated as companion pieces by Seibold (1995, 2005) and Seibold and Meyers (2012). Rather, in this treatment of my consulting projects I seek five other ends: to distinguish my consultations from the service engagements that also were part of earlier discussions; to use my consulting experiences as representative of those of other communication scholars; to draw from my consultations (and those of others) inferences about communication scholars' unique perspective on organizational consulting; to use these projects as a platform for discussing CAD and consulting as design (neither of which were part of my earlier discussions); and to emphasize even more than before the links between theory and practice in these consultations.

COMMITTED TO RESEARCH <-> CONSULTING COMMITMENTS

Commitment to Socially Relevant Communication Research

As initially discussed in Seibold (2005), my commitment as an academic researcher long has been to conducting theoretical studies that are methodologically rigorous *and socially relevant*. Like most communication faculty members, I view my role as a professor to teach students to solve communication-related problems for the betterment of society, and to engage in scholarship that has the potential to improve society through consumption by organizational and community members or through application by practitioners. Thus, and in combination with efforts at theory development (Ballard & Seibold, 2003; Seibold & Meyers, 2007; Lewis & Seibold, 1993; Poole, Seibold, & McPhee, 1996; Seibold, 1975) and theory testing (e.g., Ballard & Seibold, 2004; Lemus & Seibold, 2008), much of my scholarship also has been *applied* in nature (Seibold, 2015; Seibold, Lemus, Ballard, & Myers, 2009). Representative applied research studies across the past 40 years include investigations of interpersonal and mediated processes through which persons learn of newsworthy events such as assassination attempts

(Steinfatt, Gantz, Seibold, & Miller, 1973); procedures for making meetings more successful (Seibold, 1979); persuasive strategies for increasing charitable donations (Cantrill & Seibold, 1986); communication approaches to addressing alcohol problems in personal relationships, in friendships, and in the workplace (Seibold & Thomas, 1994; Thomas & Seibold, 1995); processes and effects of 're-engineering' in an aerospace organization (Krikorian, Seibold, & Goode, 1997); communication practices related to innovation adoption (Lewis & Seibold, 1996); jurors' rules for decision making (SunWolf & Seibold, 1998); consultant-client relationships (Seibold, 2001); working with organizational members to co-create research (Simpson & Seibold, 2008); argument in naturally occurring jury deliberations (Meyers, Seibold, & Kang, 2010); business process modeling (Franken & Seibold, 2010); a coach's leadership tactics with members of a collegiate basketball team (Kang & Seibold, 2014); and factors that influence work-life balance among couples who own and manage their own firms (Helmle, Botero, & Seibold, 2014).

My professional profile, as outlined above, is not unique among communication consultants. Indeed, most of the authors in this volume have pursued both theoretical scholarship and applied research, *and* bought both to bear in their consulting—which is a unique feature of communication scholars' consultations. Far from bifurcating "basic" and "applied" research, communication faculty members see them as inherently connected. Those who then consult appropriate each as needed, and view the arena of consulting practice (and clients' challenges) as opportunities for informing or reforming theory (e.g., see chapters by Sostrin; Daly; Folger; Seibold; McCann; Kreps; Boster; Waldeck, Plax, & Kearney; and Stephens & Waters).

Consulting and Social Relevance

Throughout my career, being engaged in socially relevant research and practice also has meant consulting with organizations. Over the course of more than 35 years, I have consulted with 75 organizations and at over 100 locations. Approximately 65 percent of these consultations involved work with for-profit organizations ranging from minority-owned small enterprises to *Fortune 500* corporations. They have been in diverse sectors (energy, technology, telecommunications, hospitality, retail, professional services, consumer goods, agriculture, financial services, insurance, and entertainment) and their products include technology, utilities, clothing, and food. Roughly 30 of the consultations have been with government and nonprofit organizations in numerous areas (e.g., education, philanthropy, transportation, environmental protection, international development, health, and human services), and with a few professional associations. The balance have been consulting projects in which colleagues and I offered services to organizations unable to undertake them on their own (e.g., a hospice, charities, and civic organizations).

Especially between 1983 and 2000 I committed nearly a day each week, most vacations, and the majority of summer recess in a variety of roles with at least 3000 persons from nearly fifty countries. These consultations included serving as executive coach, strategic planning consultant, facilitator, technical advisor, program evaluator, trainer, curriculum designer, process consultant, and featured speaker. The following are representative of my consulting projects with non-health organizations and health-related organizations, which I then relate to the unique qualifications and perspectives of communication consultants generally.

Non-health organizations. My consultations with non-health organizations (not including those discussed in Chapter 11 in connection with team development projects) have included collaborating with members to improve communication in a family-owned trucking firm; conducting staffing audits and human resources needs assessments; mediating conflicts; facilitating problem-solving discussions among quality circle participants in a tool and die plant; working with supervisors seeking to improve relations with employees; offering training workshops on strategic planning, assertive communication, managing conflict, interpersonal influence, and facilitation techniques; improving Human Resources professionals' consultative skills with their internal clients; collaborating with line and personnel managers in the design of organizational change interventions for a computer applications group, for several scientific research teams, and for a business services unit; assisting sales managers with presentation skills and providing training for sales representatives; consulting with a national firm concerning the acquisition and restructuring of a technical services subsidiary; working with members of an employee stock ownership (ESOP) organization to improve performance and productivity; troubleshooting organizational communication problems; evaluating and redesigning a major consulting firm's employee opinion surveys; conducting and reporting internal communication audits in a variety of retail, service, and technological organizations; designing and conducting a survey to assess the communication effects of a telecommunication company's decision to centralize operations; designing and implementing an intervention at all management levels for improving internal communication in a utility company; designing and implementing a program to improve managers' skill in communicating strategic goals to employees; training and facilitating top managers in strategic planning; coaching executives concerning leadership skills; and consulting with top management concerning communication plans for reorganization.

Health organizations. I also have had opportunities to serve as a consultant, evaluator, and trainer for numerous health-related government agencies and health services organizations. My roles have included assisting with the design, implementation, and analysis of formative and summative evaluations of administrative teams and their plans, health education specialists' activities, and health communication programs (e.g., inquiries from the public, mass communication campaigns, publicity efforts, continuing education for health professionals); providing training in communication and conflict management skills for technicians and supervisors in five departments of a hospital laboratory; investigating causes for volunteer turnover in a hospice care program; conducted a staffing audit and organizational assessment of the communications office of a large federal agency; training and development work with health executives, managers, professionals, and lay volunteers; acting as national project evaluator for a federally funded three-year project to improve the pre-professional training of education and allied health professionals who serve children with disabilities; working with other communication researchers to facilitate introduction of an interaction design model of external communication at a federal agency.

Nearly all of these engagements involved linking theory/research with my/our practices (Seibold, 2005). For instance, in a course I was teaching on field methods of research and program evaluation research, graduate students and I collaborated with administrators and health educators in a regional health center to assess their programs' effectiveness, including a widely disseminated newsletter. Given adequate time to design the evaluation, we examined research literature on media and health communication campaigns. The theoretical frameworks there aided us in designing the study, facilitated interpretation of findings, and enhanced our ability to share them with program personnel in perspectives and terms on which health educators relied (Seibold, Meyers, & Willihnganz, 1984). This consultation raised questions that encouraged us to examine the marketing research and program evaluation literatures and led to the utility of an integrative model of health organizations as a framework for program assessment that these administrators and educators embraced (Meyers, Seibold, & Willihnganz, 1983) and alternate market segmentation approaches for understanding consumers' utilization of health services (Meyers & Seibold, 1985).

Again, my portfolio of consulting engagements is not unique among communication scholars. While it may be longer as a result of my age and longer tenure in the field, it is no more varied or involved than most of the authors in this volume and many others of whom I am aware. And this is another unique aspect of communication scholars' organizational consulting. That is, given the breadth of the field, the added breadth that accrues from the multidisciplinary orientation of its members, the comfort (and commitment) of communication scholars to theory-practice relationships, and of course the communication aspects of nearly all consulting projects, communication scholars have the potential to become involved in a very wide range of projects—wider than I have witnessed among scholars from other disciplines.

Consulting: Partnerships, Premises, and Principles

Partnerships. In most of the cases above I was partnering with the organization to aid members in some agreed upon ways (and in many others that were emergent). Usually this was as a paid consultant (working alone or for a consulting firm contracted to the organization and subcontracting to me to perform the service). Sometimes it was pro bono as a member of the community served by the organization, and occasionally as a university teacher offering engaged learning experiences for college students.

A vital component for meaningful organizational consulting and for serving as well as I/we could was drawing upon theoretical research findings (and methods) and linking theory and practice (a key point in this chapter). This was not a process of bringing theory *to* the consultations. It was a recursive process as opportunities for theory development arose *in* and *from* the engagement (two examples are reviewed in the next section). Furthermore, and as Jackson and Aakhus (2014) propose concerning the CAD perspective that was explicit or implicit in all of my consulting, these engagements have the potential to stimulate powerful new theoretical concepts. That certainly proved true in many of my projects in which I/we 'discovered' relationships that could be investigated in the context of the engagement and that had the potential to advance scholarship concerning interpersonal influence, groups, health, and organizations. For example, an extended consultation concerning turnover of oncology nurses in a hospice led to a theoretical contribution concerning role conflict reported in Berteotti and Seibold (1994) and insights into volunteer motivations discussed by Seibold, Rossi, Berteotti, Soprych, & McQuillan (1987). A pro bono/engaged learning project concerning organizational restructuring and changes work practices in a food processing plant led to proposing the innovation modification model introduced by Lewis and Seibold (1993). And a series of consultations with managers and professionals seeking to improve how they delivered constructive negative feedback to peers and subordinates led to challenges to the research literature on criticism-giving provided by Mulac, Seibold, and Farris (2000). These are but a few of many examples in which opportunities to inform or reform theory via academic publications emerged from practices observed in the course of my organizational consulting, which is another relatively unique facet of communication scholars' approach to organizational consulting. In most cases, of course, the same amount of effort was devoted to consultations that were of no overt or immediate scholarly value.

As noted elsewhere (Seibold, 2005), my impulses to partner with organizations in the ways mentioned above were varied. I engaged in these consultations *for the members of the organization* (sometimes for managers or administrators but more often for the teams of employees); *for the cause* (to aid those who could not find help and whose aims I believed to be vital or admirable); *for the experience* (a new problem, a new location, new persons); and, yes, *for the reward* (remuneration, appreciation, advancement).

To conclude this portion of my personal account and reflections, I know of numerous communication scholars who have had careers like mine (including many of the authors in this volume): balancing active and visible academic roles with intensive organizational consulting, and integrating those commitments as much as possible. In the following two sections I reflect on premises and ethical principles that have become foundational to my approach to organizational consulting.

Premises. My consultations, and those of many communication scholars, do not involve narrow specialization but invite or require *breadth* of expertise and skills. As Seibold (2005) observed, organizational members' challenges revolve around autonomy and control, inclusion and marginalization, order and change, participation and decision making, structure and flexibility, planning and innovation, information and communication, climate and conflict, performance and productivity, evaluation and motivation, power and reward, ambiguity and ambivalence, profitability and social responsibility, internal and external environments, and a host of other dynamics that do not neatly fit narrow specializations or divisions in our field—including "organizational communication." The organizational consultations in which I became involved—and I suspect this is true for most communication scholars—were similarly complex and multidimensional. In turn, they encouraged insights from scholarship concerning organizational communication certainly, but also from communication research on interpersonal relationships (including family communication), instructional communication, persuasion, conflict, gender, groups, intercultural and intergroup communication, health communication, global communication, and new workplace communication and information technologies. In my experience, substantive organizational communication consulting demands a broad perspective, not a narrow approach— and this is a unique feature of communication scholars' organizational consulting more so than the 'specialists' I have witnessed from other disciplines.

Organizational consulting also requires communication scholars to understand theoretical perspectives, research literatures, and practices *beyond our own discipline.* I have found it crucial to keep informed about scholarship and popular literature in management studies, in public administration, and in health behavior. Not only are those the constructs and frames employed by clients with whom I most often engage (and hence within whose discourses I need to communicate), but those perspectives offer important frames for interpreting the practices I encounter. Organizational consultations by communication scholars also can be aided through awareness of *meta-theoretical perspectives* whose axiological, ontological, and epistemological tenets can illuminate our consultations. As described in Seibold (2005) my early education in systems theory (Farace, Monge, & Russell, 1977) enjoins me to encourage the design of (positive) interdependencies into new structures organizational members create, to appreciate uncertainty and equifinality, to reinforce the importance of maintaining permeable boundaries, and to co-construct mechanisms for scanning relevant environments and creating feedback processes. My sensitivity to organizational paradoxes (Stoltzfus, Stohl, & Seibold, 2011) invites discussion with stakeholders about tensions, oppositions and contradictions in organizational practices. Sometimes these were my personal frames of reference, and sometimes they were shared with stakeholders who occasionally utilized them to address problems (Seibold, 1995). My long-term commitment to structuration theory (Giddens, 1984) directs me to examine how structures of power are produced and reproduced, meanings legitimated, and norms institutionalized.

Finally, *organizational scholars must manage an exquisite balance between scholarship and consulting*. The challenge is one of both depth and balance. Consultations are not simply a process in which we are transformed, but must be deep enough to transform others—our client organizations and our students. Yet as we become immersed in the transformational aspects of engagement, we cannot lose—that is, must balance—our commitment to scholarship. In my opinion, we must fulfill our commitment as scholars in the discipline no matter how enticing, ennobling, entraining, or even enervating our organizational consultations may be.

Principles. Closely associated with the assumptive premises above concerning organizational engagement is a set of principles that guide my consultations with organizations. They may or may not align with others' codes of conduct. However, in the spirit of Keyton's (Chapter 3) encouragement of transparency concerning the ethical basis of consultations, I review mine in the hope that they motivate other communication scholars to reflect on their own principles (and to challenge me to higher standards).

I do not advertise or otherwise market my services for I am a full-time employee in another realm. Consulting firms invite me to collaborate in serving their clients, and clients I take on personally find me through word of mouth or their own research. Once an opportunity arises, and although it may be appealing for any of the reasons above, I do not take on any project unless I can believe I can significantly aid organizational members and/or stakeholders. There is an additional responsibility to that commitment: thorough preparation regarding the client's philosophy and practices through personal research, archival work, observation, and interviews with individuals and focus groups (see Waldeck, Plax, & Kearney, Chapter 7). Furthermore, while I attempt to aid I also continue to scan in order to ensure that I have done no harm—especially unintended consequences. If that happens, my topmost and most immediate goal is to correct things as much as possible (which also offers clients the opportunity to learn the importance of "ownership" and to develop skills for dealing with other problems they face). I hold myself accountable not simply to the person(s) with whom I am consulting (e.g., a person whom I am coaching, a dyad seeking to better manage their work relationship, a group involved in team building, an organization-wide change effort), but to the system as a whole in which participants are embedded (Seibold, Hollingshead & Yoon, 2014). For that reason I do not take on consulting projects in which the participant(s) cannot be open with others about my role and our relationship. I also request permission to seek additional information that will illuminate the problem(s) for all involved and will further involve all those who care to be. These often include speaking with sources up and down levels of the organizational hierarchy, and interviewing across lateral relationships with peers, other teams, even external stakeholders. In that same spirit of candor, I encourage participants at all levels—especially to managers and administrators—to enact more transparent management to the extent possible and to create practices that increase members' voice. I work on developing organizational relationships that meet the standards of good personal relationships: integrity, honesty, availability, acceptance, respect, and trust. At times I take on the role of advocate for internal and social change (though not as reflectively nor effectively as the authors of many chapters in this book, especially Barbour, Faughn, & Husband; Folger; Sostrin; Cody; Keyton; Pettegrew; and Kreps).

I do not accept projects that will compromise my responsibility to perform my *primary* duties as an academic. However, I also try to take back to campus the "best practices" I find in other organizations to share them with my colleagues. I learn from and, while I often fail, I strive to be as effective as the best leaders I work with in these consultations. Finally, I seek most welcome projects with organizations whose products and services improve society, that evidence social responsibility and, increasingly, that demonstrate commitment to environmental sustainability. Conversely, I do not become engaged with organizations (or with those who own them) whose products or services make me uncomfortable—especially those that adversely affect the health and vitality of our communities and the sustainability of our environment.

COMMUNICATION AS DESIGN <-> DESIGNING CONSULTATIONS

As noted at the outset of this chapter, Jackson and Aakhus (2014) propose that the design of communication perspective (CAD) involves empirically examining communication problems to which existing communication theories can be applied as "design languages" (p. 131). Consistent with CAD commitments, my consultations fundamentally entail decisions concerning how I will *design* my consulting interactions (as speaker, trainer, process consultant, facilitator, evaluator) with clients around their needs, *and* how they will interact with each other and their relevant stakeholders during and after that consulting relationship. At the same time, and consistent the Yates and Orlikowski (1992) "genres" perspective (in which design is viewed as the organizing structures that guide the ongoing communicative actions of members of a community of practice), my consulting also involves seeking to understand the design routines of clients—that is, how they conceptualize and structure their communication and practices over time with each other and with salient stakeholders. Understanding their designs helps me to track problematic issues (about which they may be aware or may not even realize), and helps me reflect more on how I will design my consulting interactions with them. Next, I review two areas of consulting in which I utilized theory/ research from many areas of the discipline as bases for *design* of both training and development activities in organizations.

Designing Presentation Skills Training <-> Presentation Skills Design Languages

Especially during the first 30 years of the nearly 40 years I have consulted, but occasionally still, I deliver presentational skills training as an external consultant contracted by organizations. As noted in Seibold (2005), the workshops are quite similar to those offered by other communication consultants. Participants typically have made many informative and persuasive presentations, but wish to be more effective. The two-day sessions emphasize audience analysis and assessing rhetorical challenges; controlling anxiety; optimum preparation; schema for organizing content; use of evidence; crafting introductions and conclusions; utilizing visuals support and technology effectively; responding to audience members' questions; identifying speaking strengths and weaknesses; changing ineffective delivery dynamics (e.g., volume, rate, animation, variation, eye contact, dynamism, gestures, diction and pronunciation, and so forth); and developing a program for continued growth. In addition to my own presentations, group discussion, and feedback methods used to address these issues, the 8–12 participants in each session deliver a variety of presentations that are videotaped, replayed, and analyzed by all participants and by me. Hence, the objectives, format, content, and methods of these workshops probably are quite similar to the presentation skills training programs other communication consultants provide. What is unique is the way that *all* communication consultants, compared with workshops I have witnessed by non-communication specialists, *integrate* the trifold focus on improving content persuasiveness, on delivery effectiveness, on close analysis of videotape and feedback.

In the view of CAD proponents, design work includes applying extant theories as "design languages" (Jackson & Aakhus, 2014). I regularly integrate in lectures, discussions, and feedback theory-based research findings that enable participants to understand issues they confront or suggestions I offer (Seibold, 2005). For example, participants are comforted to realize that their "stage fright" is readily explained by research on speakers' physiological responses to stressors, and they are empowered by results revealing steps for relieving psychological anxiety and for relaxing physical tension. Other participants, for whom English is a second language, begin to see that their dialect alone may not be what is challenging for listeners. Instead, it may be the interaction of dialect with their rapid rate of delivery (just as speech rate interacts with topic complexity in producing attention and comprehension difficulties for the audiences of any of the participants who must share quite technical information with nontechnical listeners). Still others witness in their videotapes the efficacy of messages reflecting language intensity and lexical diversity, as well as the deleterious effects of hedges, strong qualifiers, and a variety of nonverbal behaviors identified in the research literature. Furthermore, research findings concerning the dimensions along which speaker credibility appear to factor in audience members' judgments of presenters, together with findings concerning the role of issue reactance in producing resistance to persuasion, and of order effects in facilitating influence, all serve to enable participants to consider ways to structure their talks in order to increase their effectiveness. These and other empirical knowledge claims from communication scholarship are not centerpieces of the workshops, and typically I do not mention authors and references. Rather, I use the research findings as design languages that are incorporated into information shared and discussed across the two days. This is another consulting practice in this area of training that is relatively unique among presentation skills trainers.

Evaluation of training programs can be a basis for communication consultants' continued improvement of their programs, including reflection and the construction of ideal models to guide the design of communication practices (Craig & Tracy, 2014). Evaluation efforts also can be an opportunity to undertake research and contribute to scholarship on the impact of communication consulting. Colleagues and I (Seibold, Kudsi, & Rude, 1993), with the blessing and assistance of program sponsors, completed a two-year evaluation of these two-day presentational skills workshops. Our evaluation study focused on assessing participants' behavioral skills (not merely their satisfaction and learning). Given the rigorous nature of our research design (which was nearly a Solomon four-group design) as well as the use of co-workers' assessments, plus our efforts to reduce measurement sensitization, self-report bias, and demand characteristics, the results of our investigation increased sponsors', scholars', and my confidence that both short-term and long-term change is possible in presenters' skills.

Designs for Structuring Group Interaction <-> Structuring Group Interaction Designs

My initial interest in the field of Communication emerged in an undergraduate course in which I was enrolled. Nominally called Small Group Communication, it was an "old school" offering on discussion methods and conference leadership (with origins in textbooks that dated to McBurney & Hance, 1939). Only later, as a graduate student in the discipline, did I begin to (re)frame that course as having been focused on the design of deliberative processes in the types of discussion groups in which many citizens participate and in the types of decision making groups in which most persons engage. This realization not only spawned my theoretical commitments to understand group influence and decision processes (Canary, Brossmann, & Seibold, 1987; Contractor & Seibold, 1993; Meyers & Seibold, 2009; Meyers, Seibold, & Kang, 2010; Poole, McPhee, & Seibold, 1982; Poole, Seibold, & McPhee, 1985, 1996; Seibold & Meyers, 2007; Seibold, Meyers, & Shoham, 2010; Seibold, Meyers, & SunWolf, 1996; SunWolf & Seibold, 1998), but also motivated applied scholarship in which colleagues and I engaged concerning designs for structuring meetings and collaborative decision making (Contractor, Seibold, & Heller, 1996; Jablin & Seibold, 1978; Seibold, 1979; Seibold & Krikorian, 1997; SunWolf & Seibold, 1999).

In turn, those studies and my awareness of others' scholarship in this area (e.g., Gouran, 2003; Poole, 1991) enabled me to design consultations—for example, training sessions, team meetings addressing a multitude of issues, facilitating strategic planning deliberations—for structuring those groups' interactions. In particular, I was able to share procedures that enabled members to elect how to structure their processes to accomplish work and achieve goals. Many of these were traditional analysis-ideation techniques, which emphasize analysis of problems before generation of ideas to resolve them (e.g., Reflective Thinking, Nominal Group Technique, Delphi Method, Multi-attribute Decision Analysis, Pareto Analysis, Flow Charts, PERT). However, there also were opportunities to offer suggestions concerning ideation-analysis techniques that could be useful for generating ideas prior to members' systematic analysis (e.g., Polling, Problem Census, Brainstorming, Buzz (Sub)Groups, Risk). Essential to these suggestions was simultaneously offering evidence that enabled clients to assess the efficacy of a particular structuring procedure—and thus whether it would be a suitable design for structuring their interactions. For example, a study by Jablin, Sorenson, and Seibold (1978) showed that groups in which members brainstormed alone and before they brainstormed as a group outperformed groups in which members brainstormed together immediately. Similarly, explaining that the "four rules" of brainstorming (criticism is taboo, the wilder the idea the better, hitchhiking is welcome, and quantity is wanted) function to counteract dysfunctional processes in groups that seek to be creative (inhibition due to criticism, premature evaluation, egoism, and overly narrow discussions respectively) enabled clients to envision potential problems in their interactions and how to design structures that would counteract them.

Finally, in connection with my current scholarly, pedagogical, and service commitments in the Technology Management Program at UCSB, I have become interested in how innovators and entrepreneurs are designing collaborative information sharing and communication in start-ups and new ventures. As with any business process, founding team members need to design the processes, methods and tools necessary for the venture to succeed. As I work with some of these start-ups in consulting and pro bono service engagements, and view their work routines within a life cycle of data needs that require generation, capture, evaluation, development and launch information and communication activities, I frequently observe new venture founders and their teams appropriating intriguing tools that are linked to mind maps, to idea databases, to IP search and protection, and to rapid prototyping, among many others. What they are doing, from both CAD (Aakhus & Jackson, 2005) and genre (Orlikowski & Yates, 1992; Orlikowski, 2000) perspectives, is making design decisions concerning how they will interact around their data needs. Furthermore, they increasingly are enabling new product development and launch through the design of interaction that includes the appropriation of structured and structuring software products (e.g., Bright Ideas, Imaginatik, Sopheon, OVO Incubator). No doubt other communication consultants are designing their interactions with organizational clients around how those clients have designed their interactions concerning critical processes—and especially clients' choices and uses of advanced information and communication technologies to enable and maintain those interaction structures. And that is another relatively unique feature of communication scholars' organizational consulting: a theoretical awareness and practical appreciation for the interpenetration and structuring potential of technology and interaction (Jackson, Poole, & Kuhn, 2002; Rice & Leonardi, 2014).

CONCLUSION

In this chapter I have sought to describe how and why communication scholars with an interest in organizational training and development are well suited to consulting. I hope I have encouraged scholars and other readers to think critically about the nature of a communication scholar's perspective, knowledge, and skills, as well as several ways that the perspectives communication scholars brings to bear on consulting projects differ from other experts' orientations in ways that add particular value to organizations and/or increase consultants' effectiveness.

First, given the breadth of the field, the added breadth from our multidisciplinary orientation, the comfort of communication scholars to theory-practice relationships, and the communication aspects of nearly all consulting projects, communication scholars have the potential to become involved in a very wide range of projects—wider than experts from other disciplines. Second, and related to the first, substantive organizational communication consulting demands a broad perspective not a narrow approach—and this is a unique feature of communication scholars' organizational consulting more so than the 'specialists' I have witnessed from other disciplines.

Third, opportunities to inform or reform theory via academic publications that emerge from practices observed in the course of consultations is another relatively unique facet of communication scholars' approach to organizational consulting. This is especially the case given that "basic" and "applied" research are seen as inherently connected in the discipline. Fourth, the best communication scholars whose consulting I have witnessed use strong research findings as design languages that are incorporated into information shared and discussed. Fifth, and in light of organizations' increasing reliance on advanced information and communication technologies, communication scholars possess a distinctive theoretical awareness and practical appreciation for the interpenetration and structuring potential of technology and interaction. Sixth, given the dual commitments of the communication discipline to theory and practice, the consultations of which I am aware that are conducted by communication scholars have a distinctive *design* orientation that are at the nexus of extant theory and practice/performance.

To put a finer point on these observations, training and development consultants often lack credibility with organizational members because they offer "off the shelf" programs or presentations that are not responsive to the needs of participants in particular organizational contexts. They have not engaged the organization sufficiently. Their lack of credibility also may stem from members' perception that many consultants offer recommendations without 'evidence' for them. Integrating research findings into consultations inoculates against that perception and bolsters communication scholars' credibility. Of course scholars must concomitantly move beyond that expertise to collaborative learning and problem solving *with* participants—a point that Folger (Chapter 10) discusses with great insight. Making transparent the theoretical warrants for recommendations greatly increases organizational members' learning—a dynamic I witnessed repeatedly in the presentation skills workshops noted above. In turn, that deepened understanding aids participants in subsequent problem solving and in developing their own strategies for decision making—as was evident in the many times I worked with team members who were interested in improving their meetings.

Finally, I have sought to preview the many chapters in this volume that richly identify both general and task-specific skills that communication scholars bring to organizational consulting. By way of complement to them, I reflected on my code of ethics and wide range of roles as potential aids for others concerning how to develop and maintain a credible identity as both a scholar and a practicing consultant. At the heart of that dual challenge is maintaining a commitment to socially relevant engagement—as a scholar or consultant—and a commitment to looking for opportunities for theory and practice to be reciprocally enhancing.

REFERENCES

Aakhus, M., & Jackson, S. (2005). Technology, design, and interaction. In K. Fitch & R. E. Sanders (Eds.), *Handbook of language and social interaction* (pp. 411–436). Mahwah, NJ: Erlbaum.

Ballard, D. I., & Seibold, D. R. (2003). Communicating and organizing in time: A meso-level model of organizational temporality. *Management Communication Quarterly, 16*(3), 380–415.

Ballard, D. I., & Seibold, D. R. (2004). Organizational members' communication and temporal experience: Scale development and validation. *Communication Research, 31*(2), 135–172.

Barge, J. K. (2001). Practical theory as mapping, engaged reflection, and transformative practice. *Communication Theory, 11*, 5–13.

Barge, J. K., & Craig, R. T. (2009). Practical theory in applied communication scholarship. In L. R. Frey & K. N. Cissna (Eds.), *Routledge handbook of applied communication research* (pp. 55–78). New York: Routledge.

Berteotti, C. R., & Seibold, D. R. (1994). Coordination and role-definition problems in health care teams: A hospice case study. In L. R. Frey (Ed.), *Group communication in context: Studies of natural groups* (pp. 107–131). Hillsdale, NJ: Lawrence Erlbaum.

Canary, D. J., Brossmann, B. G., & Seibold, D. R. (1987). Argument structures in decision-making groups. *Southern Speech Communication Journal, 53*, 18–37.

Cantrill, J, & Seibold, D. R. (1986). The perceptual contrast explanation of sequential request effectiveness. *Human Communication Research, 13*, 253–267.

Contractor, N. S., & Seibold, D. S. (1993). Theoretical frameworks for the study of structuring processes in group decision support systems: Adaptive structuration theory and self-organizing systems theory. *Human Communication Research, 19*, 528–563.

Contractor, N. S., Seibold, D. R., & Heller, M. A. (1996). Interactional influence in the structuring of media use in groups: Influence in members' perceptions of group decision support system use. *Human Communication Research, 22*, 451–481.

Craig, R. T. (1989). Communication as a practical discipline. In B. Dervin, L. Grossberg, B. J. O'Keefe, & E. Wartella (Eds.), *Rethinking communication* (pp. 97–122). Newbury Park, CA: Sage Publications.

Craig, R. T. (1995). Applied communication research in a practical discipline. In K. N. Cissna (Ed.), *Applied communication in the 21ˢᵗ century* (pp. 147–155). Mahwah, NJ: Lawrence Erlbaum Associates.

Craig, R. T. (1999). Communication theory as a field. *Communication Theory, 9*, 118–161.

Craig, R. T. (2006). Communication as a practice. In G. J. Shepherd, J. St. John, & T. Striphas (Eds.), *Communication as...: Perspectives on theory* (pp. 38–47). Thousand Oaks, CA: SAGE Publications.

Craig, R. T., & Tracy, K. (1995). Grounded practical theory: The case of intellectual discussion. *Communication Theory, 5*, 248–272.

Craig, R. T., & Tracy, K. (2014). Building grounded practical theory in applied communication research: Introduction to the special issue. *Journal of Applied Communication Research, 42*(3), 229–243.

Farace, R. V., Monge, P. R., & Russell, H. M. (1977). *Communicating and organizing.* Reading, MA: Addison-Wesley.

Franken, L., & Seibold, D. R. (2010). Business process modeling at the Internal Funding Office: Structuring group interaction processes to structure business processes. In L. Black (Ed.), *Group communication: Cases for analysis, appreciation, and application* (pp. 17–24). Dubuque, IA: Kendall Hunt.

Giddens, A. (1984). *The constitution of society: Outline of the theory of structuration*. Berkeley: University of California Press.

Gouran, D. S. (2003). Communication skills for group decision making. In J. O. Greene & B. R. Burleson (Eds.), *Handbook of communication and social interaction skills* (pp. 835–870). Mahwah, NJ: Lawrence Erlbaum Associates.

Helmle, J. R., Botero, I., & Seibold, D. R. (2014). Factors that influence perceptions of work-life balance in owners of copreneurial firms. *Journal of Family Business Management, 4*(2), 110–132.

Jablin, F. M., & Seibold, D. R. (1978). Implications for problem-solving groups of empirical research on 'brainstorming': A critical review of the literature. *Southern Speech Communication Journal, 43,* 327–356.

Jablin, F. M., Sorenson, R. L., & Seibold, D. R. (1978). Interpersonal perception and group brainstorming performance. *Communication Quarterly, 26,* 36–44.

Jackson, M. H., Poole, M. S., & Kuhn, T. (2002). The social construction of technologies in studies of the workplace. In L. A. Lievrouw & S. Livingstone (Eds.), *Handbook of new media* (pp. 236–253). London: Sage Publications.

Jackson, S., & Aakhus, M. (2014). Becoming more reflective about the role of design in communication. *Journal of Applied Communication Research, 42*(2), 125–134.

Kang, P., & Seibold, D. R. (2014). Demanding leadership of a collegiate basketball team: Courting Goals-Plans-Action (GPA) theory. In C. J. Liberman (Ed.), *Casing persuasive communication* (pp. 69–85). Dubuque, IA: Kendall Hunt Publishing Company.

Krikorian, D., Seibold, D. R., & Goode, P. L. (1997). Re-engineering at LAC: A case study of emergent network processes. In B. D. Sypher (Ed.), *Case studies in organizational communication* (2nd ed., pp. 129–144). New York: Guilford.

Lemus, D. R., & Seibold, D. R. (2008). Argument development versus argument strength: The predictive potential of argument quality in computer-mediated group deliberations. In T. Suzuki, T. Kato, & A. Kubota (Eds.), *Proceedings of the 3rd Tokyo conference on argumentation: Argumentation, the law and justice* (pp. 166–174). Tokyo, Japan: JDA.

Lewis, L. K., & Seibold, D. R. (1993). Innovation modification during intra-organizational adoption. *Academy of Management Review, 18,* 322–354.

Lewis, L. K., & Seibold, D. R. (1996). Communication during intra-organizational innovation adoption: Predicting users' behavioral coping responses to innovations in organizations. *Communication Monographs, 63,* 131–157.

McBurney, J. H., & Hance, K. G. (1939). *The principle sand methods of discussion*. New York: Harper & Brothers.

Meyers, R. A., & Seibold, D. R. (1985). Consumer involvement as a segmentation approach for studying utilization of health organization services. *Southern Speech Communication Journal, 50,* 327–347.

Meyers, R. A., & Seibold, D. R. (2009). Making foundational assumptions transparent: Framing the discussion about group communication and influence. *Human Communication Research, 35,* 286–295.

Meyers, R. A., Seibold, D. R., & Kang, P. (2010). Examining the argument process in naturally occurring jury deliberations. *Small Group Research, 41*(4), 452–473.

Meyers, R. A., Seibold, D. R., & Willihnganz, S. C. (1983). Using an integrative model of health organizations as a framework for program assessment. *Journal of Applied Communication Research, 11,* 28–44.

Mulac, A., Seibold, D. R., & Farris, J. (2000). Female and male managers' and professionals' criticism-giving: Differences in language use and effects. *Journal of Language and Social Psychology, 19*(4), 389–415.

Orlikowski, W. J. (2000). Using technology and constituting structures: A practice lens for studying technology in organizations. *Organization Science, 11*(4), 404–428.

Pearce, W. B. (2007). *Making social worlds: A communication perspective.* Malden, MA: Blackwell.

Poole, M. S. (1991). Procedures for managing meetings: Social and technological innovation. In R. A. Swenson & B. O. Knapp (Eds.), *Innovative meeting management* (pp. 53–109). Austin, TX: 3M Meeting Management Institute.

Poole, M. S., McPhee, R. D., & Seibold, D. R. (1982). A comparison of normative and interactional explanations of group decision-making: Social decision schemes versus valence distributions. *Communication Monographs, 49*, 1–19.

Poole, M. S., Seibold, D. R., & McPhee, R. D. (1985). Group decision-making as a structurational process. *Quarterly Journal of Speech, 71*, 74–102.

Poole, M. S., Seibold, D. R., & McPhee, R. D. (1996). The structuration of group decisions. In R. Y. Hirokawa & M. S. Poole (Eds.), *Communication and group decision making* (2nd ed., pp. 114–146). Thousand Oaks, CA: SAGE Publications.

Rice, R. E., & Leonardi, P. M. (2014). Information and communication technologies in organizations. In L. L. Putnam & D. K. Mumby (Eds.), *The SAGE handbook of organizational communication: Advances in theory, research, and methods* (3rd ed., pp. pp. 425–448). Thousand Oaks, CA: SAGE Publications.

Seibold, D. R. (1975). Communication research and the attitude-verbal report-overt behavior relationship: A critique and theoretic reformulation. *Human Communication Research, 2*, 3–32.

Seibold, D. R. (1979). Making meetings more successful: Plans, formats, and procedures for group problem-solving. *Journal of Business Communication, 16*, 3–20.

Seibold, D. R. (1995). Developing the "team" in a team-managed organization: Group facilitation in a new plant design. In L. R. Frey (Ed.), *Innovations in group facilitation techniques: Case studies of applications in naturalistic settings* (pp. 282–298). Cresskill, NJ: Hampton.

Seibold, D. R. (2001). The admiral and the loose cannons. In S. DeWine, *The consultant's craft: Improving organizational communication* (2nd ed., pp. 337–339). New York: Bedford.

Seibold, D. R. (2005). Bridging theory and practice in organizational communication. In J. L. Simpson & P. Shockley-Zalabak (Eds.), *Engaging communication, transforming organizations: Scholarship of engagement in action* (pp. 13–44). Cresskill, NJ: Hampton.

Seibold, D. R. (2015). Applied communication research. In W. Donsbach (Ed.), *Concise encyclopedia of communication* (pp. 27–29). Oxford: Blackwell Publishing.

Seibold, D. R., & Flanagin, A. J. (2000). Potential 'sites' for building common ground across metatheoretical perspectives in organizational communication. In S. R. Corman & M. S. Poole (Eds.), *Perspectives on organizational communication: Finding common ground* (pp. 175–182). New York: Guilford Publications.

Seibold, D. R., Hollingshead, A. B., & Yoon, K. (2014). Embedded teams and embedding organizations. In L. L. Putnam & D. K. Mumby (Eds.), *The SAGE handbook of organizational communication: Advances in theory, research, and methods* (3rd ed., pp. 327–349). Thousand Oaks, CA: SAGE Publications.

Seibold, D. R., & Krikorian, D. (1997). Planning and facilitating group meetings. In L. R. Frey & J. K. Barge (Eds.), *Managing the tensions of group life: Communicating in decision-making groups* (pp. 272–305). Boston: Houghton Mifflin.

Seibold, D. R., Kudsi, S., & Rude, M. (1993). Does communication training make a difference? Evidence for the effectiveness of a presentation skills program. *Journal of Applied Communication Research, 21*, 111–131.

Seibold, D. R., Lemus, D. R., Ballard, D. I., & Myers, K. K. (2009). Organizational communication and applied communication research: Parallels, intersections, integration, and engagement. In L. R. Frey & K. N. Cissna (Eds.), *Routledge handbook of applied communication research* (pp. 331–354). New York: Routledge/Taylor & Francis.

Seibold, D. R., & Meyers, R. A. (2007). Group argument: A structuration perspective and research program. *Small Group Research, 38,* 312–336.

Seibold, D. R., & Meyers, R. A. (2012). Interventions in groups: Methods for facilitating team development. In A. B. Hollingshead & M. S. Poole (Eds.), *Research methods for studying groups and teams: A guide to approaches, tools, and technologies* (pp. 418–441). New York: Taylor & Francis/Routledge.

Seibold, D. R., Meyers, R. A., & Shoham, M. D. (2010). Social influence in groups and organizations. In C. R. Berger, M. E. Roloff, & D. Roskos-Ewolsen (Eds.), *Handbook of communication science* (2nd ed., pp. 237–253). Thousand Oaks, CA: SAGE Publications.

Seibold, D. R., Meyers, R. A., & SunWolf (1996). Communication and influence in decision making. In R. Y. Hirokawa & M. S. Poole (Eds.), *Communication and group decision making* (2nd ed., pp. 242–268). Thousand Oaks, CA: SAGE Publications.

Seibold, D. R., Meyers, R. A., & Willihnganz, S. C. (1984). Communicating health information to the public: Effectiveness of a newsletter. *Health Education Quarterly, 10,* 263–286.

Seibold, D. R., Rossi, S., Berteotti, C., Soprych, S., & McQuillan, L. (1987). Volunteer involvement in a hospice care program. *American Journal of Hospice Care, 4,* 43–55.

Seibold, D. R., & Thomas, R. W. (1994). Rethinking the role of interpersonal influence processes in alcohol intervention situations. *Journal of Applied Communication Research, 22,* 177–197.

Simpson, J. L., & Seibold, D. R. (2008). Practical engagements and co-created research. *Journal of Applied Communication Research, 36*(3), 265–279.

Steinfatt, T. M., Gantz, W., Seibold, D. R., & Miller, L. (1973). News diffusion of the George Wallace shooting: The apparent lack of interpersonal communication as an artifact of delayed measurement. *Quarterly Journal of Speech, 59,* 402–412.

Stoltzfus, K., Stohl, C., & Seibold, D. R. (2011). Managing organizational change: Paradoxical problems, solutions, and consequences. *Journal of Organizational Change Management, 24*(3), 349–367.

SunWolf, & Seibold, D. R. (1998). Jurors' intuitive rules for deliberation: A structurational approach to communication in jury decision making. *Communication Monographs, 64*(4), 282–307.

SunWolf, & Seibold, D. R. (1999). The impact of formal procedures on group processes, members, and task outcomes. In L. R. Frey (Ed.), *The handbook of group communication theory and research* (pp. 395–431). Thousand Oaks, CA: SAGE Publications.

Thomas, R. W., & Seibold, D. R. (1995). Interpersonal influence and alcohol-related interventions in the college environment. *Health Communication, 7*(2), 93–123.

Witte, K., & Roberto, A. J. (2009). Fear appeals and public health: Managing fear and creating hope. In L. R. Frey & K. N. Cissna (Eds.), *Routledge handbook of applied communication research* (pp. 584–610). New York: Routledge.

Yates, J., & Orlikowski, W. J. (1992). Genres of organizational communication: A structurational approach to study communication and media. *Academy of Management Review, 17*(2), 299–326.

CHAPTER THREE

Many Paths

The Role of the Consultant's Paradigms, Values, and Ethics

JOANN KEYTON

North Carolina State University

Consulting is an omnibus, or sweeping, term. It conjures positive and negative evaluations. It references individuals who consult occasionally for extra money as well as mega-consulting firms. Consulting is also seen as a powerful process that benefits some and disadvantages others. This volume, in general, addresses a number of questions relative to consulting, such as: Who can be a consultant? What does a consultant do? What are the goals of consulting? More specifically, meaningful consulting requires an understanding of the paradigms and values from which the consultant works. The goals of this chapter, then, are to (a) distinguish among different structures through which consulting is accomplished, (b) explain the distinction between expert and process consulting, (c) explore the consultant's philosophical perspective in approaching consulting activities, and (d) examine the importance of values and ethical principles.

TYPES OF CONSULTING AND A WORKING DEFINITION

Generally speaking, there are three types of consulting. The first is *in–house consulting* (i.e., a unit within an organization that provides an array of consulting activities across organizational functions). Some large organizations (Rouen, 2012) designate employees as consultants to keep significant decisions within the organization, and to keep external consultants from threatening the organization's culture.

In-house consulting is sometimes seen as a pathway to top management positions, as these employees/consultants provide are expected to learn about and provide assistance to all of the organization's activities (e.g., marketing, finance, human resources, information/technology, operations). For example, American Express CEO Ken Chenault, CEO at American Express since 2001, started his career in its internal consulting department (Rouen, 2012).

The second type is *internal consulting* (i.e., a designated organizational unit that provides consulting expertise or processes to other organizational units). In many ways, an organization's human resources department performs internal consulting functions. Using their specialized expertise on employment issues and job performance, HR personnel can coach supervisors and employees in other departments, as well as provide advice about best practices. I served as a member of Operations Review, an internal consulting team at the Federal Reserve Bank of Kansas City. The Bank provides financial services to depository institutions. The Review team focused only on analyzing and improving technology and communication associated with operational workflow issues (e.g., cash, check, and treasury bill, notes and bond management). Our scope of work was quite narrow and similar across the different operational units served. This internal consulting team followed the process and practices associated with commercial bank deposits from when they entered the Bank to when they exited the Bank. Because of the volume and value of activity, each exchange among employees was to follow a specific protocol. The team watched employees execute the protocols, talked with employees about the protocols, and made recommendations on how protocols could be improved. Team members also observed employees operate equipment (e.g., check sorting machines) to identify if operational efficiency was distracting from security. Eventually, each protocol was finalized in a written procedure. For this organization, the internal consulting team was the way the Bank continuously improved its processes.

Both in-house and internal consulting are less expensive than hiring external consultants and provide some specific advantages (Cerisano, 2014). For example, internal consultants (a) have an integrated understanding of the organization, (b) are able to follow a project from conception to implementation to evaluation, and (c) are able to proactively think about and plan for the future.

The third type is *external consulting*. Here, consulting services are provided by an economically independent individual, team, or large consulting firm that works under contract to the organization. This type of consulting is contracted, often for a specific period of time and for a specific project. Being outside the organization, external consultants bring advantages as well. Primary among these is being able to draw upon diverse and high-level expertise, and bringing an outsider's, including an industry, view of the issues. For this reason, many large consulting organizations focus on specific industries.

For this chapter, I adopt Steele's (1975, pp. 2–3) definition of consulting: Consulting is "any form of providing help on the content, process, or structure of a task or series of tasks, where the consultant is not actually responsible for doing the task itself but is helping those who are." This definition encompasses several important points. First, this definition does not focus solely on communication consulting as a paid activity for profit organizations for which the consultant earns a fee for services performed. Communication consulting can be performed for nonprofit or government organizations for which some consultants work pro bono.

Second, this definition does not privilege organizational communication consulting in which the consultant directly helps an organization become more efficient or effective. Rather, communication consultants may, for example, do research with consumers to help profit and nonprofit organizations understand societal trends, assist government entities in crafting public safety or health warning messages, prepare a political candidate for debate, or help attorneys prepare for trial. Communication consulting is a broad based problem-solving activity—both in types of activity and context. But "at its core, [consulting] is always regarded as being about interaction concerned with the process of giving and taking advice" (Rottger & Preusse, 2013, p. 103).

A third important dimension of Steele's definition is that it includes the premise that the consultant has significantly limited, or no, decision power in the organization. The consultant may make recommendations, but cannot take steps to enact them. Of course, some consultants do enact decisions and perform organizational activity on behalf of their client. In this latter case, however, the so-labeled consultant is performing professional services that are no longer consultative or advisory. When a professional is working as a consultant in an advisory role the focus of the work is primarily about what could or should be changed about client activities, and how those changes should take place. Thus, a number of issues related to underlying approaches or paradigms, values, and ethics must be addressed. But, first let's distinguish between expert and process consulting.

EXPERT AND PROCESS CONSULTING

Typically, the first issue that consultants must address is the approach to the consulting activity. Research on consulting has coalesced around two primary paradigms: expert consulting and process consulting (see Grossman, 2011; Zerfass & Franke, 2013).

Expert consulting is content-related consulting based on the consultant's professional expert knowledge and experience. That is, expert consulting focuses on the *what*. For example, I was once contracted to review all the materials and pre-trial depositions collected in a case of gender discrimination. The attorney representing the complainant was trying to assess the strength of the case. My analysis would influence the approach he took in pre-trial negotiations. I content analyzed hundreds of pages to identify themes; and then performed a second analysis to evaluate the degree to which themes from the complainant and defendant testimony agreed or conflicted. More specifically, the client wanted to know (a) if gender discrimination occurred; (b) if gender discrimination occurred, what the exact nature of it was; and (c) what the effect of that discrimination was.

Alternately, *process consulting* focuses on the *how*. In this case, the consultant helps facilitate the client's problem solving, or decision making, by leading or coaching the client through a process that reveals or reflects the client's underlying assumptions or blind spots. In its ultimate form, process consulting enables the client to work effectively on its own. For example, I was contracted to assist an organization's team of lawyers with understanding how an organization's sexual harassment policy and procedures could be interpreted differently by supervisors and subordinates. More specifically, I helped the attorneys (a) explore if and how one policy could be interpreted differently by different groups of people; (b) examine how these different interpretations would influence the likelihood of employees reporting sexual harassment when it occurs; and (c) project how unreported incidents of sexual harassment would influence the organization's culture. In this case of consulting, my role was to use different frames of reference to help the attorneys assess the likelihood that the policy would be used as they intended. In other words, I helped them to see the policy not as attorneys, but in the ways organizational members would.

In both cases, my expertise was demonstrated by my professional education and position. Primary evidence of my expertise was the empirical research I had conducted and published about sexual harassment in organizations. Interestingly, presentations I had been invited to make to non-academic organizations about organizational culture, sexual harassment, and gender discrimination—and the specific audiences to which those presentations were made (e.g., attorneys)—were often the way my expertise was discovered.

As others have noted (Grossman, 2011; Kubr, 2002; Zerfass & Frank, 2013) both expert and process forms of consulting can be effective. One may be more effective than the other depending on the circumstances. Sometimes both forms of consulting will be required, with one form of consulting becoming a springboard for the other type of consulting.

PARADIGMS OF CONSULTING

Earlier, consulting was believed to be a type of intervention to help organizations stop destructive or ineffective processes (DeWine, 1994). This *deficit* model of consulting has largely been replaced by an *improvement* model in which consulting is intended to help clients improve on some standard (i.e., become more effective or efficient, improve meeting management, improve messages about consumer food choices, increase fundraising through more effective campaigns). Whether one takes a deficit or improvement view of consulting, consultants also use their underlying philosophical assumptions—and, these are often the same as the assumptions associated with their research activities. Each philosophical position carries with it a set of ontological, epistemological, and axiological assumptions that direct how consultants identify problems, develop potential solutions, and interact with members of the client organization. These assumptions, consciously or not, lead consultants to a perspective that frames their work. When a consultant operates from a legitimate paradigm or theoretical framework, his or her work becomes tenable, defensible, and credible across contexts. The communication discipline offers consultants a number of useful paradigms; what follows is an explanation of three common perspectives for approaching a consulting project, along with examples of each from my consulting work.

Systems Perspective on Consulting

Much consulting is developed from a systems perspective because problems to be solved and their solutions affect one or more entities directly, and numerous others indirectly. There are many levels from which to analyze consulting practices. As the largest frame, systems theory—or some derivation—is used to position consulting activity within the broader context in which consulting occurs. Systems theory (van Bertalanffy, 1968) is essentially a theory of change in complex environments based upon the interdependence, or interrelatedness, of components involved in change. Systems theory offers consultants two important premises. The first premise is that sets of interacting components comprise a system. Thus a consultant could look for and analyze ways in which units within an organization interact with or depend on one another. This type of investigation can reveal when a problem or opportunity in one part of the system intentionally or unintentionally influences a problem or opportunity in another part of the system. Frequently, employees and managers become experts at *their* work and fail to notice the systemic influences of what they do. A second premise of systems theory is that there are multiple ways to accomplish the same end point. That is, there is no *correct* way for consulting to be enacted. Moreover, the consultant cannot directly influence the client system without some willingness of the organization (or its members) to change. This paradigm positions both the consultant (and his or her system of entities and influences) and the organization or client (and its system of entities and influences) as interdependent systems comprising a more macro consulting system (e.g., giving and receiving influence from each other; Rottger & Preusse, 2013).

Relative to consulting, systems theory positions the consultant in two ways (Rottger & Preusse, 2013). First, the consultant is an outsider to the system in which the consulting is to occur. And it is this position from which consultants "derive their legitimacy as providers of advice" (p. 105). Second, the consultant is connected to the client, or organization, by the practice of consulting, which is believed to be a problem solving process requiring learning and reflection by both the consultant and the client. Central to a systems theory perspective for consulting, the consultant is never an actor or co-actor in the organizational system; rather the consultant "maintains a reflexive distance from the client system" (Rottger & Preusse, 2013, p. 115).

The systems perspective was central to much of the sexual harassment consulting I did in the mid to late 1990s. Organizations were interested in reducing sexual harassment claims and, ironically, less concerned about reducing the occurrence of sexual harassment. In initial meetings with potential clients, I routinely drew a systems view of their organization to demonstrate that a better way to reduce claims was to take a multi-step approach to reducing harassment. I advocated that sexual harassment policy, reporting procedures, and training were essential to changing the organization's culture. I also emphasized that changes in these formal communication policies alone could not make this happen. Next I layered on systems of informal communication systems, including the day-to-day conversations between supervisors and subordinates, as well as conversations among employees. At that point in time, sexual harassment claims prominently featured in the news were made by subordinates based on their supervisors' behaviors. Using the systems perspective gave me the tools to demonstrate that this one type of harassment was the most visible aspect of a much bigger problem. That is, there was evidence that supervisors were sexually harassing subordinates, and that a hostile work environment had likely developed that encouraged sexual harassing communication among employees. The systems perspective allowed me to illustrate how one subsystem (sexual harassment from supervisors to subordinates) was also contributing to sexually hostile communication among employees. Simply, my advice was: addressing a single type of sexual communication in the organization would not solve the problem, a more comprehensive approach would be needed.

Interpretive Perspective on Consulting

Another distinct approach to consulting is the interpretive paradigm. The interpretive perspective of organizational communication views organizations as social sites in which members use communication to socially construct their reality (Cheney, 2000; Putnam, 1983). Day-to-day interaction among organizational members creates their organizational reality. Thus, people construct their own organizational realities as they go about their daily work practices. Realities are individual and meaning centered. In consulting work from this perspective, the consultant must interact with and collect data from organizational members and value their interpretations of organizational life. Thus, the point of view of organizational members is privileged over the point of view of the organization or the consultant.

For example, the interpretive perspective informed a consulting project with which I was involved in important ways. A major research hospital invited me to consult to help them design their application for the Best Places to Work™ competition, which is essentially a benchmarking process of organizational culture. Because I had little understanding of the hospital's culture as an outsider, I asked for examples of their written external and internal communication and a tour of the facility. After agreeing to consult on this project, the human resources team showed me their employee survey results and their draft design of their application package. As I compared the numeric survey results and employees' written comments with the application that the organization had prepared for submission, I struggled to find a relationship between the two. The employee survey results clearly demonstrated employees' high regard for the organization, and its values and mission. But, the application package was positioned figuratively as a recorded message—similar to that of the television series *Mission: Impossible*. In that scenario, once the mission was revealed, the recording self-destructed. I continued to struggle to see how the self-destructing recording represented the very favorable employee survey scores. In further discussions with the HR team, I discovered that they envisioned a catchy theme to be important for the judging panel who made the first-pass decisions about applications. I asked questions about what themes, or narratives, could be used to package the application and represent the favorable survey results. Finally, I remarked, "You don't want the voices of the employees to disappear. You should use their written comments to find your theme. To be effective, narratives need to resonate with one another. And, the strongest narratives you have comes from your employees." Drawing upon an interpretive explanation of communication, I encouraged them to find a more authentic and representative voice or story for their application.

Symbolic Convergence Perspective on Consulting

A third paradigm for framing consulting work is symbolic convergence theory. As Bormann (1982) described it, "symbolic convergence provides a description of the dynamic tendencies within systems of social interaction that cause communication practices and forms to evolve" (p. 51). In general, and for consulting, symbolic convergence occurs during communication between or among communicators, in which two symbolic worlds overlap. For example, in an interaction as the client explains the problem which has directed her consulting need, the consultant explains how his expertise supports or reinforces the client's understanding of the problem. Through conversation, the client and consultant can achieve mutual understanding (or very overlapped symbolic systems). When symbolic systems overlap, both client and consultant see the problem in highly relatable ways allowing them to "sympathize, empathize, and identify with one another (Bormann, 1982, p. 51).

Why are overlapping symbolic systems so important to consulting? First, shared symbolisms position interaction between the client (and organizational members) and the consultant as primary. From and through their interactions, the two parties share a common social reality about necessary initiatives or plans; for example, when convergence exists, organizational members are likely to agree, for example, on the need for a public relations campaign to introduce a company's new service. The shared social reality is deepened when both parties share how they talk about the problem and ways in which a public relations campaign might work (or fail). Narratives, or accounts or a story about events, help to shape the relationship between client and consultant, and drive creative, effective potential solutions for which there is widespread support. Second, when the consultant interacts with the client and organizational members (see Cragan & Shields, 1992), she learns the *symbolic landscape* that allows her to understand the problem in the way the client and organizational members do. For example, if the consultant is to develop persuasive public relations (or advertising or a political campaign), she must develop messages that relate in some way (advance or repair) to the existing narratives.

When symbolic realities do not converge, the consultant is at a disadvantage in terms of competently completing her work. For example, when I received a call from a law enforcement official asking me to do a presentation on sexual harassment for his officers, I asked him a few questions about his views on sexual harassment and how problematic he believed sexual harassment to be within his organization. His responses clearly indicated that sexual harassment was not a problem in his jurisdiction, and if it were, he would have taken care of it. At that moment, I realized we did not share the same symbolic reality about sexual harassment, especially the type of pervasive sexual harassment and gender discrimination that can occur in power-laden organizations. I also had difficulty believing that this potential client was able to know the extent of sexual harassment when most of his officers worked in remote locations, away from his direct oversight. Looking for a fresh start to the conversation, I asked about the number of female officers and number of women in administrative positions. He replied again with "*sexual harassment is not a problem* and *if it were, I would have taken care of it.*" Perplexed, I asked why he wanted the presentation; he replied that a presentation would count as sexual harassment training. It was clear to me at this point that our symbolic representations about the potential presence of sexual harassment in this work environment were different, as were our symbolic realities about the role of sexual harassment training. Finally, I asked if I could interview a few male and female members of both the administrative and patrol staff before making the presentation. He firmly refused my request indicating he just wanted the presentation. I did not believe it was ethical of me to use his narrative about sexual harassment (which I viewed as power-laden and dismissive about the potential that sexual harassment could occur without his knowledge) to develop a presentation for other members of the organization. Thus, I declined the opportunity.

Across this brief phone conversation, I tried several times to assess the degree of convergence (or where convergence might be) between the potential client and me. Convergence in meaning is not something one starts with or ends with. Rather, convergence is developed as people interact. If had chosen to work with this client, I would have needed to assess our convergence as I developed the training, when I delivered the training, and in the evaluation of the training. When consultant and client cannot achieve symbolic convergence, one or both parties are likely to be unhappy with the process and outcomes.

Critical Perspective on Consulting

Some scholars work from a philosophical perspective that consulting privileges those in power (see, for example, Buzzanell, 2000). Communication scholars who draw upon the critical perspective—sometimes labeled *activist consulting*—often use action research or participatory research as the basis of their consulting activities. Drawing upon the critical perspective, action researchers work inside the organization, but also as consultants who can raise questions about power and privilege, especially the taken-for-granted structure and systems that shape our society. Crabtree and Ford (2004) provide a rich description of their research from an activist perspective that positions consulting as a social justice activity within the affected community. Crabtree describes her journey with a sexual assault nonprofit agency from facilitating a classroom project for students to community activism (as well as her own healing). Admitting that her activist activities "eventually looked a lot like a consultancy" (p. 258), and consistent with feminist theorizing, Crabtree had difficulty in separating her roles as personal, professional, political, academic, or activist. Her coauthor, Ford, also describes how a feminist perspective provided a lens from which to evaluate the nonprofit's structural problems. For example, Ford acknowledged the positive interpersonal communication among the leader and her staff. At the same time, this closeness "severely restricted open discussion about the long-term interests of the agency" (p. 259). Similarly consultants who are also organizational insiders, or sympathetic to an organization's social justice mission, may have difficulty distinguishing between their personal and professional roles, and their respective actions within those roles. Being organizational insiders in some form is typical for scholar-consultants who work from critical or related perspectives.

Communication Perspective Summary

Depending on the scope of the consulting project, consultants may draw from various perspectives, as different approaches are required for different aspects of projects. As some of the previous examples have demonstrated, consultants, including myself, tend to rely on one perspective in a particular consulting project or activity. If the perspective chosen is not well aligned with the client's project or their intended outcomes, then the consultant may be unable to fulfill the client's needs. On the other hand, when the consultant brings a different perspective than that of the client, the consultant opens up the solution space in a way that encourages the client to see the problem, and potential solutions, in a different way.

When problems are particularly complicated or perplexing, the consultant is well advised to use his or her analytical ability to view the problem from different perspectives. Sometimes, demonstrating a different way of looking at a problem is illuminating for the client. For example, Hart, Esrock, and Leichty (2008) describe the various theoretical foundations they relied on as they helped a nonprofit agency improve messaging with the goal of raising a state's excise tax on tobacco. As the project developed, their involvement included "participation in strategy and operations meetings, reviews of media coverage of the campaign, analysis of campaign documents, and interviews with campaign leaders and key legislative allies of the excise tax increase proposal" (p. 436). Bringing multiple philosophical or competing theoretical explanations to consulting activity can be useful, as many problems in organizations and client systems are paradoxical—or sites of incompatibility.

On a more sober note, Suchan (2006) draws our attention to the fit between consultant's theoretical knowledge, theories-in-use by members of the client system, and theoretical knowledge needed to complete the consulting activities. He describes that consultants may possess the necessary theoretical knowledge for a specific issue, but not appropriate theoretical background to direct change of that issue. In his instance, Suchan was asked, and agreed, to assess and improve an organization's written reports. He advocates that all consultants need understanding of how to initiate changes and why change is resisted. He makes a very good point. Beyond the theoretical and methodological knowledge consultants bring to any setting, they must also be able to dislodge current communication processes to allow new ones to become normative. Suchan also points out that consultants cannot rely on leaders or others in power to fully understand this process, as they rarely "take time to reflect on their own and the organization's communication assumptions and practices because they are under pressure to respond quickly" (p. 24).

Regardless which communication perspective(s) a consultant takes, consultants are rhetors in their attempts to change organizational or client systems. That is, "consulting requires persuasive communication" (Lange, 1984, p. 51)—whether that be in the form of the consultant persuading a client to enter into a consulting contract, convincing a client that he or she is competent, or advocating for a particular plan of action. In any of these instances, clients may resist the consultant's claims or suggestions. Using scholarly research on enthymemes and participative decision making, Lange (1984) describes how to overcome client resistance, and even seek resistance so formerly unstated objections can be addressed.

CONSULTING ETHICS

A consultant's ethics are as important, and in some cases, more important than his or her knowledge when consulting with a client. Consultants may not know the information needed to help the client, but most consultants are well versed in tracking down information and learning new concepts and processes. In many of my consulting activities, I had to learn about my client's industry practices and principles, and become knowledgeable about information and topics with which I had little or no background. A consultant's expertise is valuable, but often incomplete. Indeed, a consultant that believes he or she knows everything may be dangerous.

On the other hand, a consultant's ethics are the bedrock of the consulting practice and process. Five ethical principles are absolute. Not adhering to these principles can damage consulting relationships beyond repair.

First, *consultants must protect clients' proprietary, confidential information.* Consulting work generally provides consultants with access to confidential and proprietary information that belongs to the client. A consultant may have access to the client's customer or supplier list, manufacturing processes, technical or financial information, or software and databases. While not routinely shared outside the organization, the client may divulge some of their intellectual property to the consultant so that he or she can perform the contracted work. Clients require that consultants sign a contract that includes a confidential and proprietary information clause to prohibit the consultant from revealing this information to anyone. This is this first ethical principle of a consultant.

In their overview of the legal and ethical issues that consultants face, Montgomery, Heald, MacNamara, and Pincus (1995) and Stolle and Studebaker (2011) identify other principles that define a consultant's professional responsibility. Each deserves attention. First is fidelity and veracity. *Fidelity*, or the allegiance, faithfulness, or commitment a consultant brings to a project, speaks to the consultant's relationship with the client. *Veracity*, or integrity or truth, speaks to the type of information the consultant provides to the client. That is, a consultant creates a verbal or written contract with the client, and the consultant must adhere to that negotiated relationship for the designated time period. The consultant must also be truthful in his or her communication with the client, and provide the client with complete and accurate information.

Second, *consultants must protect client autonomy* (Montgomery et al., 1995). Clients retain their powers over decision making, both in the hiring of the consultant, selecting what activities the consultant will engage in, and in using his or her advice or input. Before a contractual relationship begins, the client should have full disclosure from the consultant about his or her background, education, experience, and expertise. Clients must also be informed about "what the consultant is doing and why" including any real or perceived costs or benefits associated with the consultant's activities (Montgomery et al., 1995, p. 376). Thus, in a consulting relationship, the client makes the final determination of what the consultant will (or not) do. Client autonomy is supported when the consultant provides a full description of of his or her expertise and experience, expected range of activities, timeline for completion of these activities, and the costs to accomplish these activities.

Third, *consultants must be committed to beneficence and nonmalfeasance* (Montgomery et al., 1995). Much like the institutional review board requirements scholars use in their research, consultants also must also protect the well-being of organizational members during their consulting activities. Consulting outcomes must do no harm. As Montgomery et al. (1995) explain, "in their actions, consultants should consider that the courts, in general, have taken what might be described as a 'risk-aversive stance'—they will act to minimize risk even if that action might deprive others of a potential benefit" (p. 376).

Fourth, *consultants have a duty to not benefit* (Montgomery et al., 1995). Although a consultant may receive a fee for his or her work, consultants cannot receive or take other monetary or nonmonetary benefits. Nonmonetary benefits include using data from consulting for publishing without the express permission of the client (and, of course, IRB approval when appropriate). It is also recommended that consultants not "become intimately involved with a client" (Montgomery et al., 1995, p. 377). These and similar activities could be seen as exploitation—something a consultant should always avoid.

Finally, *consultants must ensure acceptability of the consulting activity or intervention* (Montgomery et al., 1995). If the consultant's activities are legally questioned by the client, the *reasonable standard of care* would be the litmus test. That is, what the consultant did would be evaluated against what a reasonably prudent consultant (under similar circumstances) would do. This principle is context- and community-centered such that "techniques, methods, and even language acceptable in one setting may be unacceptable in another" (Montgomery et al., 1995, p. 378).

Although many professional associations (e.g., Association for Business Communication, Institute of Management Consultants USA, International Association of Business Communicators) offer members a set of ethical guidelines, neither the International Communication Association or the National Communication Association provide ethical practice guidelines for communication consultants. Yet, the high value both organizations place on ethics and ethical communication suggests that anyone presenting themselves as a communication consultant would conduct themselves ethically in their consulting activities (see the National Communication Association's Code of Professional Ethics for the Communication Scholar/Teacher). Conflicts of interests, like those listed above, should be avoided. Communication consultants can minimize these conflicts if they do not assume a role that (a) impairs their objectivity, competence, or effectiveness, or (b) exposes any person or organization to harm or exploitation. Of course, consultants working in specialized areas (e.g., trial consulting) should seek and follow any ethical principles espoused for that particular type of work.

One ethical area that is not well defined concerns *work product*, or any deliverable (e.g., training) produced for a client. Clients often insert a *work made for hire* clause (see U.S. Copyright Law) in a contract declaring that everything related to or produced for the contracted activity belongs to the client who ordered or commissioned the work. But this can be limiting for the consultant who wishes to use, for example, scales or training modules she developed for one project for another. A consultant can ask for a change to the contract to explicitly state that he or she is not an employee of the company, as well as a clause that states that work product belongs to the consultant. Negotiating the contract or agreement is part of a consultant's responsibility (see Waldeck, Plax, & Kearney, Chapter 7). Doing so, and having an attorney review the contract before signing can help consultants avoid questions about scope of duty and ownership.

Regardless of the setting, consultants should address each of these principles before finalizing a consulting contract. Some of these topics may be difficult to bring up. But it is a consultant's duty to address these before signing a contract or making a verbal agreement to do consulting work. Consultants manage risks in consulting activities by knowing and considering the acceptable standards of their consulting practices, engaging the client in a conversation about these issues, and securing agreement on these principles. While it may be more comfortable to seek a verbal agreement, documents in writing (i.e., general service agreements, contracts) are preferable. Organizations of all types and sizes regularly use written documents for the purposes of securing outside services. Communication consulting should be no different. Although the examples are specific to trial consulting, Stolle and Studebaker's (2011) review of conflicts of interest and contract issues is a productive primer in these issues. Considering the hypothetical scenarios they provide can help communication consultants analyze risks in their existing and potential consulting relationships.

CONCLUSION

There is no official or legal designation of competence to designate oneself as a communication consultant. To effectively consult, we must have widespread theoretical knowledge and a set of assumptions to guide and legitimate our work. We must hold ourselves to a consistently high level of values and ethics. Should communication consultants wish to develop a set of standards based on values and ethics, we would be wise to follow the advice Exton (1982) offered to management scholars in setting standards for the professional practice of management consulting. He recommends that (a) professional standards be developed, (b) training programs be utilized to advance the knowledge (of information and processes) of those who consult, (c) a code of ethics be developed with provisions for those violate the code, and (d) a pledge of commitment to a standard of professional and ethical excellence be utilized.

Currently, there is not a professional association that supports or credentials communication consultants. Thus, each consultant is responsible for consulting ethically with excellence. Communication consultants can demonstrate excellence by enriching the practice of communication within their client organizations. Drawing upon competing and complementary perspectives, as well as a variety of methodologies, communication consultants are positioned to integrate knowledge across communication's subdisciplines when translating scholarly knowledge to client needs. Communication consultants can also develop new techniques, processes, or knowledge not only for clients, but also adding contributions to the scholarly study of communication. Plax (1991) argued that "there are clear conceptual and operational parallels between what high quality university communication researchers do in a simulated setting and what high quality communication consultants do in the field" (p. 56). Perhaps now more than ever before, scholarly studies of communication take place in field settings. But a communication consultant's integration in a client context is often for a longer period of time and is more robust than institutionally approved empirical examinations (see, for example, Chandler & Wallace, 2008). Thus, communication consultants' contributions to the body of communication knowledge should be encouraged.

REFERENCES

Bormann, E. G. (1982). The symbolic convergence theory of communication: Applications and implications for teachers and consultants. *Journal of Applied Communication Research, 10,* 50–61.

Buzzanell, P. M. (Ed.). (2000). *Rethinking organizational and managerial communication from feminist perspectives.* Thousand Oaks, CA: Sage.

Cerisano, R. (2014, June 6). Internal versus external consulting: Advantages and disadvantages. Retrieved from http://www.9lenses.com/internal-versus-external-consulting

Chandler, R. C., & Wallace, J. D. (2008) Crisis communication consultation of the Federal Reserve Bank System. *Journal of Applied Communication Research, 57,* 443–451. doi:10.1080/03634520802245345

Cheney, G. (2000). Interpreting interpretive research: Toward perspectivism without relativism. In S. R. Corman & M. S. Poole (Eds.), *Perspectives on organizational communication: Finding common ground* (pp. 17–45). New York, NY: Guilford Press.

Crabtree, R. D., & Ford, L. A. (2004). Community activist and communication consultant. In L. R. Frey & K. M. Carragee (Eds.), *Communication activism: Communication for social change* (Vol. 1, pp. 249–285). New York, NY: Hampton Press.

Cragan, J. F., & Shields, D. C. (1992). The use of symbolic convergence theory in corporate strategic planning: A case study. *Journal of Applied Communication Research, 20,* 199–218.

DeWine, S. (1994). *The consultant's craft: Improving organizational communication.* New York, NY: St. Martin's Press.

Exton, Jr., W. (1982). Ethical and moral considerations and the principle of excellence in management consulting. *Journal of Business Ethics, 1,* 211–218.

Grossman, R. (2011). Delineating the paradigm shift. In A. F. Buono, R. Grossman, & H. Lobnig (Eds.), *The changing paradigm of consulting: Adjusting to the fast-paced world* (pp. 3–17). Charlotte, NC: Information Age.

Hart, J. L., Esrock, S. L., & Leichty, G. (2008). Blowing smoke and billowing logic: Consulting on cigarette excise tax increase messages. *Communication Education, 57,* 434–442. doi 10.1080/03634520801983078.

Kubr, M. (Ed.). (2002). *Management consulting: A guide to the profession.* Geneva, Switzerland: International Labor Office.

Lange, J. I. (1984). Seeking client resistance: Rhetorical strategy in communication consulting. *Journal of Applied Communication Research, 12,* 50–62. doi:10.1080/ 00909888409365246

Montgomery, D. J., Heald, G. R., MacNamara, S. R., & Pincus, L. B. (1995). Malpractice and the communication consultant: A proactive approach. *Management Communication Quarterly, 8,* 368–384. doi:10.1177/0893318995008003005

Plax, T. G. (1991). Understanding applied communication inquiry: Researcher as organizational consultant. *Journal of Applied Communication Research, 19,* 55–70. doi:10.1080/ 00909889109365292

Putnam, L. L. (1983). The interpretive perspective: An alternative to functionalism. In L. L. Putnam & M. E. Pacanowsky (Eds.), *Communication in organizations: An interpretive approach* (pp. 31–54). Beverly Hills, CA: Sage

Rottger, U., & Preusse, J. (2013). External consulting in strategic communication: Functions and roles within systems theory. *International Journal of Strategic Communication, 7,* 99–117. doi:10.1080/ 1553118x.2013.765437

Rouen, E. (2012, January 11). Inside job: Consultants don't need to be outsiders. *Fortune.* Retrieved from http://fortune.com/2012/01/11/inside-job-consultants-dont-need-to-be-outsiders/

Steele, F. (1975). *Consulting for organizational change.* Amherst: University of Massachusetts Press.

Stolle, D. P., & Studebaker, C. A. (2011). Trial consulting and conflicts of interest: An introduction. In R. L. Wiener & B. H. Bornstein (Eds.), *Handbook of trial consulting* (pp. 351–369). Boston, MA: Springer.

Suchan, J. (2006). Changing organizational communication practices and norms: A framework. *Journal of Business & Technical Communication, 20,* 5–47. doi:10.1177/ 1050651905281038.

van Bertalanffy, L. (1968). *General system theory.* New York, NY: George Braziller.

Zerfass, A., & Franke, N. (2013). Enabling, advising, supporting, executing: A theoretical framework for international communication consulting within organizations. *International Journal of Strategic Communication, 7,* 118–135. doi: 10.1080/1553118X.2013.765438

PART TWO

Creating a Consulting Experience That Matters: The Groundwork

CHAPTER FOUR

The Importance
of Context, Situation
and Setting in Consulting

LOYD S. PETTEGREW
University of South Florida

> *Every moment—every blink—is composed of a series of discrete moving parts, and every one of those parts offers an opportunity for intervention, for reform, and for correction.*
> —MALCOLM GLADWELL, *BLINK, 2005*

INTRODUCTION

Understanding in an unambiguous way the differences between context, setting and situation is a necessary coin of the realm for successful consultants. This chapter supports Hymes's (1974) argument that communicating competently is context dependent. Doing so necessitates the ability to understand and differentiate context from setting and situation and incorporate this understanding into actual consulting practice. The differences are neither semantic nor trivial for the consultant-scholar who wants to make a difference *through* research (Frey, 2009, p. 209). The downside of treating context, setting and situation as interchangeable is that you miss important dynamics that both enable and constrain communication.

A number of years ago I was asked by a national media company to present a proposal that would deliver customer service training to its newspaper division. This was a huge and potentially lucrative contract, so I picked a colleague I had worked with before and who was an excellent trainer. The company had just read research by the Medill School of Journalism at Northwestern University that presented national data showing newspapers having the highest customer satisfaction ratings were also the most profitable. My colleague and I had done customer service training for Yamaha USA, a national restaurant chain, and Arthur Andersen (before the Enron debacle). She insisted we use these existing training materials and adapt them for the new audience, saving us preparation time, and the client considerable money. I understood that print journalism and print journalists were such a different animal that any successful training program had to be "one off," designed specifically for this audience and organization. We continued to struggle over these conflicting viewpoints. Hers would be efficient and less costly; mine necessitated background research with a representative sample of newspaper employees, cost three times as much and take four times longer to complete. My position prevailed though I was afraid the price tag would eliminate us from the running. In the end, we were awarded the contract; I was both elated and apprehensive because it was an unproven program and a great deal of work for two people. My friend at the company's corporate headquarters revealed that we were chosen over bigger, national companies. He revealed, "Our S.V.P. of Newspaper Operations said we need a training program tailored *exactly* for us and you were the only group that did just that. He trusted you would come to know us more intimately." Our research at the various newspapers, revealed that not unlike many academics, newspaper journalists doubt they even have customers, so customer service was anything but a given and the audience would be challenging. Understanding the context, setting and situation and this particular audience made the difference in our consulting.

The academy (social sciences, business, and communication in particular) has long tolerated an equivocal approach to using the terms, context, setting and situation. All three words pervade the literature with egalitarian imprecision. An essay in *Communication Quarterly* by Goodall (1984) is illustrative. In the first page of the article, he uses context and situation interchangeably, yet never defines either term. Goodall is not alone. I conducted a Google Scholar search finding 3,010,000 articles using context, 3,300,000 articles using setting and 3,430,000 articles using situation. I randomly sampled 65 articles and the majority failed to carefully consider or define how these respective words were being used or their precise meaning in the research. Like the communication phenomenon itself (see Hopper, 1981), context, setting and situation are habitually taken for granted.

In this chapter, I argue that social science and business deserve better. In fact, consultant-scholars have a much more phronetic (see Tracy, 2007), if tacit, understanding of context, setting and situation, allowing them to traverse successfully the communication complexities they encounter in their consulting roles. The following model of context, setting and situation is offered to further my argument and illustrate the important differences of these terms.

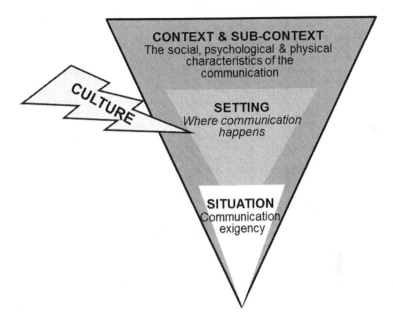

Figure 1: The Model.

Figure 1 shows that setting and situation are imbedded in context and sub-context, but are conceptually distinct. Embodied in this model is the idea that communication in contexts, be it healthcare, education family or others will also vary by setting and situation; all are affected by the larger culture in which they operate.[1] As consultants, if we are to understand any context more fully we must also attend to setting and situation in our research and practice. Setting is the site where communication happens, and within setting is situation—the exigency for communication. In other words, if you are going to discuss context, you must also account for where the communication takes place and its purpose. Both are distinct, but inseparable from the contextual whole. An example from my years at University Medical Center (UMC) will help illustrate this model.

When at UMC, I worked with an ER team, not unlike that described by Eisenberg, Baglia & Pynes (2006). The context was healthcare and the sub-context was a large academic medical center in the southeast. During a quiet Tuesday evening, interaction among team members was relaxed and informal; routine cases were triaged and treated. An hour later, in this same context, sub-context and setting, a call came in from the airport. A regional jet had crashed on landing and multiple trauma victims would be medevac'd to the UMC ER. The context, sub-context and setting remained the same but the situation had changed, moving from routine to STAT. Ease and informality of staff communication were replaced by hierarchical, technical and directive communication led by the chief of emergency medicine. It had become a decidedly different world communicatively. Hours later, the chaos had subsided; the trauma patients had been treated and released or triaged to the multiple ORs or the ICU. When the ER team went off duty, they decided to have something to eat at the medical center cafeteria. While the context and sub-context remained the same, both the setting and situation were changed. Team interaction was no longer role-driven, directive, and hierarchical with a STAT character; it became informal and darkly humorous. Here, setting and situation had a profound effect on communication within the same healthcare context and academic medical center sub-context.

This model holds that context is influenced by the even larger cultural phenomenon. For example, in past years when Toyota USA achieved its profitability projections, all employees at its U.S. headquarters were released from work for a 2-hour, decidedly Japanese celebration where the CEO from the parent company congratulated the employees and performed celebratory Japanese cultural rituals. When employees returned to their desks, a bonus check greeted their accomplishment. It is doubtful that an American automobile company would accomplish such logistical precision or celebrate success this way.

Culture

Contexts are indeed affected by the larger cultural milieu. This is particularly important for consultants who must deal with organizational divisions in foreign countries. For example, I performed training for both Yamaha U.S.A. and Yamaha Canada. Fortunately, I had several colleagues and family who were Canadian and had visited our northern neighbor many times. Even though both the USA and Canada divisions involved the same company, culture demanded a different approach and I toned down the presentation theatrics and adjusted the program content for the predominantly male Canadian audience by using a less stereotypically "John Wayne" American approach. Making these changes helped me create stronger identification with my Canadian audience.

THE IMPRECISION OF CONTEXT

A representative example of how context, setting and situation have been confounded in academe comes from the popular textbook, *Organizational Communication: Balancing Creativity and Constraint*, by Eisenberg, Goodall and Trethewey (2006). Within one chapter the reader is led to believe that context is (a) "*where* communication occurs" (p. 35), (b) "*situated* individual behavior" (p. 37),

(c) "a set of constraints limiting creativity and individual freedom" (p. 37), and (d) "multiple settings that frequently come in conflict" (p. 38). In the final chapter we learn that innovation will vary, depending on aspects of the context of the situation. Such loose definitions of context and situation are reminiscent of Bitzer's (1992, p. 1) concept of rhetorical situation where he writes, "When I ask, 'What is the rhetorical situation?', I want to know the nature of those contexts…" He references anthropologist Bronislaw Malinowski (1922), then proceeds to discuss "the context of situation" (p. 4) where within any given scene, utterances are bound up with the context of situation and with the aim of the pursuit. Such is the academic habit throughout social science and business.

Context is perhaps most often used by academicians in the sense of the verb, *contextualize*—to place or understand something within a particular social milieu or usage. This falls short of what most scholars attempt to convey when referring to organizations or hospitals as contexts. Confusion is compounded when context is used synonymously with setting and situation. Lest the reader believe I am being semantically intemperate, I refer you back to the millions of scholarly research citations using these terms, and as we have seen with some of the communication field's finest scholars, in an unnecessarily careless manner. Consultants can't afford such imprecision among all these moving parts.

Other examples abound. Young and Rodriguez (2006) examine narrative text, context and subtext in end-of-life care responses by V.A. primary care providers and their patients about life-sustaining treatment, terminal condition, decision making capacity and state of permanent unconsciousness. The V.A. hospital is the implicit sub-context of these interventions, but we learn nothing about either the V.A. hospital, or the institution's likely effects on these interviews or the participants. Implicitly we are led to believe end-of-life care giving and communication aren't affected by where the care is provided. Given the ongoing patient care quality turmoil across the much of the V.A. system, the research validity, devoid of any representation of where it takes place, is suspect. Further, research designs seldom lend themselves to accurate comparison with other healthcare facilities. Making such assumptions in the academic world may be de rigueur, but in consulting could label one seriously uninformed.

Two credible attempts have been made to unravel context. Spitzberg and Brunner (1991) attempted to integrate context with communication competency, positing that any theory of communication competence must explicate the social context in which the communicator functions. The second is the Relational Health Communication Competence Model offered by Kreps (1988) for healthcare which he correctly presents as a context of communication. He accurately differentiates context from situation but neglects setting, except for discussing a study of four relational nurse settings in his literature review (Worobey & Cummings, 1984).

As I point out in the next section, scholarly shortcomings emanate from melding context, setting and situation, instead of defining them uniquely and treating them as distinct but related constructs.

Implicit Generalizability of Context

Implicit within the confusion of context, setting and situation is the academic desire to produce generalizable findings that apply broadly if not universally. While generalizability is a warranted ideal for academic research, it can be the death knell for consultants who must carefully consider exactly how the organization they are working with differs from others, and as Malcolm Gladwell said in the beginning of this chapter, its discrete moving parts.

Melding context, setting and situation provide neither clarity nor generalizability for consultant/scholars. Successful consultants quickly learn about the risks of generalizing uncritically from one setting to another. For example, in an academic study of U.S. nursing homes, Davis, Weech-Maldonado, Lapane & Laberge (2014) refer to the nursing home industry itself as a context. Yet those familiar with nursing homes recognize the incredible diversity in what they do, how they operate, their physical plant, and their differential impact on patients and their families. Generalizing across nursing homes without detailing differences between the respective institutions mistakenly assumes commonality where none may exist (see Nussbaum & Robinson, 1990).

A notable exception to this uncritical generalizability of sub-contexts comes from a study by consultant/scholars Waldeck, Seibold and Flanagan (2004). The study examined the impact of advanced communication and information technologies (ACITs) on organizational assimilation across four different types of for-profit organizations (two hotel groups, one bank and one real estate company). The authors understood that hotels, banks and a real estate company could be remarkably different organizational sub-contexts and tested for, but found no significant differences across them. With deserved confidence, the authors suggest that ACITs appear to be quite important to efforts to organizational assimilation across very different types of organizations.

Communication Competence and Context

Communicators who are able to read the situation and audience have been identified as competent or rhetorically sensitive by the communication field. More specifically, Spitzberg (2013, p. 128) warns that "It is therefore this evaluation, and *not the skill itself* that constitutes competence…" For Bitzer (1992) rhetorical sensitivity involves situations in which the speaker or writer creates effective rhetorical discourse. Like Spitzberg, Bitzer places communicator ability or success in the eyes (or ears) of the audience. Hart and Burks (1972) developed a construct, and later a measure of rhetorical sensitivity (Hart, Carlson & Eadie, 1980). Prominent within this construct is the ability to undergo adaptation, recognize ideas can be rendered in multi-form ways and choose information appropriately to effect human understanding and social cohesion. To accomplish this end the communicator must be adept at understanding the interaction context, situation and setting. Plax and his colleagues (Plax, 1991, p. 59; Plax, Kearney, Allen & Ross, 2006) advance an "applied" communication perspective, where the researcher feeds back results to management and employees about valuable and useful insights. While the treatment of context, setting and situation in these accounts still suffers from imprecision, there is concurrence that the effective practitioner is able to adjust her/his messages to unique audiences across multiple contexts, settings and situations.

CONTEXTS AND SUB-CONTEXTS

I offer seven main contexts: healthcare, organizational, familial, educational, religious, political, intimate and legal. Certainly there could be other contexts as well. Each of these both enable and constrain human communication in distinctive ways. For example, you and a person with whom you have a romantic aspiration go out for a first dinner date at an intimate little bistro with jazz and great wine; your communication behavior is directed toward intimacy. The next day your mother telephones you to see how things went. You express your delight and your mother says you have to bring your new friend over to the house that evening for dinner. While the evening replicates the original date in some ways, the communication is likely to very, very different. This is because the setting (parent's home) and situation (parental inspection) have changed the intimate context to a familial context that necessitates markedly different communication behavior to be socially acceptable to the family. In other words, there are larger social-psychological elements of healthcare, organizations, family, legal and other contexts that condition how people will communicate. Each context, setting and situation constrained and enabled the couple's human communication. Understanding these moving parts is a prerequisite for being effective as a consultant…or with your family.

Sub-contexts

Now the reader might ask what happens when you have an overlap between two or more contexts, say a healthcare organization, or in the example above, the intimate and familial contexts. These are sub-contexts. Sub-contexts in organizations have occasionally been referred to as sub-cultures (see Gregory, 1983; Sackmann, 1992; Schein, 2010), but the work exploring them has often failed to deal substantively with both setting and situation. As we have seen, context, situation and setting are frequently used interchangeably or at least uncritically in scholarly work. For example, Diaz (1999) talks about contexts of risky sex but uses the term "sexual ecology," suggesting that context and place (setting) are somehow synonymous. Sarangi (2007) explicates the narrative context in medicine but it could have more accurately been replaced with situation. Gillotti, Thompson and McNellis (2002) refer to the delivery of medical bad news as a context; the model above would identify it as a particular situation, especially since those delivering bad news to mock patients were third-year medical students and the real context was educational. Nonetheless, the word context is used approximately 25 times in this research, interchangeably with setting and situation.

Humana Inc. is a decidedly different context than regulated monopolies like Comcast and Time-Warner, or high-tech companies like Google. Even though all are large organizations, they are hardly comparable sub-contexts. Even within healthcare organizations, there is considerable diversity that is seldom accounted for in academic research. Failing to understand such differences can lead practitioner-consultants to be less effective and helpful to their client organization. Dan Costello and I (Costello & Pettegrew, 1979) offered a comprehensive review of healthcare organizations, pointing out that academic medical centers (a sub-context of health, educational and organizational contexts) were a very different phenomenon than other medical centers. We would spend six years becoming intimately familiar with how different this sub-context was. What about a Catholic hospital? This involves three sub-contexts: healthcare, organizational and religious. While many academics ignore the complexity of such hospitals, treating their research findings as if they came from any hospital, consultants must keep this sub-contextual complexity carefully in mind if they are to succeed optimally.

The Bell Labs sub-context. To illustrate how sub-context can be remarkably different, I offer an example from my consulting with AT&T American Transtech (AT). AT was the first AT&T division to operate exclusively as a non-regulated enterprise after the federally mandated break-up of the Bell System in 1984. Since its inception in 1877, AT&T (Ma Bell) had been a regulated telephone monopoly. It was the only U.S. company to be regulated by how much profit it could make, not by rates charged to the customer. Like universities (that spend excess money at the end of their fiscal year so the next year's budget allocation won't be cut), AT&T would spend lavishly before the fiscal year end to lower its profitability level. AT had been created to perform the Bell System break-up work, including shareholder services for AT&T and seven regional Bell operating companies. By 1989, AT&T was under tremendous financial pressure to become profit-driven, something not in its organizational DNA. Because of AT's profitability experience, AT&T CEO Robert Allen assigned responsibility to AT for spreading its competitive culture across the AT&T system. Since I was a consultant for AT with nonprofit academic ties (and therefore could potentially aid employees with a better understanding of their dilemma), they thought I would be able to help with the re-acculturation.

One of the first divisions targeted for transformation was Bell Labs, home of 8 Nobel Laureates including Arno Penzias and Robert Wilson who were the first scientists to find evidence of the big bang theory of the universe. The AT&T headquarters in Basking Ridge, New Jersey was a paean to button-down corporate America—dark suits, starched white shirts, polished shoes, conservative neckties, and well-coiffed haircuts. Bell Labs was nestled 38 miles away in a different sub-contextual universe. I first met the Bell Labs representatives at AT&T headquarters. As they marched in, the classic southern phrase to interlopers came to mind: "You ain't from around here, are you, boy?" They were AT&T employees, but just didn't think, look, behave or sound like they were. The Bell Labs guys had obviously put on suits for the occasion, ill-fitting, rumpled, clip-on ties, socks that didn't match, and looked extraordinarily out of place among the real suits. This was a remarkably distinctive sub-context of AT&T. My efforts with AT to re-acculture them to the profit motive was about as well received as the old high school prank of throwing a Baby Ruth candy bar into a crowded swimming pool. The AT team and I spent 5 months working in vain with the Bell Labs folks trying to get them to understand that their pure science had to become profitable. It was reminiscent of Tompkins's (1993) work with NASA. Even with my years of academic culture, our efforts failed and Bell Labs went through a series of downsizing; its population declined from 30,000 employees to 1,000, and is now a division of Alactel-Lucent. Bell Labs' sub-context was so dramatically different that it couldn't survive AT&T's existential upheaval toward profitability. Had I been able to communicate a clearer understanding of this sub-contextual disconnect, I might have kept AT&T from spending valuable resources to push through the impossible. A consultant has to know his limits.

SETTING

The healthcare context has been an important area for human communication study and consulting (Babrow & Mattson, 2011; Costello, 1977; Kreps & Thornton, 1992; Nussbaum, 1989; Pettegrew, 1988; Pettegrew & Logan, 1987; Smith, 1989; Thompson, Parrott & Nussbaum, 2011; Zook, 2011). Some researchers have drilled down deeper, carefully examining specific health settings like special needs summer camps (Frohlich, 2012), refugee camps (Conquergood, 1988), cosmetic surgery offices (Mirivel, 2008), V.A. medical centers (Howren, Cozad & Kaboli, 2015), gay bath houses (Rotello, 1997), an urban hospital ER (Eisenberg, Baglia & Pynes, 2006), community AIDS education diffusion campaigns (Kreps, this volume), and a hospital rehabilitation unit (Scholl & Ragan, 2003) to name a few.

Setting is where communication actually takes place and is the performative stage of human interaction. Anyone who has attended a business meeting in a corporate board room senses the typical solemnity of this setting. It is not a place conducive to open interaction, especially if employees from lower organizational levels are present. If the consultant wants open and honest communication, there are far more conducive settings. My favorite strategy is to pick the area from which the lowest level employee in the group is represented and arrange the meeting there. We did this almost exclusively at UMC. Employee comfort and openness is always much better than in the executive suite where they may feel important, but terrified.

SITUATION

Situation is the communication exigency—the forces that bring about the reason for communicating. Situations vary from the mundane and routine to critical and threatening. True situational studies are relatively uncommon because most communication in organizations is routine, non-generalizability, with low publication potential. Two situations have garnered the most research attention. The first is the takeover of one business by another. Gutknecht and Keys (1993) studied employee communication during merger and acquisition (M&A) and Stahl and Sitkin (2005) examined trust between employees of Ciba-Geigy and Sandoz during their M&A. The second is organizational crisis. King (2002) studied teamwork and communication during crisis. Yu, Sengul and Lester (2008) examined the spill-over effects of crisis on people both within and outside of organizations. Tompkins & Tompkins (2004) detailed crises and decline in the NASA space program. Yet it is often more routine employee-management communication that consultants must dissect the moving parts.

Oftentimes, the exigency presented by top management is markedly different that those one finds from interviewing lower level employees. For instance, I was once brought in to a national restaurant company where the president told me there were systemic communication problems that needed fixing or the company would lose its market share in the industry. This situation seemed dire. I told him I would sniff around for several weeks and see what I could discover and get back to him with a plan and a fix. He sent around a memo giving me access to the entire organization as I deemed necessary. After 10 days of face-to-face and telephone interviews, it appeared that the president was woefully mistaken. I couldn't detect any systemic problems, but I did learn that the president was a big fan of Tom Peters's *Thriving on Chaos*. Some very credible managers and employees told me that every few years the CEO felt he needed to shake things up by fixing things that weren't broken. In turn, this process made his intervention necessary and I was being used to further the chaos. I met with him after I had completed my preliminary report, told him I found no systemic communication problems and resigned.

The situation I was hired to help fix was manufactured by the company president, and most employees both recognized and discounted it. Crisis had become an episodic phenomenon manufactured by the president to stir things up so they would need his leadership. Reading situations necessitates skill and insight. The situations we actually find frequently aren't what they are advertised to be. Ethnographic research skills and gaining employee confidence help the consultant read such situations correctly.

CONCLUSIONS

Consultants are confronted with a myriad of discrete moving parts in their efforts to understand and help improve their client organizations. The model of context presented in this chapter is designed to help illuminate some very important pieces to the consulting puzzle. It is time the academic side of social science and business be more precise, and ultimately descriptive, when using terms like context, setting and situation. I have tried to demonstrate that each is unique and should be differentiated from the others, even while recognizing that each is a vital part of what both constrains and enables human communication. Doing this requires a change in perspective and is no easy task since context often operates at a tacit level. Successful consulting demands that this tacit understanding become more explicit.

The role and importance of understanding the crucial interplay between culture, context, setting and situation is aptly illustrated by the work of some of the consultancies associated with the Big Four accounting firms. I had the opportunity to work with Accenture (formerly part of Arthur Andersen) during my days at AT. Often, these groups, reflecting their rule-driven parent companies, operate by the Law of the Hammer. Give someone a new tool and everything needs fixing with it. The accounting-based consulting firms have a propensity for the same process. If it worked for one company, they would use it for another (saving time and development costs). This is the antithesis of what context, setting and situation demand. It is my belief from 40 years of experience as an academic researcher, informed by my consulting, that consciously considering the model presented in this paper requires you to understand the organization first and then discern the most appropriate solution.

To understand organizations and other contexts optimally, we must bring greater rigor to what we refer to as context, setting and situation. This includes sensitivity to sub-contexts, where two or more different contexts overlap as well as where the communication takes place and its exigency. Consulting is complicated and what we see is often colored by the words we use. Consultants would do well to follow Gladwell's (2005, p. 241) advice in this chapter's introduction, to attend to, understand, and take advantage of life's many moving parts.

NOTE

1. Zook (2011, p. 367) discusses the impact of socio-cultural influences on the healthcare context.

REFERENCES

Babrow, A. & Mattson, M. (2011). "Building health communication theories in the 21ˢᵗ century." In T. Thompson, Parrott, R. & Nussbaum, J. (eds.). *The Routledge handbook of health communication, 2ⁿᵈ Edition.* New York, NY: Routledge, 18–35.

Bitzer, L. F. (1992). The rhetorical situation. *Philosophy and Rhetoric, 25*(1), 1–14.

Conquergood, D. (1988). "Health theatre in a Hmong refugee camp: Performance, communication and culture." *TDR, 32,* 174–208.

Costello, D. (1977). "Health communication theory and research: An overview." In B. Ruben (Ed.), *Communication yearbook 1.* New Brunswick, NJ: Transaction.

Costello, D. & Pettegrew, L. (1979). "Health communication theory and research: An overview of health organizations." In D. Nimmo (Ed.) *Communication Yearbook 3,* New Brunswick, NJ: Transaction.

Davis, J., Weech-Maldonado, R., Lapane, K. & Laberge, A. (2014). "Contextual determinants of US nursing home racial/ethnic diversity." *Social Science & Medicine, 104,* 142–147.

Diaz, R. (1999). "Trips to fantasy island: Contexts of risky sex for San Francisco men." *Sexualities, 2,* 89–112.

Eisenberg, E., Baglia, J., & Pynes, J. (2006). Transforming emergency medicine through narrative: Qualitative action research at a community hospital. *Health Communication, 19,* 3, 197–208.

Eisenberg, E., Goodall, H. & Trethewey, A. (2006). *Organizational Communication: Balancing Creativity and Constraint,* 5ᵗʰ Ed. Boston, Ma: Bedford-St. Martin's.

Frohlich, D. (2012). "People supersede illness." *Health Communication, 27,* 623–627.

Frey, L. R. (2009). What a difference more difference-making communication scholarship might make: Masking a difference from and through communication research. *Journal of Applied Communication Research, 37*(2), 205–214.

Gladwell, M. (2005). *Blink; The power of thinking without thinking.* New York: Back Bay Books.

Gillotti, C., Thompson, T. & McNellis, K.(2002). "Communicative competence in the delivery of bad news." *Social Science & Medicine, 54,* 1011–1023.

Goodall Jr, H. L. (1984). The status of communication studies in organizational contexts: One rhetorician's lament after a year-long odyssey. *Communication Quarterly, 32*(2), 133-147.

Gregory, K. L. (1983). Native-view paradigms: Multiple cultures and culture conflicts in organizations. *Administrative Science Quarterly,* 28 (3), 359–376.

Gutknecht, J. E., & Keys, J. B. (1993). Mergers, acquisitions and takeovers: Maintaining morale of survivors and protecting employees. *The Academy of Management Executive, 7*(3), 26–36.

Hart, R. P., & Burks, D. M. (1972). Rhetorical sensitivity and social interaction. *Communications Monographs, 39*(2), 75–91.

Hart, R. P., Carlson, R. E., & Eadie, W. F. (1980). Attitudes toward communication and the assessment of rhetorical sensitivity. *Communications Monographs, 47*(1), 1–22.

Hopper, R. (1981). The taken-for-granted. *Human Communication Research, 7*(3), 195–211.

Howren, M. B., Cozad, A. J. & Kaboli, P. J. (2015). Considering the issue of dual-use in Veteran Affairs patients: Implications & opportunities for communication and counseling. *Health Communication, 30*(3), 838–842.

Hymes, D. (1974). *Foundations of sociolinguistics: An ethnographic approach.* Philadelphia: University of Pennsylvania Press.

King III, G. (2002). Crisis management & team effectiveness: A closer examination. *Journal of Business Ethics, 41*(3), 235–249.

Kreps, G. L. (1988). Relational communication in health care. *Southern Speech Communication Journal, 53*(4), 344–359.

Kreps, G. & Thornton, B. (1992). *Health communication theory and practice (2ⁿᵈ ed).* Prospect Heights, IL: Waveland.

Malinowski, B. (1922). *Argonauts of the Western Pacific: An account of native enterprise and adventure in the archipelagoes of Melanesian New Guinea.* London: Routledge.

Mirivel, J. (2008). "The physical examination in cosmetic surgery: Communication strategies to promote the desirability of surgery." *Health Communication, 23,* 153–170.

Nussbaum, J. (1989). "Directions for research within health communication." *Health Communication, 1,* 35–40.

Nussbaum, J. F., & Robinson, J. D. (1990). Communication within the nursing home. In D. O'Hair and G. Kreps (Eds.), *Applied communication theory and research* (pp. 353–369). Hillsdale, NJ: Erlbaum.

Pettegrew, L. S. (1988). "The Importance of Context in Applied Communication Research," *Southern Speech Communication Journal, 53,* 331–338.

Pettegrew, L.. & Logan, R. (1987). "Communication in the health car context." In C. Berger & S. Chafee (Eds.), *Handbook of Communication Science* (pp. 675–710). Beverly Hills, CA: SAGE.

Plax, T. G. (1991). Understanding applied communication inquiry: Researcher as organizational consultant. *Journal of Applied Communication Research, 19*(1–2), 55–70.

Plax, T. G., Kearney, P., Allen, T. H. & Ross, T. (2006). Using focus groups to design a nationwide debt-management educational program. In *Facilitating group communication in context: Facilitating group task and team communication* (L. R. Frey, Ed.). Creskill, NJ: Hampton.

Rotello, G. (1997). *Sexual ecology: AIDS and the destiny of gay men.* New York: Dutton.

Sackmann, S. A. (1992). Culture and subcultures: An analysis of organizational knowledge. *Administrative Science Quarterly, 37* (1), 140–161.

Sarangi, S. (2007). "Editorial on the narrative context." *Communication & Medicine, 4,* 129–130.

Schein, E. H. (2010). *Organizational culture and leadership* (Vol. 2). New York: John Wiley & Sons.

Scholl, J. and Ragan, S. (2003). "The use of humor as promoting positive provider-patient interactions in a hospital rehabilitation unit." *Health Communication, 15,* 319–330.

Smith, D. (1989). "Studying health communication: An agenda for the future." *Health Communication, 1,* 17–27.

Spitzberg, B. H.(2013). (Re)Introducing communication competence to the health professions. *Journal of Public Health Research, 2*(e23), 126–135.

Spitzberg, B. H. and Brunner, C. C. (1991). Toward a theoretical integration of context and competence inference research. *Western Journal of Speech Communication, 55* (1), 28–46.

Stahl, G. K. & Sitkin, S. B. (2005), Trust in mergers and acquisitions. In G. K. Stahl & M. E. Mendenhall (Eds.). *Mergers and acquisitions: Managing culture and human resources.* Stanford, CA: Stanford University Press.

Thompson, T. L., Parrott, R., & Nussbaum, J. F. (Eds.). (2011). *The Routledge handbook of health communication.* New York, NY: Routledge.

Tompkins, P. K. (1993). *Organizational communication imperatives: Lessons of the space program.* Los Angeles: Roxbury Publishing Company.

Tompkins, P. K., & Tompkins, E. V. (2004). *Apollo, Challenger, Columbia: The decline of the space program: A study in organizational communication.* Los Angeles: Roxbury Publishing Co.

Tracy, S,. J. (2007). Taking the plunge: A contextual approach to problem-based research. *Communication Monographs, 74*(1), pp. 106–111.

Young, A. & Rodriguez, K. (2006). "The role of narrative in discussing end-of-life care: Eliciting values and goals from text, context and subtext." *Health Communication, 19,* 49–59.

Yu, T., Sengul, M., & Lester, R. H. (2008). Misery loves company: The spread of negative impacts resulting from an organizational crisis. *Academy of Management Review, 33*(2), 452–472.

Waldeck, J., Seibold, D. & Flanagin, A. (2004). Organizational assimilation and communication technology use. *Communication Monographs, 71*(2), 161–183.

Worobey, J. L. & Cummings, H. W. (1984). Communication effectiveness of nurses in four relational settings. *Journal of Applied Communication Research, 12*(3), 123–141.

Zook, E. (2011). "Embodied health and constitutive communication: Toward an authentic conceptualization of health communication" (pp. 344–377). In S. Deetz (Ed.). *Communication yearbook 17.* Thousand Oaks, CA: Sage.

CHAPTER FIVE

Building an Evidence-Based Practice

Conducting Valuable Needs Assessments

PETER F. JORGENSEN
Western Illinois University

Asking the right questions takes as much skill as giving the right answers.
—ROBERT HALF, FOUNDER AND PRESIDENT OF ROBERT HALF INTERNATIONAL

The art and science of asking questions is the source of all knowledge.
—THOMAS BERGER, AMERICAN NOVELIST

Not all knowledge is considered equal. Some knowledge may be timely whereas other knowledge is not; some knowledge may be relevant, whereas other knowledge may be interesting yet tangential to the scope of inquiry. Some claims of knowledge are more accurate, effective, or useful than others. In short, "good" knowledge has the power to foster effective organizational decision making, improve communication processes, strengthen organizational cultures, and generally lead to healthy, satisfying, productive and successful organizational environments. Conversely, the utilization of "poor" knowledge can result in flawed decision making that can be costly in terms of organizational time, money, resources and relationships.

Organizational needs assessments represent the consultant's first step in attempting to gain a better understanding of organizational attitudes, processes and problems. Needs assessments are a critical component for helping practitioners build a foundation of responsible knowledge related to interactional and attitudinal processes, without which consultants would be forced to proceed on the bases of perceptual frameworks held together by intuition, conjecture, hearsay, and/or biased observation. When conducted properly, needs assessments are a necessary and valuable part of building a basis of valid, reliable knowledge from which to develop strategic action plans in order to enhance organizational performance.

From a pragmatic standpoint, needs assessments can be conducted relative to a variety of organizational processes and can range from very specific efforts (e.g., assessing the listening effectiveness of line supervisors) to more global assessments (e.g., evaluating the outcomes of diversity programs). Such research might be conducted in order to identify and address a potential lack of competency at the individual, department, and/or organizational level, and may include a focus on measuring attitudes, knowledge, affect, behaviors and/or processes. Needs assessments are a common fixture in organizational training efforts, as such evaluations provide for establishing both a baseline of current individual behavior as well as helping to clarify what constitutes reasonable and achievable training objectives. For communication consultants, needs assessments might focus on communication competencies of individuals and units, communication channels utilized within the organization, information flow, the impact and use of various communication and information technologies, the functionality of decision processes, and the efficiency and effectiveness of a variety of communication networks both internal and external to the organization.

A prevailing theme in this book is that effective consultants must acquire and develop a wide range of skills, and they must be credible in the execution of their diverse roles. In order to conduct effective needs assessments, a consultant must be flexible and competent in fulfilling a number of roles throughout the process. One of the primary roles a consultant must effectively enact is that of detective when conducting assessments. Indeed, Steele (1985) identified many similarities between detectives and consultants that are still as true today as they were then, including the need for both to actively and carefully search for clues and evidence in order to build their cases. It is important to note that, like detectives, consultants must do more than simply search for data and information; they must be able to build a convincing case based on evidence that suggests a possible course of action for organizational change efforts (see Waldeck, Plax, & Kearney, Chapter 7).

This chapter will begin by developing an understanding of what needs assessments are and why they are worth the initial investment of organizational time and resources. Then, the process of conducting needs assessments will be explored, identifying common foci of such efforts as well as examining the advantages and disadvantages associated with a variety of methodological approaches. Finally, the chapter will conclude by discussing the ongoing vital role of needs assessments in the organizational development process.

WHAT IS A NEEDS ASSESSMENT?

A needs assessment is, at its core, a process of conducting a "gap analysis" of where the organization currently is in regard to member attitudes, behaviors, processes, structures and/or culture, and where the organization would like to be. Within this definition are three components that help to differentiate a needs assessment from other kinds of organizational evaluations: needs assessments as process; a current evaluation point; and organizational goals.

First, a needs assessment is a *process*, involving multiple stakeholders and systems. Conducting needs assessments can be complex, complicated, and may go through several iterations as data are gathered, organizational goals are identified and clarified, and information is interpreted relative to the data at hand. Hence, these are not "one-shot" data collection efforts designed to evaluate organizational performance. In practice, a needs assessment may begin with interviews with high-level managers or administrators in an effort to gain an understanding of the perceived shortcomings of organizational processes. From there, a consultant may wish to conduct focus groups of employees to establish if the problems articulated by management are perceived similarly or differently from how upper-level management may see them, and if such perceptions differ, additional interviews/surveys may be required in order to more clearly understand the issues being identified as problematic. In Chapter 6 of this volume, Plax, Waldeck, and Kearney explore these assessment procedures in greater depth.

As needs assessments are being defined here as a "gap analysis," two additional components are required for this definition in order to determine if a gap exists: an initial evaluation point (e.g., "where we are as an organization right now"), and an ideal comparison point consisting of either immediate and/or long-term organizational goals (e.g., "where we want to be as an organization"). The consultant's role is to help the organization determine its current status in regard to behaviors and processes of interest, clearly identify immediate and/or long-term goals related to those specific areas of interest, and then provide a convincing narrative supported by empirical data detailing where the organization is, where it wants to be, and offer courses of action based on the consultant's area of expertise on how the gap between current performance and expected performance might be narrowed.

Needs assessments share many similarities with Patton's (2012a, 2012b) utilization-focused evaluation process, but also reflect subtle differences. Utilization-focused evaluation begins with the premise that the value of evaluations lies in the pragmatic utility associated with such efforts; hence, such evaluations should always be conducted with an eye toward how the information can and will be used by the sponsoring stakeholders. Such stakeholders might include management, employees, clients, customers, community members, and/or internal/external decision makers. The focus in utilization-focused evaluation, as defined by

Patton (2012b), is on the "intended use by intended users" (p. 366), and describes a process that is a collaborative effort on the parts of all stakeholders and the consultant to generate information that is both relevant and actionable to the organization. Needs assessments share the same emphasis on information utility that utilization-focused evaluation does, although needs assessments are generally conducted at the behest of management and may be less inclusive of stakeholder input in regard to the measurement process. Like utilization-focused evaluation, needs assessments should also be conducted with the goal of helping the organization select the most appropriate methods, instruments, theory, and samples frame their inquiry. But in some instances, needs assessments may rely more heavily on readily marketable prepackaged measurement instruments and surveys, consultants with very specifically defined areas of expertise, or pre-existing theoretical philosophies more so than utilization-focused evaluation approaches would typically employ. The last difference between needs assessments and utilization-focused evaluations might be best clarified as a difference in outcome expectations; the process of utilization-focused evaluations is not just about discovering information and generating usable knowledge, but it also seeks to actively involve the intended users in the development, the use, the interpretation and the application of such information (Patton, 2012a). The focus of most needs assessment activities, in contrast, is not so concerned with transforming the intended users into evaluators, as it is concerned with collecting information that can be used to generate knowledge regarding organizational attitudes and/ or performance.

To clarify how needs assessments may differ from other forms of organizational inquiry, consider the following case. I was approached by a former client, a large midwestern manufacturer of mechanical equipment used in a variety of agricultural and industrial settings, with a request to design and offer a full-day workshop on maintaining professional relationships within the workplace. After some initial conversations with management, it became clear to me that there was an agenda at work; the request for the workshop was being made in an effort to curb the bullying behavior of a few individuals who were having a detrimental effect on the rest of the administrative and support staff. Some additional conversations with my principal contact as well as other Human Resources staff confirmed that the bullying behavior was the problem that management wanted to address, but they were uncertain as to how to go about it. A further review of the organization's evaluation standards for annual employee appraisals identified the lack of any mention of promoting workplace civility and respectful behavior toward fellow employees in the evaluation criteria, so management did not feel that they had the grounds for addressing these issues with the employees involved as the offending behaviors were not technically prohibited in the appraisals. Ultimately, I argued against the need for running 200 employees through a professional workplace relationship workshop, offering empirical evidence that such a workshop would be costly to the organization in terms of loss of productivity and would likely do little to address the central problem of the bullying behavior. Instead, I recommended a two-pronged approach to address the problem based on the data: revise existing employee behavioral standards to include rewarding workplace civility and respect for fellow employees, and to offer coaching to the individuals who were engaging in the bullying behavior. The client expressed appreciation and immediately acted to implement both suggestions.

This particular case highlights a number of important characteristics of needs assessments. First, the initial solicitation for the professional relationships workshop did not indicate that a needs assessment would be required, but conversations with management about the purpose of the workshop strongly suggested that a needs assessment might be in the best interests of the organization (as well as helping the consultant to try to figure out what was actually going on!). Second, initial data gathering efforts consisting of unstructured interviews with managers and a few employees who happened to be available at the time of my on-site visit focused on assessing the perceived quality of existing workplace relationships as well as the presence of bullying behavior. When the data showed that most of the employees felt that their relationships with their coworkers were congenial and respectful with a few notable exceptions, and that there was empirical evidence of some employees being bullied, a picture began to emerge of where the organization was now in regard to these behaviors. After additional formal interviews with employees and management, and after discussions involving the desired future state of affairs for the company (i.e., an elimination of the bullying behavior and encouraging building satisfying workplace relationships for employees), the third and final step of the initial analyses focusing on the gap between current practice and desired end-states could be identified and potential solutions could be offered and evaluated.

In summary, then, a needs assessment is an interactive, often iterative process whereby an initial evaluation of an organizationally defined issue is undertaken, benchmarks or ideal standards are determined, and the differences between the initial evaluation and the stated goals of the organization are analyzed and interpreted with the expressed intent of reducing or eliminating any empirically defined gaps. The focus of the needs assessment may involve employee/managerial knowledge, attitudes, feelings, performances, processes, culture and/or behaviors. The procedures employed may vary in terms of the type of data collected (i.e., quantitative, qualitative and/or process data), design utilized (experimental, naturalistic), and method undertaken (interview, survey, observational, or content analysis). Ultimately, the needs assessment is a process of identifying and empirically substantiating the existence of an organizational problem, and is a critical first step in planning strategic interventions.

WHY CONDUCT NEEDS ASSESSMENTS?

In a perfect world, organizational decisions would be logically and rationally based on sound, unbiased data; but we do not live in a perfect world. Indeed, in the modern economy, organizations are challenged every day to do more with less, to act more quickly than their competitors, to constantly innovate while maintaining some level of stability in their companies, and to maintain optimal organizational performance. Key organizational resources including time, staffing, and money are always stretched to the limit, and always seem to be in short supply and in high demand.

Engaging in the needs assessments process is a useful activity for a number of reasons. Specifically, Brown (2002) found that performing needs assessments can help organizations to identify:

- *Organizational goals and effectiveness in achieving these goals.* Needs assessments can help organizations to more clearly articulate important goals central to the organization, which in turn can provide a better understanding of whether or not such goals are being achieved once such goals are more clearly defined.
- *Gaps or discrepancies between employee skills and the skills required for effective job performance.*
- *Problems that may not be solved by training.* Not all problems can be solved by training; problematic organizational practices which derive from existing organizational policies or procedures will require top management to intervene in the system in order to make necessary changes.
- *Conditions under which the training and development activity will occur.* It may be that the organization experiences difficulties only in certain sectors, divisions, shifts, or some other subset of the organizational system. Rather than subjecting all organizational employees to a generalized training regimen, needs assessments may help to identify which of the employee/leadership groups might require and/or benefit from more focused training efforts.

Additionally, Rossett (1987) explained that needs assessments are useful tools when seeking information about: (a) optimal performance or knowledge, (b) actual or current performance or knowledge, (c) feelings/affective states of organizational stakeholders, (d) problem causes, and (e) potential solutions. In essence, then, needs assessments should not be viewed as a process of collecting mere information, but rather the true value of needs assessments involves converting organizational *information* into organizational *knowledge* that provides the organization with both direction and rationale to enact positive change interventions.

Despite the value in conducting needs assessments and its payoff (in the form of responsible knowledge), managers commonly decide that the costs associated with a needs assessment, such as time and effort, may be too high. Management may perceive that the cost associated with conducting a proper needs assessment outweighs the potential benefits to be gained by such an endeavor, especially where organizational leadership may already be convinced that the causes and nature of a problem are widely understood. At times like these, a consultant must change her/his professional hat to become an advocate in order to convince management that the time and energy invested in performing a needs assessment is worth the time and effort in order to generate actionable knowledge.

There are a number of arguments for conducting needs assessments that a consultant might use to gain the approval of a reluctant client. First, needs assessments generate relevant data that can be used to define or confirm suspected problems. During the initial stages of working with a client organization, members (including both management and employees) often claim to "know" the nature or the causes of the problem facing the organization. The catch is that these individual perceptions and explanations are not wrong per se, as multiple interpretations of these problems will exist concurrently between the members of the organization. Not surprisingly, although some perspectives may be similar, others may differ radically when attempting to explain a performance deficiency. Calling to mind the bullying case discussed previously, individual employee opinions regarding the lack of satisfying work relationships in that unit were alternatively attributed to poor interpersonal communication practices, a lack of leadership, a lack of discipline, an organizational culture permissive of bullying, and in one case a complete denial that anything was amiss within the unit. A needs assessment involves collecting data from multiple sources in order to confirm or disconfirm certain presumptions of causes and problems, as well as to provide evidence of other issues that may be related to the focus of the assessment. On a more pragmatic note, McArdle (1998) claims that when properly done, needs assessments represent a wise investment for the organization, as the outcome can focus precious organizational resources on the right problems.

The second argument for the value of conducting a needs assessment is that the client and the consultant can gain a better understanding of the scope and range of potential solutions. Not all solutions will be appropriate or implementable for a given organization; the process of conducting a needs assessment can help the consultant and the client understand what options may be available to them in addressing any perceived gaps. For instance, is the nature of the problem one that can be best addressed by training programs, organizational policy changes, process changes, or by all three? If the problem is caused by lack of adequate staffing, poor system processes or inadequate resources, training options are not effective solutions (Sorenson, 2002). While conducting the research, the consultant may gain insight into what kinds of interventions might be supported by both management and employees given the organizational culture, available resources, and company history.

The third argument for justifying the cost of conducting a needs assessment is that the process can create an atmosphere of cooperation and support for organizational change efforts. As organizations have become flatter, relying more on team-based processes and less on hierarchical structure for day-to-day decision making, employees have become less accepting of "top-down" change mandates (Arnold & McClure, 1996; Michael, Neubert & Michael, 2012). Proposed organizational changes that lack input from employees at all levels of the organization are likely to be met with resistance. Since the most valuable needs assessments rely upon member input from all levels of the organization, the inclusion of multiple voices in the data collection process and the invitation to organizational members to participate in the assessment process fosters a sense of commitment and stake in the enterprise, thereby lessening resistance and building support for the change efforts (Kaufman & Guerra-Lopez, 2013). Additionally, since needs assessments are based on empirical data and not merely opinion or hearsay, this information is often perceived as a more legitimate and more trusted basis for justifying impending changes. Employees are more likely to trust data than they are management "vision" or expertise when confronted with unexpected change, and the use of objective, responsible data to justify change efforts goes a long way in helping to build coalitions of cooperation and support in future change efforts.

HOW ARE EFFECTIVE NEEDS ASSESSMENTS CONDUCTED?

With an increasing interest in change management and organizational development over the past two decades, there have been numerous books and toolkits published designed to help practitioners conduct effective needs assessments in organizations. The purpose of this chapter is not to provide a step-by-step description of how to conduct actual needs assessments, but rather to argue that needs assessments should be framed as evolving arguments in which the collection and interpretation of data and evidence plays the key role. Readers seeking more of a hands-on practical guide or specific advice on conducting needs assessments are referred to works such as those by Kaufman and Guerra-Lopez (2013), Sleezer, Russ-Eft and Gupta (2014), and the excellent five-volume set on conducting needs assessments authored by Altschuld and his colleagues (Altschuld, 2009; Altschuld & Eastmond, 2009; Altschuld & Kumar, 2009; Altschuld & White, 2009; Stevahn & King, 2009). These works are similar in that they describe many of the theoretical models driving the practice of needs assessments, as well as providing numerous tips and pragmatic advice on how to implement and conduct such assessments in real-world settings.

Altschuld and Witkin (1999) argue that the needs assessments process should take place in three phases: pre-assessment, assessment, and post-assessment. This chapter will adopt that same approach and describe key issues associated with each of these phases in generating valuable needs assessment data that can be used to develop useful organizational knowledge.

Phase 1—Pre-Assessment

Drawing upon the comparison described earlier about the similarities between a consultant and a detective, the pre-assessment phase for the consultant is analogous to when the detective arrives on the scene of the crime for the first time. Generally, the scene may be chaotic and confusing; there are multiple witnesses who may have stories that overlap each other in some instances, yet may contradict each other on other key points. Witnesses will describe their personal versions of the events surrounding the crime scene, while other law enforcement specialists are noting and marking any existing evidence which may be linked to the crime. The detective does not have a good handle on what actually occurred as of yet, and must start putting the pieces of the story together in order to understand what happened. At this beginning phase of the investigation, the detective must answer some important basic questions, such as: What do we know about what happened here? What evidence exists to support or disprove initial witness testimonies? Who was involved?

For the consultant, the pre-assessment phase is primarily concerned with gaining an understanding of what kinds of issues the organization is seeking to address. Altschuld (2004) describes the pre-assessment phase as involving "getting organized and focusing on potential areas of concern, finding out what is already known or available about the foci, and deciding to collect in-depth information in a formal needs assessment" (p. 11). The client organization's members, including your management contact(s), probably have some inkling of what issues need to be addressed. However, the concerns stated by the organization may reflect more of a concern with outcomes rather than process (i.e., "We need to improve our customer satisfaction numbers"); symptoms rather than causes (i.e., "Our employees seem to be under a lot of stress lately"); or issues that may not require a needs assessment (i.e., "We want you to help us roll out a new culture for our organization").

In the pre-assessment phase, the consultant has two primary responsibilities: (a) to identify a focus for the client's area of interest, and (b) to determine whether or not a formal needs assessment is warranted based on the nature of the focus and/or by a review of any existing data. The first responsibility of the consultant is to ascertain the general scope and nature of the client's problem, and to identify the variables and questions to focus on. Part of this responsibility is to gain an initial understanding of what the problem may be, and what other possible issues may be associated with it. Importantly, at this point of the process, these efforts represent just the initial attempts to identify the needs of the client, and the original conception of the problem and needs may change as the process evolves. Just like a detective, the consultant and the client must be willing to alter their understanding of the issue based upon the evidence available at the time.

The initial evidence available to a consultant may not be sufficient to gain a clear focus on the issue. This first phase of the needs assessment process may require some initial data collection, which may include interviews, focus groups, surveys, and/or a review of institutional research/organizational assessment data in order to try to narrow down the target of the assessment. The better the understanding of the initial issues, the better the questions that can be asked to generate information, which in turn leads to superior knowledge.

At this stage, the consultant may clarify with management what the ideal standard for performance is that management would like to attain. If management's purpose in conducting the needs assessment is to reduce customer satisfaction complaints to less than 2% of all customer service interactions, such knowledge can steer a consultant in the direction of investigating how customer service complaints are recorded and evaluated. Similarly, if the comparison point is a published industry standard, deconstructing how that measurement was conducted will assist the consultant in understanding what questions need to be asked in order to develop a comparable metric.

The second responsibility of the consultant is to determine whether a formal needs assessment is warranted once the preliminary issues have been identified and defined. Data may indicate that a needs assessment may not be appropriate based on the task or process being examined, perhaps because there is no clear definition of the future state desired by the client ("I just want to improve morale at the company. It can be better than it is currently!") or because the problem being studied may be better approached using a task analysis (i.e., a focus on maximizing efficiency in repetitive processes as opposed to human interactions) or some other organizational evaluation process. Additionally, depending on the depth and quality of the existing data, the consultant may feel that enough information already exists to proceed directly to the post-assessment stage without any additional data collection. For instance, if an organization has recently conducted an in-house annual survey of employee concerns and the analysis of that data clearly shows that a particular problem exists, or if recent dialogues between management and employees have mutually identified and agreed that the organizational members are facing a specific problem that needs to be addressed, then it may not be beneficial to the organization to spend valuable resources simply to confirm what recent data already suggest.

Just as the detective builds a case based on the evidence available, so too does a consultant begin by building a case for a needs assessment by identifying a specific set of skills, knowledge and/or feelings, proposing a means whereby to measure those areas of interest, and ultimately determine whether the assessed competency levels meet organizational/professional standards in those areas. The central questions that a consultant would want to have answered in the pre-assessment phase include:

- What is/are the potential area(s) of concern, based on the evidence available?
- What do we KNOW about these areas, and what do we THINK we know?
- Would a formal needs assessment be appropriate? (i.e., are we fundamentally looking at evaluating some level of knowledge, emotion, behavior and/or process, and do we have an organizational benchmark/ideal to which it can be compared?)
- What questions do we need to ask to develop more specific data about these concerns?

Phase 2—Needs Assessment

Once our detective has examined the initial crime scene and determined that a crime has indeed taken place, the next step would be to begin to follow up on any leads in an effort to gather more evidence. The detective may even have some initial suspicions as to who the culprit may be, the motives that prompted the crime, and/or the means whereby the crime was committed. But at this stage of the game these represent starting points, not conclusions, based on the available evidence. From this point on out, the detective will continue to collect evidence in an effort to prove or disprove several hypotheses, ultimately working toward a case where the preponderance of the evidence yields a clear, compelling, and internally consistent narrative that identifies the who, the how, and the why of the criminal act.

In the second phase of conducting formal needs assessments, the consultant must continue to enact the role of detective as in the metaphor we have established. The consultant needs to ask good questions in order to produce good data, data that can be used to develop valid knowledge about organizational behaviors and practices. However, the process begins with realizing that the questions we ask, in part, determine the answers that we receive; hence, the utmost care must be taken in developing research methodologies for collecting data.

Asking the "right" kinds of questions. The quality of all data collection efforts is largely defined by two measurement criteria: validity and reliability. Good data are data that are both reliable and valid; poor data fail to meet one or both of these standards. Measurement validity refers to the extent to which a given measure (e.g., an interview or focus group question, or an item on a questionnaire) adequately captures and reflects the concept being measured. In one sense, "accuracy" might be considered a synonym for validity. Hence, a valid measure is one that measures what the question intended to measure. For instance, if a consultant were interested in creating a measure of job stress, she/he may develop an item that asked the question "How stressed do you feel today?" Suppose that a respondent answered "Whew! VERY stressed!" Can the consultant conclude that she/he has a good answer to the question? Probably not. Unfortunately, such a question could not be considered a valid measure of job stress; although the respondent may have indicated a high level of stress and the answer seemed to be appropriate on the surface, the respondent's reply was not necessarily associated with workplace stress. The respondent may have been experiencing a high degree of stress due to a family member being ill, relational conflict at home, or harboring a deep fear of being questioned by consultants!

The definition of a valid instrument may assume slightly different meanings depending on whether one is collecting quantitative versus qualitative data. In the case of quantitative data, where measurements are reflected by numbers, validity is still defined by the degree to which a question measures what it is intended to measure. In the case of qualitative data, however, validity may take on a slightly different meaning. Lincoln and Guba (1985) argue that validity in qualitative measurements might be better conceptualized as "credibility" as opposed to "accuracy," insofar as the purpose of qualitative research is to describe or understand the phenomena of interest from the respondent's unique perspective. Since the respondents are the only ones who can legitimately judge the accuracy of their responses, trying to establish validity from the point of view of the researcher may be difficult (Krueger & Casey, 2009). Hence, validity in qualitative measures might be better associated with the degree to which respondents feel like they understood and answered the question being asked.

Reliability, on the other hand, refers to the degree to which an assessment tool is stable and consistent in measuring what it is intended to measure. Reliable questions are questions that people will interpret similarly; i.e., that the question elicits a similar meaning in people who are presented with the measure. Note that the standard of reliability depends upon consistency, not accuracy, in the interpretation of such measures. Hence, a reliable measurement is one that, if repeated a second time, will give the same results as it did the first time.

Again, however, how reliability is operationalized differs between quantitative and qualitative measures. The traditional quantitative view of reliability is based on the assumption of replicability or repeatability, with the assumption that a measure could be deemed reliable if we would obtain identical results if we measured the same thing twice. The criterion of reliability for qualitative research might be better construed as "dependability," or "trustworthiness," as opposed to consistency. Dependability emphasizes the need for the researcher to consider the ever-changing context within which the measurements are gathered, recognizing that what may be an honest answer from a respondent on a given day may change due to changes in the environment. For instance, if a consultant is using a qualitative approach in measuring an employee's communication satisfaction with her superior by conducting interviews, during an initial interview the employee may respond that she has always found her superior to be honest, forthcoming, and fair. However, the next week there are some unexpected organizational changes that create some difficulties for the employee, and in a follow-up interview she may have changed her opinion of her superior due to the inability of the superior to keep her informed. From the standpoint of dependability, even though the employee's answer changed and may not have been consistent from the previous week, the different response was due to changes in the external environment, not ambiguity associated with the question itself. From this perspective, 'reliable' qualitative data is denoted by trustworthy and honest responses on the parts of the respondents.

Obviously, the best data are gained from measures which can be established as being both reliable and valid. There are numerous preexisting, prepackaged measurement instruments focusing on such diverse variables as leadership behavior, emotional intelligence, conflict management styles, and organizational culture that could be useful for conducting needs assessments. Such measures will include data and arguments establishing their validity and reliability, but the consultant would be wise to remember that even these instruments may need to be modified based on the requirements of any given organization.

In regard to improving the validity of the measures used, consider the following guidelines:

- Questions should be clear, unambiguous, and phrased using language and terms that the respondents will easily understand.
- Double-barreled questions (i.e., asking two questions rolled into one) will create problems and should be avoided.
- Every question asked of a respondent should be an attempt to elicit information about a specific variable/theme; the more clearly that a question targets a specific kind of knowledge from the respondent, the better the validity.
- The most effective consultants assume a "respondent-centered" approach to question design; how is the respondent likely to interpret the question? Is the intent of the question clear?
- Questions should be written in objective, nonjudgmental ways, and clinically worded in order to foster honest and accurate responses.

In terms of improving the reliability of measures associated with data collection, a consultant should:

- Ask the same question of each respondent; don't reword/rephrase questions, as changing the wording may change the intent of the question.

- Use multiple related questions when possible to measure a given construct; don't rely on a single item "global scale" to measure a concept of interest, as in most cases the likelihood of respondents interpreting a single question differently is significant.
- Keep the interviews/focus groups/questionnaires to a reasonable length.

Asking the "right" kinds of people. In addition to the validity and reliability of the questions used to collect data, the consultant must be aware of the implications of the methodologies utilized to collect the data. As Table 1 demonstrates, there are a variety of research methodologies available to consultants, each with its own advantages and disadvantages. The table provides a quick explanation for each of the methods, their advantages and disadvantages, when each might be most appropriate, and some tips to keep in mind when using each method. Further, Keyton (this volume) explores the epistemological assumptions that indicate the use of particular theoretical frameworks and methodologies when consulting.

One of the central concerns of the consultant in conducting any needs assessment data is making certain that a representative sample of stakeholders is included. It is the consultant's job to make certain that there is sufficient participation in the needs assessment to assure that the data being gathered can be generalized to the appropriate organizational system, whether the targeted system is a department, a division, or an entire organization. Using poor sampling techniques can introduce unwanted bias into the data collection process, skewing the data to the point where the data are unusable.

The importance of utilizing proper sampling techniques (or more accurately, the perils of NOT using sampling effectively!) might be best established by a prior experience. A former client of mine once contacted me to put together a full-day training workshop on improving interpersonal communication competence in the workplace. My training partner and I decided to meet with the full management team of this organization to find out what kinds of topics and issues they wanted us to focus upon. Over the course of our meeting with them, a number of different goals for the training session were suggested and discussed, including a section devoted to helping the employees more effectively utilize the email system of the organization. According to the input from management, employees were inundated with hundreds of emails from coworkers every day. Employees were not using priority flags to indicate urgent or priority messages, various informal messages and jokes were being forwarded indiscriminately and were clogging the system, and the email system itself did not seem to be used efficiently. Each of the managers shared personal horror stories of "email fails," all of which reinforced the idea that some kind of protocol for using the email system more effectively and efficiently might indeed be a useful component of the training session. Armed with such knowledge, my partner and I set to work preparing the training workshop.

Table 1.

Method	Description	Advantages	Disadvantages	Best for:
Questionnaires	• Can be used in either online or in paper form. • Can consist of a variety of question formats. • Predominantly quantitative in nature.	• Can efficiently survey a large population. • Are inexpensive. • Are easily summarized and quantified. • Are anonymous.	• Responses are constrained; no chance to elaborate or explain. • May yield low response rates.	• Gathering quantitative data from a large number of respondents. • When time is limited to collect data.
Interviews	• Can be formal/structured or informal/unstructured. • Can be face-to-face or over some form of interactive media. • Qualitative in nature.	• Can get at individual motivations, perceptions, causes and potential solutions. • Yields very "rich" data. • Adaptable.	• Requires significant amount of time to collect data. • Requires significant amount of time to analyze data. • No anonymity in responses.	• Gathering data related to individual perceptions, perspectives, and understandings. • Exploring areas of concern unknown to the researcher.
Focus Groups	• Group interview conducted by a moderator. • Can be formal or informal. • Ideally consist of 10-12 participants. • Qualitative in nature.	• Participant interaction can lead to generation of new ideas. • Yields "rich" data • Adaptable	• Lack of anonymity • Some members may decline to participate in the discussions. • May require significant time to analyze data.	• Idea generation or problem solving. • Building consensus.

Method	Description	Advantages	Disadvantages	Best for:
Documents/ Previous Organizational Research	• Consists of organizational documents such as organizational chart. Newsletters, minutes, and annual reports.	• Easily collected. • Provides objective data as to organizational operations and policies. • Can identify and track problem histories. • Does not negatively impact worker productivity.	• Data can be difficult to analyze. • Data may be outdated and no longer valid relative to understanding current difficulties.	• Providing historical background on problem.
Observations	• May be focused on behaviors or processes. • Can be either qualitative or quantitative.	• Collects data on actual behavior or processes, not self-report data. • Does not negatively impact worker productivity.	• Can only study overt behavior. • Presence of observer may bias behaviors.	• Objectively measuring actual behavior or processes.

On the day of the workshop, our training session seemed to be going well and well-received by the participants. As we transitioned into the final section of the workshop which focused on email etiquette, we began the section by asking the participants "On average, how many emails do you receive a day?" Obviously, we were prepared to deal with groans and immediate numbers into the hundreds as employees sought to outdo each other in terms of who suffered the most abuse at the hands of the evil email system, so when we received answers such as "eight," "twelve," and "between 10 and 20 a day," my partner and I looked at each other in shock. Our training session on email use had been predicated on the assumption that these employees were overwhelmed with mostly irrelevant emails on a daily basis, and that valuable organizational time was being lost due to the lack of an efficient use of this medium to communicate with other organizational members. What had happened?

What had happened was that my partner and I had failed to base our needs assessment on an appropriate sample. All of the stories that we gathered relative to the problems with email use were from the *managers* of the organization, not the employees; and the training session was intended for the employees. This is an example how management's perspective on organizational processes can often vary from other employees' experience, and why proper sampling of the individuals who are expected to participate in the session is important. Although my partner and I were able to salvage some important points from the final section of our session, it was not nearly as effective as it could have been had we done a better job of sampling our workshop participants.

There are two general types of sampling techniques available to the consultant: probability and nonprobability sampling. Probability sampling involves the use of random sampling techniques, whereas nonprobability sampling does not. The advantage of using probability sampling (including simple random sampling, systematic sampling, and stratified sampling approaches) is that the data collected from smaller, randomly selected participant pools can be generalized to the larger organization as a whole; nonprobability samples (such as convenience samples, quota sampling, and purposive/judgment sampling) cannot. When using nonrandom samples, there is no way to determine sampling error, or how much the sample might differ from the target population—which could result in biased data.

Each sampling method has advantages and disadvantages associated with the technique, as depicted in Table 2. In general, probability sampling techniques are usually the best way to go to minimize intrusion into the organization while maximizing the generalizability of the results generated by the data collection, but random sampling is also more costly in terms of time and effort than nonprobability samples. However, probability sampling techniques may be unnecessary or inappropriate for collecting certain kinds of qualitative data, such as when gathering data from focus groups or reviewing organizational documents and publications in order to identify prevalent themes. Additionally, the focus of the needs assessment may not demand the effort needed for a random sample if the needs being assessed are already well-known and readily apparent to key organizational members, or if the organization is small enough that a purposive sample of everyone is a viable possibility. In short, using an appropriate sampling methodology will help to assure that the consultant has a representative basis of information from which to draw conclusions about organizational attitudes, feelings, behaviors and processes.

Comparing "what is" to "what is desired." The final step of the needs assessment phase is the comparison of the accumulated data to the industry benchmarks or organizational ideals regarding the concepts being assessed. Up until this point, the needs assessment has been no different than any other form of organizational evaluation; foci have been identified, questions have been asked, and data have been collected. What makes the needs assessment process unique is the direct comparison of the gathered data to a predefined standard of performance. The data collection provides an answer to the question "Where is the organization now?" with regard to the focus of the research; the standards provide the answer to "Where does the organization want to be?" This final step of the needs assessment involves determining the difference, or gap, between the observed data and the given standard, prioritizing needs, and identifying possible solutions for any observed gaps in performance.

During this step, all of the information gathered during the assessment process is transformed from data to knowledge. Information is not the same thing as knowledge; the raw numbers and the qualitative responses do not in and of themselves reveal what is or is not taking place in the organization. Instead, it is the skill of the consultant in understanding the meaning of the measures of central tendency and indices of dispersion revealed in numeric data, and the repetition and prevalent themes that emerge from narrative data, and the tendencies and trends noted in observational data that ultimately allow for the consultant to develop an interpretation of the data into meaningful knowledge. Data in themselves do not have any meaning; the value of data lies in their ability to serve as evidence in developing arguments for the interpretations of organizational realities. When data are valid and reliable, when the sampling procedures are appropriate for the task, and when the interpretation of the data is responsible, then strong arguments can be made as to what we "know" about the given processes of an organization, and by default what gaps exist in the performance of various organizational responsibilities.

Returning to our crime metaphor, the detective has now accumulated a wealth of evidence and data. Based on the detective's observations, witness testimonies, physical evidence, and follow-up research, the detective now needs to find a way to fit all of the available facts together in order to understand what happened. The evidence will be used to build a case against the culprit, with the evidence playing the key role in determining guilt or innocence.

Table 2.

Sampling Method	Description	Advantages	Limitations	Best used when:
Simple Random Sampling	• All given members of a population have an equal chance of being selected. • Typically, all members of the population are assigned a number, and then numbers are randomly generated. • Probability sampling	• If sample size is sufficient, results from random samples should generalize to the larger population. • Ensures a high degree of representativeness.	• All members of a population must be known and listed to avoid bias. • The sample selected may create difficulties accessing potential participants due to geographic location or work shift.	• The population members are similar to one another on important variables.
Systematic Sampling	• A form of random sampling that selects participants on the basis of a systematic criteria such as every 10th person on a predetermined list. • Probability sampling	• Ensures a high degree of representativeness. • Does not require a random number generator/table.	• Less randomized than simple random sampling. • Possibility of losing vital information from the population.	• The population members are similar to one another on important variables.

Sampling Method	Description	Advantages	Limitations	Best used when:
Stratified Sampling	• A population is broken down into subgroups of interest, such as Management/ Employee, shift, and work facility. Random samples are then drawn from each group. • Probability sampling	• Ensures a high degree of representativeness from all of the identified groups in the population. • Generally considered to be superior to random or systematic sampling due to reduction in possible sampling error.	• Time consuming	• The population is diverse and contains different groupings of individuals, and that group identification could significantly impact the variables of interest.
Convenience Sampling	• Participants are recruited based on ease of contact and availability. • Nonprobability sampling	• Convenient • Quick • Inexpensive	• Degree of generalizability of the findings is questionable	• Time, support, or ability to reach more sophisticated samples is limited.

Sampling Method	Description	Advantages	Limitations	Best used when:
Judgment Sampling	• The researcher chooses a representative sample based on their understanding of the population as a whole, such as meeting with top management to determine organizational priorities. • Nonprobability sampling	• Is relatively quick and inexpensive. • Participants known to have knowledge of the variables/processes of interest are approached, thus preventing distortion of the data from uninformed sources.	• Subject to researcher biases. • The group selected may not accurately reflect the range/intensity of the variables of interest. • Degree of generalizability of the findings is questionable.	• Time, support, or ability to reach more sophisticated samples is limited. • When the researcher, based on his/her experience, believes that the judgment sample can provide quality information which is representative of the rest of the population.
Quota Sampling	• A population is broken down into subgroups of interest, such as Management/Employee, shift, and work facility. Then a convenience sample is taken from each group. • Nonprobability sampling	• Ensures some degree of representativeness of the groups of interest in the population.	• Degree of generalizability of the findings is questionable.	• Important grouping factors are present that may affect the variables of interest but stratified sampling is not possible or is impractical.

Much like the detective, the consultant must use the data collected from the needs assessment to tell a story. The knowledge gained from an analysis of the data must be used to support a coherent narrative of what was measured, where the organization rates relative to that focus, and the gap between where the organization is and where it wants to be. The argument developed by the consultant must be supported by the majority of the available evidence, and the narrative shared with the organization must do a better job accounting for the collected evidence than any other rival explanations or interpretations of the data. In this sense, the needs assessment becomes an exercise in building a quality research argument, where the quality of the evidence will in large part determine the strength of the argument.

Phase 3—Post-Assessment

The post-assessment phase involves analyzing the knowledge gained from conducting the needs assessment to applying that information as a means of creating and arguing for planned interventions designed to reduce observed gaps in performance. Such interventions might consist of training solutions, process changes, and/or organizational structural changes designed to address these deficiencies/problems. Additional elements of the post-assessment phase include implementing proposed solutions and evaluating such interventions as well as the overall needs assessment process itself (Altschuld, 2004).

Although the needs assessment data have been collected, interpreted, and shared with the organization by this point, the post-assessment phase represents an opportunity for both the consultant and the organization to learn from the needs assessment process. What worked well? What could have been done better? Where did unexpected barriers arise, and were there ways that such challenges could have been minimized with additional care, forethought or planning? What questions were answered, and what new questions were raised? The time spent in addressing such issues represents an investment in the organization and will help the assessment process to run more smoothly in future change cycles.

Additionally, the opportunity to build future networking opportunities and to enhance professional credibility can be increased by taking the time to evaluate the needs assessment process with the client. DeWine (2001) describes four criteria that can be used for evaluating the effectiveness of the consulting process. The first criterion focuses on evaluating the consultant's effectiveness from the client's point of view, and centers on questions of professional conduct, responsible behavior, and effective communication with the client. The second reflects the consultant's own satisfaction with her or his own efforts and performance with the client. The third criterion is based upon Holtz's (1989) work which seeks to evaluate the impact of the consultant's work on the organization by assessing the consultant's enthusiasm, leadership, presentational ability, efficiency, effectiveness and openness with the client. Finally, evaluating the project outcome is a means whereby to evaluate the effectiveness of the consultant. In Chapter 7 of this volume, Waldeck, Plax, and Kearney elaborate on the importance of evaluating consulting processes and outcomes.

WHAT HAVE WE LEARNED?

The purpose of this chapter was to illustrate that organizational needs assessments are best conceptualized as arguments that depend on reliable, valid data to serve as evidence in supporting the claims of the consultant. Furthermore, valuable needs assessments depend not so much on the answers gained from such research, but rather upon the quality of the questions that are asked to elicit those responses. In short, effective needs assessments depend on asking the right questions, not just getting answers. The kinds of questions that are asked, how they are asked, and who is asked to respond to the questions all affect the quality of the evidence used to determine organizational gaps in skills, emotional states, processes and/or structures.

REFERENCES

Altschuld, J. W. (2004). Emerging dimensions of needs assessments. *Performance Improvement, 43* (1), 10–15.

Altschuld, J. W. (2009). *Needs assessment Phase II: Collecting data.* Thousand Oaks, CA: Sage.

Altschuld, J. W., & Eastmond, J. N. (2009). *Needs assessment Phase I: Getting started.* Thousand Oaks, CA: Sage.

Altschuld, J. W., & Kumar, D. D. (2009). *Needs assessment: An overview.* Thousand Oaks, CA: Sage.

Altschuld, J. W., & White, J. L. (2009). *Needs assessment: Analysis and prioritization.* Thousand Oaks, CA: Sage.

Altschuld, J. W. & Witkin, B. R. (1999). *From needs assessment to action: Transforming needs into solution strategies.* Thousand Oaks, CA: Sage.

Arnold, W. E., & McClure, L. (1996). *Communication training and development.* Prospect Heights, IL: Waveland.

Brown, J. (2002). Training needs assessment: A must for developing an effective training program. *Public Personnel Management, 31* (4), 569–578.

DeWine, S. (2001). *The consultant's craft: Improving organizational communication.* Boston: Bedford/ St. Martin's.

Holtz, H. (1989). *Choosing and using a consultant: A manager's guide to consulting services.* New York: Wiley.

Kaufman, R., & Guerra-Lopez, I. (2013). *Needs assessment for organizational success.* Alexandria, VA: ASTD Press.

Krueger, R. A., & Casey, M. A. (2009). *Focus groups: A practical guide for applied research* (4th ed.). Thousand Oaks, CA: Sage.

Lincoln, Y. S., & Guba E. G. (1985). *Naturalistic inquiry*. Newbury Park, CA: Sage.

McArdle, G. (1998). *Conducting a needs analysis*. Menlo Park, CA: Crisp Learning.

Michael, B., Neubert, M. J., & Michael, R. (2012). Three alternatives to organizational value change and formation: Top-down, spontaneous decentralized, and interactive dialogical. *Journal of Applied Behavioral Science, 48*(3), 380–409.

Patton, M. Q. (2012a). *Essentials of utilization-focused evaluation*. Thousand Oaks, CA: Sage.

Patton, M. Q. (2012b). A utilization-focused evaluation approach to contribution analysis. *Evaluation, 18*(3), 364–377.

Rossett, A. (1987). *Training needs assessment*. Englewood Cliffs, NJ: Educational Technology Publications.

Sleezer, C. M., Russ-Eft, D. F., & Gupta, K. (2014). *A practical guide to needs assessment*. San Francsico: Wiley.

Sorenson, S. (2002). Training for the long run. *Engineering Systems, 19* (6), 32.

Steele, F. (1985). Consultants and detectives. In C. R. Bell & L. Nadler (Eds.), *Clients and consultants: Meeting and exceeding expectations* (pp. 176–190). Houston: Gulf.

Stevahn, L. A., & King, J. A. (2009). *Needs assessment Phase III: Taking action for change*. Thousand Oaks, CA: Sage.

CHAPTER SIX

Collecting and Using Narratives That Matter

TIMOTHY G. PLAX
California State University, Long Beach

JENNIFER H. WALDECK
Chapman University

PATRICIA KEARNEY
California State University, Long Beach

There are a number of ways that consultants collect information that will aid them in designing useful and effective solutions for clients. In addition to survey and archival data, many practitioners rely on the insights provided by organizational stakeholders through their personal narratives or stories. Seidman (2013) recalls, "recounting narratives of experience has been the major way throughout recorded history that humans have made sense of their experience" (p. 8). Browning and Morris (2012) point to the power of narrative for making sense out of organizational behavior and events. Indeed, people's experiences with a particular issue of interest to an organization, and how they make sense of and behave relative to those experiences, are often deeply rich, worthwhile accounts to consider when consulting. The stories people tell matter.

In the preface to a now-classic explication of what was then a little-known research activity, Merton (Merton, Fiske, & Kendall, 1956/1990) argued that "the focused interview" elicits these stories in a unique and highly effective way that allows the "emergence and transmission of knowledge...[and] the diffusion of knowledge from one sociocultural world to another." Specifically, as a means of generating understanding of the various "worlds" that exist in and around organizational environments, we, the authors of this chapter, have used focus groups extensively in a wide range of settings, and with diverse populations. Focus groups have helped us to transfer information in consumable format from employees to management, from one type of work team or job function to another, from consumers to agencies that provide products and services, and even from speakers of one language to another. So, in this chapter, our purposes are to define the nature of focus groups in consulting work; examine the purposes that they serve for consultants, clients, and participants; discuss the methodology and logic underlying a rigorous, systematic focus group sample and facilitation protocol; explore the communication dynamics of focus groups and the challenges that working with clients and participants poses to facilitators; and explain the data analysis techniques most commonly applied to focus group responses, including how these may be triangulated with other types of data the consultant collects.

Our team, collectively and individually, has used focus groups in unique and large-scale ways to support our consulting work for several decades, beginning with Plax's internal consulting role at Rockwell International in the 1980s, and Plax and Kearney's work for the California State Teachers Retirement System. Waldeck did her first focus group work in the early 1990s as part of the large-scale Disneyland Job Accountability Profile project. In the mid-1990s, Plax and Kearney, with others, began a multi-year engagement with the student loan guarantor industry (EdFund, USA Funds, and Sallie Mae) to explore why students default on their educational loans. They conducted 39 focus groups with college students, alumni, parents, and student loan administrators from US colleges and universities from the eastern, southern, midwestern, and western regions of the United States. The data they obtained informed the development of a nationally used financial literacy and debt management educational campaign known as Life Skills ™ (Plax, Kearney, Allen, & Ross, 2006). Waldeck was involved in the transcription and coding of some of those data, and later went on to use focus groups both as a needs assessment tool and as a way to collect research data for clients of her then-employer's firm and, more recently, in her own engagements.

For example, Waldeck (2008) utilized focus groups to discover the learning needs and preferences of members of a large national professional association, and then utilized what she learned in designing an overall performance improvement strategy and specific training curriculum. Later, she facilitated focus groups to assess consumer perceptions of the US automotive industry, to evaluate employee readiness for a large-scale change in a Tier 1 supplier for the US Big Three automotive manufacturers, and in the needs assessment phase for a leadership development initiative and intercultural communication training for public safety officers. In addition to the educational loan project, Plax has substantial experience using focus groups to generate information for the purposes of managerial decision making and program design in the aerospace industry (Plax & Cecchi, 1989); and Plax and Kearney have used focus groups in a number of consultations with California agencies involved in environmental protection work, including the Air Resources Board (Plax, Kearney, Ross, & Jolly, 2008), the Integrated Waste Management Board, the city of Fremont's Environmental Services Division, and the city of Folsom's Hazardous Materials Division. This is just a sample of the variety of projects in which the authors have collected stakeholder narratives over the years through the use of focus groups. Based on existing literature and our own experiences, we have developed a breadth and depth of expertise that uniquely qualifies us to share this chapter. Throughout it, we will offer specific examples from our experiences, as well as lessons we have learned in doing this important, meaningful, and difficult work.

DEFINING THE NATURE OF FOCUS GROUPS IN CONSULTING WORK

What Is a Focus Group?

By focus groups, first, we mean *groups of people that are moderated or facilitated by a trained individual to discuss a specific issue or set of issues relevant to the question, problem, or need that the consultant has been asked to address.* More specifically, this discussion is guided by a series of 7–10 carefully prepared questions designed to yield consistent data on the same focused topic. Our experience suggests that focus groups are most productive with a minimum of 5–10 participants but no more than 12. The consultant should determine group size based on his or her own facilitation skills and experience and the complexity of the topic(s) to be covered. The group should be small enough such that participants feel comfortable and sharing their experiences and perspectives, but large enough to allow for a broad range of shared narratives (Krueger & Casey, 2009). Plax recalls one focus group he facilitated that turned into a one-on-one interview when only one individual showed up, and others with close to 15 people. There are challenges associated with building trust and extracting meaningful information in settings that include too few and too many people, even for very experienced facilitators.

Second, participants in a focus group must *meet some criteria for inclusion and possess some similarities with one another, based on the purpose of the focus group.* For instance, Waldeck's then-employer, The Scher Group, was hired to develop a sustainable, ongoing training and development solution for a national association of landscape/green industry employees. As the lead consultant on the project, she used focus groups to discover these employees' needs, their proficiency with using the Internet for learning, and their preferences for online learning experiences. In order to participate in a focus group, employees needed to meet several *screens* (Krueger & Casey, 2009). Specifically, their position had to require a minimum number of continuing education credits per year (i.e., employees without ongoing training requirements were excluded from the discussions), and have access to the Internet (participants with no Internet proficiency or access would continue to participate in instructor-led face-to-face training). Further, participants were screened for their English language proficiency—because a large number of employees required a translator to participate, they were put into groups together based on this shared characteristic. In another example, Plax and Cecchi (1989) selected engineers within a large corporation and organized them into focus groups on the basis of their work groups and management levels. Participant similarities to one another on these characteristics allowed for meaningful discussion of their experiences with the organization's performance appraisal process, and enabled the facilitator to elicit participants' input of functional, work-specific criteria that would enable the consultants to recommend a new evaluation process. These two illustrations showcase how focus group participants are selected based on their possession of some characteristic (e.g., group membership, level of education, job function, experience) and then often subsequently grouped according to their similarities on these characteristics with one another. A great deal of focus group work we have read relies on inadequate samples. As a result of some of this work, there is a widely held belief that focus group research is invalid and unreliable due, in part, to lax sampling procedures. Later in this chapter, we will revisit the importance of proper sampling procedures for ensuring the rigor of the group's design and validity of conclusions.

Third, focus groups are, in fact, *focused* in the nature of their discussions. These are not random groups of individuals brought together to have an informal chat. Focus groups are, as we just discussed, brought together in a systematic way. And, their interactions are carefully and expertly facilitated in such a way that the consultant(s) can gather valuable information that can otherwise be elusive and difficult to access. Therefore, focus groups are strategic: Questions are researched, pre-written, often pilot-tested, and logically structured. The effective facilitator then works hard to achieve a comfortable environment in which these conversations *seem* informal, natural, and unplanned in order to bolster levels of trust and authentic conversation. But, make no mistake: No matter how comfortable, casual, and spontaneous a focus group's interactions may seem, if the facilitator has designed and carried out the group to maximize extraction of usable information, he or she has paid the same level of attention to detail and applied principles of rigor as would be characteristic of a laboratory experiment.

Why Do Consultants Use Focus Groups?

Although focus groups were first introduced and used by the iconic social scientist Robert Merton in his studies of troop morale during World War II, the technique lay somewhat dormant for a number of years—ignored by academics and practitioners with a social science focus, first discussed in a scholarly forum by Merton et al. (1956/1990), and then used predominantly by market researchers beginning in the 1950s. Business enterprises began using focus groups to gather consumer data on products, packaging, design, and advertising strategies—and suddenly, Merton's research technique was a tool being used to advance the interests of business (Greenbaum, 1988). To this day, many major shopping malls have some type of focus group facility, and numerous research firms specialize in "mall intercepts"—one-on-one and group interviews with retail consumers. But the uses for focus groups by consultants have multiplied both in number and the depth of their sophistication since they were first used in the 1950s for these commercial purposes.

Overall, consultants use focus groups to gain information from employees, customers, and other stakeholders about the nature of the status quo, including what works and what problems and needs they experience. And, through focus groups, consultants learn what participants know and don't know. This information can then be used for a variety of purposes, such as to support decision making, resource allocation, program development and evaluation, and strategic performance improvement and change.

What follows is a list of some of the reasons why consultants utilize focus groups. These are not mutually exclusive. Uncovering needs can lead to the generation of information important to decision making and program development, for example. We cannot think of a focus group in which we have not learned a lot about communication dynamics and organizational climate even while probing seemingly technical, non-personal issues like oil recycling habits. The skilled focus group facilitator, above all else, in our view, is equipped to use the technique to generate valuable information.

Identifying individual, team, and organizational needs and problems. In some engagements, we use focus groups as part of a larger needs assessment designed to identify strengths, weaknesses, opportunities, threats, and structural dynamics which permeate all levels of analysis within an organizational setting. Based on the data obtained and the themes we identify in our analysis, we make recommendations and facilitate interventions designed to address what we learned through the focus groups and any other types of data you may have accessed.

Focus groups oriented toward needs assessment may be conducted with employees of the client organization, external stakeholders, or both. For example, Plax facilitated focus groups with employees of a state teachers' retirement agency on internal issues of organizational development; simultaneously, he conducted another series of groups with external stakeholders—the teachers themselves—about their experiences with the agency, their concerns about saving for retirement, and their understanding of the financial aspects of planning for retirement. The information gathered through these groups enabled the consulting team to: (a) create a survey intended to further explore these issues among invested stakeholders, and (b) facilitate the design and deployment of frequent, strategic messages intended to enhance stakeholders' understanding of the agency's practices regarding management of their investments. As this example indicates, information gleaned from focus groups can help a consultant determine what strategic changes might position an organization for improved performance or stakeholder perceptions, and then recommend and facilitate activities such as training and education, team building, or planned change within the organization.

Gathering information to support decision making and problem solving (Albrecht, Johnson, & Walther, 1993; Plax & Cecchi, 1989). The attitudes and experiences that aerospace engineers shared with Plax, for example, guided corporate leadership's thinking and decision making about development of a more effective performance appraisal system. This represents a somewhat indirect way that focus group data inform decision making; but in some skillfully facilitated focus groups, the participants contribute to decisions and problem solution in direct ways. Waldeck once moderated a group discussion about a recurring and pervasive organizational problem with accessing a particular available resource. She guided participants in answering questions like "What would you do, if you could, to remove the barrier?" "What conditions would you create to solve this problem?" and "Ideally, what would need to happen in order to for this challenge to go away?" Through the discussion, participants actually served as architects of the plan that would ultimately be implemented by the organization's leadership.

Guiding program or product development and evaluation (Greenbaum, 1988; Plax et al., 2006). In a project for the California Air Resources Board, Plax and Kearney used focus group data to develop a media outreach/social marketing campaign for educating truckers about the state's diesel exhaust reduction regulations. Through those groups, they were able to learn about the factors that shaped truck drivers' attitudes about environmental protection and compliance with existing laws. This knowledge helped them develop a campaign to raise awareness, shape new attitudes, and create knowledge about environmentally responsible practices among the target population. Then, the team was able to demonstrate through follow-up focus groups that post-campaign participants had internalized (received, reinforced, perceived, and remembered) the intended messages. In another example, Plax et al. (2006) used focus groups to talk with current and former college students, parents, and financial aid professionals about the problems and challenges associated with timely repayment of student loan debt. From those discussions, the consulting team developed a five-module instructional program for college students on topics surrounding debt management and financial literacy that is used at more than 500 institutions of higher education in the United States.

The literature is full of examples relevant to product development and evaluation. Most of the published work on focus groups is concerned with its use in market and product research. Greenbaum's (1988) *Practical Handbook and Guide to Focus Group Research* is an excellent resource for consultants working in product development, testing, and evaluation.

Learning about the climate, communication dynamics, human behavior, and roles characteristic of the organization (Albrecht et al., 1993). Focus groups offer the consultant and clients a unique perspective on life is really like for members of organizations, and how that life differs across teams, units, and levels. Discussions often illustrate the complexity and messiness of an organizational life that looks logical on paper. For instance, Waldeck was part of a consulting team hired by a large resort to review managers' responsibilities. The client requested review of managers' job functions as they compared to written job responsibilities with the goals of heightened accountability, individual job satisfaction, coordination, control, efficiency, and performance effectiveness. The consulting team grouped managers according to their unit, and guided a discussion about managers' job responsibilities. Questions focused on the documented nature of the participants' jobs, as well as the unwritten functions they performed outside of their formal job descriptions. The consultants then reconciled these verbal accounts with existing written job descriptions to create updated job descriptions, and highlight areas where managers were being stretched past their capacities or competencies. We uncovered a wide range of discrepancies and inconsistencies between what people were "supposed" to be doing, and what the current realities of their system demanded from them—and made recommendations accordingly.

In other projects, we have found that when situated in a well-facilitated focus group, employees feel that it is fairly easy and cathartic to share details of the organization's communication network (i.e., who talks to whom), identify obstacles to effective communication, and discuss their concerns. Additionally, when the issue under investigation is subjective in nature, participant responses tend to be much richer than the kinds of data we obtain through surveys or in one-on-one interviews. For instance, skilled focus group facilitators can leverage the ideas shared by Folger (Chapter 10) to transform intact teams' communication relative to conflict, and Sostrin (Chapter 9) to get group members to share their stories—including those they routinely tell, those they avoid telling, and those that might not be known until the group's guided interaction sheds light on them. In the earliest work on this technique, Merton et al. (1956) discussed the counterintuitive point that focus groups participants might be *less* inhibited in the group setting than they would be if they were interviewed individually. Plax and Kearney recall focus groups where participants actually stayed an hour past the scheduled end because they were enjoying discussing the issue with others so much.

Make general and specific recommendations relative to action steps an organization should take to accomplish its prioritized objectives (Plax & Cecchi, 1989; Waldeck, Kearney, & Plax, 2013). For example, Plax et al. (2008) reported on a consultation for a client interested in promoting environmentally friendly energy choices and consumption behaviors. They used focus group results to make recommendations to the client regarding the messages, communication channels, and media techniques that would be most effective in influencing consumers to purchase or lease clean-air and alternative-fuel vehicles.

What Can Focus Groups Do for Consultants?: Types of Information Available

Consultants who have never used focus groups in their consulting work may be wondering how the information they yield is different or in some cases better than what they currently collect using other methods. Of course, the nature of the questions should direct decisions about which technique(s) to employ; but for certain issues and questions, focus groups offer a unique way to collect a lot of useful data which actually become more interesting and more useful as a result of the facilitation process itself. We will explore these ideas in this section.

Krueger and Casey (2009) suggest that focus groups are useful when a consultant or researcher wants to:

- Elicit a range of ideas or feelings that people might have about something.
- Understand differences in point-of-view across categories of people.
- Reveal factors that persons' influence opinions, behaviors, or behavioral intention.
- Generate ideas and solutions, the quality of which could be enhanced by group synergy.
- Pilot test ideas, products, designs, or policy changes.
- Acquire information, such as language commonly used and understood by the target population, which can be used to design messages or quantitative assessments like surveys.
- Uncover qualitative observations which can help make sense out of quantitative data already obtained by other means.
- Build relationships with and get input from a target audience that is highly valued by the client.

Further, focus groups are useful in helping participants retrieve distant experiences from memory, or reconstruct those for which their attitudes and feelings might be somewhat inaccessible. Whereas in survey research we would be concerned about the threats to validity associated with participants interacting with one another, focus groups *depend* on those conversations. As consultants, we must understand the socially constructed nature of organizational stories and narratives: People come to realize and make sense out of "how things are around here" through their interactions with others (see Sostrin, this volume). In other words, people make the choices and engage in the behaviors they do, and understand their organizational realities, based in large part on their relationships with others—and the communication that characterizes those relationships. They do this in meetings and in their day-to-day activities, and they do it during focus groups. So, if we operate from the assumption that organizational stakeholders engage in sense-making about their environments through their interactions, we now have a critical realization about focus group work. It can be a powerful aid in encouraging participants to recall and reconstruct events, and to access their own attitudes. As they then share their own narratives and listen to others', the group connects and "mutually [develops], a substantive 'story' (as their response)" (Albrecht et al., 1993, p. 58).

Focus groups also reveal for the consultant and client the nature of participants' interactions with one another. Sometimes, strangers are selected for focus group participation on the basis of some common characteristic. Observing their communication with one another can reveal interesting and helpful insights. But when we facilitate intact groups or groups of stakeholders who routinely interact, the competent consultant can extrapolate valuable information about how these individuals relate to one another in the organizational context—particularly around issues important to them. For instance, a facilitator might detect unresolved power and dominance issues through the verbal and nonverbal interactions among employees discussing an organizational issue. Focus group observers, usually situated in a special soundproof observation room (and particularly observers from the client organization familiar with the participants) may be able to shed even more light on patterns the facilitator notices, or point out things that the facilitator didn't detect.

Thus, based on our interpretation of the literature and our experiences, we believe the most defensible rationale for using focus groups lies in the organic, generative function of this unique group process and the nature of the information it produces—the synergy and richness of responses that are created when "multiple respondents perform together" (Greenbaum, 1988, p. 17). The interaction among group participants, who have been assembled based on their commonalities relevant to the issues you are interested in, enhances the quality of information you obtain in important ways. In fact, the success of a focus group depends on that interaction.

A properly planned and facilitated focus group will reveal several very important things to the astute consultant who has chosen to use this technique. Put another way, skilled planning, design, and facilitation are necessary conditions for generating the following types of highly useful, insightful, synergistic data:

- *What participants know.* Individuals will respond to questions based on their knowledge of and experience with the issue under investigation. In

Waldeck's formative research with landscape industry employees, she was able to determine their existing level of knowledge about the range of topics her client had requested training on. Further, through her focus groups, she learned what knowledge was truly relevant to these people's job performance. For example, although the client had recommended training on email proficiency, focus group discussions revealed that participants were already fairly literate in the effective and appropriate use of email, and that email was an unnecessary job skill for the vast majority of the employees who would be enrolled in the program. Those who did use email, such as business owners and managers, were already highly proficient. As Jorgensen (Chapter 5) indicates, clients sometimes have a misinformed or misguided sense of what they really need. Listening to the stories of what stakeholders really think they know, and what they think they need, can help consultants design meaningful interventions.

- *What participants don't know.* Participants will reveal directly or indirectly what gaps exist in their thinking relative to the issues, including underdeveloped skills and/or knowledge. Consultants may also discover opportunities for response shaping (Miller, 1980) when a participant or group appears to have little information or bias. For example, in one set of interviews designed as a formative evaluation tool, Waldeck discovered that employees were unaware of a set of online resources their employer had created to assist them in a challenging administrative task. This alerted her to the opportunity to shape this audience in positive ways toward the resource since they had no prior experience or knowledge relative to it. She factored this revelation into the message design recommendations she made to the client. In the project focused on educational loan debt management, Plax and Kearney discovered through the responses they obtained "just how unprepared young adults really are in terms of their ability to manage their financial lives and survive on their own while in school" (Plax et al., 2006, p. 96). This conclusion guided their development of the Life Skills ™ educational program.

- *How participants think about what they know.* Through their responses, consultants will learn about participants' attitudes about the issues you are discussing (including whether they are neutral, when a position is preferred). You will learn what influenced and continues to influence how they think about what you are asking them about, and who they talk to (and potentially influence) about these issues. And, you have the opportunity to explore their thought processes surrounding the issues, and how they use or could use the focus of your conversation in their work. For example, one especially valuable question we use which generates this type of information is: "Assume for a moment that you are a highly paid consultant expert on this topic/in this industry. What is the most important piece of advice you would give?" Listening to the responses and probing, if necessary, to find out why that information is valuable to them, will yield important data regarding how your participants think about this particular topic.

- *How participants think about what they don't know or understand.* Focus groups provide a venue for learning about how participants make sense of the things they don't know. We also learn about the procedural, structural, and cognitive barriers that may lead to a lack of knowledge. For example, in the Life Skills ™ consultation, students offered a variety of reasons why they were so unsophisticated in their financial literacy. But a primary theme the consultants identified was that borrowers evaluated the educational materials available to them as highly ineffective. We learned that their negative perceptions of and unwillingness to use these resources contributed to their overall poor financial management skills. Learning more about students' thought processes and attitudes regarding the things they didn't know or understand helped to substantiate a need for more effective educational resources. And, it informed the message strategies employed in the new resources.

- *How participants think through what others say about what they know.* Merton et al. (1956/1990) noted that one of the primary advantages of focus groups is their ability to ascertain variance in positions and responses. Although an individual could certainly report her opinions in a survey or a one-on-one interviewer, when she does so in a group setting, the consultant is afforded the opportunity to encourage and facilitate others' responses to that individual's statement. In this way, focus groups not only yield exponentially more data than other information-gathering techniques, they create different kinds. This is the synergistic, snowball effect of focus groups we have been referring to.

- *How participants think through what others say about what they don't know or understand.* Focus groups provide us with an opportunity to facilitate an interesting dynamic when members fill gaps for others who report low information or misunderstanding about the topic. This is an illustration of *sensegiving*, through which organizational members influence one another to attribute particular meanings and view organizational reality in particular ways (Gioia & Chittipeddi, 1991).

- *How participants revise how they think about something when they listen to others talk about it.* Focus group discussions sometimes lead to individual participants shifting their thinking (i.e., what they know, how they act, or how they feel) about the issue as a result of the social interaction of the group. We have experienced this phenomenon when a group member reports frustration with a task, technology, policy, or procedure and another participant shares their own successful coping tactic. Or, a participant might share a highly negative experience he had with organizational change. If another (particularly if that other is an opinion leader, cf. Katz & Lazarsfeld, 1955) talks about her own positive experience with change in convincing, informative, and passionate enough terms, the skeptic may begin to think about the idea under discussion a little differently. This aspect of focus groups offers consultants and their clients a window into the influence and information-generation processes of a particular team or the organization as a whole.

- *The overall impact of the focus group experience on how participants think and feel about certain issues.* Warren Bennis and Burt Nanus wrote that "all organizations depend on the existence of shared meanings and interpretations of reality, which facilitate coordinated action" (1997 p. 37). A well-facilitated focus group, as we have seen, is a deeply sociological experience. It influences its participants; it gets them thinking, talking, and interacting with one another. The byproduct of these discussions can be a valuable form of *sensemaking* (Weick, 1995): As focus group members reason through the things that they hear in the setting, construct their own responses, and verbalize those responses, they are engaging in a complex type of social construction. They come to know what they think by saying it and observing the interactions that flow from that point. This potent aspect of focus groups is explained, theoretically, by the schools of symbolic interactionism (Mead, 1934), phenomenology (Schutz, 1967), and social constructionism (Berger & Luckmann, 1967). All of these frameworks highlight the social context and relational nature of thought and behavior which focus group discussions enable.

LESSONS LEARNED

There are plenty of credible contemporary "how-to" resources available for using focus groups as a data collection technique (cf. Bloor, Frankland, Thomas, & Robson, 2002; Greenbaum, 1999; Krueger & Casey, 2009; Morgan & Krueger, 1997) that we recommend for the step-by-step considerations of conducting focus groups, as teaching focus groups as a research method is outside of our scope of purpose. Additionally, Plax et al. (2006) walk the reader through an entire focus group project from the genesis to evaluation, clarifying issues to consider and challenges to anticipate. Here, we will now turn to some of the critical lessons we have learned through our work in each of the key areas of designing, facilitating, analyzing, and reporting on focus groups.

Designing a Focus Group Protocol

Research focus and interview questions. The major lessons we have learned about designing focus group protocols reside not in the method itself, but in our interactions with our clients regarding the objectives of our work. As experienced consultants know, clients can be very opinionated in how they represent their needs, but the way in which clients articulate what they want is often neither (a) concrete enough from which to launch a valid, systematic research investigation, nor (b) in line with the organization's actual problems and needs. Some common problems we have encountered include clients who are generally unsophisticated about research, seem unwilling to share enough background on the issue, and push us to explore too many topics and/or use too many questions in a single focus group study.

We spend a great deal of time working with our client, over multiple conversations and meetings, clarifying their objectives and what they would like us to explore. Our goals in these conversations are to help them think through their objectives and crystallize their thinking, and to formulate about three overarching testable research questions. In our experience, this is the maximum number of related issues that can be explored with a single focus group study. We expend a great deal of time and energy on the development of research questions up front over the course of many meetings because, in our experience, "a well-formulated research question is a half-answered one." From the research questions, we work in a fashion nearly identical to how we would conduct an academic research study. First, we write a pool of interview questions designed to answer the research questions, and we pilot test them.

In terms of generating the questions, we find that the process is much like that of generating items for objective-type instruments. We begin by identifying the specific feelings, perceptions, attitudes, beliefs, knowledge, and experiences we want to assess. The importance of determining exactly what we need to measure in order to address our research questions is no less important in this type of work than in any other type of research. Then, we formulate several questions that target the topic, using slightly different language. In other words, we ask the same question in several different ways. We then submit those questions to a range of pilot procedures, refine and streamline them, and eventually arrive at the list we intend to use. We have found that 7–10 questions typically yield consistent data on the same focused topic, and that 7–8 are best. The lower number minimizes the likelihood of data *saturation* (the point at which you don't get any new information) (Krueger & Casey, 2009) and prevents the focus group from taking too much of participants' time (a barrier to participating for many qualified focus group prospects). Further, shorter sessions minimize facilitator and participant fatigue. Plan a series of questions that will take about 60 minutes to facilitate; a group may last 90 minutes, but this is a bit longer than we find productive and preferable. Through our pilot testing procedures and years of experience, we find that the best questions are *open-ended, concise, clear, short, focused on a single subjective issue,* and *use language and jargon familiar to participants.* We also recommend creating a wide range of questions, from low-level inquiries that will be very easy for participants to answer, to more difficult ones that will require participants to think harder. The answers to those very basic questions may not contribute much to the analysis, but they will go a long way toward building trust and affinity with the group and creating momentum through early participation.

This last characteristic of good focus group questions raises another important point about the design of useful protocols. Effective consultants and focus group facilitators do extensive background research on the industries in which they work. We have become literate in a range of sectors and concerns that our advanced degrees in communication never would have prepared us for. Waldeck, for instance, can have a great conversation about the science and safety issues of tool forging! Make an effort to learn the language that your participants use in order to build trust and credibility with your participants. Plax found this particularly important when interviewing Latino truckers about their oil recycling habits. By using the terms and jargon in his questions that his participants use, he went a long way toward resolving any trust issues they may have had with a white male academic consultant asking questions about their work. Attempting to write questions without becoming fluent in the industry and foci of the group will inhibit data collection efforts. The groups themselves help educate and enlighten the facilitator, but he or she must enter the room with a base level of knowledge that will get participants talking.

Sampling and working with focus group facilities. We have conducted focus groups in classrooms, conference rooms, cafeterias, sparse empty rooms in shopping malls and business parks, and luxurious commercial focus group facilities with the most sophisticated recording equipment and participant comforts available. We have generated our own samples, used 100% of the population an organization provided us with, and relied on the samples generated by the professional focus group suites we've dealt with. Who generates the sample and where the discussion is held is largely dependent on the size and scope of a project and the resources available to the consultant through the contract.

When a consultant is responsible for selecting participants, Kruger and Casey (2009) give in-depth advice on setting screens, designing the recruiting process, generating a pool of potential participants, and then randomly selecting from the pool. In forming our own samples, we strive for a *homogenous sample with maximum variation.* Although this may sound like a contradiction, it is the foundation to effective focus group research. You are looking for members of the target population (e.g., individuals who work for the same company, are in the same industry, participate in the same retirement plan, belong to the same professional association, are consumers of certain goods) who *share some characteristic or set of characteristics in common* (e.g., they all intend to buy within the next six months, work in middle management, have student loan debt, or use smartphones). But after identifying people who meet these criteria or screens, you also want to assemble groups that will allow for a *range of experiences on the topic and contrasting opinions*. For example, in the student loan debt project, we formed separate focus groups for currently enrolled college students with outstanding educational loans and alumni already in repayment of their loans. This accomplished the homogeneity requirement. Then, we sought college students who were both male and female, came from diverse socioeconomic backgrounds, and were in different phases of their college careers. In this way, we achieved variation. Similarly, we sought college alumni (the shared characteristic) with high-paying jobs as well as low-income participants, those working in professional and non-professional fields, and from all major geographic regions of the United States. These latter characteristics helped maximize the diversity of responses and experiences we were able to extract from the groups.

Sometimes, on sizable projects with equally big budgets, consultants contract with a commercial focus group facility that handles the logistics. Online directories for identifying these professionals by city and state are available at http://www.quirks.com/directory/focusgroup/ and http://www.greenbook.org/market-research-firms/focus-group-facilities. Focus group facility services include screening the population list using the consultant's criteria, recruiting, scheduling the groups, managing payment of participants, providing refreshments, and administering questionnaires or usability tests associated with the focus group. The facility offers facilitation space, observation space, audio and/or video recording equipment, and a comfortable lounge area for participants. Facilities vary in their amenities—how much participant and observation space there is, how high-end the furnishings and amenities are, the location (i.e., convenience to freeways, airports, or other important criteria), and the technology available. A consultant considering use of a professional facilitation site should explore the facility's services and space in comparison to the project's needs and budget before contracting with a particular firm.

In evaluating and selecting focus group facilities, the most important thing to look at is their sampling and recruiting process. We have learned through experience that we would rather conduct a group in a low-tech room with folding chairs than in a high-end facility which does not sample and recruit participants properly. We have had projects go over budget and behind schedule due to facilities that produced poor, inadequate samples. So, ask detailed questions about their practices, and seek references. Find out if they are competent at assembling qualified focus groups that meet the screens of your project. This is particularly important when dealing with participants who are external to the client's organization, such as the truck drivers in our emissions study for the Air Resources Board, or the consumers in our "clean-air" vehicle project. The facility should recruit more prospects than are actually needed for a group, and provide the consultant with background on all of the participants they assemble (including how they responded to each screening question or filter). The facilitator or consulting team then makes the final decisions about who to retain, and the facility will compensate anyone not chosen and send them home.

This raises a final logistical issue related to sampling. The larger question is "What will incentivize members of this population to participate?" but the specific consultant concern is "how much should we pay?" When consultants interview employees of the client organization, they typically do not compensate them financially. But what other incentives might motivate them to participate? Refreshments? Mileage reimbursement to and from the focus group site? Can their employer mandate that they participate? These are issues consultants should negotiate with the client to encourage participation. When we recruit members of the public, we compensate them. Consultants must determine this number in advance and figure it into the cost projection for the consultation. Typically, depending on the nature of the data we want to collect and the population itself, we pay between $75 and $200 cash per participant.

Facilitating Focus Groups

Important moderator skills. The ability to extract the deep, rich accounts we described earlier in this chapter is highly dependent on the facilitator's skills. In fact, Greenbaum wrote: "The quality of the moderator is the most important element that determines the ultimate usefulness of the output of focus group research" (1988, p. ix). First, consultants must be physically and mentally ready for the rigors of focus group work. Groups can be very tiring (and for this reason, we recommend never scheduling more than two per day). Further, facilitators need to be articulate, good listeners, and competent interpersonal and organizational communicators (Beebe, Chapter 8). Effective facilitators allow for some deviation from a semi-structured interview protocol; in fact, because they are astute listeners, they explore responses that they find confusing, vague, potentially passive aggressive, surprising, and so forth, with follow-up questions that may not have been part of the initial script. Facilitators must be good time managers. This is one of the most challenging aspects for inexperienced facilitators. Keep conversation flowing and do not allow it to dwell on any one question for so long that the group runs overtime or the facilitator has to eliminate questions.

Many of the same behaviors that are effective in encouraging and managing conversation in our classrooms work well in facilitating focus groups. We find that audience analysis, confirmation behaviors, affinity-seeking, prosocial compliance gaining strategies, and immediacy behaviors work especially well (see Beebe, Chapter 8; Houser, Chapter 12). Excellent facilitators also notice nonverbal behaviors that indicate nervousness, conflict, or are out of sync with participants' verbal behaviors. Sarcasm, some laughter, eye rolling, facial expressions, very relaxed or very rigid posture, lack of eye contact, fidgeting, or leaving the room can all be telling behaviors that the good facilitator will sensitively probe.

Additionally, *facilitators must be adept facilitating the entire group*. By this we mean that the facilitator must pay attention to everyone, encourage equal participation, and manage both dominant and apprehensive members. Inexperienced facilitators often favor the dominators because they talk freely and seem to make the group flow easily, and allow apprehensive participants to remain quiet. However, experienced facilitators recognize the importance of drawing everyone present into the conversation in order to generate the greatest amount of useful data. A group's narrative is not complete unless everyone contributes meaningfully.

Similarly, we often have to work hard not to become annoyed with and exclude certain personalities. Facilitators quickly learn the importance of validating everyone as a way of encouraging the organic process of conversation. Say things like "That's very interesting!"; "Now that's a new idea to me—help me understand"; "That seems really useful—can you say just a bit more?" "What did the rest of you think of that idea?" or "Now three of you seem to be in agreement. Would you say this is a fairly common or popular belief around here?" Further, be prepared to modify questions for groups that have trouble understanding them. Sometimes, the course of a long project, changes in the external environment may render questions more or less relevant. But as you edit questions, be careful to always maintain the original purpose of the question.

One important conclusion about facilitation that we have drawn taken from our years of focus group experience is that *participants don't know that they know as much as they know until you validate and further probe what they share*. Participants may arrive believing they have little to contribute, but through the facilitator's careful questions and interaction with other group members, everyone in a properly sampled focus group has something meaningful to contribute. On the other hand, inexperienced facilitators who lack competence in the facilitation skills we are discussing here are likely to obtain unreliable, incomplete, inauthentic data.

Building trust. Despite the necessity of all of the communication skills we have just discussed, we view them as insufficient conditions for truly effective focus group outcomes. The most important thing a facilitator must do early and throughout his or her time with each group is to *establish trust*. Some populations and individuals may distrust researchers and consultants. They may view us as different from them in ways that predispose them negatively to us and our presence. They may perceive a focus group facilitator or consultant as a distraction from their work, too far removed from who they are and what they do, too old or too young, too erudite, or aligned too closely with management or other groups they dislike or distrust. They may worry that other individuals or groups will retaliate against them for their comments, or that someone outside (such as supervisors or social friends and acquaintances) the group will find out what they said. This can be particularly true when the topic of the group is of a sensitive personal or political nature. For example, in the educational loan groups, we heard from several parents who were burdened by such large amounts of debt that they experienced embarrassment, depression, and fear. In another project examining attitudes about using re-refined oil, we experienced resistance due to mistrust surrounding this highly controversial, politically sensitive topic.

We have already mentioned several strategies for creating trust with groups: learning the unique language of participants, using competent communication strategies that validate participant responses, and expressing care and concern through affinity-seeking behaviors and verbal and nonverbal immediacy. Overall, *facilitators must be authentic.* Walk into the room with the attitude that you care about these people and what they have to share with you. Make some small talk with them, express interest, and deemphasize any status differences. Never be condescending. Remind and reassure them that their anonymity will be protected. Encourage them through the process. Say things like: "I'm a college professor, not an expert in what you do. I know a lot about solving problems, but I know nothing about you or your daily life and work. To be effective here and to ultimately help you, I need you to teach me and feed me information." "I don't have an agenda here. I'm here as a third party to listen and get as much information from you as I can and to protect your anonymity. Nothing you say will be associated with you or your name." "People in my groups enjoy themselves. You are going to get to talk about yourself, your opinions, and your experiences and get paid to do it. This is going to be a really positive hour together." As participants open up and tell their stories, reinforce them. They may vent, and you will need to manage that and keep them focused, but commiserate with them a bit—"that really happened to you?! Tell us more. Has that happened to anyone else?" to continue the flow of conversation and keep building the trust. This type of reinforcement is to be avoided in scholarly research interviews, but is critical to establishing a comfortable, open climate in consulting interviews. The very best questions asked in the most clear and straightforward ways by the most affable consultants will still result in inaccurate, inauthentic, or incomplete narratives if trust is low.

A final point about trust is the importance of not only establishing trust between facilitator and participants, but to encourage participants to trust one another. Low trust among participants can lead to low willingness to communicate and low quality or dishonest data. Therefore, facilitators must establish ground rules which encourage focus group participants to speak openly and honestly. Remind participants that everything shared should be confidential and is not to be discussed outside of the focus group room. Additionally, we have asked participants to help generate ground rules that would help them feel more comfortable with responding candidly. Overall, though, in our history of facilitating focus groups, we have had more positive than negative experiences with group members interacting: We've seen participants network and connect with one another, leaving with valuable contacts and new relationships they did not have prior to the session.

The role of observers. Consultants often assign a member of the team to sit in an adjacent room and monitor the discussion through a two-way mirror or via video feed. Even though the group might be recorded, the observer should take notes. Kearney observes all of the groups Plax facilitates; she records particularly enlightening sentences or phrases and nonverbal activity (Kruger & Casey, 2009). The observer also records his or her own opinions, thoughts, or questions on the stories participants tell, and may pass questions on to the facilitator to ask before dismissing the group. Sometimes the client or other stakeholders will want to observe, too, and this can have both negative and positive impacts on the process (see Plax et al. [2006] for more explanation).

Analyzing the Data and Writing the Report

Nearly all of our focus group work has involved triangulating multiple types of data from which we make our conclusions and recommendations. Prior to the focus group interviews, we administer surveys among the population as well as participants, and sometimes conduct phone or face-to-face one-on-one interviews. These yield data which, when tabulated and analyzed, supplement, reinforce, and extend the interview data; additionally they serve the important function of stimulating participants' thinking about the issues we're interested in prior to their focus group. Further, we often examine archival data (e.g., existing student loan default rates or written job descriptions).

To analyze focus group responses, we use a thematic analysis process. We transcribe, analyze, and code all data obtained. Coding procedures typically involve three coders who separately (and then together) analyze the transcripts and document common, overlapping responses known as *response themes* to questions posed by the facilitator. When there is a question about the validity of a particular response theme, coders view the relevant segments of the videotapes again and discuss disagreements with the goal of maximizing intercoder reliability. We then select representative narratives, examples, and quotes to illustrate each theme.

Most clients request a formal report summarizing the results of archival research, survey responses, and focus group interviews. The client may provide a standard format or template that the consultant must work with; in our experience, this can be challenging and if possible, should be avoided. No two focus group study reports we have produced have adhered to the same format, and attempting to standardize reports is a limiting way of portraying findings and making recommendations. Although it may have more or fewer sections which are labeled in slightly different ways, in general, the report should include the following:

- Abstract
- Executive summary
- Introduction
- Methods and materials
- Results
- Conclusions
- Recommendations
- References
- Copies of surveys, interview guides, and any other stimuli used in assessing participant knowledge, attitudes, and/or skills.

The report should be written authoritatively, logically, and persuasively (much like any other research report). It should be concise and consumable, with language that will be understandable to the client (who may be unfamiliar with research terminology). (Much of the same advice Waldeck, Plax, and Kearney (Chapter 7) suggest for proposal writing is useful in writing the report, as well). Keep in mind that, as Boster (Chapter 14) notes, we cannot always deliver the results that a client hopes for. Sometimes we cannot be as definitive as clients would like in drawing conclusions; thus, as part of our ongoing relationship with the client, it is important to manage their perceptions and expectations carefully. Waldeck et al. (2013) argue for the importance of being able to "translate" our work as consultants for clients, and this includes helping them understand the scientific standards required to produce valid conclusions—including our ethical responsibilities not to overstate our conclusions or make recommendations for which there aren't sufficient supporting data.

Finally, as you produce your report, be aware that it will serve as a political document inside the client organization. In it, you are making potentially controversial recommendations about resource allocation, organizational culture, strategy, relationships, power, leadership, change, and initiatives that may privilege and showcase some units over others. Thus, you cannot ignore the context in which the need for your consultation emerged and the impact that your recommendations will have.

CONCLUSION

Scholars and practitioners should find this chapter helpful in understanding the power, value, and nuances of collecting narratives through focus group facilitation. In it, we defined the nature of focus groups in consulting work and offered examples of how we have used the technique in many of our own engagements. We shared our perspective on when the method can be meaningfully used, and what consultants can learn through the stories and experiences participants share. We noted the theoretical foundations of this type of work in the fields of sociology and communication. Finally, we discussed a number of the lessons we have learned over the years in planning and designing focus groups, facilitating them, analyzing the data, and assembling reports. In reflecting on the seminal focus group work conducted by Merton, Lazarsfeld, Kendall, and others at Columbia University's Bureau of Social Research, Gollin points out that "much of our knowledge of social, political, and economic life" (Merton, Fiske, & Kendall, 1956/1990, foreword, para. 3) during post-World War II years was gained through this method. Indeed, the practice has important implications for our continued understanding of organizational systems—how they function internally, and how they interact through the exchange of products, services, and messages with external stakeholders. Masterful focus group facilitation begins, evolves, and ends with an understanding of social science theory, research, and best practices in communication as consultants work with clients and participants.

REFERENCES

Albrecht, T. L., Johnson, G. M., & Walther, J. B. (1993). Understanding communication processes in focus groups. In D. L. Morgan (Ed.), *Successful focus groups: Advancing the state of the art* (pp. 51-64). Newbury Park, CA: SAGE.

Bennis, W. G., & Nanus, B. (1997). *Leaders: The strategies for taking charge* (2nd ed.). New York, NY: HarperCollins.

Berger, L. & Luckmann, T. (1967). *The social construction of reality.* New York, NY: Doubleday.

Bloor, M., Frankland, J., Thomas, M., & Robson, K. (2002). *Focus groups in social research.* London, UK: SAGE.

Browning, L., & Morris, G. H. (2012). *Stories of life in the workplace: An open architecture for organizational narratology.* New York, NY: Routledge.

Gioia, D. A., & Chittipeddi, K. (1991). Sensemaking and sensegiving in strategic change initiation. *Strategic Management Journal, 12,* 443–448.

Greenbaum, T. L. (1988). *The practical handbook and guide to focus group research.* Lexington, MA: Heath.

Greenbaum, T. L. (1999). *Moderating focus groups: A practical guide for group facilitation.* Thousand Oaks, CA: SAGE.

Katz, E., & Lazarsfeld, P. F. (1955). *Personal influence.* New York, NY: Free Press.

Krueger, R. A., & Casey, M. A. (2009). *Focus groups: A practical guide for applied research* (4th ed.). Thousand Oaks, CA: Sage.

Mead, G. H. (1934). *Mind, self, and society.* Chicago, IL: University of Chicago Press.

Merton, R. K., Fiske, M., & Kendall, P. L. (1956/1990). *The focused interview: A manual of problems and procedures* [Kindle edition]. Retrieved from Amazon.com.

Miller, G. R. (1980). On being persuaded: Some basic distinctions. In M. Roloff & G. R. Miller (Eds.), *Persuasion: New directions in theory and research* (pp. 11–28). Beverly Hills, CA: SAGE.

Morgan, D. L., & Krueger, R. A. (1997). *The focus group kit: Volumes 1–6.* Thousand Oaks, CA: SAGE.

Plax, T. G., & Cecchi, L. F. (1989). Manager decisions based on communication facilitated in focus groups. *Management Communication Quarterly, 2,* 511–535.

Plax, T. G., Kearney, P., Allen, T. H., & Ross, T. (2006). Using focus groups to design a nationwide debt-management educational program. In *Facilitating group communication in context: Facilitating group task and team communication* (L. R. Frey, Ed.). Creskill, NJ: Hampton.

Plax, T. G., Kearney, P., Ross, T. J., & Jolly, J. C. (2008). Assessing the link between environmental concerns and consumers' decisions to use clean-air vehicles. *Communication Education, 57,* 417–422.

Schutz, A. (1967). *The phenomenology of the social world.* Evanston, IL: Northwestern University Press.

Seidman, I. (2013). *Interviewing as qualitative research* (4th ed.). New York, NY: Teachers College Press.

Waldeck, J. H. (2008). The development of an industry-specific online learning center: Consulting lessons learned. *Communication Education, 57,* 452–463.

Waldeck, J. H., Kearney, P., & Plax, T. G. (2013). *Communication consulting: What skills do I need?* In *Business and professional communication in a digital age* (pp. 311–335). Boston, MA: Cengage.

Weick, K. E. (1995). *Sensemaking in organizations.* Thousand Oaks, CA: SAGE.

CHAPTER SEVEN

Planning and Proposing Consulting Work

JENNIFER H. WALDECK

Chapman University

TIMOTHY G. PLAX AND PATRICIA KEARNEY

California State University, Long Beach

INTRODUCTION

The proposal is a powerful vehicle for influencing clients to begin the exciting venture of change, development, progress, and improvement that truly excellent consulting work can usher into an organization. Consultants rarely obtain work without a well-done proposal, written to define the scope, rationale, and cost of a consulting project for a client, and ultimately, to obtain the work. An effectively crafted proposal is well-organized, well-written, visually attractive, and persuasive. The most successful proposals are created with the client in mind; they are carefully customized for the client and reflect what the consultant has learned about the organization's structure, political climate, strengths, weaknesses, external environment, opportunities, and needs. This chapter offers consultants insights on creating proposals that not only win business, but mobilize and motivate clients to make important changes that enhance what they do and how they do it. In it, we will discuss the content of most consulting proposals, the process and principles we follow for creating strong proposals, and some advice for writing and presenting proposals persuasively.

In overview, a consulting proposal addresses six primary topics in some structured format:

- The consultant (or consulting team's) credentials, experience, and technical ability to deliver the proposed services
- The objectives of the proposed work
- A detailed description of the consulting plan—the intervention(s), programs, activities, and/or other deliverables the consultant is proposing based on an assessment of the client's needs (see Jorgensen, Chapter 5; Plax, Waldeck, & Kearney, Chapter 6)
- A timeline for implementing the planned interventions along with logistical details of project management
- The estimated costs and expenses associated with the project; and
- The method(s) for evaluating the effectiveness of the proposed plan

Figure 1 features a suggested structure that can be adapted for most consulting proposals, into which these six topics can be situated. Not all proposals will include all of these sections; and some will include other sections as required by the client. Sometimes, clients provide a proposal template that the consultant must adhere to. To produce the most relevant, impactful proposal, we spend extensive time collecting background information relevant to the project that helps us determine what information decision makers need, and how they want it presented.

Title Page
Transmittal Letter
Table of Contents
Executive Summary

Introduction and Overview
Provide relevant history of the project
Overview needs assessment methods and summarize results
Establish firmly a compelling need for action, development, change, or improvement based on data collected through all methods
Illustrate the consulting team's credibility relative to the specific project (include professional bios and vitae as Appendices)

Project Objectives & Scope
Provide carefully constructed observable, measurable, attainable, and specific objectives (individual intervention objectives, such as those associated with a training recommendation, will be spelled out in a later section)
Summarize the target audience for the consultation overall (target audiences for various interventions will be discussed in a later section)
Estimate the length of the project

Recommendations
List and describe the specific intervention(s) the consultant (or team) is recommending to address the needs established in Overview
Substantiate each recommendation with evidence from the needs assessment
Provide carefully constructed observable, measurable, attainable, and specific objectives for each recommended intervention
Specify groups and/or individuals from the organization who will be involved in each recommended activity
Explain any considerations such as employee time away from work, space, or physical resources the client should be aware of

Timeline
Provide a descriptive, visual timeline for the entire consultation. When will each recommendation be launched? How long will each phase take?
Be transparent about project management: How will the logistics of the project be managed? Who is accountable for project management in the multi-stage, longitudinal consultation?

Methods of Evaluation
Specify how each recommended intervention will be evaluated in terms of process, content, and delivery
Explain how evaluations will reveal whether project objectives were accomplished and enable clients to realize a return on investment (ROI)
Address both formative and summative evaluation techniques

Budget and Costs
List, explain, and justify amounts requested for the consultation

Summary and Conclusion
Summarize the overall purpose of the project, close warmly, and ask for the business

Appendices
Bibliography

Figure 1. Suggested Table of Contents for Consulting Proposals

Project Background Matters

How the consultant arrives at the point of writing a proposal serves as an important backdrop for how he or she constructs the document and generates evidence for his or her recommendations. Exactly what to include in the proposal and how to package it depends highly on whether it is being developed in response to a *Request for Proposal* (RFP) or after a thorough, systematic needs assessment using methods such as those suggested by Jorgensen (Chapter 5) and Plax et al. (Chapter 6) in this volume. An RFP is an invitation to qualified organizations or individuals to bid for specific work, typically without the benefit of a thorough needs analysis. Waldeck often consults with a team on government contract work—for example, to deliver leadership development and/or communication skills training within government agencies. These proposals can be very challenging to create, because they must be written based on what is frequently limited or general information provided in the RFP. The naïve or inexperienced consultant address only that content, but the experienced consultant becomes good at doing a great deal of "reading between the lines" and networking with insiders to create an influential document that stands out to the agency. The agency states its needs in a fairly straightforward, general way, and the consultant responds with an offer to provide services, in the format specified in the RFP. Although the agency typically designates an employee who will respond to consultants' queries (usually by email), the specificity and depth of information that individual offers is nothing like the type of information consultants can acquire through a needs assessment (see Jorgensen, Chapter 5) and by establishing an ongoing communication relationship with a prospective client.

Most of the work that the authors of this chapter do collectively and individually is for clients with whom we have preexisting relationships and work history. These clients often approach us with a particular need or needs. Our history does not pave the way for automatic acceptance of our bid; nor does a relationship mean we do not encounter resistance to certain recommendations we make. Therefore, the proposal remains a critical element of our work. It must be persuasive, well-evidenced, technically perfect, and certainly strategic. Most frequently, we write the proposal based on our knowledge of the client acquired over time, needs assessment data, and frequent meetings and in-depth conversations with our contact person(s) inside the organization. The principles underlying the process we follow are discussed in the next section.

SIX PRINCIPLES FOR PREPARING A CONSULTING PROPOSAL

Principle 1: The Proposal Should Be Based on Frequent Communication with the Client

Whether interacting face-to-face or by leveraging communication media (see Stephens & Waters, Chapter 13), we rely on frequent, in-depth communication over time with clients to produce the best proposals. We cannot emphasize this point enough. Consultants must work closely and check in with the client as they develop each element of the proposal. Client input helps us identify and define problem situations, spot strengths and opportunities for organizational development, specify target objectives for the consultation, design appropriate interventions meant to generate buy-in, and understand the client's budget so that we can prepare a realistic proposal. Sometimes clients are too busy to be hands-on, or (mistakenly) believe that hiring an external consultant means that they should stay out of the process. In contract work that consultants bid in response to an RFP, there may be little opportunity to cultivate a strong consultant-client relationship prior to the award; but, still, communication helps us obtain helpful insights from program officers during the proposal process.

To maximize the success of the project and ultimate client satisfaction with our work, we encourage clients to stay closely connected to the project and we seek substantive input from them. The more engaged the client is in the entire process, beginning with the formulation of the proposal, the more likely the client will be satisfied with consulting results. When the client is disconnected, the consultant will have a difficult time getting buy-in and approval. In our experience, less involved clients find more to be critical of than engaged ones because they lack an appreciation of both the process and product. As a result, the relationship becomes strained, the process becomes more effortful than it could be, and the client may not fully benefit from the consultation.

Some clients, on the other hand, may want to be *over-involved* and may attempt to micromanage or control the direction of the project. The tactful consultant can hear this client's concerns and address them in the proposal, while still making recommendations based primarily on an objective assessment of the organization's needs. Whether clients are aloof or enthusiastic, the best consultants manage useful interactions with them. They listen carefully, educate clients about the consulting process and each stakeholder's role in it, and utilize the information they acquire to write a targeted proposal. We have experienced successful consulting outcomes, acquired additional contracts, and built long-term relationships with organizations when we integrate our clients into the work, beginning at the proposal stage. Successful consultants build time into their consulting plans for these important exchanges.

Principle 2: The Proposal Must Be Strategic and Aim for Perfection

Consulting proposals must be prepared with a great deal of thought and attention to detail. First, the proposal should be a highly customized document. Every line of the proposal must target the reader and his/her organization and needs; *great consultants never use boilerplate language.* Even standard aspects of our work—for example, the written description of how we construct a survey or facilitate a focus group study—are customized for the client using specific, targeted language and references to the focus of the engagement. Second, we support the project in general and each recommendation in particular with clear, convincing each intervention connects to one or more of the overarching project objectives, defined in a consumable way for the intended reader(s), and substantiated with needs assessment data and/or a theoretical or research-based rationale from the literature. Third, the strategic proposal is a perfect document, both in terms of content and presentation. The grammar, punctuation, sentence and paragraph structure, and document format should be polished and flawless.

For all of these reasons, proposals should undergo several drafts and revisions before the consultant submits them. We have even added professional editors and proofreaders to our consulting teams to ensure the technical perfection and useful formatting of our proposals. Although the work of writing and editing is primarily the responsibility of the consulting team, we again point to the value of working closely with a contact inside the organization. The larger the project or the bigger the client organization, the more challenging and labor-intensive the process will be to create an acceptable proposal, and working closely with your client will be very helpful. This may mean an activity as superficial as asking a program officer a procedural question about the RFP. But, in many cases, consultants who effectively integrate clients into proposal development will, as a result, obtain a valuable resource for evaluating aspects of the bid before it is submitted in final form. For example, our proposal for the Life Skills™ consulting project described in Chapter 6 took approximately six months. As the agenda for the project became clear, various stakeholders reviewed aspects of the proposal and weighed in on the details, creating an increasingly refined portrait of how the consultation would proceed. The final proposal, then, anticipated and addressed the concerns and suggestions of key decision makers within the client organization. As a result, the project met the client's expectations and we fulfilled the consulting goals established at the beginning of the project.

Although aspects of technical perfection such as grammar, use of evidence, and organization constitute skills inexperienced consultants may have already mastered, other facets of proposal strategy take time and effort to learn, often through trial and error. For example, Waldeck's group of subject matter experts responded to close to a dozen RFPs from a particular agency before there was any interest expressed in our ideas and services. Our proposals were organized and written well, and the consultants were highly qualified for the work. But, as any experienced consultant knows, a lot of work goes into figuring out the "secret sauce" to getting one's foot in the door. In our case, the principal consultant spent *years* learning the political landscape of this government agency, performing fairly small-scale training programs, getting to know decision makers, seeking feedback on failed proposals, and acquiring inside information about the agency's expectations. Only after all of this effort did the group have a good understanding of how to create a successful proposal to do larger, interesting, and impactful projects for this particular client.

Thus, consultants must understand that sound proposals require a substantial investment of time, effort, and sometimes direct expense (e.g., payment to professional editors to polish our work). Yet, the consultant receives no payment toward the recommended project unless the contract is awarded. New or inexperienced consultants must be aware that the costs of developing proposals for work not awarded are simply out of pocket. It takes time to learn the process of strategic proposal development. In spite of the risks inherent in expending resources on proposals that might not be funded, as a consultant becomes more adept at constructing proposals and builds relationships with clients, the more likely he or she is to win profitable contracts. As the saying goes, "it costs money to make money."

Principle 3: The Proposal Thoroughly Documents the Nature and Extent of the Client's Needs

Without a clear understanding of the client's current status and needs, consultants are hindered in their ability to create a viable consulting plan (Jorgensen, Chapter 5). This understanding might be based solely on what the client includes in the RFP and any insider information and background research the consultant may be able acquire . For most projects, however, consultants identify needs and diagnose problems through a formal needs assessment. A consultation's objectives, and each recommendation the consultant makes, then, must be logically tied to those documented needs. For instance, Waldeck's group responded to an RFP that specified particular communication and leadership courses the client required (this curriculum represented the client's need). Their proposal, then, offered a persuasive argument that the team had credible experience and the technical ability to design and teach each course in an appropriate fashion for this agency's employees. In another project, Plax and Kearney used formal needs assessment data, collected through focus groups, to substantiate the need for financial literacy education for college loan borrowers. So, whether the consultant learns about client needs through an RFP, background research on the client, formal needs assessments, or informal discussions, he or she must use these needs in persuading the client that the recommended interventions will be worth the effort and financial investment.

Principle 4: The Proposal Specifies Target Objectives

Once the consultant identifies the client's needs and defines them, he or she must translate those into desired outcomes. In collaboration with the client, we must determine:

- What specific outcomes should result from the intervention(s)
- What changes should come about as a byproduct of the consultation; and

- How organizational members should think, behave, or feel differently as a result of the project.

Writing useful consulting objectives requires a great deal of thought of and time. They are observable, measurable, attainable in the agreed-upon timeframe and with the available resources, and specific (Beebe, Mottet, & Roach, 2013). Objectives that meet these criteria give the consultant direction on what kinds of intervention activities will be effective, because they specify what should result from the engagement. In a project that involved leadership curriculum development, Waldeck and her client agreed that the client's existing courses were largely populated with outdated, unsubstantiated "pop" advice about leadership. Thus, her objectives included updating and strengthening the curriculum with greater emphasis on peer-reviewed research and the thinking of credible leadership experts. With these objectives in mind, she reviewed literature published in the prior five years for research findings to include in the courses, and selected a formal theoretical framework for the curriculum. Having a theoretical framework enabled her to organize the content, material that was not consistent with the selected theory, and ensure that what remained was credible and reflected scholarly rigor. She then wrote specific learning objectives for each course—statements of what training participants should know and be able to do after completing the course. Taken together, the objectives ultimately enabled her to evaluate the success of the program.

In another example, Meyer, Roberto, Boster, and Roberto (2004) defined specific objectives for an intervention known as *Get Real About Violence*®, meant to reduce adolescents' verbal and physical aggression (e.g., insulting and fighting) and to reduce behaviors that research show promote or encourage violence (e.g., watching others fight and spreading information about a fight that is going to happen). They used the Theory of Reasoned Action to drive content and process development, designed a 12-lesson curriculum to promote their two primary objectives, and evaluated their intervention specifically with respect to whether their objectives were realized among the adolescents enrolled in the coursework.

A consulting intervention might involve, as in the two examples just mentioned, training and education; or, it might recommend team building, leadership development, strategic planning, process design, and/or organizational restructuring, for instance. Regardless of the consultant's focus, developing objectives allows him/her to create, implement, and then evaluate a solution.

Principle 5: The Proposal Recommends One or More Appropriate Interventions

Once the problem is defined and project objectives are specified, the consultant's task is to describe in clear, concrete detail, his or her recommendations for solving the problem and meeting the client's needs. In addition to describing the intervention(s), the proposal should be specific in indicating a timeline for implementation and delivery, controls for keeping the project on schedule, and assignments of accountability to members of the team. The proposal should also discuss issues of project management, specifying who will perform functions such as scheduling people and space or ordering supplies and making other requisitions.

In discussing each recommendation, the consultant should offer compelling evidence. For example, in a consulting project described in Waldeck (2008), a range of skill inventories administered during a needs assessment revealed employees' competence gaps in several areas. Using statistical data extracted from these assessments as a rationale, the consulting team recommended training and other educational initiatives designed to close those gaps.

This volume explores a variety of consulting interventions, including team building, transformative mediation, training, and research. Consultants might recommend curriculum development, an educational or informational campaign, research and development, strategic planning, an evaluation of some kind, or large-scale system-wide organizational change, depending on the unique nature of the client's needs. Interventions might address human behavior, processes, or organizational structures. Although they come in a variety of forms, a consultant's recommendations include some type of product, service, or other deliverable, *and must be well-substantiated.* The client must be able to see the link between the recommendation and the need. The proposal must further demonstrate the efficacy of the solution. For instance, in their work for the educational loan industry, Plax and Kearney devised a solution designed to address the problem of students defaulting on their loans. Based on clear evidence collected from their target population indicating that existing educational materials were inadequate, their proposal went well beyond simple resources such as brochures, posters, and brief workshops. They recommended a multistage, curriculum-based solution to the problem of financial illiteracy that was scalable for diverse audiences including undergraduates, graduate students, professional students, and recent college graduates.

The question of consultant expertise and relevant skills is key to any project that promises comprehensive programs and solutions designed to address complex organizational problems. Plax (2008) wrote, "No one person can expect to do everything. Part of being able to market what you can do is putting together a team of experts that make your weaknesses irrelevant" (p. 243). Our work is typically focused on large, complicated, multistage, mixed-method interventions. These projects require a consulting team with relevant individual skills. For example, we often need to bring together instructional designers, media specialists such as video producers, experts from different subject matters to create content, writers, editors, statisticians, qualitative data analysts, facilitators, trainers, and more. The best consulting teams have members with the necessary backgrounds, skills, and training that operate in unique and complementary ways. The team approach not only allows a consultant to tackle large projects that one person could not complete on time, but it introduces the range of experiences and skills necessary to address multidimensional issues. Thus, the proposal should be specific in describing each member of the consulting team's roles and related background qualifications so that the reader believes that the recommendations are logistically possible (since one individual cannot likely perform all aspects of a complex consultation), realistic in terms of the team's expertise (since one individual is not likely to have all of the skills and required knowledge to carry out all aspects of a large engagement), and superior to other teams' qualifications and talents.

Principle 6: The Proposal Must Indicate How the Consultation Will Be Evaluated

A thorough, convincing proposal addresses exactly how the consultant plans to assess the effectiveness of all interventions recommended. The goal of evaluation is to provide useful feedback to key stakeholders impacted by the consultant and his/ her work. Evaluative feedback provides clients with evidence that their investment in the project was worthwhile, often in the form of a critical metric known as *return on investment* (ROI). Such evidence allows clients to argue for additional resources, programs, or continuation of any of the initiatives begun. Evaluation offers consultants feedback on what worked and what did not, and it speaks to whether or not the project's objectives were realized. Without a proper evaluation, consultants cannot know how to improve their facilitation skills or the nature of their programs, and clients can only make guesses about the value inherent in the work that was done. In the absence of a systematic evaluation plan, all that stakeholders can do is base their conclusions on anecdotal evidence of questionable reliability and validity.

The approach we take in evaluating our consulting work relies heavily on the scientific method. As a result, we obtain data that are fairly objective, reliable, valid, and impartial. We also collect open-ended, subjective, qualitative data. In addition, we find that organizational decision makers appreciate and understand the results of quantitative measures when it comes to demonstrating bottom-line success of a consultation. That said, every consultant needs to determine what types of evaluative methods to employ based on a careful "audience analysis" of key decision makers within the client organization.

Further, we conduct both formative and summative evaluations. *Formative evaluations* assess participant reactions to the interventions *as they are implemented*. We rely on frequent formative evaluations to revise and refine our consulting interventions as they are occurring. For instance, we ask participants to use fairly simple feedback forms with Likert-type and semantic differential scales for evaluating the content, delivery mechanism, and clarity of a particular intervention; their reactions to a trainer or facilitator; and their overall evaluation of a program. We also rely on metrics available from the organization relevant to the intervention. For example,

Waldeck examined employee attendance as one measure of the effectiveness of an initiative designed to heighten employee engagement, identification, and loyalty.

Summative evaluations are conducted after a program has been implemented. Typically more formal in design than formative evaluations, summative evaluations measure the outcomes of an intervention and are linked to program objectives. Consultants should investigate the availability of existing instruments that assess attainment of each objective, or create their own reliable, valid assessments. Common summative evaluation techniques include tests or demonstrations, anonymous surveys, exit interviews, and both short- and long-term outcome indicators that measure impacts, benefits, or changes brought about by the specific elements of the consultation. Clients often show interest in the long-term impacts of consulting—that is, how valuable interventions are at specified intervals after the intervention concludes. There may be a sleeper effect associated with improvements (i.e., the value of the intervention isn't measurable immediately), or clients want to know if the immediate value lasts or even grows. For example, Waldeck was involved in the development of an e-learning initiative for corporate employees that included videos of motivational keynote speeches delivered by well-known business leaders. At the conclusion of each talk, participants were asked to complete a specific goal-setting exercise based on the speaker's content and overall program objectives. Follow-up emails at 4-week, 6-month, and 1-year intervals prompted them to complete summative assessments of their progress toward established goals in areas related to the focus of the program. In other projects, our team has identified individual, team, and organizational performance metrics to examine at specific intervals over time, and created self-report instrumentation designed to evaluate the long-term impact of planned change.

Principles of Proposal Development: Summary

Taken together, these six principles of proposal development should suggest several important take-away points to readers. First, consulting requires careful, strategic planning. Effective consultants think through every possible detail of planning, facilitating, and evaluating an intervention prior to writing the proposal. Although we discuss the importance of brevity and clarity in a later section, the proposal must nonetheless be very detailed. Well-crafted proposals anticipate readers' concerns, questions, and objections. Second, high-quality proposals furnish credible, compelling evidence relevant to each recommendation. They convince the reader that the recommendation will work, and they minimize client objections or concerns about implementation by clarifying the consultant's expertise and ability to facilitate the interventions smoothly. Third, successful proposals illustrate in logical fashion a series of objectives and precisely how the consultant's recommendations will help the organization realize those objectives—and how the team will know (i.e., through what evaluation methods). Finally, the proposal must be a technically flawless document. Any errors, gaps in reasoning, editorial mistakes, or missing information necessary for the client's decision making process will result in the proposal being discarded in favor of one that has been thoughtfully prepared. One of the most important details a client will need involves the costs associated with the project.

HOW MUCH SHOULD I CHARGE? ADVICE FOR ESTIMATING COSTS AND DETERMINING YOUR WORTH

Academics who perform consulting services can be masterful at identifying issues, proposing solutions, and facilitating interventions because they are scholarly experts in process and content. They are often good writers who can produce a solid proposal that is persuasive and readable. But, many lack the skills to accurately cost out their services in a way that satisfies the client and ensures a profit. Our colleagues and students with training or consulting opportunities often ask us, "How much should I charge?"—a question for which there are no easy, straightforward answers. Plax (2008) offers consultants advice for determining what they can charge, and we summarize his recommendations here and contextualize them in terms of the task of writing the proposal.

First, we caution consultants that the most common mistake we have made and observed others making involves underestimating the time associated with a project. A careful proposal makes an accurate estimate of what is exactly required to carry out the project; but inexperienced consultants are sometimes shortsighted in thinking through all that is involved. For example, a one-day training workshop involves much more than the eight hours spent at the training site. Determining the time associated with any project becomes more difficult the larger and more complex the consultation is. For any engagement, Plax (2008) advises that consultants carefully consider:

- *Preparation time* (e.g., assessing the target audience for the interventions, formally meeting with the client, conducting a formal needs analysis, identifying project objectives, research, designing messages, preparing and editing materials, generating evaluation measures).
- *Delivery time* (e.g., the actual intervention delivery, such as delivering the workshop, conducting the focus group, facilitating the strategic planning; setting up the physical environment for the intervention; arranging for participant comforts such as food and beverages; parking and commuting expenses).
- *Debriefing time* (e.g., analyzing evaluation data, writing a report, briefing the client).

The consultant should also consider that costing out time for a proposal does not include the time spent finding the work, writing the proposal, talking informally with the client, or negotiating the terms. To some extent, as we mentioned earlier, consultants incur some indirect costs in proposing and acquiring work—but this series of background tasks we complete can be factored in to the rate we charge for the project. Estimating our time according to the three activities of preparation, delivering, and debriefing can help us be accurate in computing how many hours we will spend on a particular project. As a general rule, you should overestimate your time; in our experience, everything takes longer than we anticipated and projects often grow in unexpected ways as clients ask for more and as contingencies arise. The question then becomes what dollar amount to affix to the time associated with a consultation.

Plax recommends that consultants just starting out calculate an hourly rate based on their salary as a college professor. More experienced consultants will likely charge a great deal more. But, before using that hourly fee to multiply by time spent to calculate a total project cost, the consultant must also consider that:

- Consulting work is contract work, which does not include benefits normally associated with permanent employment. If the consultant does not have health insurance or a retirement benefit from another employer, he or she will need to fund them from consulting fees.
- Consulting fees are taxable, yet the payment a client makes is pre-tax money; the consultant will need to set aside a portion of what is earned to pay taxes owed.
- The consultant's fee must cover any expenses not specified elsewhere in the contract.
- The fee is a one-time payment for services rendered, and because there is no guarantee of future work with this client, the consultant will spend more time and money to generate additional work at the conclusion of the project or the next time a consulting opportunity arises.

All of these considerations suggest that consultants must be careful to account for the costs associated with their work in order to generate a profit. So, using Plax's formula, for example: If your base salary at your academic institution is $70,000, that works out to $1,458.33 per week and $36.46 per hour based on a 40-hour work week. But when you take into account the issues we've just discussed and subtract these projected expenses from $36.46, you are left with a very small number.

Thus, Plax recommends adding additional time into your initial estimate; for instance, although each day of training typically requires 40 hours of total (i.e., preparation, delivery, and debriefing) time, he advises adding another 20 hours (which brings the hourly rate in the above example to about $125.00) to calculate an overall cost of the project that will cover expenses and yield a profit for the consultant. (If you are not a full-time faculty member at a college or university, you can use the average gross annual salary figure for that position for your geographic

region and your discipline; or, you can calculate a similar hourly figure by researching what consultants in your area of expertise are paid by consulting firms).

Realize, too, that our sample calculation was the cost of *one consultant* and
would need to be multiplied by the number of people working on the project. The
fees paid to some contractors, such as graduate students hired to code or enter data
or graphic designers who produce materials for the project, will be different than
what the consultant charges for his or her services, but the costs of their services
need to be considered in the budget. We are not suggesting that you provide clients with a projected hourly accounting of your project (unless one is requested);
but we are offering a formula for thinking about how to determine the *categories* of
expense for which you will need to charge clients, *time spent* on these activities, as
well as how to calculate a *total cost* for your services.

Costing out the budget for a consulting project is not a pure science. Many
factors influence what consultants can charge, including:

- *Their history with the client*: Consultants who have established relationships
  with clients characterized by a track record of trust, reliability, and liking
  can charge more than consultants with a less solid history with any particular client. We have performed *pro bono* work and helped many clients with
  small, low-profit jobs in order to establish our value. Over time, the client
  learns what we can do and how well, and offers us the opportunity to propose bigger projects with more interesting implications and greater profit.
  For example, Waldeck conducted a program evaluation for a state agency
  interested in health literacy among minority youth. The agency had a very
  small budget for the initiative of interest, so she did not charge for this
  service (which also provided a community partnership experience for a class
  that she was teaching). Later, when the agency was awarded a grant (based,
  in part, on results of the evaluation), they came back to her for additional
  work, for which she was compensated.
- *The client's perception of the value inherent in the consulting team's skills*: When
  a client really *needs* what the consultant has to offer, they will pay more than
  situations in which the consultant's recommendations are targeted at low
  organizational priorities. Here, the consultant can build his or her client's
  perceptions of value by building a compelling sense of need, and communicating it persuasively and strategically. When the proposal is crafted in
  such a way that client needs are well-documented and supported with data,
  and recommendations are clearly tied to those needs, the consultant will
  heighten the client's perceptions of his or her value.
- *The consultant's credentials and experience*: Consultants must be able to
  illustrate their expertise. Those with terminal degrees, such as a Ph.D. or
  M.F.A., can typically charge more than those without them. Clients are

typically impressed by other metrics of a consultant's expertise, such as research publications and books, an affiliation with a prestigious university or firm, and prior consulting experience. These all go a long way toward establishing what the client will be willing to pay.

Finally, Plax defines the ability to *communicate a sense of self-confidence, worth, and credibility* as a critical characteristic that distinguishes seasoned and highly paid consultants from those who cannot charge as much. "Projected self-confidence is worth money. Individuals who come across as experts, confident in what they know and what they can do, are also those the client is likely to hire and be willing to pay the most" (2008, p. 246). Effective consultants write proposals that communicate their expertise and self-confidence in terms that the client will understand and appreciate. In this way, the proposal will maximize client confidence that not only is the proposal a good one, but that the consulting team is the right one for implementing the recommended changes.

STYLISTIC ADVICE FOR CREATING A WINNING PROPOSAL

As this chapter has established, effective proposal writing affords the consultant the opportunity to do many things: establish credibility, define needs and problems, propose solutions, persuade prospective clients to accept recommendations, and more. Effective proposals enable us to present ourselves well, as a valuable asset to the client who recognizes the organization's needs and is able to make sensitive recommendations for addressing them. They are also written in a style that appeals to their audience—organizational decision makers who may not fully understand the research-based and theoretical approaches we take to our work, but are concerned with improvements and outcomes. Over time, we have established some stylistic guidelines that we have found to be effective in writing proposals for clients in a wide variety of industries and settings.

- *Follow the instructions in the RFP if you are working from one.* If the RFP suggests or requires a structure, use it. If you deviate from the prospective client's requirements at this stage in your relationship, you are demonstrating that you may not listen later. To establish credibility, provide what information the RFP requests in the required format.
- *Be very clear in addressing the client's needs.* Driving the proposal should be an articulate expression of exactly how the recommendations will solve problems and meet client needs.
- *Customize the proposal to the client.* Avoid boilerplate language (standardized business text that can be recycled for different purposes without

being changed much). The only acceptable boilerplates are standard contract language, rate sheets, and proprietary and nondisclosure statements (Wreden, 2006).

- *Consider your specific readers.* Most high-level decision makers in organizations value brevity and conciseness. This is certainly true, for example, with people who review government contract bids. However, through interactions with the client, effective consultants learn something about how the client makes decisions and will know what level of detail and description is required. The consultant's goals should be to (a) provide a proposal that the client will read with enthusiasm, not annoyance because it is too long or filled with too many details; and (b) provide enough detail that will allow the client to make an informed decision or ask good questions and keep the relationship moving forward.
- *Write objectively, accurately, and concretely.* Be thorough and exact in presenting facts, and support claims and recommendations with evidence.
- Use influence and argumentation skills to build a persuasive case.
- *Use a consistent scheme of lists and italicized, boldfaced, and underlined text to emphasize important information.* Adopt a style guide to guide the format of proposals.
- *Use logical paragraphs and headings to keep the proposal organized.* We find that deductively structured paragraphs are most effective. Be sure that paragraphs are coherent and flow with one another smoothly.
- *Use internal previews, summaries, and signposts to keep the reader oriented.*
- Provide visuals and graphic illustrations such as tables, figures, graphs, and other images where appropriate to enhance the visual appeal and readability of the proposal.
- *Follow the principle of "chunking."* Present ideas in small, digestible units that will be easy for readers to comprehend and remember. Miller (1956) found that readers may be able to cognitively process between just five and nine units of information at a time. Thus, structure proposals with this in mind.
- Revise the proposal until it is clear and concise; features the correct tone for the audience and purpose; is accurate and readable; contains proper attributions for all external sources; is free of passive voice, spelling, punctuation, and grammatical errors; and relies on language and concepts the client will understand.
- "Translate" areas of your own expertise that might be unfamiliar to the client. Effective consultants are able to write proposals that make their recommendations, often framed by esoteric theory and/or research, relevant and consumable to diverse readers in applied settings.

CONCLUSION

The ability to write a clear, persuasive, thorough, and marketable proposal constitutes the foundation for effective consulting work. Successful consultants are able to create proposals that demonstrate compelling, substantiated needs within the client organization; advance appropriate objectives; and make relevant and realistic recommendations. Additionally, a good proposal gives the client confidence in both the consultant and his or her recommendations by demonstrating credibility and an evaluation method. Finally, consultants must master both the science and the art of proposal development. The science involves sound business writing skills and logical formatting. The art involves understanding one's work and one's client in a meaningful way. This understanding allows us to create a document that truly speaks to its reader and will favorably influence the decision making process.

REFERENCES

Beebe, S. A., Mottet, T. P., & Roach, K. D. (2013). *Training and development: Communicating for success* (2nd ed.). Boston: Pearson.

Meyer, G., Roberto, A. J., Boster, F. J., & Roberto, H. L. (2004). Assessing *Get Real About Violence®* curriculum: Process and outcome evaluation results and implications. *Health Communication, 16*, 451–474.

Miller, G. A. (1956). The magical number seven, plus or minus two: Some limits on our capacity for processing information. *Psychological Review, 64*, 81–97.

Plax, T. G. (2008). Raising the question #2: How much are we worth? Estimating fees for services. *Communication Education, 55*, 242–246.

Waldeck, J. H. (2008). The development of an industry-specific online learning center: Consulting lessons learned. *Communication Education, 57*, 452–463.

Wreden, N. (2006). Making your proposal come out on top. *Written communications that inform and influence* (pp. 29–38). Boston, MA: Harvard Business School Press.

CHAPTER EIGHT

Communication Skills for Consulting Excellence

STEVEN A. BEEBE

Texas State University

Warren Buffet, one of the richest persons on earth, once announced to MBA students at his alma mater, Columbia University, that he would offer $100,000 to any student in return for 10 percent of their future earnings. He then announced that if the student would take a communication class, he would increase his offer to $150,000. According to Buffet, taking a communication course was one of the best investments he had ever made (Toogood, 2010). Buffet's advice is just as relevant to consultants as it is to MBA students; communication skills are highly valuable assets in the consultant's tool kit. All consultants, regardless of their subject matter expertise, need a set of core communication competencies that will enhance all they do—from needs assessment to proposing the consulting project, to executing and evaluating it. This chapter presents several communication skills that a professional consultant should master and use frequently.

Although being a skilled communicator and consultant involves the performance of specific behaviors, communication effectiveness involves more than mere technique. Effective communication is anchored in theoretical assumptions about competent communication (Morreale, 2009; Spitzberg, 1983, 2000, 2006), as well as decades of communication research and communication theory (Littlejohn & Foss, 2008; Salem, 2012). From a theoretical perspective, competent communication is based on a learner possessing three things: knowledge, motivation, and skill (Morreale, 2009; Spitzberg, 1983, 2000, 2006).

In addition to mastering knowledge (cognitive domain), motivation (affective domain) and skill (behavioral domain), a competent communicator achieves two additional criteria: Effectiveness and appropriateness (Spitzberg, 1983, 2000, 2006). *Effectiveness* is the degree to which a message is understood (the degree to which a message expressed is the message interpreted) and the communicator achieves his/her intended communication goal (e.g., to inform or persuade). *Appropriateness* refers to whether the message is adapted to the situation, context, culture, expectations, and needs of the individuals involved in the communication. Embedded within being appropriate is the concept of being an ethical communicator, critical to the consulting endeavor (see Keyton, Chapter 3). According to the National Communication Association's Ethical Credo, "Ethical communication enhances human worth and dignity by fostering truthfulness, fairness, responsibility, personal integrity and respect for self and others" (2014). Thus, to be a skilled communicator is be both *effective* and *appropriate,* guided by a clear ethical framework. This chapter focuses on three communication contexts important for consulting and where competence defines the consultant's ability to be effective: interpersonal, group, and presentational communication.

INTERPERSONAL COMMUNICATION SKILLS

Interpersonal communication is a distinctive, transactional form of human communication involving mutual influence, usually for the purpose of managing relationships (Beebe, Beebe & Redmond, 2014). Being able to effectively relate to clients is vital for professional longevity as a consultant. I obtained a major consulting contract with a Fortune 500 company in part because I listened to precisely what the client wanted, paraphrased the desired deliverables, and then wrote a proposal that included exactly what the client wanted. Yet one of my most challenging consulting experiences occurred when I was facilitating a focus group of angry employees who were having their benefits reduced. I engaged in careful listening as a route to an authentic relationship with group members, and my listening skills were vital in helping to diffuse a tense situation. Three essential interpersonal skills presented here include listening, establishing rapport, and coaching.

Listening Skills

Listening is the complex process of selecting, attending to, creating meaning from, remembering and responding to verbal and nonverbal messages (Beebe et al., 2014; International Listening Association, 2014). Listening typically tops the list as among the most valued communication skills in business contexts. Hawkins and Fillion (1999) found that listening skills were the single most valued skill needed by those who work in groups and teams. Surveys of personnel directors find that communication skills in general, and listening skills in particular, are among the most coveted communication competencies (Windsor, Curtis, & Stephens, 1997). Listening skills, then, are requisite for consultants charged with facilitating improvement and development among individuals and teams. They are especially important when assessing a client's needs, during facilitation and focus group sessions, and when managing conflict and easing relational tensions.

The communication literature on enacted support, or what is said and done in the course of talking with a person experiencing trouble (Goldsmith, 2004), sheds light on what a consultant can do in listening to clients to fulfill the role of helping professional (DeWine, 2001). For example, although active listening comprises both verbal and nonverbal behaviors, Bodie, Vickery, Cannava, & Jones (2015) suggest that consultants may be well served to emphasize their *verbal* listening behaviors with clients. Specifically, Bodie et al. found that listeners' verbal behaviors (e.g., paraphrasing and asking open questions) signal greater awareness and may promote improved outcomes among people disclosing challenges than listeners' nonverbal behaviors (e.g., immediacy, vocal pleasantness, and animation). With the importance of listening and verbal listening behaviors established, what follows is a summary of listening-related skills critical to competent consulting.

Adapting to others' listening styles. Listening researchers have identified styles or ways we consistently process the information we hear (Bodie & Worthington, 2010; Kiewitz, Weaver, Brosius, & Weimann, 1997; Watson, Barker, & Weaver, 1995; Worthington, Bodie, & Gearhart, 2011). Knowing your listening style and being able to adapt to clients' listening styles is especially important when you have cultural, experiential, educational, or other differences that could be a hindrance to effective communication. Listening research has identified four listening styles: relational, analytical, critical and task-oriented listening (Bodie & Worthington, 2010; Worthington et al., 2011).

First, *relational listeners* prefer to focus on emotions and feelings communicated both verbally and nonverbally by others. They search for common interests (like listening to stories), and are empathic. For example, if your client indicates to you that he or she is interested in creating or maintaining a positive relationship between management and employees, the client may have characteristics of a relational listener. Adapt your own listening style to show interest in feelings, emotions and relationships when communicating with clients you have determined are relational listeners. Mirror this style in communication with your client, and be sure that your broader needs assessment activities, and eventual interventions, address this important client concern.

Next, *analytical listeners* typically withhold judgment; they listen to all sides of an issue and want to hear the facts before reaching a conclusion. They tend to listen to the entire message before determining the accuracy and reliability of what they hear. In the consulting context, analytical listening can be important when there is detailed information to understand and assess. Be attuned to the needs and preferences of analytical listeners in your design and presentation of consulting activities. They will likely expect a detailed, multi-faceted presentation of facts and an analysis of data you gather during the needs assessment or post-consulting assessment phase of a project. This type of listener will object to a one-sided message, instead preferring to hear all aspects of an issue.

Critical listeners generally prefer to listen for evidence, data and facts to support key conclusions; they look for the underlying logic of a message and are attuned to listen for discrepancies, inconsistencies and errors. They will be more inclined to rely on the evidence you offer than to want to analyze the message themselves (as analytical listeners would) in making a decision or taking action. Because critical listeners appreciate facts and data, effective consultants recognize the importance of ample details and well-documented evidence when presenting conclusions and recommendations to a client.

Finally, *task-oriented listeners* are focused on determining what action needs to be taken based on what they hear. They look at the overall structure of a message when determining what needs to be done with the information. They tend to like brief, clear, and efficient messages. A client with a task-orientation to listening will be especially interested in your recommendations. Make sure you have clear, accurate and precise verbs that describe the deliverables of your consulting conclusions. They want to know both what you will do as well as what they should do to achieve the consulting goals. Action steps and task lists are effective formats that will resonate with task-oriented clients. On the other hand, relational listeners might perceive this action-oriented approach to be too rushed and believe that it overlooks important concerns, and analytical and critical listeners will want you to back up and give more rationale and evidence for the plan.

Researchers caution that there is no single best listening style; but being able to "style flex"—adapt your listening style to different listening situations— is the ideal listening strategy. Watson et al. (1995) found that about 40% of listeners have a primary listening style. In addition, 40% of listeners typically use more than one style. About 20% of listeners do not have a single listening style preference. There is also evidence that females tend to have a preference the relational listening style (Kiewitz et al., 1997). Understanding your listening style as well as the listening style of those with whom you communicate—including your primary contact as well as all members you encounter in the client organization—is the first step toward being able to adapt your listening style to others. Achieving style flexibility will enable you to better model effective communication behaviors for clients, address specific needs, successfully acquire and maintain client relationships, and communicate in ways that build buy-in and support for your recommendations.

How to listen for accuracy. Being aware of your listening style and the style of your partner is a prelude to the skill of listening for accuracy. As noted, some listeners have a task-oriented and action approach to accomplishing a consulting goal, but *all* clients expect to be understood accurately. Research indicates that the best predictor of being perceived as an effective leader is to be perceived as an effective listener (Romig, 2001). You will have more credibility and influence as a consultant if you are perceived as an effective listener. Your clients will *expect* you to model effective listening skills when the focus of your engagement is communication! To be an accurate listener, research suggests there are several important behaviors to master. Halone and Pecchioni (2001) found that accurate listeners put aside their own thoughts; are mentally prepared to listen because they consciously focus, mindfully, effortfully concentrate; they take their time in conversation and avoid rushing the speaker, and are patient. Indeed, Ruyter and Wetzels (2000) studied professional call center employees, and found that customers preferred listeners who seemed focused and gave them their full attention. Further, researchers (Acheson, 2008; Halone & Pecchioni, 2001) found some very specific characteristics of people perceived because they others as good listeners: They avoid interrupting, contribute the conversation, provide nonverbal reinforcement such as nodding, and offer verbal indicators of listening such as saying "yes" or "I understand."

Also important to the consulting context, Bodie et al. (2015) found that active listening behaviors contribute little or nothing to a troubled person's perceptions of the listener's ability to solve problems or offer useful advice. In other words, active listening can establish positive affect between consultant and client. Further, listening well will enable you to collect information critical to your work within the organization. However, in order to maximize your effectiveness, research suggests that you cannot rely on your listening skills alone as you interact with members of the client's organization. You have to contribute ideas, demonstrate expertise, and generate an action plan that resonates with your client to make valuable contributions and facilitate improvement-oriented outcomes. Listening is a necessary, but insufficient condition for good consulting work.

In sum, the listening research has at least three implications for consultants. First, in direct face-to-face interactions with clients, such as those necessary for obtaining foundational information about the organization's status quo and the contact's perceptions of need, consultants must be prepared to respond *verbally* based on the disclosures made. Although nonverbal listening behaviors, such as natural eye contact, nodding, and an interested facial expression are useful ways to encourage ongoing dialogue, the consultant's verbal listening behaviors will improve conversational outcomes. Further, listening behaviors should mirror the concerns and style that the consultant detects from the client. These recommendations extend to the consultant's communication with other members of the organization.

The listening skills we have just reviewed remain important for consultants beyond the initial phase of determining and defining client needs as they facilitate interventions and conversations among organizational members. For instance, active, supportive listening behaviors based on the recommendations made here will enhance your ability to engage in mediation work with individuals in conflict, and successfully facilitate group interactions in engagements which involve team building or strategic planning.

Finally, a consultant's own listening skills and sensitivity to the importance of listening in organizational settings will aid him or her in training, coaching, and advising clients on how to develop and practice better listening skills themselves. For example, building your own listening skills and awareness of the listening research will assist you in coaching managers to listen more effectively when they interact with their subordinates. Consultants who are master listeners will be able to "hear" the concerns of organizational members who feel "unheard" by others and coach or train them to better analyze these individuals and their listening styles and preferences, and to subsequently design and deliver more appropriate, effective messages. When consultants are aware of the most current research on topics such as listening and use it in their conversations with clients and interventions (both through their own practices and what they teach or recommend), they enhance the substance and credibility of what they do.

Rapport-Building Skills

When you have the required technical qualifications for a consulting engagement, you will enhance your likelihood of getting and keeping the client when you also prioritize establishing *rapport*. Rapport is the ability to develop a positive relationship between two or more people that results in liking and mutual positive feelings. In our consulting roles, we need to recognize that our clients want our expertise and skills; but, additionally, they often need a confidante and colleague who listens, serves as a sounding board, and can help solve problems in an objective fashion. This kind of relationship evolves when we consciously build necessary rapport. To have rapport is to be emotionally supportive and to be verbally and nonverbally in sync with another person. There are several specific skills for establishing rapport.

How to establish rapport verbally. For several decades, researchers have studied the types of verbal messages that communicate positive support and result in mutual perceptions of rapport. At the heart of establishing rapport is unconditional acceptance of another person (Rogers, 2012). Two ways to communicate this acceptance are through the use of supportive verbal messages and affinity-seeking behaviors. A classic work on supportive messages (Gibb, 1961) offers these specific research-supported (Tandy, 1992) guidelines for engendering supportive, rather than defensive, reactions in others:

- *Describe your feelings and observations; avoid evaluating the behavior of others.* For example, try using "I" language. This technique involves using the word "I" as a prelude to describing your own feelings and thoughts about a situation or event. The more evaluative "you" language begins a sentence with an accusatory "you" such as, "You are making a lot of mistakes with this strategy." A person using "I" language would rephrase the sentence this way: "I have observed your strategy, and have some recommendations for refining it." This approach frames the conversation with your client as a collaborative, solution- and progress-oriented one, rather than as an accusatory, ego-defeating one.
- *Seek to solve problems; avoid appearing to control others.* A problem solving approach will require you to draw upon your listening skills and to listen more and talk less. As a consultant, you may think you should immediately propose a solution to assert control. Instead, think about issues that come up as problems to solve collaboratively and over time, rather than assuming you need to have immediate answers. Ask questions, seek input from multiple stakeholders, and listen carefully.
- *Appear genuine and authentic, rather than premeditatedly manipulative.* Your nonverbal messages will signal that you are interested and genuinely supportive. Nonverbal immediacy behaviors (such as eye contact, open posture, natural forward lean) are especially useful in communicating openness. Goodwill or caring is an often overlooked component of consultant credibility; you will build rapport in addition to client perceptions of your expertise when you demonstrate that you genuinely care about the organization's best interests.
- *Empathize, rather than appearing detached and aloof.* Empathy involves your ability to understand the other communicator's perspective in a situation. You are more likely to be perceived as empathic if you listen and ask follow up questions rather than interrupting or responding immediately to client questions or concerns. Empathic communication is another way to demonstrate authentic caring and, as a result, enhancing your credibility and creating rapport with members of your client organization.
- *Maintain flexibility rather making than rigid, certain pronouncements.* For example, in discussing proposed initiatives and interventions with a client, seek input rather than offering inflexible ideas that the client may perceive as unrealistic. Consider offering offer options for the client to consider when developing recommendations.

- *Present yourself as equal rather than superior.* For example, although your credibility is important, clients will become defensive if they perceive you as an expert with a superior, know-it-all attitude. Although you do need to let your client know about your credentials, when possible and appropriate, let your good work speak for you. Always seek to balance people's perceptions of your expertise with their perceptions of your trustworthiness and goodwill.

In addition to building a supportive climate, effective consultants know how to use affinity-seeking cues for creating rapport with clients and organizational members. Affinity-seeking behavior communicates a positive regard for another person. Research has identified seven specific affinity-seeking behaviors that enhance the relational climate whether in individual or group contexts (Frymier, 1994; Frymier & Thompson, 1992; McCroskey & McCroskey, 1986), and these are relevant to consulting in a number of areas (e.g., training [see Houser, Chapter 12], presenting proposals and findings, and making recommendations to clients):

- *Assume equality:* Present yourself as an equal rather than all-knowing and superior. After all, you have been hired for your unique expertise and knowledge, so this dimension of your credibility is established. As a consultant, you can accomplish a climate of equality by being a good listener, building rapport, and communicating in ways that establish closeness, rather than distance and superiority. Find ways to let people know that you want to understand them, you are listening, you care about what they are experiencing and have to say, and that you are there to help. Of course, you will want to be cautious about sacrificing or damaging your credibility in your efforts to build perceptions of equality.
- *Be perceived as comfortable:* Appear relaxed and at ease. One way to verbally this goal is through appropriate self-disclosure and small talk. Your nonverbal behavior is also helpful for establishing a comfortable climate. Smiling, a relaxed posture, touch appropriate for the context, and removing barriers between you and other communicators (such as avoiding use of a podium, or arranging the room so that you are not sitting behind an imposing desk when interacting with clients) will help. We will explore nonverbal predictors of rapport in the next section.
- *Keep conversational rules:* Don't change topics too quickly. Avoid interrupting clients in one-one-one settings or trainees in a group session.
- *Practice dynamism:* Be active and enthusiastic in your interactions with everyone you encounter in the client organization. Avoid appearing bored or tired. Members should easily detect that you enjoy working with them.
- *Invite disclosure from others:* Ask others to share appropriate information about themselves following the cultural rules of self-disclosure. To learn

more about cultural self-disclosure expectations see Beebe, Beebe & Redmond (2014) and Ting-Toomey & Chung (2012).
- *Encourage enjoyment*: Tell appropriate stories, use humor appropriately for your audience, and establish a comfortable environment. When you set the tone for a consulting engagement as one of openness, dynamism, and enjoyment through your own behaviors, those around you will be more comfortable mirroring you.

According to research conducted in instructional settings, affinity-seeking behaviors enhance the learning climate and increase motivation to learn (Frymier, 1994; Frymier & Thompson, 1992; McCroskey & McCroskey, 1986). Similarly, consultants who employ affinity-seeking behaviors will influence members of client organizations to accept their recommendations; internalize desired attitudes, beliefs, and values; and motivate them to engage in recommended behaviors.

Establishing rapport nonverbally. In addition to the verbal strategies that we have already discussed, nonverbal behavior can help consultants build rapport with members of their client organizations. To establish rapport nonverbally involves monitoring and mirroring the posture and position of others. This doesn't mean that you have to meticulously mimic everything your partner does. That would be disingenuously awkward. Yet being in nonverbal sync with someone does involve being attentive to your partner's nonverbal displays, monitoring your own posture, and displaying a general symmetry of position and movement. Establish nonverbal rapport early in a consulting-client relationship to enhance the likelihood of a positive, ongoing relationship.

Besides being nonverbally in sync with someone, Rogers (2012) suggests that client rapport is enhanced if nonverbal mismatches are avoided. To enact a mismatch is to break rapport with distracting, disconfirming, or unsynchronized messages. Mismatches include:

- *Looking at your watch or clock or fiddling with your watch*: May communicate impatience and rushing the speaker
- *Staring at the client*: A too-long stare can communicate aggression
- *Crossed arms and legs*: May communicate closed mindedness
- Leaning back when the other person is leaning forward: May communicate lack of interest
- *Turning your chair away from the speaker*: May suggest lack of interest or self-assurance
- *Fidgeting of fingers, toes or twiddling a pen or pencil*: May communicate lack of interest and disengagement
- *Touching your face or mouth while talking*: Can suggest timidity, insincerity, or untruthfulness

Although we should typically try to avoid mismatches, there may be times when you may want to change the topic or mood of the room, and punctuate what you say by deliberately mismatching (Rogers, 2012). For example, when facilitating a strategic planning session you may find that group participants will get off track, or become overly negative. Mismatching can assist the consultant in redirecting and refocusing the team's energy and attitude. For example, to bring the group back to the agenda, you might physically orient your body away from participants (a behavior we usually try to avoid) and toward a PowerPoint slide with an outline while telling the group it's time to be get back on track. Similarly, you can avoid eye contact and turn away from participants who dominate discussions, or use a deliberate stare to let participants engaged in negative side-talking that they need to "come back" to the primary discussion.

COACHING SKILLS

Building on the skills of listening and establishing rapport, coaching skills help clients identify their goals and take appropriate action to achieve their goals. Rogers (2012) defines coaching as:

> *A partnership of equals whose aim is to achieve speedy, increased and sustainable effectiveness through focused learning in every aspect of the client's life. Coaching raises self-awareness and identifies choices. Working to the client's agenda, the coach and client have the sole aim of closing the gaps between potential and performance* (p. 7).

The overriding goal of coaching is to help the client make appropriate and effective choices relative to their personal and professional goals based on increased self-awareness. Coaching skills include goal setting, listening, rapport building, problem solving, questioning, and feedback skills. Some communication consultants explicitly offer coaching as a consulting method for helping a client achieve his or her goals. But even if you don't consider yourself to be a coach or executive coach (someone who works with top leadership), you will undoubtedly find yourself working informally in this capacity. Coaching is a "managed conversation" (van Nieuwerburgh, 2014) that can help a client change, learn, or develop. Chances are, coaching will be an integral part of what you do as a communication consultant even if you do not label it as "coaching."

The GROW model of coaching, an acronym for four key coaching processes proposed by Whitmore (1992), is an often-referenced description of the coaching process that can help you frame your conversations and enact this important consulting skill:

- *Goal*: What is the desired outcome?
- *Reality*: What is the current reality in relationship to the goal?

- *Options*: What are the options you have for achieving the goal in the context of the current reality?
- *Will*: What will you do as a result of the coaching session to help you achieve the goals?

The overall purpose of a coaching session, based on the GROW model, is to increase awareness and develop a sense of personal responsibility (Whitmore, 2009) to help the client move forward to achieve the desired goal. The most effective coaches have the skill to get to the essence of the issues that a client faces. Rogers (2012) suggests the following prompts for coaching conversations:

1. *What's the issue?*
2. *What makes it an issue now?*
3. *Who owns this issue/problem?*
4. *How important is the issue on a 1–10 scale?*
5. *How much energy do you have for a solution on a 1–10 scale?*
6. *What are the implications of doing nothing?*
7. *What have you already tried?*
8. *Imagine this problem has been solved.*
9. *What is standing in the way of that ideal outcome?*
10. *What is your own responsibility for what's been happening? (pp. 84–85)*

There are no surefire or "magic" communication strategies that always achieve the desired results. The most effective coaches are those who have the sensitivity required to accurately interpret what a client is saying and feeling, as well as the skills to help the client develop insights and create options to achieve desired goals. The ten prompts listed above can help you create an effective coaching practice.

GROUP FACILITATION SKILLS

In facilitating groups and teams (see Seibold, Chapter 11), consultants should ensure that group discussion taps the wisdom of the group in an orderly way. To effectively facilitate a meeting or any other type of group interaction, the conversation needs a balance of two things: structure and interaction. Even if you are not participating in a formal meeting but rather, collaborating with two or more clients, facilitation skills are useful. Facilitation skills are beneficial whenever there are more than two people having a task-oriented conversation.

Structure consists of the agenda other techniques and procedures to help a group stay on task. A small group with the appropriate structure has a more focused discussion and avoids shifting from topic to topic. An unstructured discussion is one in which participants don't listen to one another, are thinking about their own comments rather than what the group is discussing, and there are frequent interruptions and often confusion. Effective consultants are alert to problems related to structure, and can guide participants in finding a structure that works well for their needs.

Interaction is the give-and-take conversation that occurs when people collaborate. Meetings, team sessions, and small group discussions tap the knowledge and experience of the group members. Interaction is vital for achieving group goals. A group with no interaction resembles a speech in which one person talks and the others listen. In contrast, a group with too much interaction is marked by people talking over one another, little connection among contributions, and conversation that doesn't stick to the topic at hand.

The goal when facilitating a group or team discussion is a balance of structure (focus) and interaction (talk). For example, when I was facilitating a high-level meeting of oil industry executives, the group consistently got off task to focus on issues that were not on the planned agenda. As they would wander off task, I would gently point out that they were off task (bringing their lack of structured conversation to their attention) and ask if they wanted to return to the agenda. It is acceptable if a group wants to deviate from the agenda, but they should do so mindfully. Facilitating group discussion involves raising group awareness of what it is doing at a given point in time, and helping group members make a conscious decision about what they would like to discuss.

How to Provide Structure for Group Discussion

Group communication researchers have found that groups with no planned structure or agenda have difficulty accomplishing their tasks (Kerr & Tindale, 2004). Specifically, without structure, groups will take more time to deliberate than groups with structure, prematurely focus on solutions, hop from one idea to the next, put themselves in a position to be controlled by a dominating group member, and experience heightened levels of unmanaged conflict (SunWolf & Seibold, 1999).

Importantly, research across contexts and group foci indicates that any method of structuring group discussion is better than no method at all (Beebe & Masterson, 2015; Witte, 2007). Researchers have found that groups shift topics about once a minute (Berg, 1967; Poole, 1983) unless there is structure to keep the group focused. Groups benefit from a variety of consultation methods and techniques for keeping the discussion focused on the task. The primary tool for providing group structure is an *agenda*.

Why is having an agenda so important for a communication consultant? If an organization is paying you well for your consulting services, it is to their advantage that your time with them remains on task and not follow conversational trails "into the woods." Although all meetings should have an agenda, it is especially important for communication consultants to use a meeting agenda to provide meeting focus. Having an agenda models effective meeting management principles and also increases the likelihood of goal accomplishment. Beebe and Masterson (2015) offer guidelines for creating and using agendas that I recommend to the reader of this chapter. Understanding these guidelines will help consultants effectively plan and facilitate group interactions.

How to Facilitate Group Interaction

In addition to structure, groups need a counterbalance of synergistic dialogue (Pavitt, Philipp, & Johnson, 2004). Through talk, groups accomplish tasks and desired outcomes. But the consultant must carefully manage these conversations by enacting certain roles and behaviors with the group. First, consultants should act as *gatekeepers*. A gatekeeper manages the flow of conversation by encouraging less talkative members to participate and limits lengthy contributions of group members who talk too much. The key skills of a gatekeeper are to listen, encourage those who contribute less frequently for ideas, and appropriately ask those who over-verbalize to hold their thoughts until others have spoken. During one group session that I was facilitating, there was one young man who seemed quiet and pensive. Although he appeared alert and seemed to be following the conversation, he didn't make verbal contributions. At one point when the group was generating options, I specifically asked him if he had an idea to contribute. Although he spoke with a soft, quiet voice, his idea was stellar and eventually solved the problem the group was addressing. "Opening the gate" to encourage a quite group member can yield important results. However, there have been many times when I've also had to "close the gate" to discourage "over-verbalizers" from monopolizing the conversation.

Second, consultants should *summarize frequently* and *keep the group focused on its mission*. Summarizing and focusing help remind the group where it is (and where it isn't). The most experienced, skilled facilitators orient the group toward its goal, help them adapt to what is happening in the group at any given moment, and involve the group in developing an agenda for the meeting (Ludwig & Geller, 1997). Simply reminding the group what the goal is can help them stay on task. During one meeting I facilitated, the group seemed especially prone to getting off task. When my verbal suggestions for focusing on the goal weren't successful, I walked to the whiteboard and wrote the goal on the board. I didn't chastise the group for getting off task, but merely pointed them back to their self-developed goal. The group responded well and there were fewer tangents and more on-task talk.

A third essential facilitation skill is the use of *metadiscussion*. Metadiscussion literally means discussion about discussion. One important metadiscussion activity involves establishing ground rules before a discussion. During discussion, a metadiscussional statement is one that focuses participants on the discussion *process*, rather than on the specific topic under consideration. Examples of metadiscussion include "I think we are straying from the agenda," and "I don't think we are addressing the key issues." Research supports the importance of metadiscussion; simply having someone periodically reflect on where the group is on the agenda and review what has been accomplished helps the group remain aware of the topic and issues at hand (Gouran, 1969; Kline, 1972). Metadiscussion can play an important role after meetings, as well. For example, try asking participants to informally evaluate the discussion process and reflect on how they could make changes to be optimally effective at reaching goals in future meetings.

Other suggested strategies for consultants involved in facilitating groups and teams through discussion and meetings include:

- *Display known facts for all group members to see.* When consulting, if you find that the group is struggling to reach agreement, it is especially useful to summarize data and information on a whiteboard for all to view.
- Listening for group-oriented (we, us, our) rather than self-oriented (I, me, my) pronouns to provide clues about the group's sense of cohesiveness and identity. Be sure to use "we" language in your interaction with the group to model cohesiveness.
- Seeking clarification of group member misunderstandings.
- *Emphasizing areas of agreement.* Since one of your consulting goals is to help clients reach agreement or consensus, catching clients agreeing is especially important for building a positive group climate and achieving goals.
- *Encouraging discussion and deliberation.* Great consultants understand the value of disagreements and differences of opinion, and are able to facilitate these so that they do not create dysfunction or toxicity among the group. If the group seems to agree *too* quickly, ask probing questions, play devil's advocate, or implement other strategies to keep the discussion going to be sure the group avoids dangerous groupthink.
- *Monitoring and managing time.* Think of your agenda as a map that charts the course of what you want to accomplish. Think of the clock as your gas gauge for the trip; it lets you know the amount of fuel you have to get where you need to go.
- *Structuring interaction.* One way of ensuring that all group members participate in a discussion is to structure the conversation by having members provide written responses before they provide oral responses. For example, rather than using traditional brainstorming where members verbally share ideas, have members first write their responses. This increases participation in a group to 100 percent and gives members who may be apprehensive or generally quiet a way to contribute.

PRESENTATION AND INSTRUCTIONAL SKILLS

Consultants and trainers need to be able to connect to listeners not only in interpersonal and small group settings, but also when presenting material to an audience. Although e-training and distance learning continue to grow in popularity because of their efficiency, the ability to present training or other formal messages in person is an essential consultant communication skill. Effective communicators focus on the needs and interests of their audience; they adapt their content and delivery to meet the needs and expectations of their listeners. (Waldeck, Kearney, and Plax [2013] discuss the delivery of briefings and other formal presentations in the business context, as well as training, as important presentational activities of consultants).

One of the most important things to remember is that presentations should be interactive to the greatest extent possible, given your time limitations. Interactivity is especially important for training engagements, where active engagement (versus passive listening) are important for learning and skill acquisition. Overall, a consultant's presentations should be more like jazz than classical music, in that the consultant should respond to the clients/trainees, and customize the message to those listeners—even making adaptations during the presentation.

The purpose of this chapter is not to give you a comprehensive education in public speaking skills. Rather, I direct you to the vast array resources available within the communication discipline for building your presentation skills and becoming a master speaker and trainer who encourages interactivity, critical thinking, and action. Houser (Chapter 12) discusses important skills for consultants working in the training context. One area, however, is of particular importance, and deserves special understanding by consultants working as trainers, speakers, and educators, and thus, attention in this chapter. Specifically, considerable research suggests that the ability to communicate in *influential* ways in educational and training settings is critical to learning outcomes and the success of consulting interventions.

How to Use Instructional Power and Influence Skills

Power is the ability to influence the behavior of others (Franz, 1998; French & Raven, 1968). In a consulting context, for example, a trainer may ask trainees to participate in activities, read material, and invite them to participate in a variety of learning activities. Additionally, a consultant may need to influence negatively biased or jaded organizational members to view change more positively, or to participate in strategic planning discussions with open minds. A line of research suggested how instructors use power cues to influence learners in the classroom (Plax, Kearney, McCroskey, and Richmond, 1986). These same behaviors, called behavior alteration techniques (BATS), are useful to consultants and trainers. When used appropriately, BATs create a prosocial climate and motivate communicators within that climate to engage in recommended behaviors and to adopt particular attitudes. The most effective behavior alteration techniques consultants can employ during group facilitation sessions, focus group meetings, presentations, and other consulting situations in which cooperation and compliance are important include:

- *Offering both immediate and deferred rewards.* For example, you might suggest how implementing a specific recommendation will result in benefits to the organization and/or a specific team or individual.
- *Making positive comments about an employee's self-esteem as appropriate.* For instance, during an individual coaching session, you might commend an executive for implementing a specific personal growth plan.
- *Making positive comments about the relationship between the consultant and client.* In general, you can accomplish this by expressing your positive regard for the client and that you are enjoying the engagement. Even more specifically, you might try verbally reinforcing a client for following your advice and achieving a positive result: "Thanks for giving that a try. I see that strategy really worked for you."
- *Appealing to a sense of responsibility on the part of the client organization's leadership and membership.* For example, you may induce cooperation when you suggest that training participants have a *responsibility* for participating in training and applying skills learned to their everyday work. This technique is most useful when you know your audience has a high degree of loyalty and commitment to the organization.
- *Using trainee and trainer modeling.* You can be influential in eliciting cooperation through your own actions and by noting others' actions that are consistent with your recommendations. For example, in a public speaking skills training engagement, be specific in pointing out what trainees are doing well in their delivery of presentations, and which of their actions represent desired skills and behaviors. And, of course, practice excellent presentation skills yourself.
- *Drawing on consultant expertise.* This is an easy strategy for most consultants. Much of what we do and say is based on our prior credible experience. When you can illustrate that those prior instances are relevant to your client, you will achieve influence. So, wherever possible, let your audience know that what you are recommending has worked well for people or organizations similar to the client. And be sure to point out those similarities.
- *Being responsive.* Responsiveness involves many of the interpersonal communication skills we discussed earlier in this chapter, including rapport-building, affinity-seeking, and effective listening. During a facilitation session, be mindful of responding to participant input in positive, confirming ways. Empirical

evidence suggests that when you are responsive to those around you during a consultation and during training, you will elicit positive attitudes toward your material and heightened motivation and cooperation among participants.

Research in instructional contexts also reveals a number of antisocial power behaviors which tend to reduce learning effectiveness, perceptions of instructor immediacy, and related learning motivation. We might expect these behaviors to work against consultants' efforts to influence clients, as well. Some antisocial BATs and relevant examples include:

- *Punishment or retribution.* For example, I once heard about a trainer who dismissed a participant from the training room and refused to allow him to continue the workshop because he displayed a negative attitude. This approach is counterproductive to consulting and training goals and may have a negative impact on those who remain. Other related behaviors to avoid include demeaning participants in any way, purposefully embarrassing or humiliating them, and unfairly and/or consistently criticizing trainees.
- *Expressing dislike for the client organization or any of its members.* There will always be difficult participants in the consulting process, but the effective consultant avoids making statements or using nonverbal behaviors that overtly communicate dislike. (See DeWine, 2001 for additional strategies and resources for dealing with difficult clients).
- *Appealing to higher authority or the consultant's authority.* Avoid variants on the statements "Do this because I'm the consultant and I say so," or "Management is requiring this; I can't make any changes."
- Appealing to some sense of debt on the part of the client or employees of the organization by saying (implicitly or explicitly) "You owe me" or "You promised to do this." It should be evident that as a consultant, you are owed cooperation, respect, and the agreed-upon fee. Avoid references to these commitments in your routine interactions with clients. If the consulting relationship breaks down to the point that these basic commitments aren't being honored, you will need to have a sensitive discussion with the client about your contract. You will also need to make some difficult decisions about whether to continue the engagement. Several chapters in this book mention consulting experiences that ended because the consultant felt ethically compromised or because the professional relationship was irreversibly damaged. These things can and do happen.

In thinking through the substantial amount of research on communication and influence, we can conclude that consultants need a wide range of communication skills to elicit client cooperation, but should emphasize productive, supportive, prosocial tactics. In one compelling research study that supports my assertion, Teven concluded that "prosocial power use and nonverbal immediacy were positively and significantly related to subordinates' self-reported satisfaction, liking for the supervisor, and work enjoyment" (2007, p. 170). The bottom line: Use more prosocial communication behaviors and fewer antisocial behavior alteration techniques to maximize your influence.

CONCLUSION

The majority of problems that a communication consultant addresses, whether related to relationships, structures, or processes, are "people problems." Workplace problems often involve communication solutions. Skilled consultants need to master skills to facilitate effective interventions in a variety of consulting situations. This chapter described selected skills sets in three communication contexts—interpersonal, group, and presentational communication—that consultants use when engaging with clients.

Interpersonal skills include listening, establishing rapport and coaching individuals to achieve their potential. Group facilitation skills include how to provide group structure through an agenda and manage interaction through such skills as gatekeeping, focusing on the goal, and metadiscussion. Finally, the chapter offered several strategies for delivering presentations including instructional communication skills such as verbal and nonverbal immediacy, affinity-seeking communication and prosocial influence messages to maximize the learning climate.

As you develop your consulting practice, mastering these key skills will enhance your repertoire of services and make you more effective in all of your engagements.

REFERENCES

Acheson, K. (2008). Silence as gesture: Rethinking the nature of communicative silence. *Communication Theory, 18, 335–355.*

Beebe, S. A., Beebe, S. J., & Redmond, M. V. (2014). *Interpersonal communication: Relating to others.* Boston: Pearson.

Beebe, S. A., & Masterson, J. T. (2015). *Communicating in small groups: Principles and practices.* Boston: Pearson

Beebe, S. A. Mottet, T. P., & Roach, K. D. (2013). *Training and development: Communicating for success.* Boston: Pearson.

Berg, D. M. (1967). A descriptive analysis of the distribution and duration of themes discussed by task-oriented small groups, *Speech Monographs, 34,* 172–175.

Bodie, G. D., Vickery, A. J., Cannava, K., & Jones, S. M. (2015). The role of "active listening" in informal helping conversations: Impact on perceptions of listener helpfulness, sensitivity, supportiveness, and discloser emotional improvement. *Western Journal of Communication, 79,* 151–173.

Bodie, G. D., & Worthington, D. L. (2010). Revisiting the listening styles profile (LSR-16): A confirmatory factor analytic approach to scale validation and reliability estimation. *International Journal of Listening, 24,* 69–88.

DeWine, S. (2001). *The consultant's craft: Improving organizational communication.* New York: Bedford/ St. Martins.

Franz, R. S. (1998). Task interdependence and personal power in teams, *Small Group Research, 28,* 85–93.

French, B. H., & Raven J. R. P. (1968). The bases of social power. In Cartwright, D. and Zander, A. (Eds.) *Group dynamics: Research and theory* (3rd ed.) (pp. 259–269). New York: Harper & Row.

Frymier, A. B. (1994). The use of affinity-seeking in producing liking and learning in the classroom. *Journal of Applied Communication Research, 22,* 87–105.

Frymier, A. B., & Thompson, C. A. (1992). Perceived teacher affinity-seeking in relation to perceived teacher credibility. *Communication Education, 41,* 388–399.

Gibb, J. R. (1961). Defensive communication. *Journal of Communication, 11,* 141–148.

Goldsmith, D. J. (2004). *Communicating social support.* New York: Cambridge University Press.

Gouran, D. S. (1969). Variables related to consensus in group discussions of questions of policy. *Speech Monographs, 36,* 385–391.

Halone, K. K., & Pecchioni, L. L. (2001). Relational listening: A grounded theoretical model. *Communication Reports, 14,* 59–71.

Hawkins, K. W., & Fillion, B. P. (1999). Perceived communication skill needs for work groups, *Communication Research Reports, 16, 167–74.*

International Listening Association (2014). *ILA home page.* http://www.listen.org.

Kerr, N. L., & Tindale, R. S. (2004). Group performance and decision making, *Annual Review of Psychology, 55,* 623–655.

Kiewitz, C., Weaver, J. B., Brosius, B., & Weimann, G. (1997). Cultural differences in listening style preferences: A comparison of young adults in Germany, Israel, and the United states. *International Journal of Public Opinion Research, 9,* 233–248.

Kline, J. A. (1972). Orientation and group consensus. *Central States Speech Journal, 23,* 44–47.

Littlejohn, S. W., & Foss, K. A. (2008). *Theories of human communication.* Belmont, CA: Thompson Wadsworth.

Ludwig, T., & Geller, E. S. (1997). Assigned versus participatory goals setting and response generalization: Managing injury control among professional pizza deliveries. *Journal of Applied Psychology, 82,* 253–261.

McCroskey, J. C., & McCroskey, L. L. (1986). The affinity-seeking of classroom teachers. *Communication Research Reports, 3,* 158–167.

Morreale, S. P. (2009). Competent and incompetent communication. *21st century communication: A reference handbook* (pp. 444–453). Los Angeles: Sage.

National Communication Association. (2014). NCA credo for ethical communication. Retrieved from https://www.natcom.org/uploadedFiles/About_NCA/Leadership_and_Governance/Public_ Policy_Platform/PDF-PolicyPlatform-NCA_Credo_for_Ethical_Communication.pdf

Pavitt, C., Philipp, M., & Johnson, K. K. (2004). Who owns a group's proposals: The initiator or the group as a whole? *Communication Research Reports, 21,* 221–230.

Plax, T. G., Kearney, P., McCroskey, J. C., & Richmond, V. P. (1986). Power in the classroom VI: Verbal control strategies, nonverbal immediacy, and affective learning. *Communication Education, 35*, 43-55.

Poole, M. A. (1983). Decision development in small groups III: A multiple-sequence model of group decision development. *Communication Monographs, 50*, 321–241.

Rogers, J. (2012). *Coaching skills: A handbook* (3rd ed.). New York: McGraw Hill Open University Press.

Romig, D. (2001). *Side by side leadership: Achieving outstanding results together.* Austin: Bard.

Ruyter, K. & Wetzels, M. G. (2000). The impact of perceived listening behavior in voice-to-voice service encounters. *Journal of Service Research, 2*, 276–284.

Salem, P. J. (2012). *The complexity of human communication.* (2nd ed.). New York: Hampton Press.

Spitzberg, B. H. (1983). Communication competence as knowledge, skills, and impression. *Communication Monographs, 32*, 323–329.

Spitzberg, B. H. (2000). What is good communication? *Journal of the Association for Communication Administration, 29*(1), 103–119.

Spitzberg, B. H. (2006). Preliminary development of a model and measure of computer-mediated communication (CMC) competence. *Journal of Computer-Mediated Education, 11*, 629–666.

SunWolf & Seibold, D. R. (1999). The impact of formal procedures on group processes, members, and task outcomes, in Frey, L. (Ed.). *The handbook of group communication theory and research* (pp. 395–431). Thousand Oaks, CA: Sage.

Tandy, C. H. (1992). Assessing the functions of supportive message. *Communication Research, 19*, 175–192.

Teven, J. J. (2007). Effects of supervisor social influence, nonverbal immediacy, and biological sex on subordinates' perceptions of job satisfaction, liking and supervisor credibility. *Communication Quarterly, 55*, 155–177.

Ting-Toomey, S. & Chung, L. C. (2012). Understanding intercultural communication. New York: Oxford University Press.

Toogood, G. N. (2010). The new articulate executive: Look, act, and sound like a leader. New York: McGraw-Hill.

van Nieuwerburgh, C. (2014). *An introduction to coaching skills: A practical guide.* Los Angeles: Sage.

Waldeck, J. H., Kearney, P., & Plax, T. G. (2013). *Business and professional communication in a digital age.* Boston: Cengage.

Watson, K. W., Barker, L. L. & Weaver, J. B. (1995). *The listener style inventory.* New Orleans, LA: Spectra.

Witte, E. H. (2007). Toward a group facilitation technique for project teams. *Group Processes and Intergroup Relations, 10*, 299–309.

Worthington, D., Bodie, G. D., & Gearhart, C. (2011, April). *The listening styles profilerevised (LSP-R): A scale revision and validation.* Paper presented at the Eastern Communication Association, Arlington, VA.

Whitmore, J. (2009). *Coaching for performance: GROWing human potential and purpose: The principles and practice of coaching and leadership* (4th ed.). London: Nicholas Brealey.

Whitmore, J. (1992). *Coaching for performance: A practical guide to growing your own skills.* London: Nicholas Brealey.

Windsor, J. L., Curtis, D. B., & Stephens, R. D. (1997). National preferences in business and communication education: A survey update, *Journal of the Association for Communication Administration, 3*, 174.

PART THREE

Facilitating a Consulting Experience That Matters

CHAPTER NINE

A Collaborative Approach to Examining and Addressing Organizational Challenges

The Coordinated Management of Meaning as Practice

JESSE SOSTRIN

California Polytechnic University

Successful consultants solve problems, but problems are like holes in the ground. Our solutions fill them with dirt, but that only gets us back to level ground. As more show up, we repeat the cycle. If it continues then two inevitabilities emerge: Our inability to resolve the underlying issue slowly erodes our credibility; and the client eventually loses faith in our process and effectiveness. If you want to do more than exchange recurring problems for temporary solutions, then you need a collaborative approach that offers more than just shovels and dirt.

Regardless of the type of consulting and the context in which it is delivered, the fundamental pursuit is a *solution that addresses the core issue and provides lasting, substantive value.* Unfortunately, whether the goal is a new leadership behavior, a sweeping culture change, or a straightforward process improvement, a top cause of failure in management and organization development consulting engagements is the inability to change the system that keeps old, unwanted circumstances and behaviors in place (McLean, 2006). When this kind of *tampering* occurs, new behaviors quickly revert to old patterns and the initial gains from the consultation are easily lost (O'Connor & McDermott, 1997). To counter this tendency, a more dynamic and collaborative approach to consulting is required—one that simultaneously leverages meaningful participation from the stakeholders affected by the issue and harnesses a potent force embedded within every consultative scenario—*patterns of communication and interaction.*

Communication is an intrinsic aspect of organizational life, and there is not a single collaborative initiative one could pursue that does not require some form of communication with others. In a rapidly changing business environment that is more undefined, virtual, and hypercompetitive than ever, getting communication right is increasingly important as a competitive advantage (Sostrin, 2013). Yet despite the significance of communication, it is often treated like an afterthought—little more than an ancillary issue to address once the primary consulting work is finished. This is because communication itself is habitually overly simplified and taken for granted. While general themes regarding communication are not unfamiliar to experienced consultants, the understanding of communication's profound impact on organizational life in general and consulting outcomes specifically remains under-unexplored (Pearce, Sostrin, & Pearce, 2011).

The goal of this chapter is to offer consultants a set of tools to identify and integrate hidden communication dynamics into their practice. It introduces a consultative framework that can be used to transform unwanted patterns of communication and interaction into more preferred patterns that simultaneously resolve organizational issues and enable consulting solutions to stick. Drawn from innovative communication theory, research, and practice, the framework can be deployed by both internal change agents and external consultants across a variety of disciplines. The chapter begins with an overview of the theoretical underpinnings of the framework, including how it contrasts with conventional approaches to understanding communication in the world of work. It then provides a breakdown of the methodology and a brief case example that demonstrate its application.

CMM: A DEEPER PERSPECTIVE ON COMMUNICATION

My consulting approach is based on a variety of methodologies, but one of the most influential traditions of theory and practice is The Coordinated Management of Meaning, or CMM. Originally introduced in 1976, CMM is a system of ideas used as an interpretive heuristic in interpersonal communication contexts to understand the complexities of socially constructed relationships (Pearce & Cronen, 1980). Over time, this unique vein of communication theory became known as much for its practical application as it is for its vanguard role offering a macro theory of face-to-face communication (Griffin, 2009).

The core contribution of CMM, and perhaps the appeal it holds for consultants, comes from its distinctive way of seeing communication, namely: The patterns of communication in which we participate are not simply neutral instruments by which we exchange information, accomplish tasks, and influence other people (Pearce, 1994). Rather, the patterns themselves are the forces that shape our identities and relationships with other people and literally construct organizations and our experiences within them (Sostrin, 2013).

To illustrate this, imagine a scenario in which two colleagues stop in the hallway to engage in an impromptu conversation about their project. Each one has updates to offer, and they both would like to figure out the next steps they should take. On the surface, the interaction seems simple enough as they each talk and listen to the other and compare notes about the status of the project and the remaining tasks that must be completed. However, at a deeper level the communication process itself also makes something. Further, the precise character of this pattern of interaction also creates a condition in which certain experiences and outcomes are either more or less likely to occur.

To visualize this, imagine that our two colleagues in the hallway conversation have worked together long enough to establish a few habits in their interactions. For example, if they enjoy a sense of positive regard toward one another, if they believe the other is sincere, and if they habitually offer their candid opinions and insights to each other in a free-flowing manner, then you might say they have a condition of *trust*, which is conducive to effective teamwork and collaboration. Hypothetically, if you were hired as a consultant to assist these two individuals with the process of implementing new procedures required by an operational change, you could easily imagine how this preexisting condition of trust would serve as an enabler to successfully make other required changes.

Alternatively, if the two colleagues do not hold each other in high esteem, if they do not believe the other is credible or sincere, and if they do not regularly communicate in transparent ways, then you can anticipate the kind of challenges you will face in your consulting role as you attempt to facilitate the required changes amidst this underlying *condition of distrust*. Rather than the preferred pattern of trust that promotes collaboration and change, this pattern and its related conditions naturally limit the potential for effective teamwork and collaboration. The critical insight here is that patterns never rest on a plateau; they unfold continuously in a process of being built up or eroded one interaction at a time. As anyone in a trustworthy working relationship knows, one breach of that trust can undo years of positive, respectful experience. And likewise, one trustworthy episode in an otherwise distrustful relationship can set a new course for something better.

When applied to organizational life, CMM provides a meaningful way to look at individual relationships, team dynamics, and organizational cultures with a focus on these generative dynamics of communication. Within this view, hallway conversations are not just hallway conversations. As people talk, individuals simultaneously make their own meaning and take coordinated action based on those interpretations. The perceptive filters organizational communicators use to interpret their experience provide the parameters for their conclusions, and the inherent framework of rules they use to make sense of the situation, give structure to the actions that they ultimately take. Two such rules that people apply in the communicative situation include: (a) constitutive rules, which are used to interpret or understand an event or message; and (b) regulative rules, which determine how each person will respond or act based on their interpretation (Littlejohn, 1996). Returning to the example of our two trusting colleagues, the preexisting pattern of trust is the context they act out of so when one colleague says to the other "I'm struggling with my deliverable and I know that my delay is holding things up..." the rules used to interpret the message likely produce a positive assumption and equally collegial response "Don't worry about it, we knew it would be a challenge. How can I help you...?"

With complex dynamics like these revealed, CMM exposes the elemental nature of communication and shows how communication itself is substantial and the tangible patterns of communication we engage in represent something meaningful to look at, not just through. In CMM, these elemental concepts are often referred to as taking the *communication perspective* (Pearce, 1989). When consultants take a communication perspective and help their clients isolate and transform their unwanted patterns of communication, they transfer powerful leverage for creating lasting change in the organization.

Despite the potential within this perspective shift, the task of transferring of CMM's core concepts to consultants is challenging because of the complexity of its academic terminology and the lack of meaningful examples that could bridge the theory with the real world of work. The practitioner-centric introduction offered in this chapter is itself an effort to bridge that gap and reduce the opportunity cost of applying its insights and tools. To begin building that bridge, an efficient way to highlight the pragmatic potential CMM has for consultants is to contrast it with a prevailing communication theory.

Beyond the Transmission Model

The transmission model, or standard model of communication, was established in 1949 by Claude Shannon and Warren Weaver (1948) of Bell Laboratories. The model suggests that communication is a simple process of sending and receiving messages for transferring information from one person (sender) to another (receiver). This views communication as *information transfer* and the process of communication itself is little more than a static pipeline through which raw information transactions occur from person to person and the roles of sender and receiver are distinct as messages are encoded and decoded independently (Axley, 1984). The influential communication theorist, Robert Craig (2001), describes the transmission model in this way:

> In the simplistic transmission model that is so often taken for granted in everyday discourse, communication is conceptualized as a process in which meanings, packaged in symbolic messages like

bananas in crates, are transported from sender to receiver. Too often the bananas are bruised or spoiled in transport and so we have the ubiquitous problem of miscommunication: The message sent is not the message received; the sender's meaning does not come across. In order to improve communication, according to this model, we need better packaging and speedier transportation of messages. Good communication is basically a technical problem. (p. 125)

Because this conventional wisdom focuses primarily on what people say and how they listen to each other, it is extremely limited in its utility. For "good" communication to occur, the sender of the message must choose his/her words carefully and the receiver of the message must listen well to decode the message in order to understand what it means. If one or both people are distracted, or if there is too much going on around them, the message cannot be accurately transmitted. Additionally, any unexpected element that potentially disrupts the flow of information and the effectiveness of the transmission (e.g., information overload, distortion, and ambiguity) similarly derail the process.

Furthermore, we know now that different people can interpret the same message differently. And we know that even the same person can interpret the same message differently at different times depending on factors such as context, prior experience, and assumptions. To complicate things even more, as individuals, we hold onto our own private thoughts and feelings, at times we can confuse and mislead others, and we can be ambiguous—even deceptive—in our communication and interactions in certain circumstances (DeVito, 2001). Above all of this, we know that our life experience and the contexts in which we communicate have a significant impact on how we make meaning from our communication with others (Pearce, 2007).

Despite its limitations, the transmission model is still infused in the vast majority of professional development programs and popular business books that attempt to illuminate the challenges of workplace communication. You can see the essence of the transmission model in this conventional wisdom shared by leaders who offered their advice about how to create effective communication at work: *choose your words carefully, consider the listener as you craft the message, actively listen until the other person is done speaking, don't forget about the power of nonverbal cues, set aside your own emotions in order to hear the speaker's message when things get tense, communicate assertively by advocating for your own ideas without shutting others down, and be persuasive by mirroring other people's style of communication* (Sostrin, 2013).

These prescriptions have roots in the transmission model of communication and their prevalence creates a treadmill effect where, too often, the solution for organizational issues related to "miscommunication" simply calls for more communication. While increases in communication efforts cannot hurt in general terms, for non-routine, hard-to-define, complex problems, simply stating the need for more of the same kind of communication is the epitome of the *shovels and dirt* I referred to in the opening of this chapter. When consultants and organizational change agents adhere to this simplified picture of communication, they lose the potential to leverage the core influence of communication. To harness the potential of communication in ways that simultaneously resolve organizational issues and enable consulting solutions to stick, consult from a communication perspective.

CONSULTING FROM A COMMUNICATION PERSPECTIVE

Consulting from a communication perspective means that regardless of the presenting problems and issues the client draws your attention to, you remain focused on the underlying patterns of communication and interaction of the people who are stakeholders to those issues. You do not separate communication from the consulting agenda; you simultaneously work with a substantive issue of concern along with the embedded habits of interaction of the involved players. Again, this is the recognition that any organizational issue that your client can point to was made over time through a series of recurring interactions that created the condition for the issue to emerge.

Adopting this fluid perspective requires you to overcome the false assumption that organizational dynamics are fixed. For example, when we interact with organizations (either as members or outside stakeholders), they often appear *reified*. This means that we are unable to recognize the subtle ways they are made and changed continuously. In other words, we fall victim to the client's certitude that the consultation-worthy issue they identified exists apart from them and the people affected by it. On the contrary, consulting from a communication perspective provides an alternative, fluid way of thinking about issues and the organizations that house them: *organizations and their concerns are made through the ongoing and combined interactions of their people.* Therefore, if you want to change anything about the organization, you begin with the relevant interactions of its people.

The three key aspects of this shift include the beliefs that the: (a) clients' experience in the workplace are not predetermined or fixed, but are literally shaped by the nature of their ongoing patterns of communication and interaction; (b) stories the clients tell about the issues of concern are infused with complexity and have multiple meanings that each reveal a unique aspect of the situation; and, (c) core issue that they seek your consultation to resolve can be potentially be remade into a more rich and satisfying experience when the underlying patterns that influence them are commensurately shifted.

Creating Conditions that Support Consulting Objectives

Once this perspective shift is in motion, the consultant must leverage the generative influence of communication. The primary objective at this point is to draw the client's exclusive focus away from consulting outcomes, and invite them to give attention to the conditions required to achieve them. This is a shift from looking primarily at the endpoints that define the success of the consulting engagement to seeing a broader picture of what gives rise to the concerns which prompted the consultation in the first place.

Conditions themselves are value-neutral until we assign judgment to them. Generally speaking, we label them as "preferred" when they produce the kinds of experiences and outcomes we want, or we call them "unwanted" when they block us from accomplishing them. Unwanted conditions go by many names and descriptions. They are unhealthy, unproductive, limiting, destructive, confusing, and out of sync with priorities and goals. Likewise, preferred conditions also have many labels. They are useful, productive, healthy, energizing, and aligned. They reflect what is important to us, and although they may take time to cultivate, they are worth the effort because they allow us to both contribute and receive something valued. Conversely, unwanted conditions drain capacity. They are just plain difficult and ultimately they prevent us from both contributing and achieving the things we value.

Sometimes a condition develops quickly; other times it evolves slowly over a longer period of time. Either way, conditions are made and re-made through the ongoing patterns of interaction we engage in with others. As a consultant, it is your job to understand the client's unique situation and to determine the balanced mix of conditions that will produce an environment conducive to their objectives. There are too many combinations of factors to list all possible conditions, but here are several examples of useful conditions that simultaneously resolve common organizational challenges while also establishing the environment for the consulting solution to stick:

- *Flexibility*: The capacity to adapt to continuous change.
- *Readiness*: The preparedness to act at the right time.
- *Innovation*: The willingness to fail in pursuit of opportunities to change.
- *Development*: The commitment to continuous learning and growth.

Learning how to create the conditions you need is a powerful way to align the consulting engagement's big-picture goals with the day-to-day behaviors and interactions required to carry them out. Returning to CMM's focus on turn-by-turn communication analytics, the three sequential elements that produce a given condition are turns, episodes, and patterns (Sostrin, 2013). In the following description of these elements, notice the continuum approach I use to describe the labels we often place on them. Nothing is ever absolutely good or bad, but rather in a fluid process of moving closer to or further away from what is desired.

Turns are the step-by-step communication exchanges we have with other people. What you say or do before, during, or after an interaction, is a turn. Turns can be fragmented or aligned with our values and goals. With turns, there is typically an action … reaction pattern, so what happens in the current turn invariably influences what happens in the next (e.g., you said this, so I said that, you did this, so I did that, etc.). When you exchange a few turns with noticeable start/end points, you can give it a name and call it an episode.

Episodes can be open or closed toward the experiences and outcomes you want. For example, you may have experienced episodes such as "the difficult conversation that went sideways" (closed), "the failed task delegation that got our wires crossed" (closed), or the "excellent performance appraisal that renewed your commitment to the company" (open). If you string a few related episodes together that can be described with by a common theme, then you have a *pattern*.

Over time, our *patterns* of interaction become our conditions, and they can be preferred or unwanted. Figure 1 shows what these interaction analytics look like, going from the basic turns we take from conversation to conversation, and how they accumulate in the episodes and patterns that shape our overall experience. Once you look within patterns more carefully you notice that the sequence of turns and episodes form a structure that acts somewhat like a blueprint. Just like an architectural blueprint provides a picture of the structure and form of the edifice, the blueprint of a pattern reveals the way in which the communication and interactions combine to shape the experience of those involved.

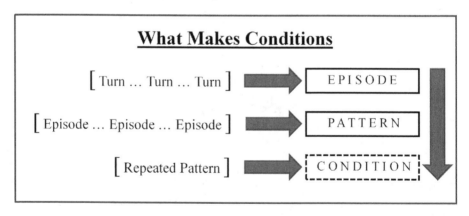

Figure 1. The CMM-Inspired Building Blocks of Conditions.

For example, consider the condition blueprint in Figure 2. An experienced manager, Susan, wanted to get out in front of some major industry disruptions that she knew would challenge her team. She brought me in as a consultant to work with her team to prepare for the uncertainty ahead. Using the desired condition of "readiness" as a guide, Susan pulled a few team members together and we created this framework—beginning with the everyday turns—that served as a roadmap to establish the episodes and patterns necessary for the team's success.

Condition: *Readiness*

As a team we will do the little things that enable us to remain present, observant, and responsive to changing circumstances. During meetings we will openly discuss issues and encourage alternative perspectives. We will stick with the hard questions, not rush past them. And we will use our network to gain insights that extend our capacity.

▆▆ The Blueprint ▆▆▆▆▆➤

Turns – *In our everyday interactions we will challenge assumptions, take time to confirm our understanding, and be patient as each of us processes change at our own speed.*

Episodes – *Building on these turns, we will use critical meetings to thoroughly explore multiple scenarios. We will not rush or get caught up by the pressure to charge ahead. We will move swiftly and deliberately.*

Patterns – *These episodes will establish healthy habits of focus, clearer understanding of complexity, and honest assessments about the implications of change. The pattern will keep us <u>ready</u>.*

Figure 2. Creating the Condition of Readiness.

Preexisting Patterns

Susan's concern was how to get her team to proactively work in ways that would help them be ready for industry shifts, rather than complacent to the realities they faced. In your consulting work, regardless of the identified presenting problem that prompted the consultation in the first place, you never start with a blank page. Anytime a consultant enters an organization, he or she invariably encounters a wide range of preexisting patterns and the various conditions they produce. Particularly when it is early on in the consultation, a consultant can listen for and explore these preexisting patterns because they are the silent, powerful forces that expand or limit what is possible within the team or organizations capacity to respond to the consulting intervention. I have spent a large part of my career refining my capacity to quickly listen for the clues to understand patterns. The following additional examples are provided to help guide your efforts to quickly see patterns in the organizational systems you enter.

Surrendering creativity for consensus. At first glance, this is a pattern that can seem positive. However, when people prematurely surrender their own divergent perspective in the pursuit of consensus or convenient agreement, they often miss out on the potential for creativity and innovation. The kinds of recurring episodes that produce patterns like these include: cutting meetings short to avoid sensitive topics and withholding honest opinions to avoid disagreement and conflict. The creative dissent that potentially emerges when disagreements are worked through in open, direct ways can be a catalyst for positive change and deeper respect for others. However, when the turns that individuals take result in silence or avoidance of their difficult conversations they can produce this dysfunctional pattern (Caproni, 2005).

Excessive collaboration. This pattern results from collaborative action that serves no performance-based rationale. In contrast to leveraged collaboration, which is the intentional choice to partner with others when the combination of skill, ability, and available resources can create a more effective outcome than is possible alone, sometimes teamwork is implemented for the sake of teamwork (Sostrin, 2013). When episodes of over-collaboration occur, you see people holding value-less meetings, creating duplicative efforts, and producing ambiguous accountabilities. Although the intent of collaboration may be noble, empty collaboration can slow down productivity and produce a negative impression of the true value of collaboration when it is legitimately warranted.

Just within these two examples you can see that if one were to zoom in on the habits of communication and interaction you would see an entire web of turns and episodes that ultimately combine to make the overall pattern. And once the pattern takes effect, it produces the related conditions that make it either more or less likely that other outcomes will develop. As you begin to consult from a communication perspective, you will see your actual role as consultant shift. In addition to the presenting issues that must be addressed, it is your job is to help the client examine and reconsider the unwanted patterns and conditions that are sustaining their negative outcomes while simultaneously creating a new set of preferred patterns and required conditions that will produce and sustain desired results of the consulting objective. The communication-driven framework I created to help consultants accomplish this is the M-A-I-D sequence.

The M-A-I-D Sequence

The body of scholar-practitioner work on CMM has produced a wide array of distinctive tools for describing, understanding, and guiding people-in-conversation so that they can more intentionally use communication to make better social worlds, however they may define it. The more well-known and traditional tools in CMM include the "hierarchy" model of embedded stories; the "serpentine" model that plots the unfolding of episodes; the "daisy" model that maps conversational textures of events, people, and objects; "strange" and "charmed" loops among the complex, often contradictory stories we tell; and the "logical force" that describes the sense of "should or ought" that an individual might attribute to the reasons why they do or do not do something in a given situation (Pearce, 2007). Consultants interested in understanding the more elaborate application requirements of these heuristics should refer to the *CMM Solutions Field Guide* (Pearce, Sostrin, & Pearce, 2011).

Inspired by these early heuristics developed by CMM scholars and practitioners, I created the simpler M-A-I-D sequence as a guide for consultants who want to quickly expand their capacity to work from a communication perspective. Rather than a prescriptive formula to follow, the four-part sequence is an array of reference points that initiate close collaboration between consultant and client as they explore the generative elements of communication that can accelerate the organizational change they seek. It includes the following:

- *M*ap influential patterns of communication and interaction
- *A*ssess the quality of the experience and outcomes produced by those patterns
- *I*dentify candidate patterns to re-make
- *D*etermine the collaborators and sequence of action necessary to re-make the patterns

Regardless of your consulting specialization or the issues presented to you in a given consultation, the M-A-I-D sequence offers a versatile, flexible way to bring influential patterns of communication to the surface. The model is truly collaborative in that the consultant does not identify problems on her own; organizational members identify them through facilitated discussion and application exercises. Similarly, the consultant does not act as an expert who fixes or repairs problems; rather, he guides the participants to create their own solutions by re-making the unwanted patterns of communication in preferred ways. Several of the most common uses for this model include:

- Evaluating the general status of individual and team relationships
- Identifying patterns that are inconsistent with desired organizational changes

- Reviewing specific episodes that produced unwanted outcomes or experiences
- Exploring the next step or turn that will begin to create desired conditions

To understand the versatility and application potential of the model, a closer examination of each phase is required. The following summary provides an overview of each milestone.

Map influential patterns of communication and interaction. The first phase involves looking closely at specific episodes of communication and focusing on distinct patterns of interest. Consultants may recognize these patterns of interest as recurring topics that the client mentions or as the sensitive topic that seems too delicate to discuss without specific questioning from the consultant. Either way, bringing this focus to a specific set of interactions allows you to punctuate episodes and determine where a given pattern starts and stops. This is important because our working lives can often feel like one continuous, interconnected pattern with little difference between the conversations and interactions that take place throughout the day. The mapping process takes a big job—disentangling influential patterns of communication—and breaks it down into a smaller and more manageable starting place.

Assess the quality of the experience and outcomes produced by those patterns. This phase involves an honest review and assessment of the impact of the pattern across two dimensions. First, look at the impact it has on the quality of the client's experience. Does it diminish or enhance their working life in some way? Does the overall experience act as a catalyst for you to engage more fully in your work and express your best contributions more consistently, or does it cause you to shrink back, disengage, and limit your performance? Second, look at the outcomes produced by the pattern. Do they contribute to effective learning, high performance, and success at work? Do they enable effective collaboration? Do they directly or indirectly lead to high quality work? Do they foster aligned relationships which produce synergy? Do they impact the bottom line?

These questions assess the task and relationship levels of communication, both of which are important to analyze. At the relationship level, you are looking for clues about the impact of the pattern on people. Does the pattern seem to strengthen the bond between people and result in increased trust, positive regard, and likelihood of productive interactions, or does it disrupt teamwork and reduce the likelihood of trust-based partnering on future projects and activities? At the task level, you are focusing on the actual activities and work flows that are accomplished. In other words, does the pattern make something useful that is required to achieve the priorities and goals of the people engaged in it (e.g., increased innovation, improved decision making, better meetings, and enhanced products/ services), or does it complicate matters and work against stated goals?

Identify candidate patterns to re-make. In the next step of the model, we facilitate a careful process of selecting patterns to potentially re-make based on a set of criteria that you choose. Although this is technically the third step in the sequence, it often happens simultaneously with the first two stages of M-A-I-D. The identification of potential patterns for re-making can include comparing the potential advantages and disadvantages of re-making them. Facilitate discussions with questions like:

- If we altered the communication habit, would it improve a relationship, outcome, or other important aspect of the quality of our work?
- How critical is that potential improvement right now?
- How entrenched is this pattern and who else must be involved to change it?
- What available time, energy, and motivation do we have for re-making the pattern?
- Are there any risks associated with engaging others to re-make this pattern? If so, what are they?
- Can we afford not to attempt to re-make it?

Answering questions like these—whether individually or in small groups—requires decisive judgment about what matters, and what will help close the gap between what characterizes the organization currently, and its desired objectives. The consultant has multiple options regarding how these questions can be presented. The consultant can lead the discussion, or the consultant can share the process and ask that client stakeholders interview each other to explore the questions and answers. Transferring the capacity from the consultant to the client is a learned skill. The most important aspect of the process early on is to identify candidate patterns that are equal parts "headache and frustration" and "positive potential for something better."

Determine the collaborators and sequence of action necessary to re-make the patterns. In this final step, you ask "who," then "what." You begin by determining the stakeholders who must be included to re-make the pattern. Once you know the "who," then you focus on the what—the specific sequence of actions necessary to re-make the pattern. For every diverse issue you face, there is an equally diverse range of potential sequences to employ. When determining sequence and approach, I suggest the simplest combination of tools and approaches that can be used to most effectively alter the underlying system of attitudes and behaviors that holds the unwanted pattern in place.

With this framework as a guide, the following case example is offered as a practical example of consulting from a communication perspective. It offers a closer look at the power of communication to shape the experiences and outcomes of organizational life, including the specific ways in which a consultant can empower clients to recognize this in other aspects of their work that go beyond the consulting parameters.

Case Example: A Sales Team Stuck in a Pattern of "Change Traps"

Although the scope of this chapter is only sufficient for an introduction to CMM and its application to consulting, the following case example is intended to provide a concrete demonstration of how several of the core concepts were used in a real-world consultation that I led with a small sales team.

I was invited to consult with Brent's team because they faced slumping sales and, in his words, they needed to quickly "jumpstart their innovation." Once considered a shining example of stellar performance in the growing company, a period of relative stability in the market coupled with a string of successful accounts caused the team to lose focus on executing their sales process with the same rigor and intensity that produced their initial success. Despite the fact that Brent, Rebecca, and Zach all chose the sales profession because they thrived on the challenging pursuit it presented, over time they seemed to grow comfortable with the status quo and that acutely affected their productivity. Using the M-A-I-D sequence to identify and shift the unwanted patterns of communication and interaction that produced their condition of complacency, I led the team through a three-hour collaborative process that resulted in clear performance expectations, increased sales, and a greater depth of resiliency to face similar future issues.

Listening for Stories

After introductions, I spoke briefly about the power of stories, including the ways they explain our deeper ideas and beliefs about work. Within CMM, there is a deep history and focus on using the complexity and richness of stories to show that there is always more going on below the surface. This is because stories have the unique capacity to give meaning to past, present, and anticipated future events in our lives (McAdams, 1997). Making and managing meaning in order to achieve coherent stories about ourselves, other people, and the world around us is an inherently human feature. You do not have to teach a person how to put their life experiences into stories and to sort through those stories; in fact, you cannot stop them from doing it.

CMM and its related tools make it easier for consultants to explore this instinctive sense-making and story-telling capacity in specific situations (Pearce, Sostrin, Pearce, 2011). Additionally, the complexity of interpersonal interactions can be seen in the tension between the stories people live and the stories people tell. One reason for this difference is that stories told tend to have a narrative unity or coherence, while stories lived are contingent on what two or more people do—each with their own varying stories—in specific sequence and in particular circumstances (Pearce, 2007).

When these gaps between the story "told" and the story "experienced" surface, they can be explained by revealing the unknown, unheard, and untellable stories, which themselves are the consultant's critical insight to figure out what the tension between them suggests (Sostrin, 2013). I invited Brent, Rebecca, and Zach to tell their own stories about their working lives. With the two questions in Table 1 as a guide, they were able to express their stories in ways that pointed me to the more prominent patterns of communication and interaction. After discussing individual perspectives, I narrowed in on a few recurring themes that gave me the opportunity to reveal the tension between the unknown, unheard, and untellable stories— including the gaps between what they talked about vs. what they actually experienced. Table 1 shows the consolidated version of what we collectively documented by naming the gaps among stories.

Table 1. *Unknown, Unheard, and Untellable Stories.*

Type of Story	If there is a story, what does it mean?	What is the impact *of the story?*
Unknown Story	"We are actually losing ground to our competitors—it is slow, but noticeable."	"I didn't know the story, so I assumed that continuing with our regular efforts was enough."
Unheard Story	"We have been relying on our past success and the hunger has faded a little."	"I didn't hear the story, so I felt we were just in a slight dip and things would balance out soon."
Untellable Story	"The incredible energy and hard work we invested to make the last few years so successful may have left the tank empty."	"I didn't imagine the story, so I would not have thought the grind may just be too much or that we are resistant to change and okay with the status quo."

By revealing these unknown, unheard, and untellable stories Brent, Rebecca, and Zach made a few more discoveries about the work-related experience they created together. As I collaborated with them to name and explore things, I quietly but consistently enabled them to gain some objective distance between their own judgments and interpretations of what was going on in order to see a wider perspective larger than their own. It turned out that each of them had been feeling quite similar to the others, but the sales culture in their group was one that prompted them to "always be up" and to project "steady confidence" in the face of adversity. The consequence of this was that there were quite a few stories that needed to be heard. This is a brief excerpt from the conversation that took place during the exercise de-brief:

Brent: "This is really interesting to see. We have all been feeling and acting a certain way, but we were not talking about it with each other. I hope you both know that we can talk about things like this. Getting re-motivated and relying on the support of the team is an important aspect of sales success."

Zach: "I'm glad we're doing this too. It really seems like our celebration of success in 2010 evolved into resting on our laurels. We weathered the financial crisis of 2008–2009 and we did have a lot to be proud about. But, now that we have to hustle more, we're really slow to get off the starting block."

Rebecca: "Well, it's not like we haven't been working. In fact, I've been as busy as ever. I know you both have too. It seems like the unheard story about *losing market share* is the wakeup call. We will need to work differently now. And honestly, I don't know if I'm up for the 70-hour weeks we pulled back then."

Zach: "I hear you. It seems like we have more of a balance now, which is nice. The fact is that maybe we are just not as hungry."

Brent: "I think I've been as guilty as the next guy of sweeping some of these signs under the rug. It definitely seems like we are at a turning point. Maybe we need to look at how we structure our work in relation to our changing position in the market."

Consultant: "Listening to this open exchange reminds me about the high level of trust you have with each other. I think this willingness to share what is real will help you through the transition. Before we shift gears to the strategy and tactical work flow issues, I think it would be valuable to look specifically at how these *unheard, unknown,* and *untellable* stories have actually found their way into the everyday patterns of communication and interaction you engage in."

Brent: "Okay, that sounds good. It may help us to see more about what is going on here before we try to leap into change mode."

Deconstructing Patterns

With momentum established for a sophisticated analysis of communication patterns within Brent's team, I introduced an activity to help the team deconstruct a specific pattern of communication. This provided the concrete demonstration of how turn-by-turn communication leads to episodes, which ultimately shape the patterns of experience for the team. This simple exercise gives the consultant a practical tool to help clients visualize (with a greater degree of objectivity) their episodic communication.

To begin, I invited the team to brainstorm the kinds of interactions they engage in and what words and phrases they would use to describe them. As people spoke, I wrote out a rough description of the emerging pattern on the white board. In an informal way, I invited comments to adjust the wording and intent as needed so that each contribution was refined. This is an example of what they produced:

- We stay busy but we do not really address bigger, strategic issues.
- We talk a lot about the past (i.e., how good we were), but we do not really focus on the future.
- Our meetings follow the same routine updates without venturing into more challenging topics.
- We avoid honest conversations about the increased efforts and accountabilities that might be required to meet our priorities.

This common language provided sufficient context to begin deconstructing the pattern. In order to construct the anatomy of this unwanted pattern, we needed to first map its outcomes/results, and name the underlying attitudes, beliefs, and behaviors that promoted it. To start this sequence, I simply asked: **What is the pattern of communication and interaction making? Responses included:** "Superficial collaboration where we avoid certain issues"; "Good work/life balance and reasonable stress levels"; and "potential disaster if we do not make changes to get more competitive." **Next, I asked: What possible name(s) could you give to this experience?** Zach's response illustrates the power of naming: "It was a good ride, but we have to call it like we see it … we're all getting a little complacent!"

This powerful recognition proved to be an important turning point. It acknowledged the general attitude of the team, but it did so in a way that was more of a call to action rather than just a stark criticism. From then on, the clients truly owned the process of naming their challenges in a more systematic way. As a result, they became more deeply invested in figuring out how to change it. Using the worksheet in Table 2, each person independently completed their version. As individuals shared their responses, I consolidated their thoughts into one document that reflected the common themes that each individual expressed.

Table 2. *Deconstructing a Pattern of Complacency.*

Presenting Level		
Who is involved in making the pattern and when/where does it seem to take effect?	*What challenges or difficulties does it produce—specifically, how does it impact us?*	*Even if it is contradictory, does it produce any benefits for the people who make it?*
We are all involved in making this happen. Although we have met the numbers in such a way that has satisfied corporate, we know we need to be doing more.	We are losing market share and have not done enough to boost the new business pipeline. If we do not make adjustments, this could have long-term effects.	Yes, it seems like by clinging to our past success, we avoid the need to confront changes in the market. This preserves the balanced pace we have come to rely on.
Constructing Level		
If there is an episode that captures what the pattern is all about, what would it be called?	*In this episode, what are the critical turns where specific communication sustains the pattern?*	*What types of values, attitudes, and behaviors fuel these turns and hold the pattern together?*
The episode that captures this best is probably our weekly sales meeting. Knowing what we know now, it is almost comical that we just go through the motions—everybody knows it but nobody says anything.	Whenever we talk about high-potential pitches that failed to close the deal, we avoid talking about the honest reasons why: We are failing to innovate. Instead, one of us will say something about the good accounts we still have or the fact that those prospective customers don't get it.	We seem to have all of these "get out of jail free cards" and nobody is willing to speak up about the ways we are falling short. We have all worked together for a few years; and so it is done out of genuine regard for each other.

If you look carefully at their work, you can see that Brent, Rebecca, and Zach got to an even deeper level of conversation about the pattern of communication and interaction that dominated their recent work experiences. Looking at the last question (i.e., values, attitudes, and behaviors that fuel their turns and resulting episodes and patterns), I shared the concept of a *master contract*.

A master contract refers to what each communicating participant in the relationship believes he or she can expect of the other(s) in a specific episode or within ongoing patterns. These are often implied, unwritten agreements that coworkers develop with each other. I asked if anybody noticed a master contract that suggests "We Will Not Challenge Each Other." Here is the dialogue that followed:

Rebecca: "Absolutely, I see it clearly. While I know we do these things because we respect the dues that we have all paid, hearing us talk like this would have embarrassed us a few years ago."

Zach: "Rebecca is right: this must mean we are part of the old guard. If we saw a sales team take the convenient path as much as we do we would criticize them pretty hard."

Brent: I guess the thing to do is 'renegotiate the contract.' I think we can have a higher degree of truth telling without compromising the respect we have for each other. Do you both agree?"

Table 3. *Constructing a New Pattern.*

Constructing Level		
If there is an episode that captures what the pattern is all about, what would it be called?	*In this episode, what are the critical turns where specific communication sustains the pattern?*	*What types of values, attitudes, and behaviors fuel these turns and hold the pattern together?*
Substantive meetings with "Truth Telling" at our sales meetings we need to make time to dig a little deeper into why we are not closing more business.	If we revert to our old ways of covering up our shortcomings by talking about the glory days, we need to help each other make the turn that says, "That was the past, what do we need to do right now to be successful?"	Commitment to be open, honest, and engaged in our work. And, respect for our past contributions without using them to cover up our gaps.
Presenting Level		
Who must be involved to make the pattern and when/where can it take maximum affect?	*What benefits will it produce, and specifically, how will it improve the quality of your work?*	*How can additional priorities and commitments be aligned with this, so that it is not undermined?*
We all have to be in this together, consistently.	Going through the motions has caused stress by itself. Our open approach should alleviate that and help us see our challenges squarely. While we will need to work differently, it is possible that we can avoid a return to the crazy survival mode.	We already have our benchmarks for this year so we know what we need to do with the numbers. To make sure we stay on track, each of us could create personal action plans that reflect the changes necessary to stay consistent with this new approach.

As the team noticed and explored the presence of this contract, members were demonstrating a communication perspective. They understood that in order to make something different, they would have to change the fundamental drivers of their ongoing communication habits. Seamlessly, I invited them to complete the final exercise of the session. Table 3 illustrates the two levels required toconstruct a new pattern. Once your client has deconstructed a pattern and identified what it is and what it makes, you can use the *pattern constructor* to literally flip the sequence and create a plan to make something better. This straightforward tool allows you to map the moving parts of a pattern in order to more concretely and intentionally craft desired patterns of communication and interaction.

If you review the steps I took to facilitate the session, you will notice that M-A-I-D acted as a flexible guide to implement key concepts from CMM. Throughout the three-hour session, the group *M*apped an influential pattern of communication and interaction, gained a greater sense of urgency for change by *A*ssessing the quality of the experience and outcomes produced by the pattern, *I*dentified a candidate pattern to re-make, and *D*etermined the collaborators and sequence of action necessary to begin re-making the pattern. And, they accomplished all of this without ever really knowing that they were *using a process* that was based on a sophisticated, scholarly theoretical framework.

The complexity and subjective nature of communication presents one of the greatest challenges to working with it in meaningful ways. However, the approach to this consultation allowed participants to see the core building blocks in a turn-by-turn sequence and that gave them a practical perspective regarding the origins of the team challenge at hand. This neutral perspective made the hidden aspects of their communication discussable and malleable, which further empowered the consultant/client relationship to go from past-looking (blame) to forward-looking (solution-focused). Additionally, as participants exposed the architecture of their unwanted pattern, they took on a flexible learning mind-set that helped them understand the impact of their individual choices and actions and to recognize what else is required to shift the pattern. The result was an egalitarian process that simultaneously allowed individuals to express their unique perspectives on the issues while reducing the pressure to agree with to one single solution that conforms to one individual's perspective (i.e., Brent's perspective as leader of the team, or the consultant's perspective on what should happen).

CONCLUSION

This chapter is an invitation to consider the potent role of communication as both a generative force in organizational life and as a fundamental factor of success in resolving organizational issues. Approaching a wide spectrum of team and organizational issues from a communication perspective opens up collaborative opportunities to respond to both presenting issues and their underlying drivers in more systemic ways. By focusing on the way in which conditions make consulting solutions either more or less relevant and implementable, a consultant is better positioned to assist the client in the process of establishing the patterns of communication and interaction required to create them.

REFERENCES

Axley, S. (1984). Managerial and organizational communication in terms of the conduit metaphor. *Academy of Management Review, 9*, 428–437.

Caproni, P. J. (2005). *Management skills for everyday life.* Upper Saddle River, NJ: Pearson.

Craig, R. (2001). Communication. In T. O. Sloane (Ed.), *Encyclopedia of Rhetoric* (p. 125). New York, NY: Oxford University Press.

DeVito, J. (2001). *The interpersonal communication book* (9th ed.). New York, NY: Longman.

Griffin, E. (2009). *A first look at communication theory.* New York: McGraw-Hill.

Littlejohn, S. (1996). *Theories of human communication,* 5th ed. Belmont, CA: Wadsworth Publishing.

McAdams, D. P. (1997). The case for unity in the (post)modern self: A modest proposal. In R. Ashmore and L. Jussim (Eds.), *Self and identity: Fundamental issues* (pp. 46–78). New York, NY: Oxford University Press.

McLean, G. N. (2006). *Organization development.* San Francisco, CA: Berrett Koehler.

O'Connor, J., & McDermott, I. (1997). *The art of systems thinking.* London, UK: Thorsons.

Pearce, W. B. (1989). *Communication and the human condition.* Carbondale, IL: Southern Illinois University Press.

Pearce, W. B. (1994). *Interpersonal communication: Making social worlds.* New York, NY: Harper Collins.

Pearce, W. B. (2007). *Making social worlds: A communication perspective.* Malden, MA: Wiley-Blackwell.

Pearce, W. B., & Cronen, V. (1980). *Communication, action, and meaning: The creation of social realities.* New York, NY: Praeger.

Pearce, W. B., Sostrin, J. and Pearce, K. (2011). *CMM solutions field guide for consultants.* San Mateo, CA: Lulu Press.

Shannon, C., & Weaver, W. (1948). *The mathematical theory of communication.* Urbana, IL: University of Illinois Press.

Sostrin, J. (2013). *Re-Making communication at work.* New York, NY: Palgrave Macmillan.

CHAPTER TEN

Transformative Team Interventions

Using the Transformative Mediation Framework for Team Building

JOSEPH P. FOLGER
Temple University

INTRODUCTION

Approaches to team building vary significantly. The different goals, methods and grounds for measuring success of team interventions stem from different conceptions of how to be effective in altering team dynamics. As a result, it is often difficult to determine what an organization is actually requesting when it seeks team building interventions for its intact or newly formed work groups. Without thoughtful consideration and discussion of goals and objectives, it is easy to misread what clients expect. Some consultants rely on readily available approaches to team building which often fail to meet clients' expectations but seem "necessary" because they are so commonly employed. The diversity of team building approaches requires that consultants clarify their purpose in conducting such interventions and make their purpose clear to prospective clients and the team members who will participate in the events.

When I began to conduct team building sessions fifteen years ago, I immediately wrestled with the diverse and sometimes ambiguous objectives associated with this work. I have worked as a consultant since 1989, providing team building and executive coaching for a wide range of organizations. During this period I have conducted approximately 40 team building sessions for businesses, nonprofit agencies, governmental organizations, and community groups. In responding to clients' requests, I sometimes had difficulty discerning their expectations for these group interventions. This stemmed in part from the difficulties associated with a manager or human resource representative speaking for the needs of an entire group. It also stemmed from confusion about what might actually be helpful to a team.

Even when clear objectives existed, some of the standard approaches to team building seemed inappropriate or ineffective for accomplishing client objectives. Clients complained about approaches to team building that cast consultants as experts on team process who convey their knowledge to the team through a range of instructional and simulation methods. The expectation in this approach is that the team will discuss and apply this information to steer itself in more productive or satisfying directions. Although this general approach to team development is consistent with traditional classroom instruction on team dynamics, clients are often disappointed with the results. This work is one step removed from a more direct change process that team interventions are expected to deliver. Many clients are skeptical that talking about principles of team effectiveness will translate into actual change in the team's process, decision making, or quality of communication. Clients are concerned that behaviors will not change and that team interaction will not be more productive. These concerns are supported by existing research on the effectiveness of team interventions which suggests that the results of team interventions are mixed (Bradley, White, & Mennecke, 2003; Salas, Rozell, Mullen, & Driskill, 1999).

When I pressed potential clients about why they needed team building or when I interviewed members of the team, the picture became somewhat clearer. What I often heard was that team members needed to talk. Teams were not having needed conversations that might improve their process or results. There were many topics and issues that were not be discussed in productive ways despite team members' and managers' perceptions of their importance. The inability or failure to talk about key issues or topics was a key factor in reducing team members' satisfaction with their experience on the team or in limiting productivity of the team.

There are many reasons why teams do not have needed conversations. Members may avoid some topics due to their political and sensitive nature (e.g., the risk of challenging a controversial decision made by a manager). Other reasons are more mundane (e.g., over-reliance on email or voice-mail rather than face-to-face interaction, difficulties contacting people who work in different time zones). Sometimes these conversations do not occur simply because no one formulates an agenda for discussion or because the team meets too infrequently to adequately discuss the range of topics that need to be addressed. In other instances, teams proactively suppress some topics because members do not want to risk the change that might result from having the conversation or making a decision. The tendency for work groups to suppress or avoid discussion of difficult but important issues is well documented (Tjosvold, 1991; Kolb and Bartunek, 1992; Roth, 1993; Weiss and Hughes, 2005). What I often heard from those who requested team building interventions was consistent with this known tendency to leave important issues and topics unaddressed. In short, many requests for team building stemmed from self-perceived deficiencies in the team's interaction.

The development of my team intervention practice coincided with the articulation of the transformative framework for mediation practice (Bush and Folger, 1994, 2005; Folger and Bush, 1996, 2014; Folger, Bush and Della Noce, 2010). Transformative mediation rests on the premise that conflict can be viewed not as a problem to be solved, but as a crisis in the parties' interaction. The role of the mediator and the type of interventions he or she conducts follow from this view of conflict. Mediators act as facilitators of the parties' interaction in an effort to support its transformation. The goal is to help transform negative, alienating, and unproductive cycles of interaction to positive and clarifying ones—independent of any specific decision or outcome reached by the parties about the issues that may divide them.

This conception of conflict intervention resonated with what I heard in the requests for team building interventions. Organizations seeking team building interventions were, in essence, recognizing that a team's interaction was in some way deficient, destructive, or problematic and that these interaction challenges undermined team's ability to function effectively. Although the team's issues were not always about conflict *per se*, the issues were always related somehow to a deficiency in the quality of the team's interaction, as a group or across subsets of team members. As a result, it was useful to rely on the underlying premises of the transformative framework to design and conduct team building interventions within organizational settings.

Although most mediation is most often designed for two disputants, team building work requires that an intervener work with groups of all sizes. The team building interventions I have conducted have involved teams ranging in size from 6 to 65 people. The sessions varied in length from a half day to two full-day sessions. There are unique design considerations that have to be taken into account when conducting team building interventions from a transformative perspective. The various team building sessions I conducted unfolded differently based upon the twists and turns the team interaction took during the intervention itself. But all of these interventions were guided by two underlying assumptions. First, this approach assumes that the team members themselves have the expertise and knowledge to address their own problems and issues and create the outcomes that are best for them, but may lack the skills and processes for doing so. The team consultant is not an expert on the content of the team's discussions, but is skilled at helping teams discover skills and processes that will facilitate discussion about substantive issues. Thus, interventions are built on a second important assumption as well: The consultant has an important and useful role to play in supporting the constructive transformation of the team's interaction through a focus on empowerment of team members and recognition among them. Thus, the goal of this chapter is to overview an approach to team development interventions based on the underlying principles of the transformative framework.

LIMITATIONS OF INTERNAL TEAM INTERVENTIONS

Keyton (Chapter 3) differentiates among external, in-house, and internal consultants. The latter two types of consultants represent employees of the organization seeking intervention. Internal and in-house consultants often have some degree of responsibility for supporting team development and addressing performance-related challenges that teams face. For example, human resource staff or learning and development specialists are often responsible for assisting with the creation of teams and monitoring and supporting their performance. This responsibility often means that these professionals are placed in a potential team building role.

Closer to the teams themselves, managers carry the overall responsibility for their teams' performance. If there are issues or challenges a team faces, managers are ultimately responsible for team performance and the satisfaction of team members with their own team experience. Although managers and human resource professionals can have an impact on team performance through the use of evaluation tools and direct feedback to team members, they are often limited in their ability to conduct team building sessions for work groups within their own organizations.

The existing relationships that managers and human resource professionals have with team members often limit their effectiveness as interveners in team process or performance. Even in large organizations, human resource generalists or training specialists frequently have ongoing relationships with members of various teams. Their prior relationships with team members can easily contribute to perceptions of favoritism or assumptions about their investment in particular outcomes. In turn, these perceptions can have a chilling effect on team members' willingness to discuss issues. This limitation is particularly strong for managers which is one reason why managers often avoid intervening in their employees' conflicts or team dynamics (Karambyya & Bret, 1994; Katz, 1999). In addition, managers and human resource professionals are typically expected to continue their relationships with team members after a team building intervention is over. This expectation can inhibit team members, detracting from a willingness to identify team issues in the planning stages of team interventions or to discuss issues during the team building sessions themselves. Participants in a team intervention may fear that their words will be heard by someone in the organization who is in a position to influence their performance evaluations or their career paths after the team building intervention is over.

In addition to the relationship constraints, team members may view available internal third parties as representatives of the organization and its policies. Team members can easily (and sometimes accurately) assume that the third party is there to align team members behaviors with the organizations' stated core values or behavioral polices and norms. This assumption contributes to team members' perceptions that the third party is not in a position to deal with the complexities that need to be addressed. It can restrict creative interventions which could promote positive change within a team because members may assume that their communication (e.g., views expressed, challenges posed) during a team building session is itself grounds for evaluation and assessment. (See Plax, Kearney, & Waldeck, Chapter 6, for a discussion about trust issues consultants may face when facilitating groups).

Although human resource personnel typically have substantial technical expertise in areas such as employee relations, performance evaluation, and compensation, they often lack the facilitation skills needed to conduct team building interventions. Working with groups requires a skill set that goes beyond individual coaching or professional development efforts (Kaner, 1996; Schwartz, 2002). Many human resource professionals who seek help from consultants are quick to acknowledge that they do not have the personal confidence to conduct team interventions. Many do not have experience in facilitating group conflict. Even managers who have direct, frequent contact with their teams sometimes have difficulty facilitating the team as a whole and supporting the group when addressing issues that are sensitive or potentially divisive. They often have difficulty juggling their management role with a more facilitative, change agent role. They also believe that their managerial role can inhibit, rather than prompt, the kind of discussion the team needs to have. The mind-set, communication skills, and personal presence that external mediators develop is closely linked to the skills that are needed to facilitate team interaction and these skills are often not part of a manager's or human resource professional's repertoire.

Even when managers or human resource staff have confidence in their group process and facilitation skills, the organizational culture itself can sometimes override their potential effectiveness in conducting interventions. Internal efforts to shift interaction dynamics can be severely limited when trust is low in an organization or when a self-defeating culture has emerged that inhibits employee openness, acceptance of responsibility, and motivation for needed change (Beck, 1992 Halberlin, 2001; Kolb and Bartunek, 1992). Members' patterns of interaction create an organization's climate over time (see Sostrin, Chapter 9). When climate is adverse or destructive, internal third parties are often influenced by the organization in which they have been functioning (Folger, Poole and Stutman, 2013). Because internal third parties are often contributors to the patterns of interaction that created the organizational culture, their intervention efforts can be unknowingly restricted by their own past behaviors and the behaviors of their co-workers. They may not be able to see the existing patterns that are in need of change. Only someone from the outside who has not contributed to the established organizational culture may be able to objectively support team members in their efforts to change these patterns. However, even external consultants' success may be limited if the patterns are deeply entrenched and senior leadership does not support the consultant's change efforts.

Given these diverse constraints and limitations, internal third parties can actually have negative effects on teams when they design or conduct team interventions. If team building interventions are conducted by internal third parties and, as a result, team members are inhibited from speaking honestly about the issues they would like to discuss, mistrust may grow. The discussions and interactions among team members proceed on false or less than realistic premises. People recognize that what is *not* being said is more important than what is being put on the table. They sense that people are filtering and monitoring their comments and can easily attribute this lack of candor to the team members rather than the effect of the internal consultant's presence. In addition, if the third party has prior relationships with some of the team members, this can heighten defensiveness in other team members going into the team building process. Assumptions about the internal consultant's motives and biases can create relationship strains among team members.

All of the potential negative impacts of relying on internal members to create a strong case for turning to external consultants to conduct team building interventions. Many organizational leaders realize these constraints and turn to external consultants for team building initiatives that can move the team move forward and enhance productivity (Katzenbach & Smith, 1993). They also realize that team building approaches differ in design and objectives and they consider these differences when they employ the services of external consultants. Three of the major approaches to team building are overviewed in the next section, including the transformative approach which will be discussed in detail below.

THREE APPROACHES TO TEAM BUILDING

There are three well-known approaches to conducting team interventions. Each approach is guided by its own hallmarks of practice, although each can be enacted with somewhat different styles and variations. In this section, I briefly discuss these three approaches with an emphasis on the potential strengths and drawbacks of each.

Challenge Activities

One approach to team building takes teams away from their work setting and asks them to accomplish challenging tasks or to play simulation games. These tasks typically require coordination among the team members and can be used by the consultant to demonstrate principles of effective team process (Gass, Goldman, & Priest, 1992; Glover & Midura, 1992). Some challenge activities require substantial physical dexterity and coordination, such as the commonly used ropes courses. Other challenge activities are tasks that require creativity and cooperation among team members, but not athletic abilities (such as constructing a creative solution to a challenging situation or building a protective package for a fragile object) (Eller, 2004). The external consultant is responsible for designing the challenge and making sure the team understands the goal of the activity. After the team completes the activity, the consultant conducts a debriefing session that clarifies the team principles that emerged during the challenge activity. Frequently, the consultant facilitates a discussion about how the principles and practices can be implemented in the work setting.

The strengths and weaknesses of the challenge activity approach to team building are well known. On the positive side, this approach encourages the active involvement of team members. The challenge activities can spark energy and enthusiasm, thereby contributing to a positive sense about the team building process. This approach offers a change of pace from the day-to-day work environment of the team. Being away from the office or workplace is a bonus of participating in the team building event.

One of the most significant advantages of this approach is that the team challenge simulations can illustrate team principles and insights without asking team members to delve very deeply into their own challenges and problems. As a result, there can be minimal apprehension or concern about needing to discuss "real-time" issues while still allowing teams the opportunity to consider key team deficiencies or problems indirectly. In this sense, the approach can feel safe to the participants and thereby enhance participation.

The advantages of the challenge activity approach to team building are counterbalanced by several potential drawbacks. When challenge activities require physical dexterity, some people are reluctant to participate in them. People have very different levels of confidence in performing tasks that require physical skill. For some, there is potential embarrassment or anxiety associated with involvement in these activities. Even if people see parallels between the various levels of competence across team members and varying levels of competence in completing physical tasks, they can reject the activities because, in the end, the activities are not what the team is typically required to do. In addition, the more playful and "fun" aspects of the challenge activities can create an impression that the team building intervention is not a serious endeavor. Even if the activities result in insights about the team's process or needed changes, how the intervention produced these insights—the challenge activity itself—can be perceived as too playful for the seriousness of the team's work and issues. Finally, although team members may find the simulation activities useful in providing insights about their team process, they may be skeptical about whether these insights can transfer to the team's actual dynamics. In the end, the intervention may not be directly connected to the challenges that prompted the initial need for the team building.

Team Member Diagnostics

A second approach to team building relies on diagnosing the personality or communication styles of individual team members. This approach is built on the assumption that differences in team members' communication and work styles can frustrate team interaction and ultimately impede team performance. Diagnostic assessment tools, such as the well known Myers-Briggs inventory, are used as a foundation for many of these team interventions (Quenk, 2009; VanSant, 2003). The identification of personal styles and communication tendencies allows individual team members to reflect upon their own style and compare it to others on the team. This process can encourage people to see how others may approach their work in different, but equally legitimate ways, and to adjust to the differences in styles that the personality inventories reveal.

Like the challenge activity approach, this approach has strengths and weaknesses as a framework for conducting team interventions. On the positive side, this approach reveals important insights about communication style differences that may elude even the most talented individuals on a work team. Heightened awareness of different communication styles is often a key to creating deeper personal awareness of the responses that people elicit from their own behaviors. It also supports a greater acceptance of communication diversity because the styles framework assumes that no style is inherently dysfunctional or wrong. In addition, the very discussion of style differences that this approach fosters can set a precedent for future discussions about substantive differences that exist on the team. It encourages team members to assume that differences are inevitable and to work towards the accommodation of differences at many levels on the team.

Diagnostic approaches to team building have the advantage of indirectness. The team may or may not be asked to address specific issues or problems that have arisen during the course of the team's interaction. Team members are expected to link the insights about personal style differences to challenges that team members face in their day to day work. However, explicit discussions of these topics may not occur, even if some or all team members want to participate in them.

One drawback of this approach stems from its indirectness. Like the challenge activity interventions, this approach can create clear insights for team members about their own and other team members' styles. But these insights may not translate into changes that are apparent to team members after the inventories are completed and differences are identified and discussed. Awareness of personality or communication differences does not automatically provide ways for team members to adapt to this awareness or communicate with each other in new and more productive ways.

A second potential disadvantage of the diagnostic approach relates to its fundamental methodology. Identifying personal styles through inventories can create a false sense that communication styles are static or unchangeable. People are labeled as various types of communicators based on their responses to the inventories. This labeling process tends to create perceptual filters that people carry into their future interactions—they come to see each other within the static frame that the inventory has provided. In worst case scenarios, these perceptions can become stereotypes that team members use to label each other. This can create perceptions that are inconsistent with the variety of complex and nuanced ways individuals actually communicate in specific settings or situations. The static labels and perceptions can be counter-productive, and can lead to less flexibility in the team's overall interaction.

Transformative/Facilitative Approach

The third approach to team building is built on the assumption that team members' satisfaction and productivity is directly affected by the quality of interaction the team is having. This approach responds to a team's need to have conversations as an entire group or among subsets of team members. This team intervention approach addresses team members' difficulty in addressing sensitive, political or controversial issues. In some instances, the team may not be having conversations about certain topics at all, and in other cases the team's interaction may be deficient or strained in ways that challenge the productivity or success of the team. The possible deficiencies in team interaction can be explained in terms of empowerment and recognition processes, as will be discussed in more detail below. The role of the team building consultant is to help identify the conversations that team members want to have and to design ways to facilitate those conversations that are consistent with the identified needs and expectations of the team. In some instances, the consultant's role is to support the direct facilitation of the conversations. In other cases, the consultant helps to find ways for team members to have productive conversations without he or she being directly involved in those conversations.

A major advantage of this approach to team building is that it is a more direct than the other two approaches. It supports team members' ability to address their "real time" issues and thus has a greater ecological validity than training or simulation interventions. This approach creates a valued sense that the team is doing its "real work" as the team intervention unfolds. Team conversations about process, communication or expectations do not result from simulations or personal style analyses that the consultant designed and conducted. Rather, the conversations start with the topics that the team members suggest. In addition, when team members have constructive conversations about difficult issues, the team experience can be a model for future interactions the team can have on their own after the team building intervention. This approach also allows the team to address the issues it wants to address at its own pace. Because the consultant is in a facilitative rather than an instructional role, the agenda and focus for discussions are determined by the team members themselves.

There are several drawbacks to a transformative approach to team building. Because of the direct approach of facilitating discussions, team members may be threatened by this approach or perceive it as risky. They might assume that they will be forced to discuss issues that they do not want to discuss or that the outcomes of team discussions may be too unpredictable. This risk is real if the consultant imposes or requires discussions that any of the team members do not want to have or participate in. The consultant's commitment to the empowerment of all team members is crucial to allay these concerns. (Ross & Waldeck illustrate this dynamic in Chapter 19). A related drawback is that the team may raise difficult issues for discussion and these issues may require substantial attention by the team after the team building intervention is over. The issues raised may not be entirely addressed through the team building process itself. Because conversations are not predetermined by the consultant in the design of the team building intervention, the issues that team members raise are not restrained. Some team members may fear that such an approach can open a "can of worms," or raise too many issues that are left hanging. This concern can lead some team leaders or team members to resist this approach to team intervention.

This type of concern about what will be discussed in a team session arose in one team intervention I conducted with the research and development division of a large pharmaceutical firm. The manager indicated to me at the outset of the process that he wanted his team to have a positive experience throughout the team building session. He did not want team members to raise issues that might cause tension or strain. He wanted the team building session to build camaraderie and not threaten it. Specifically, he was concerned that people might raise issues about recent unmet performance expectations. He said he had discussed some of these issues individually with team members but never raised them with the group as a whole. He indicated that some of these individual conversations had not gone well and he feared that these conversations might be brought up in the team building session, thereby launching a negative, complaining tone for the day. In setting expectations with him before the team intervention, I said that the team members would have control over the topics they chose to discuss. I would not exclude any topics that team members felt they needed to address. After considering the pros and cons of allowing the team members to set their own agenda, the manager agreed (with some hesitancy) that he would support the team building session and allow people to decide what needed to be discussed. He also said that he would think through how he might respond if the performance conversations and the issues related to them were raised at the team building session. I assured him he could respond the way he thought was appropriate and helpful to the team at any point along the way.

During the session, several of the team members raised difficult and divisive issues late in the day. At that point, the manager came to me and asked me in private if I could ensure that the group ended the session on an upbeat note. I reminded him of the discussion we had during the planning stages for the event. I said I would not direct where the team went with their discussion for the rest of the day. I also said that he was free to say anything to the team about the issues and he could choose to influence the conversation if he felt he wanted to. The session ended with the team asking to schedule another session where they could more fully address the difficult issues that were raised late in the session.

TRANSFORMATIVE TEAM BUILDING: CORE GOALS AND ESSENTIAL CONDITIONS

The core goal of team building within a transformative approach is to identify and support the conversations that team members want to have in order to enhance productivity and task objectives, support team member relationships, or facilitate communication. This goal is consistent with other group and organizational interventions that focus on and facilitate the interaction of work groups (Bohm, 1996; Isaacs, 1999; Schwartz, 2002; Stanfield, 2000). In this approach, team members are responsible for identifying necessary topics of conversation. The consultant follows where team members perceive their interactions need to go, and designs team building sessions that reflect these objectives using a process that is described later in this chapter. Ultimately, the team's conversations can be about a wide range of possible topics including: the clarification of team goals, tasks, or member responsibilities, differences in work styles or communication issues, issues stemming from ethical or moral differences, concerns or challenges related to the distribution and use of power and influence, access to information, change management, differing expectations about participation or team member accountability (Geist, 1995;

Hiatt & Creasey, 2012; Littlejohn, 1995; Schein, 2009). In some instances, when the topics the team members believe they need to address are highly conflictual, they can be tied to the overall development of the life of the team (Wheelan, 2004). Throughout the process, the consultant relies on an empowerment and recognition framework to guide his/her approach to identifying and facilitating the conversations that the team has (Bush & Folger, 1994, 2005; Folger, Bush & Della Noce, 2010). That is, this approach to practice is built on the view that a team intervention might be helpful or needed because the team is experiencing a "crisis in communication." The term "crisis" is used to convey a broad sense that the interaction is problematic to some degree. It is not always the case that the team's interaction is critically challenged or in a state of extreme conflict. The problematic nature of team interaction can run through a range of intensity, from being at a true crisis point to being in need of minor changes and improvements. This crisis is rooted in team members' feelings of weakness and/or self-absorption. The consultant can help positively transform the team's interaction if team members experience a greater sense of empowerment and recognition through facilitated dialogue. Fostering empowerment and recognition means supporting greater clarity for team members about what they want to discuss, and what decisions or choices they want to make, regardless of the specific, substantive outcomes that result from the team building sessions (empowerment). It also means that team members achieve greater clarity and decisiveness while, at the same time, developing greater understanding of other team members' points of view, perspectives, or emotional reactions to the topics and issues under discussion (recognition). New understandings are woven into the decisions that the team ultimately makes.

Successful team building interventions based on this approach enable team members are able to have productive conversations that they were not able to have previously. Team members participate in conversations that create greater clarity and understanding of the team's issues and each other. Success is not contingent on the consultant's ability to have substantive influence over the decisions made, but on the opportunity he or she provides for team members to converse about topics or issues in new or productive ways. The consultant's goal is to help the team improve its conversations qualitatively, independent of the particular decisions that the team makes. This goal clearly defines the consultant's role as a facilitator rather than a substantive expert on the topics that the team is addressing. The consultant works from the assumption that the team members know what is best for them and the team as a whole.

Several essential conditions enable consultants and teams to reach the key goals of the transformative team building approach. First, there must be significant interdependence among the team members. Some work groups are within the same department or location and execute parallel tasks, but have minimal interdependence and communication. As a result, the essential goal of creating positive shifts in the quality of the team's interaction is largely irrelevant. It is only when team members' work requires interdependence—when people have to count on each other to complete tasks—that communication is vital to their success and thus warrants this approach to intervention.

Second, team members must view their communication with one another to be, to some extent, deficient or limited. In some instances, a request for team building can have little or nothing to do with the communicative needs or deficiencies of the team. For example, the productivity of a team could be challenged because it is severely understaffed and, as a result, cannot complete assigned workloads. Focusing on the communication among team members, in this instance, is unlikely to address the resource deficit that is creating frustration or morale problems on the team. It may, however, help the team members clarify the nature of the resource deficiency, consider ways to influence management about the perceived needs, or modify self-defeating perceptions that the team's performance level is linked to individual member deficiencies or accountability. If team members identify these as possible goals for a team building session, the approach may prove helpful.

Third, some degree of openness among team members must exist in order for this approach to team building to be feasible. Most teams welcome the opportunity to discuss issues that they have not previously been able to address. In some cases, however, the issues that are of concern are ones that the team members feel are too risky to address in open forums. Various reasons explain team members' reluctance to openly discuss issues. The fear of retribution for positions expressed about an issue, potential team member embarrassment, or frustration with past attempts to address an issue may inhibit team members from participating in discussions about topics that are affecting the team's performance or relationships.

Occasionally, one key member of a team may not want to participate in the team's conversation, despite the willingness of the rest of the team to discuss key issues. This is particularly problematic that individual is a senior member or leader, and if other members of the team believe that this person's participation in the discussion is critical to the discussions the team needs to have. Consistent with the premise of empowerment, the team should have the ability to indicate whether or not they want the team conversations to occur if a key member is not willing or able to attend or participate in the team building session. In some instances, this may mean that the team building session will not go forward.

Finally, this type of intervention requires time. The team must be able to set aside adequate time for team building and the organization must be willing to allocate the resources needed to support the consultation. The length of a team building session depends on the size of the team and the range and scope of the topics that the team identifies for discussion. The team leader may work with the consultant to place limits on the total time available, depending upon how long the entire team can be "off-line" at one time. Designing team building sessions from this approach requires flexibility and creativity so that the time allotted for a team building session is used to maximum potential by the team. The structure of agendas, the allocation of estimated time to discussion topics, and the possibilities for discussions among sub-groups of the team all need to be considered carefully by the consultant when designing the session. Most team building sessions within this approach last one or two full days. Multiple day sessions are sometimes done over time, usually with a one- or two-week lapse in between the day-long sessions.

An Overview of the Team Intervention Process

Figure 1 provides a broad overview of the steps a consultant takes in conducting team building interventions within the transformative team intervention approach. Like any consultation, transformative team building requires a careful needs assessment phase (see Jorgensen, Chapter 5) that involved all key stakeholders in the team's process. The first meeting is the intake meeting that occurs with a potential client—either a member of the team itself or an organizational representative such as a human resource or training specialist. The initial planning/intake meeting is important because it offers the consultant the opportunity to clarify this approach to team building and to distinguish it from challenge activities and personality approaches. The consultant obtains clear information about why team building is sought and what the expectations are for the intervention. This discussion allows the consultant to decide whether this approach to practice is appropriate, given the client's expectations and the nature of the team itself. In this first meeting, the consultant also clarifies what the steps will be in the process and provides a rough estimate of how much time will be needed to prepare and facilitate the session. It is important that the consultant clarify at the outset that the team building session may open up discussion of issues that will not be entirely finished at the end of the session. There may be a need for follow-up (not necessarily with the consultant's involvement) after the team building event. The consultant must clarify that the intervention may not result in everyone on the team being emotionally uplifted and upbeat by the end of the session. The team may explore important but difficult issues that cause some degree of conflict or stress for people. The objective is to allow the team to address issues it wants to address, even if the issues are challenging—and the client should be aware that the process might not always feel good to all team members.

The second step in the process to conduct confidential, advance interviews with the members of the team. These interviews serve several important functions. They allow the consultant to explain the team building approach to each person who will be participating in the session. The consultant needs to contrast transformative team building with other types of team building interventions for the team members. By doing so, the consultant can allay team members' fears and misconceptions about what will be expected of them based upon their previous experiences with different approaches to team building. These interviews also allow the consultant to build rapport and trust with the individual members of the team. Most importantly, these interviews allow each team member to identify the conversations or issues that he/she would like to see happen during the team building session. The consultant listens for the topics and issues that could form the basis for the discussions he or she will facilitate. If topics are sensitive or have potential negative repercussions for the team member, this time is also used to help each person become clear about what they will and will not want to say during the discussions. Further, the consultant should assure each person that every team member will make the final decision about their own level of participation in the discussions, and that their confidentiality in the interview will be honored.

When the team has more than 12 members, the consultant should consider interviewing a sample of team members or conducting the interviews in small groups of 3–4 people. If a sample of team members is interviewed, the sample should be carefully chosen to represent a cross section of roles and the issues the team faces. It is also important that the team as a whole is notified that a sub-group of the team is being interviewed. When a sample of team members is interviewed, I typically generate a written summary of the themes from these interviews and provide them to the entire team before the final design of the session is finished. Team members who were not interviewed can then provide feedback of this summary through emails or phone conversations to help shape the ultimate design of the session. These steps convey a clear intent to be as inclusive as possible and allows for the widest possible input.

- Intake/Initial Planning Meeting
  - Clarification of third party role
  - Defining expectations for success
  - Overview of the process
- Team Member Interviews
  - Defining the goals/purpose of the interviews
  - Identifying who should be interviewed
  - Summarizing themes
- Design Conversation Formats for Team Building Session
  - Agenda Setting
  - Deciding who needs to talk to whom about what
- Facilitation of Team Building Session
- Summarizing Outcomes and Possible Follow-up Steps

Figure 1. Steps in Transformative Team Building Process.

After conducting the individual team member interviews, the consultant designs the discussion formats for the team building session based upon a synthesis of the information obtained from the team members. The design of the session becomes increasingly important as the size of the team increases. Based on the information provided in the interviews, the consultant may have to prioritize topics for discussion to fit the available time for the team building session itself. The session should feature a variety of discussion formats in order to engage participants throughout the event.

Figure 2 lists several important questions that the consultant considers in designing the format and agenda for the team building session. Taken together, the answers to these questions allow the consultant to creatively design a way to support the conversations that the team has identified. Synthesizing answers to these questions is where the "art" of this approach to team building lays. The goal is to proactively follow the team members' lead in creating forums for needed discussions, while structuring and pacing the session so that the team's time is used effectively and efficiently and people are comfortable with the unfolding session. When designed well, the team building sessions tend to run themselves, with the consultant taking a background role as the team addresses the topics it has identified as important.

- What aspects of the team/organizational culture need to be considered in designing the team building session?
- Who needs to talk to whom during the session?
- What topics/issues need to be discussed and by whom?
- Are there concerns about anonymity that should be addressed through the design of the session?
- How should the session be paced?
- How much facilitation should the facilitator plan to do during the team building session?
- What advance preparation do team members need to do?
- What role will the team leader/manager play in the session?
- Will the complete design of the session be circulated before it occurs?

Figure 2. Key Questions in Designing Dialogue Formats.

For one team development project, I created a dialogue format that I called "No Question Is Too Basic." The client was a project development team of 12 people that had documented performance issues and some retention problems.

Four members had left the team and were replaced in the prior 18 months. Three of the four new members who joined the team were transferred from other divisions within the organization. The human resource coverage person for the team told me at the outset of the engagement that she felt that morale on the team was low and communication was deficient. When I conducted individual interviews with each of the team members, I heard from about half of them that they felt that they did not know enough about what other team members were actually doing on the projects. They said that some roles on the team seemed ambiguous and they lacked adequate information about individual responsibilities. Several people who raised this concern said that they were somewhat embarrassed to admit that they did not know some of this information and that they would be hesitant to express their lack of knowledge to the group as a whole, especially in front of the team's manager.

I needed to find a way for the project team to have conversations about these important issues—issues that were likely contributing to the morale and communication problems. At the same time, I wanted to honor the concerns many team members expressed. They did not want to openly admit their knowledge gaps in front of the group and their manager. I decided to give the team members blank index cards and told them they could anonymously write down any question they felt they needed answered—no question was too basic. I told the group that I would collect the cards, shuffle them, and re-distribute the cards to the group members randomly. Each group member would then read the question on their card, and anyone in the group could answer the question. I told the team members that they were free to identify their own question if they wanted to or they could leave the question unidentified.

When the team engaged in this process, the questions on the cards raised a range of issues, many of which had been reported to me in advance interviews. Some individuals identified and elaborated on their questions and others did not identify the questions they had written. I had allotted 45 minutes for this dialogue. The group spent an hour and a half answering these questions and discussing related issues that the questions raised.

At the end of the one day session, almost all of the participants reported that the "No Question Is Too Basic" discussion was extremely valuable for them personally and for the team as a whole. It was a dialogue format that allowed them to discuss issues they needed to address in the way they needed to address them.

The design of another dialogue format for a different team stemmed directly from the organizational structure of the group. I was asked to develop a team building session for a large operations division of a public utility organization. The group consisted of sixty people. The goal was to support the team's ability to function at maximum performance and to address any communication challenges the group faced. I divided the group into three sub-teams of approximately 20 people in each team. Each sub-team had its own manager, but those working under any manager had to communicate and work on a regular basis with people in the other two divisions. I interviewed a sample of team members from each of the three areas to determine what issues and challenges the group needed to address in the team building session. One important theme that emerged from the interviews was that people on all three teams worked with each other on a regular basis but each team had almost no access to or direct information from the managers of the other two teams. The three managers talked with each other regularly (and to their own teams) but not to members on the two teams that they did not directly manage. This led to misunderstandings and lack of coordination across the three teams. It seemed to some team members that the three divisions were not aligned well and that the three managers were not communicating about core direction and expectations for performance. Different teams were receiving different directives, especially those related to the prioritization of tasks. Prioritized goals and deadlines for one team were not consistent with those set for the other teams.

At the team session, I designed an opportunity for members of one team to talk with the managers of the two other teams. Each team met with the two managers of the other teams for an hour each. I asked the team members and the managers to think ahead of time about what topics they wanted to cover and what questions they wanted to ask. One person volunteered to facilitate each discussion. I observed, but did not participate in, any of these cross-manager discussions. All three teams reported that these conversations were highly useful and informative.

When the team building session occurs, the consultant plays a range of roles depending on the design of the agenda and the unfolding interaction among the team members. At the outset of the session, the consultant overviews the agenda for the entire group and explains how the agenda reflects what was heard in the interviews. At points, the consultant may be the central facilitator of the team's conversations, especially when the entire team is participating in the discussion. The facilitation of the entire team's discussion can sometimes occur in an open format with the consultant covering the responsibilities of a group facilitator. In other instances, the consultant can rely upon more structured processes for generating ideas, evaluating options, or making decisions with the entire team. The decision to rely on a structured facilitation processes is, in part, contingent on the culture of the team and the organizational climate in which the team functions. Some teams are highly intolerant of being "over-processed." They easily reject or recoil from approaches to facilitation which are perceived as too controlling. Other teams are highly dependent on structured processes in their everyday work and do not function well without clear structure during a facilitated meeting or team building event. It is important that the consultant assess the team's need for structure and guidance when designing the session. The consultant needs to proactively following the team's preferences regarding this dimension of the design.

Some discussions are not suited to the team as a whole. For these situations, the consultant can set up smaller break-out or sub-group discussions and be in a listening role as these discussions unfold. Throughout the day, the facilitator is responsible for monitoring time, gauging the pacing of the meeting, and adapting the agenda to unfolding events. This involves following unexpected directions that the team feels it needs to head in. He or she may also take on the responsibility of summarizing outcomes of the discussions, although if the group is large or if the content is complex, recorders can be used to document the outcomes of the session.

After the team building session, the consultant summarizes and reviews outcomes and recommends any follow-up steps that emerged from the team's discussion. In some cases, there is a debriefing session with the entire team, the person who commissioned the team building session, or the team's manager. When difficult issues are addressed in a team building, there is often skepticism that there will not be adequate follow-up or implementation of the decisions made or the directions set. As much as possible, the consultant needs to make sure that needed follow-up steps are taken to validate the work of the team during the consultation.

THE INNER GAME OF TRANSFORMATIVE TEAM BUILDING

The transformative approach to team development is more than a step-by-step process for supporting teams. It is a professional and, to some extent, personal engagement with a group of people who work together and count on each other in many important ways. This work is often highly challenging and at the same time very rewarding. As a process, it is respectful of people and their participation, but it is also risky and somewhat unpredictable. In most cases, it feels like a high-wire activity. Unlike other approaches to team development, it is much more participant-driven, rather than consultant-driven. It is not an off-the-shelf method that a consultant can use to create predictable and somewhat over-stated results. Because it is so responsive and unscripted, it necessitates that the consultant be self-aware of his/her own consulting style, and ability to read and understand team and organizational dynamics. To use this framework, the consultant has to be very comfortable with a process that is ultimately created by the participants. The "inner game" of this approach to team development centers on what consultants need to be comfortable with in doing this work, especially challenges like those described briefly below.

Assessing One's Own Fit with the Organizational Culture

Consultants need to have considerable sensitivity to organizational culture and climate when planning and providing team interventions. The norms of interaction and expectations for communication differ widely across different organizations and work sectors (Lafasto & Larson, 2001). To some extent, team building consultants have to adapt to these diverse norms and behavioral expectations. This adaptation can be subtle, but is critical to attaining adequate credibility with clients. A consultant's style (e.g., dress, communication style, degree of formality) is noticed and assessed in the early stages of the process by both the sponsoring stakeholders and the team members. This scrutiny usually stems from an attempt to gauge whether there will be a good fit between the consultant and the team—whether the team will be comfortable with and trust the consultant throughout the process. This means that consultants need to be aware of the kinds of organizations in which they function best as a team consultant. Although consultants can adapt to some extent, one's core style will fit well in some organizational settings and not as well in others. Consultants need to honestly appraise their styles and work with clients that suit their personal and professional presence. (See Seibold, Chapter 2, and Keyton, Chapter 3, for more discussion of the importance of a "match" between client and consultant).

Assessing Alignment with Stakeholders' Expectations and Goals

The transformative approach to team building is not always aligned with the expectations that stakeholders' have for team development. (In Chapter 14, Boster also discusses the issue of meeting client expectations). Group intervention methods that are not aligned with the needs or goals of the group are known to be detrimental to group performance (Thomas, 2010). Consultants who are committed to this approach need to be clear about what this method tries to deliver, how it contrasts with other expectations for team building, and how activities that a stakeholder might suggest for the event may be consistent or inconsistent with this focus and objectives of this type of intervention. In some instances, this requires that the consultant have frank and challenging conversations with those who are sponsoring the event and setting the goals for it. The following example illustrates the kind of issues that can arise related to alignment with stakeholder expectations.

The head of a marketing division of a large, international insurance firm wanted a team development session for the eighteen people who worked under him. He indicated at the outset that he wanted the session to be an enjoyable and fun experience for the team members. With his sponsorship, I conducted the planning interviews and I heard about a range of issues that the group felt needed to be addressed. When I summarized the themes from the interviews for the manager, I could sense that the manager thought I would not be a good fit for the kind of event he wanted to have with his team and for the climate he wanted to establish for the team building session. He showed little interest in a team building design that afforded the opportunity for these discussions. Instead, he talked with me about various challenge activities he thought *would be fun and memorable for the team to do*. I was taking a much more direct, transformative approach because I knew from the interviews with the team members that there were serious issues that the team wanted to address, including issues that stemmed from differences between senior and junior members of the team. I indicated to the manager that I would be willing to step out of the engagement at that point and that he could use the results of the interviews I conducted to organize the event he had in mind.

After the meeting with the manager, I talked with the leadership and development person who originally contacted me for the project and told her what I had discovered in the interviews and what I had told the manager. She knew about the issues on the team from her prior work with the team and felt the manager was headed in a wrong direction with his plan for the team development session. She ultimately intervened with the manager and insisted that the approach I was going to take with the team was needed. She compromised with the manager, however, by letting him lead a "survivor" type competition in the gym and pool area of the hotel where the event was being held in the evening of the first day of the team session. I designed a two-day event around the issues the team said it needed to address.

At the event, the physical challenge activity that the manager designed made several of the team members uncomfortable and several of the more senior members on the team chose not to participate in this activity. The response to the challenge activity ultimately reinforced the differences between the senior and junior members of the team that the organization was trying to bridge with the team building session. The second day of the team building session was tense and largely unproductive because of the prior evening's challenge activity. This example emphasizes the importance of having a consistent approach to the entire team event, and not including activities which can undermine the goals of a transformative approach to team building.

Working with the Political Dimensions of Team Interventions

Like any consulting intervention (see Waldeck, Plax, and Kearney, Chapter 7), transformative team building interventions require a sensitivity to the political dimensions of organizational work-life. Sometimes the very act of requesting a team building is controversial within the organization or team. Team members may fear that information they share in a team discussion will leak to other parts of the organization. Some team members will support the team building initiative, and others will question or reject it. In addition, relationships between the team and its leader can be politically charged (Conger, 1998). A manager might, for example, indicate that the team's issues have nothing to do with his or her management, although the team members have told you in the advance interviews that the team's issues are directly related to management deficiencies or decisions.

In other cases, conflict between groups within the organization may complicate team building efforts or limit their ultimate effectiveness. In situations like these, the consultant has to navigate the political realities while remaining true to the core principles and ethics of a transformative approach to intervention.

Being Comfortable with Unexpected, Sensitive, or Disruptive Events

There are often unexpected twists and turns during an unfolding team building session—including the possibility that the team will blame the facilitator for its own failures or frustrations. Consultants who conduct these team building sessions need to be comfortable with considerable ambiguity about what the team will discuss and where the team interaction will actually head during the team session. They also need to have high self-awareness of their own instinctive responses when unexpected or highly challenging situations unfold in front of them with little warning (Thomas, 2010). The advance interviews with the team members provide a general sense of the topics or issues the team might address. But the team members decide on the day of the event where the conversations actually will head. Many times the interviews only serve as a prompt for the team members to think about what they want to discuss at the facilitated session. As a result, the topics team members raise might have little to do with what they conveyed to the consultant in the preparatory interviews.

One team development session I led clearly illustrates the critical need to be ready for unexpected turns as well as difficult politically charged issues or behaviors. I was asked to work with a product sales team of 14 people in a large financial institution. When I conducted the advance interviews, team members raised a number of issues that they felt needed to be discussed, including issues related to client service standards, division of the sales regions and the current compensation model for the team. I designed an agenda for the day that allowed these issues to be addressed by the team members and the leader of the group. Portions of the day were allotted to the manager so that he could clarify his views on the issues the team raised and also discuss upcoming changes to the organization. I distributed the agenda before the event, and the team and manager provided feedback indicating that it was a good framework for the day.

On the day of the team session, there was an unexpected tone set by one senior woman on the team. Whenever the manager spoke, she pointedly challenged him and his views. Her comments were close to verbal attacks on his leadership and his management of the team. Other team members seemed surprised, uncomfortable, and embarrassed by her behavior. The manager responded to the substance of the issues she raised but was not thrown by her aggressive tone. My advance interview with this team member indicated she had a lot of issues she wanted to address with the team but she gave me no sense that she was angry or upset with the manager. At one break during the day, a member of the team asked if I was going to talk with her, implying that I should discourage or stop her behavior. I said that I would not but that any team member could address any issue he or she felt was important as the session unfolded, including the behavior of any particular individual. No one called her on her behavior and her critical and aggressive comments toward the manager continued through most of the day. After the session, the woman approached me and told me that she thought the manager was incompetent and she intentionally used the team building session to establish her credibility and vision with the team. Three months later, I heard from the human resource coverage person for this team that the manager had been removed and the woman who had challenged him throughout the team building session became the new leader.

CONCLUSION

Transformative team building interventions allow team members to address conflicts, make decisions, and build stronger co-worker relationships. These interventions can help to provide a basis for building community among team members—a quality that is frequently lost in many current work environments (Music, 2014; Sennett, 2012). Although there are potential risks to this approach to team development, it is built on the assumption that teams often need third parties to support team members as they engage in constructive confrontations about important issues (Cassidy, 2010; Fisher, 1997; Van de Vliert, 1997). This approach to team intervention practice frequently "takes the lid off" issues that the team may not have been able to address. The role of the consultant is to support the challenging interaction as it unfolds. This is a skill that transformative mediators hone in their practice (Bush & Folger, 2010). One of the upstream effects of this team building work is that team members model for each other the forms of dialogue needed to be successful in difficult organizational settings. The experience and skill of working through challenging but needed conversations can be carried beyond the team building session, thus having long-term positive impacts on the team and its future conversations and performance.

REFERENCES

Beck, P. K. (1992). *Negotiating at an uneven table.* San Francisco, CA: Jossey Bass.

Bohm, D. (1996). *On dialogue.* New York, NY: Routledge.

Bradley, J., White, B. J., & Mennecke, B. E. (2003). Teams and tasks: A temporal framework for the effects of interpersonal intervention in team performance. *Small Group Research, 34,* 353–387.

Bush, R. A. B., & Folger, J. (1994). *The promise of mediation: Responding to conflict through empowerment and recognition.* San Francisco, CA: Jossey Bass.

Bush, R. A. B., & Folger, J. (2005). *The promise of mediation: The transformative approach to conflict.* San Francisco, CA: Jossey-Bass.

Bush, R. A. B., & Folger, J. (2010). Transformative mediation: Core practices. In J. Folger, R. A. B. Bush and D. Della Noce (Eds.), *Transformative mediation: A sourcebook* (pp. 31–50). Hempstead, NY: Association for Conflict Resolution & The Institute for the Study of Conflict Transformation.

Cassidy, M. (2010). Diversity by design: Creating cognitive conflict to enhance group performance. In S. Schuman (Ed.), *The handbook for working with difficult groups* (pp. 95–111). San Francisco, CA: Jossey-Bass.

Conger, J. A. (1998). The dark side of leadership. In G. R. Hickman (Ed.), *Leading organizations: Perspectives for a new era* (pp. 250–260). Thousand Oaks, CA: Sage.

Eller, J. (2004). *Effective group facilitation in education.* Thousand Oaks, CA: Corwin Press.

Fisher, R. J. (1997). Third party consultation as the controlled stimulation of conflict. In C. De Dreu and E. Van de Vliert (Eds.), *Using conflict in organizations* (pp. 192–207). Thousand Oaks, CA: Sage.

Folger J., & Bush, R. A. B. (1996). Transformative mediation and third party intervention: Ten hallmarks of a transformative approach to practice. *Mediation Quarterly, 13,* 263–278.

Folger, J. and Bush, R. A. B. (2014). Transformative mediation: A self-assessment. *International Journal of Conflict Engagement and Resolution, 2,* 20–34.

Folger, J., Bush, R. A. B., & Della Noce, D. (2010). *Transformative mediation: A sourcebook* Hempstead, NY: Association for Conflict Resolution & The Institute for the Study of Conflict Transformation.

Folger, J., Poole, M. S., & Stutman, R. K. (2013). *Working through conflict: Strategies for relationships, groups, and organizations* (7th ed). Boston, MA: Pearson.

Gass, M. A., Goldman, K., & Priest, S. (1992). Constructing effective corporate adventure training programs. *Journal of Experiential Education, 15(1),* 35–42.

Geist, P. (1995). Negotiating whose order? Communicating to negotiate identities and revise organizational structures. In A. M. Nicotera (Ed.), *Conflict and organizations* (pp. 45–64). Albany, NY: State University of New York Press.

Glover, D. R., & Midura, W. (1992). *Team building through physical challenges.* Champaign, IL: Human Kinetics.

Halberlin, C. (2001). Transforming workplace culture through mediation: Lessons learned from swimming upstream. *Hofstra Labor & Employment Law Journal, 18(2),* 375–383.

Hiatt, J. M., & Creasey, T. J. (2012). *Change management: The people side of change.* Loveland, CO: Procsi.

Isaacs, W. (1999). *Dialogue and the art of thinking together: A pioneering approach to communicating in business and life.* New York NY: Doubleday.

Kaner, S. (1996). *Facilitator's guide to participatory decision-making.* Gabriola Island, BC, Canada: New Society Publishers.

Karambayya, R., & Bret, J. M. (1994). Managerial third parties: Intervention strategies, process and consequences. In J. Folger and T. S. Jones (Eds.), *New directions in mediation: Communication research and* perspectives (pp. 175–192). Thousand Oaks, CA: Sage.

Katz, J. J. (1999). Toward a comprehensive model for the assessment and management of intraorganizational conflict. *International Journal of Conflict Management, 10,* 268–293.

Katzenbach, J. R., & Smith, D. K. (1993). *The wisdom of teams*. Boston, MA: Harvard Business School Press.

Kolb, D., & Bartunek, J. M. (1992). *Hidden conflict in organizations*. Newbury Park, CA: Sage.

Lafasto, F., & Larson, C. E. (2001). *When teams work best*. Thousand Oaks, CA: Sage.

Littlejohn, S. (1995). Moral conflict in organizations. In A. M. Nicotera (Ed.), *Conflict and organizations* (pp. 101–125). Albany, NY: State University of New York Press.

Music, G. (2014). *The good life: Wellbeing and the new science of altruism, selfishness and immorality*. London, UK: Routledge.

Quenk, N. L. (2009). *Essentials of Myers-Briggs type indicator assessment* (2nd ed.). Hoboken, NJ: Wiley.

Roth, S. A. (1993). Speaking the unspoken: A work-group consultation to reopen dialogue. In E. Imber-Black (Ed.), *Secrets in families and family therapy* (pp. 268–291). New York, NY: Norton.

Salas, E., Rozell, D., Mullen, B., & Driskell, J. (1999). The effect of team building on performance: An integration. *Small Group Research, 30*, 309–329.

Schein, E. H. (2009). *Helping*. San Francisco, CA: Berrett-Koehler.

Schwartz, R. (2002). *The skilled facilitator*. San Francisco, CA: Jossey-Bass.

Sennett, R. (2012). *Together: The rituals, pleasures and politics of cooperation*. London, UK: Allen Lane.

Stanfield, R. B. (2000). *The art of focused conversation*. Gabriola Island, BC, Canada: New Society Publishers.

Thomas, G. (2010). Difficult groups or difficult facilitators? Three steps facilitators can take to make sure they are not the problem. In S. Schuman (Ed.), *The handbook for working with difficult groups* (pp. 339–352). San Francisco, CA: Jossey-Bass.

Tjosvold, D. (1991). *The conflict-positive organization*. Reading, MA: Addison Wesley.

Van de Vliert, E. (1997). Enhancing performance by conflict-stimulating intervention. In C. De Dreu and E. Van de Vliert (Eds.), *Using conflict in organizations* (pp. 208–222). Thousand Oaks, CA: Sage.

VanSant, S. (2003). *Wired for conflict*. Gainesville, FL: Center for Applications of Psychological Type.

Weiss, J., & Hughes, J. (2005). Want collaboration? Accept—and actively manage—conflict. *Harvard Business Review, 83*, 92–101.

Wheelan, S. A. (2004). *Group processes: A developmental perspective* (2nd ed.). Boston, MA: Allyn & Bacon.

CHAPTER ELEVEN

Facilitating Team Development in Embedded Organizational Work Groups

DAVID R. SEIBOLD

University of California, Santa Barbara

Over the course of more than three decades, working alone for the most part but occasionally with collaborators, I have formulated three methods that I use in consultations involving team development. I have employed these methods in interventions to enhance teamwork in embedded organizational work groups (Seibold, Hollingshead, & Yoon, 2014). These team development methods include "team process consultations" with one or more embedded work groups that take place over extended periods of time and include activities to develop teamwork along each of four dimensions and in a specific order; "team workouts" with single embedded work groups or cross-functional teams, or even with multiple groups simultaneously, that occur during relatively brief time periods and incorporate activities intended to aid members to identify problems in their unit(s) and how they will redress them after the intervention; and variations in these two team development interventions that promote members' and my "critical praxis and reflexivity."

As sequences of purposeful events, activities, and behaviors designed to aid these groups to improve their processes and outcomes, these team development consultations are "interventions" (Cummings & Worley, 2005), which may range from lengthy to brief, be quite complex or relatively simple, involve many or few participants, and focus on multiple levels or only one level of the organization (Bartunek, Austin, & Seo, 2008). The three team development intervention methods I discuss in this chapter range from extended to relatively brief, although they all include complex sequences of events, activities, and actions. And while my focus in all three approaches typically has been a single embedded organizational work group with six to fifteen members, I have utilized these methods with participants from multiple levels of an organization, with several interdependent groups at the same time, and even with a cross-functional group of 50 members. Nearly all of my team development consultations have been the first type of group-focused intervention that Hackman and Edmondson (2008) discuss: attempts to enhance existing teams' functioning through process-focused methods (supplemented by training for the entire group, coaching for individuals, organization-wide consultations, and conversations with stakeholders who are external to the organization). Occasionally my team development consultations involve work with one or more groups that are part of the second class that Hackman and Edmondson describe: forming new teams to resolve current organizational problems.

When these team development methods are successful, as Boss and McConkie (2008) note, team effectiveness is improved via increased member competence with tasks; increased candor in relationships and during problem solving; greater concern for each another; willingness to be accountable for commitments made during the intervention; and stronger trust within the team. Furthermore, organizational effectiveness may result if the stronger team also creates a climate in which problems routinely are acknowledged and solved; members take ownership of organizational goals and thus commitment is increased; collaboration within the team spills to other groups with which the team is interdependent; members' sensitivity to processes at the work group level leads them to be more aware of other areas of organizational functioning; and members feel empowered to redress other organizational problems.

While I discuss below, and in quite a bit of detail, each of these three approaches to facilitating development in embedded organizational groups, they are only part of my focus here and fuller treatments of the methods are available in companion pieces by Seibold (2005), Seibold and Kang (2008) and Seibold and Meyers (2012). Instead, in this chapter I emphasize the mutually informing nature of *theory/research* and these team development *practices* in the context of my consultations with embedded organizational work groups. Specifically, and as I show throughout the chapter, all three team development approaches have been informed by theory and research; and/or theory and research were appropriated at key points as they were utilized in specific consultations; and/ or use of these methods generated insights that helped me—as a scholar— to inform or reform theory and research. These links between the consulting methods and theory/research were in the background of my other treatments of these team development approaches (e.g., Seibold, 2005; Seibold & Kang, 2008; Seibold & Meyers, 2012) but will be given equal weight—even foregrounded at times — here.

Overview and Reprise

In the reminder of this chapter, I discuss four issues central to these team development interventions. First, I offer context for them by discussing the consultations in which they were part, including the number and range of organizations consulted, the types of teams aided, and the unique features of the embedded organizational teams with whom I worked. Second, I discuss the assumptions and objectives of these team development interventions. In particular, I treat ten qualities of groups with "teamwork" (and four dimensions undergirding them) revealed in research, and how my attempts to develop teams along those dimensions align with four approaches to team building also discussed in theoretical work in this area. Third, I explain each of the methods but endeavor to situate them relative to theory and research that I have most linked with each. Fourth, I conclude with how team development practice and research can be integrated.

To return to my thesis, and to set the tone of the discussion in each of the four sections in this chapter, I have found these methods of *consulting practice* concerning team development on one hand, and *theory and research* about teams and organizational interventions on the other, to be mutually informing in numerous ways. For example, in developing and making decisions during the past thirty-five years about team intervention methods of practice, I frequently turned to scholarship related to the utility and implementation of these methods that was current (e.g., Austin & Bartunek, 2003; Buller & Bell, 1986; Cohen & Bailey, 1997; Cummings & Worley, 2005; Cunliffe, 2004; Dyer, 1995; Kozlowski & Ilgen, 2006; Mathieu, Maynard, Rapp, & Gilson, 2008; Rousseau, Aubé, & Savoie, 2006; Schein, 1988). In fact, the roots of these three approaches to team development are in the theoretical and applied research of Kurt Lewin, Douglas McGregor, Chris Argyris, and Richard Hackman (Boss & McConkie, 2008).

Second, there were innumerable times during the consultations themselves when I appropriated theory and empirical findings from my own and others' scholarship to aid my own and team members' understanding of teamwork. For instance, when working to enhance team processes in organizations that were transitioning from traditional to team-based structures, I drew upon research by Lawler (1995) to assess whether there was sufficient infrastructure at the organizational level to support teams. Without evidence at the team level of members' organizational leaders modeling teamwork, an organizational philosophy that legitimated teamwork, work tasks that required teamwork, reward structures that reinforced teamwork, and training that enabled teamwork, the organization's strategic decision to implement team-based structures would have appeared to team members as "something the top of the organization told the middle of the organization to implement at the bottom of the organization"—and the teams would founder (Lawler, 1995). On other occasions I aided members of work groups to utilize Poole's (1991) procedures for managing their team meetings and techniques surveyed by SunWolf and Seibold (1999). Indeed, I have repeatedly relied on Gouran's (2003) summary of research concerning core communication competencies during group deliberations: task-related skills (problem recognition and framing, inference drawing, idea generation, argument); relational skills (leadership, climate building, conflict management); and procedural skills (planning, process enactment). On other occasions in conversations with members of self-managed teams about the normative pressures they had created (especially on members they marginalized), pressures that often exceeded any that management had exerted (Barker & Cheney, 1994), I sought to help them make sense of the tensions they were experiencing by reference to Tompkins and Cheney's (1985) paradox of concertive control.

Third, these work group interventions led me to conduct research on the methods themselves (Seibold, 1995; Seibold & Kang, 2008), and I will draw upon each of these works to illustrate the team intervention methods discussed. Fourth, I do not simply bring theory *to* each engagement; occasions for theory development arise *in* and *from* engagements. For instance, I sometimes find associations in the context of the engagement that can be tested (see Seibold, 2005) which—if supported—advance knowledge in established areas of scholarship concerning groups (for examples, see Franken & Seibold, 2010; Krikorian, Seibold, & Goode, 1997; Seibold, 1990). More generally, and like many scholars who also consult, I recognize the value of the parallels, intersections, and integration between basic and applied research and thus can speak more easily to both audiences (e.g., see Seibold, Lemus, Ballard, & Myers, 2009).

CONTEXTUALIZING THESE TEAM DEVELOPMENT APPROACHES

Since early in the 1980s, I have consulted with 75 organizations at more than 100 of their locations. Perhaps sixty-five percent of these engagements have been with for-profit organizations that include minority-owned small enterprises and *Fortune 400* corporations that offer customers hospitality, telecommunications, entertainment, insurance, and financial services and that provide consumers with technology, utilities, clothing, and food. Thirty percent of the consultations have been with government and nonprofit organizations focused on philanthropy, environmental protection, transportation, education, health and human services, international development, as well as with several professional associations. The other five percent have been projects in which graduate students and I offered services to institutions with insufficient resources to undertake them (e.g., civic organizations, charities, and a hospice).

These consultations have involved training, coaching, facilitation, formative and summative evaluation, and organizational interventions including *team development*—my emphasis here. Whether they were established work units or cross-functional groups (enduring and recurrent, or ad hoc and of brief duration), the embedded work groups and teams (Seibold et al., 2014) with whom I have worked perform tasks and accomplish goals that are important to the organization's survival and success (Greenbaum & Query, 1999; O'Toole & Lawler, 2006). Many of the work groups are *teams*, either because they possess the structural characteristics of such groups (Arrow, McGrath, & Berdahl, 2000) or because members refer to themselves that way given their high level of cohesiveness (LaFasto & Larson, 2001).

All of these groups have been "embedded" in larger organizational systems, so consulting with embedded teams requires awareness of the material and contextual influences of the embedding organization (Seibold et al., 2014): the degree of clarity of management's goals; the balance between managerial and team authority; the presence (or absence) of structures that enable success such as a motivating task, effective team composition, and metrics to track performance and alignment with organizational objectives; whether there are organizational reward and information systems that support teamwork, material resources that enable member to execute tasks such as equipment, budget and staff support; effective leadership with leadership with the potential to support teamwork in real time and at key points; and the social, political, spatial and temporal context in which teams operate including internal organizational climate, power, physical and proximal layout, and temporal factors. Furthermore, it is important to be mindful of embedded team/embedding organization relationships in terms of the degree of autonomy/dependence in teams' relationships with other organizational groups; the extent to which the organizational teams are connected formally/informally, as well as the differentiating/integrating functions they perform in their relationships with other teams; and the multiple memberships embedded team members have with other teams in the embedding organization(s) and other systems to which they are linked, as well as the impacts of their multiple organizational roles on key team processes and outcomes (Seibold et al., 2014).

The following representative examples of my team development consultations with embedded organizational work groups also undergird the three methods I discuss in the following sections: engineers concerned with team process problems in their project groups; semi-autonomous work teams in financial services firms, government agencies, and manufacturing plants pleased with their degree of autonomy but struggling with it; groups of senior executives and administrators seeking to be more cohesive and collaborative; R&D teams in the health and energy sectors with scientists interested in better coordination; professionals from four locations in a children and family services county agency forming a team; groups of university staff, faculty and administrators focused on quality of work life issues on their campus; a multidisciplinary hospice care team faced with a high rate of volunteer turnover; technicians and supervisors in five departments of a hospital laboratory addressing intragroup cooperation and intergroup coordination issues.

TEAM DEVELOPMENT → DEVELOPING TEAMWORK

The goal of each of these team development consultations was to assist each embedded work group to establish better *teamwork*. As developed in Seibold (2005), elaborated in Seibold, Kang, Gailliard, and Jahn (2009), and summarized in Seibold and Meyers (2012), groups whose practices reflect teamwork exhibit ten qualities: (1) members can articulate a shared team vision; (2) members have clear and agreed upon role expectations; (3) members have considerable role-related autonomy; (4) members establish high standards for themselves and exert considerable control over the group's procedures (versus managers' expectations and control); (5) members develop structures to respond to environmental demands, while still being organizationally appropriate; (6) members conduct decision making within the team (relative to having decisions made for them by management); (7) members share leadership among themselves and/or have a formal team leader who shares power with them; (8) members share information and interpretations with each other (including about non-task matters); (9) members reinforce each other's contributions and offer supportiveness; and (10) members convey and display mutual respect and trust.

Seibold and Kang (2008) note that these ten qualities of teamwork reflect four underlying dimensions: vision, roles, processes, and relationships. Vision includes the group's goals and objectives but also members' team identity (for themselves and for outsiders). Second, members of groups or teams characterized by high levels of teamwork also have roles that may be more or less than their job requirements. Role-related dynamics leading to teamwork entail how each member comes to understand what other members expect of him or her (and ensuing role negotiations). Third, *processes* in groups with teamwork are characterized by flexibility and responsiveness to the changing environment, more so than "standard operating procedures" implemented by managers. Furthermore, there are sufficient resources (financial, personnel, technology, and material) to sustain teamwork, as well as reward, training, and information systems that enable and facilitate members' strong teamwork (Hackman, 1990, 2004). Fourth, the relationships dimension of teamwork typically reveals members' communication to be characterized by respectful and open sharing of information, by perspective taking and valuing difference, and by allowance for both supportive and constructive negative feedback. These four dimensions, along which I attempt to facilitate teamwork, correspond respectively to the four approaches to "team building" discussed long ago by Beer (1976): goal setting perspectives, approaches to fostering clearer roles, problem solving approaches, designs focused on improving members' interpersonal relations. While those approaches have often been sole foci in others' consultations, all four are integrated in each of my three approaches to facilitating team development.

Addressing Teamwork Dimensions and In Which Order?

Incorporating all four foci into my team development interventions does not imply simultaneity in when they are addressed. Like others (Dyer, 1995), I struggled over which dimension of team effectiveness to address *first* and then *in what order* the others should be treated: vision? roles? processes? relationships? Early on, and as a communication scholar who also had surveyed research findings concerning the value of relational communication in groups (summarized in Barker et al., 2000), I emphasized better teamwork through first emphasizing the relationships dimensions. However, notwithstanding members' ensuing abilities to manage their interpersonal relationships, problems in the group often emerged from more fundamental issues related to the goals of the group (or the absence of them), challenges concerning role expectations relative to accomplishing group goals, and processes difficulties tied to ongoing structural and resource problems (which triggered relational problems periodically).

Somewhat later in my career, and relying on the rationale for the importance of goal setting designs Buller and Bell (1986), I instead focused on the vision and roles dimensions first in team development interventions. Those two dimensions needed to be dealt with together since team members did not deal with vision-related processes without talking about roles—those they wished to play and those they wished others to play. These interventions were more successful than ones in which I had first emphasized the relational dimension, since members could focus on overt goal/role issues that typically were more urgent than any difficulties in their relationships with one and other. However, members still continued to gravitate to the structural and resource-based problems that were limiting their performance as a work group.

Indeed, only after I began to aid the teams—several years later—to focus first on their operational/procedural/structural/resources problems was I assured in recommending methods I discuss below. Hackman (1990) had underscored that successful groups employ and enjoy the results of certain structural factors (especially reward, training, and information systems), material resources, and effective formal leadership. Indeed, members were most willing to enter into team development processes that promised—as their first order of business—that they could improve their own work conditions. In collaborating to ameliorate process problems associated with the group's operations, structure, and resources, the members also came to recognize the value of taking responsibility for finding solutions to their work problems, of making their own needs secondary to securing resources that helped the whole, and of holding relational issues in abeyance until operational/procedural/structural/resources problems were resolved. This was a key to the success of these interventions; members experienced the fact that their "teamwork" had improved their work conditions. These successes opened members to the value of collaborating further on matters that might improve team functioning. For example, members were *then* poised to work on a shared vision and their roles in it. And once their efforts at developing teamwork on these dimensions proved successful, focusing on relationships in their team was less onerous since members already had unequivocal evidence—from their own team development to that point having resulted from collaborating on issues on the three other dimensions—of the importance of feedback, supportiveness, respect, and trust (fundamental to developing teamwork on the relationships dimension). Hence, my reflection on each intervention, combined with my evaluation of findings from relevant research, led to a model of team development (the first discussed below) in which what I initially had addressed first (resolving challenges associated with members' relationships with each other) ultimately was addressed last among the four dimensions of teamwork (i.e., operational/structural/resources issues, then goals and roles, then relationships).

Team Development Facilitation Methods

The three approaches to team development treated next are not something I *do to* teams but activities in which I *engage with* teams. Each team often exhibits low to moderate levels of teamwork and wishes to be better, so members welcome my involvement in a joint process of developing better teamwork. These consultations may be initiated by members' feelings of difficulties surrounding procedures, goals, roles, and relationships in the team; by formal leaders' concerns about motivational or performance issues in the team; by referrals to the team or to their formal leaders who believe I can be of assistance to the team.

I do not diagnose problems, decide on lines action for the team, or make recommendations to an organization. Instead, utilizing archival data, observations, personal and group interviews, and self-report measures, I first develop a list of potential problems. I then classify them in terms the four dimensions of teamwork, next interact with members to ensure that see what sense they make of what I have seen and heard, and ultimately develop a series of structured activities in each method so that team members can prioritize their problems and engage them collaboratively. The processes reflected in these collaborative activities lead to solutions to the team's problems that also make teamwork in the group more likely, but they also offer the team with opportunities to engage in greater teamwork in order to solve their problems.

As noted at the outset, the three methods I use to facilitate the development of teamwork include: "team process consultations" with embedded work groups that take place over extended periods of time and include activities to develop teamwork along each of four dimensions and in a specific order; "team workouts" with single embedded work groups or cross-functional teams, or even with multiple groups simultaneously, that occur during relatively brief time periods and incorporate activities intended to aid members to identify problems in their unit(s) and how they will redress them after the intervention; and variations in these two team development interventions that promote members' and my "critical praxis and reflexivity." Which method is employed depends upon how long my involvement is sought by them or my availability (process consultation or workout); the amount of responsibility for the process of team development—as well as the amount of reflection—that team members wish to take on (critical praxis and reflexivity); the amount of time that members are able to devote to their team development; and the complexity of the issues they need to work on (process consultation or workout).

Team Process Consultation Method

This method includes elements of team building (Dyer, 1995) and features of process consulting (Schein, 1988), so I began to refer to it as "team process consultation" (Seibold, 1995). It typically involves immersion into the group each week for up to four months. Team members need that long to become aware of how their interactions with each other simultaneously constitute their strengths but contribute to their problems; to utilize those same interactional processes to resolve problems; and to internalize the processes and skills utilized during the team development method in order that team members will be able to use them on their own thereafter.

Consider one example of the team process consultation method that occurred during several months with the members of two large teams (representing both shifts) in a team-managed plant producing filters for the engines in construction equipment. Teams were composed of engineers and skilled technicians, most of whom had experience working in other organizations with semi-autonomous teams. The goal of this intervention, invited by the firm (BSFI) and its two parent companies, was to enhance members' already strong commitment to teams and teamwork. The preconditions for team development success existed and, in the pre-engagement process I discussed them with team members to see if they concurred. As I shared with the BFSI teams, research reveals that successful team development efforts are probable when internal tensions and/or formal group problems exist (they were contending with technical problems that were delaying production as well as coordination challenges between the shifts); commitment by the formal leader to the intervention (the plant manager highly approved); informal leaders' support for and full involvement in all team development activities; members' desire to solve their problems; reasonable expectations about the process and its outcomes; and technically competent team members who respect each other and who will take responsibility for implementing changes that result from the team development (a recent review is provided by Boss & McConkie, 2008). A complete discussion of the case and the method is reported by Seibold (1995), and some portions of that piece will be used to show the more general steps in the team process consultation approach to team development discussed next (also see Seibold & Meyers, 2012 for a discussion of assumptions of team process consultations, tenets of team facilitation, and the values surrounding interventions to which I subscribe).

Given the "order" of dimensions on which teamwork development should proceed, I first work with team members to create an "agenda" for the team's work by categorizing *problems* members say they are facing. Using qualitative procedures (e.g., members' responses to open-ended questions such as "What is preventing this team from accomplishing all it can?") and quantitative techniques (e.g., surveys and research instruments), which members elaborate on in face-to-face sessions subsequently, team members and I classify the problems along the teamwork dimensions of processes, vision, roles, and relationships.

Second, members direct their attention to *processes* related to the team's structure, operations, and procedures. From the list in the first step, members readily identify operational/procedural problems that can *they* can solve quickly and without depending on management. Members' high involvement leads them to address, first, the problems that are most important to them and they are motivated to achieve—outcomes that will improve their own job satisfaction and the effectiveness of the team (Mathieu et al., 2008). This involvement of the two teams at BFSI occurred during portions of formal group meetings each week, and in informal discussions over meals and between shifts. As members see they are capable of improving work conditions concerning matters they face and consider important, their commitment to the team and to the rest of the team process development typically follows.

Third, members attempt to develop a shared *vision*. Discussion focuses on goals that have been set for the group, often by managers and administrators, including the extent to which members are aware of them and agree with them. Members engage whether they are capable of more than has been expected, or than they have achieved, and how realistic their emerging goals are. This often results in a vision of what "the team" desires, as well as how members desire to be viewed. These conversations were significant for BFSI team members. Theirs was a new plant, so they not only needed to deal with goal ambiguities from each of their parent firms but with how they desired to be seen by those companies. Furthermore, because team members represented the plant manager in sessions with many clients, they could now speak with one voice on behalf of the plant.

Fourth, I facilitate discussions concerning *role* dynamics associated with members' vision for their team. Conversations revolve around the following questions: Does each member understand and accept others' expectations of them? How will any member's desire to act beyond those role expectations be viewed? What are the implications of these role expectations and role enactments for each member's position on the informal status hierarchy in the team? Most of these issues were quickly resolved at BFSI, where members' prior jobs in self-directing or semi-autonomous in teams led them to accept roles for the good of the team.

Fifth, I attempt to aid members to improve *relationships* within the team. Typically, the majority of the relationship issues identified in the first step have been resolved at this point in the process (or are now judged not to be serious) because members needed to work together—and to move beyond interpersonal problems—on the other issues in prior steps. Conversations now move to how dyadic and group communication can be enhanced to improve and sustain members' relationships. Sometimes this is supplemented with training for the group, or coaching for individuals, in listening, communicating non-defensively, supportiveness and climate building, offering negative feedback, affirmative conflict, dialogue, and appreciative inquiry (Barge, 2001; Barge & Little, 2008; Barge & Oliver, 2003; Gouran, 2003; Seibold, 2005). At BFSI, conflict between two central members (and supporters formed around each member—creating subgroups—that then did not cooperate either) required attention. After several mediation sessions with both members, and ensuing "behavioral contracts" between them concerning what they would and would not do (as well as next steps if either felt the contract had not been honored), the two members met with the entire team. They accepted responsibility for divisiveness that had grown in the team as a result of their relationship, and they endeavored to foster better links between their supporters.

Team Workout Method

The second method for facilitating team development, "team workouts," take place in brief periods of time (often a day-long or two-day session) and aid members to identify problems they are interested in engaging and how they will proceed afterward. I often employ this method instead of the extended "team process consultation" if members have little time, if they have relatively few issues to engage, or if this is a follow-up to earlier, more extensive work together. The relative brevity of theses consultations is why this method is a "workout" (a term suggested by a collaborator many years ago as documented in Seibold & Meyers, 2012).

Team workouts occur in retreats away from the team's work area and in which all members participate. Beforehand, I interview each team member and create a summary of what members believe to be the team's strengths as well as issues that are preventing them from working together well. Each workout commences with a conversation about members' reports of team strengths and an effort to reach consensus on a list of them. Next, and facilitated in round-robin style, each member acknowledges each other member's contributions to those team strengths—an activity that results in members feeling some support from the entire team.

I then discuss the characteristics of "teamwork" reviewed earlier in this chapter. Members dialogue about the extent to which their group possesses those characteristics and whether they desire to be a "team." I share a summary of the challenges to teamwork voiced during the individual interviews, and those results are compared with limitations just expressed in the session. Members participate (in subgroups) in an exercise designed to clarify, elaborate, and finalize the list of "team issues" that is accessed in ensuing portions of the retreat and as an agenda for members' joint efforts at continuing team development after the session.

Members transition to a structured, two-hour discussion of actions they each pledge to undertake to ameliorate problems identified earlier in the session (and that will increase teamwork). Members often find this portion of the "workout" to be significant. First, as members recognize the efforts others are willing to make on behalf of the team, they realize that they cannot avoid social comparisons (Festinger, 1954) with their own commitments. Second, since members listen to what others commit to improve but can offer recommendations concerning other actions another might undertake to enhance teamwork, the role definitions and expectations (Berteotti & Seibold, 1994) embedded in these comments lead to role negotiations (Myers, Seibold, & Park, 2011). Third, if team members later perceive a teammate to have reneged on a commitment made during the workout, they have grounds to raise their concern. Fourth, members realize that issues on the team's list of problems/limitations are remediable based on what the members do (and they become cognizant that many of those problems are constituted in their interactions to begin with). Finally, there is recognition of members' interdependence and general acceptance of the need for (and value of) communication, commitment, and collaboration if the team is to succeed and members are to be satisfied.

During the last two hours of the workout, members move beyond what is their own sphere of control to what may be in their sphere of influence (Covey, 1989). They identify persons outside the immediate group whom they need to influence in order to solve problems that are outside their own control and are adversely affecting teamwork and team effectiveness. Discussions include determination of what resources are needed to improve the team, and who can secure them. Managers or administrators participate in the ultimate session, attending to the team's requests and pledging their own commitments for how they will assist. I circulate these commitments to members the next day, together with a summary of the personal actions to which each team member committed earlier in the retreat. The list of team "issues" from early rounds, as well as the summary of all members' and all stakeholders' commitments, are critical for ensuing efforts by the team, a plan they develop together as the last activity during the workout. Colleagues and I also have employed the workout method of team development with several groups from the same organization (they work simultaneously and in parallel through these steps across two days) as part of a large-scale organizational change project.

Critical Praxis and Reflexivity

The team process consultation and team workout methods are associated with first-generation and second-generation planned change interventions in organizations (Austin & Bartunek, 2003; Seo, Putnam, & Bartunek, 2004). The team development perspective is part and parcel of third-generation approaches to interventions discussed by Bartunek, Austin, and Seo (2008), for it involves implementing—through critical praxis and reflexivity—enhanced versions of either of the two team interventions above.

Critical praxis entails continuous reflection about practice (Pedlar, 2005). More than only personal reflection, as a dyadic or group activity critical praxis also can enable members to jointly reflect on problems they are identifying. This is particularly important for understanding and facilitating *teamwork*. I do not employ critical praxis as a sequential process of activities that are distinct from each other, as with the first two methods, but as a perspective to be integrated with those methods.

As a colleague and I wrote, "we have gravitated toward critical praxis through conscious commitment to ongoing reflection on what, why, and how *we* practice team facilitation and whether, why, and in what ways *members* engage teamwork processes (those we seek to facilitate and their own)" (Seibold & Meyers, 2012, p. 434). Critical praxis invites repeated questioning, including questioning teamwork processes and structures. It inevitably brings to the foreground of consideration team members' concerns as much as their achievements. As a practice, then, critical praxis facilitates teamwork processes about which members are in dialogue, but the practice of using this perspective (Holmes et al., 2005) can also create spirit of teamwork among those engaged in joint reflection.

Seibold and Kang (2008) supply a detailed case of a municipal human services agency involving team development among members of an information support group (SST) in the agency. Throughout a period of several months in which I utilized both team process consultation and a team workout, members' reflexivity led to many alterations in how those two methods were appropriated by the SST (several examples are summarized by Seibold and Meyers, 2012, and I reprise some of them next).

For example, the team development intervention was initiated by a request to me from the team members (as I consulted with the professionals they supported), not from their manager (who had contracted for team development with only the team of professionals). Since members engaged in critical praxis are encouraged to be curious about the grounds for any policy or practice, SST members' discussion when we subsequently were working together turned to whether their manager valued them as much as the professionals whom they supported. In turn, I reflected on whether my consultations in this and other organizations were reproducing managerial bias (Deetz, 2001).

As another example of critical praxis in this team development case, during preparations with SST members for their workout retreat, team members' discussion about their roles in—and responsibility for—the team intervention (compared with mine as the facilitator) led to alterations in the team workout. Team members asked me to conduct the preliminary interviews with all members together instead of singly. Furthermore, I did not create the agenda; they did. They also formulated the outcomes they most sought from the session. Toward those ends, they also took on the role of preparing several procedures and activities that they wanted to "try out." Consequently, my role in that team development consultation changed from to co-leader and collaborator, to providing feedback, and to assisting with gathering resources. The members even invited their manager to enter into conversations with them, during which routine practices at the agency were critiqued. Thereafter, and after reflecting (Barge, 2004) on the disparity between how much she had first committed resources to development of the professionals' team, the manager increased her commitment to the SST's development (and even to teamwork in the top management team of which she was a part).

During my extended team process consultation with the SST, members' intentionally reflexive discussions during times they set aside also led to me to change my method of team process consultation with them. Members of the same subgroup that had planned the workout led the weekly follow-ups, not me. SST members of the SST all took a turn on the planning team and subsequent activities. My role became one of reflecting upon and reinforcing how members' actions were actually teamwork in and of themselves (Cunliffe, 2004). The team's processes of structured activity, evaluation/reflection, and interaction prompted them to request being reorganized into a single team. Of course, this proposal was not without tension among the members and with their manager. However, at this point in their development they also had the capability to manage intragroup conflict (although it still remains unresolved).

Many of the changes noted by Seibold and Kang (2008) and sketched above are now standard operating procedure in both the team process consultations and team workouts in which I engage. Of course, in the spirit of critical praxis, they too can be altered whenever members' reflexivity (or my own) surfaces awareness of still other issues that invite further alterations of the first two methods.

PRACTICE ⟵→ RESEARCH

A central point in this chapter is that *theory/research* concerning embedded organizational work groups and *practice* in team development consultations with such groups can be mutually informing. The discussion thus far has illustrated many ways in which I have relied on theory/research in the design, implementation, and assessment of the three approaches to team development. To these I would add that, as a scholar, I also am aware of research measures that I can utilize to support my consultations related to team development. I have utilized the Organizational Listening Survey (Cooper, Seibold, & Suchner, 1997), the Small Group Relational Satisfaction Scale (Anderson, Martin, & Riddle, 2001), and the Organizational Temporality Scale (Ballard & Seibold, 2004) as part of the multi-method first step in the extended team process consultation method. Data collected using these instruments yield sensitizing feedback to team members. They also proffer team-level diagnostics that can help "unfreeze" the group (particularly when members are accustomed to working with aggregated data, statistical displays, and population norms). I have even used these measures to evaluate overtime changes in a team.

At the same time, Seibold and Meyers (2012) discuss a number of ways in which team development interventions offer opportunities for case studies, lines of research, and theory development. In closing, I draw on several examples from that work that also were drawn from my team development consultations with embedded organizational work groups. To begin, in most consultations with teams, any data I gather with the team(s) or with individual members are confidential. When relationships with the teams have led to research reports for scholars, the publications have been case studies for the most part (e.g., interventions reported in Seibold, 1995; Seibold & Kang, 2008). Although case studies are limited to a single entity, as with the embedded organizational team(s) in my cases, since they are informed by data collected through a variety of methods and over a sustained period of time, they yield detailed analyses (Cresswell, 2003).

The insights emerging from case studies—and other qualitative approaches (Tracy & Geist-Martin, 2014)—encourage comparisons with the findings from major reviews of multiple studies of multiple groups that may prove heuristic (in the area of teamwork, cf. Kozlowski & Ilgen, 2006). Practice-based case studies also can generate research. My immersion in embedded organizational work groups over protracted periods of time has led to entire lines of research, such as that on "innovation modification" by teams participating in organizations' planned change programs (Lewis & Seibold, 1993; 1996; 1998), which was admirably extended by Laurie Lewis. These consultations also have made me aware of the "dark side" of teams and to develop a model (Seibold et al., 2009). Too, these engagements have encouraged me to publish work analyzing my practices and the genre of interventions of which they are part (Seibold, 2005), such as third-generation organizational development interventions (Bartunek et al., 2008) and relative to modes of inquiry (e.g., critical praxis in Seibold & Kang, 2008). Finally, consulting has the potential to alert scholars to ways they can or should buttress their own conceptual and theoretical stances. For example, in my own theorizing, I was led to emphasize the central role of groups in mediating individual-organization relationships (Seibold, 1998). In turn, my theoretical perspective concerning members' structuring activities and group structuration (Seibold & Meyers, 2007) has sensitized me as a consultant to processes and interactions in all three methods of team development. By extension, these consultations have strengthened my view that organizationally embedded teams are constituted in their interactions over time relative to task assignment, interdependence, goal achievement, and member satisfaction (Seibold et al., 2009). While enabled (and constrained) by the conditions of the organization in which they are embedded, team structures nevertheless are constituted in members' communication—with increasingly formal structures (and team sustainability) becoming evident across increasingly lengthy time spans of members working together.

There is a crying need for research concerning the effectiveness of team development and team communication facilitation, and Hartwig and Frey (2007) offer means for filling that gap. Furthermore, as Seibold and Meyers (2012) propose, with attention to method, careful planning, proper assessment, mutual respect, credible execution, wisdom, and experience, consultants can provide valuable insight, practical interventions, and often-successful solutions to team development puzzles. And when those consultants are scholars, there are opportunities for their research and practice to be mutually informing.

REFERENCES

Anderson, C. M., Martin, M. M., & Riddle, B. L. (2001). Small group relational satisfaction scale: Development, reliability, and validity. *Communication Studies, 52,* 220–233.

Arrow, H., McGrath, J. E., & Berdahl, J. L. (2000). *Small groups as complex systems: Formation, coordination, development, and adaptation.* Thousand Oaks, CA: SAGE Publications.

Austin, J., & Bartunek, L. (2003). Theories and practices of organizational development. In W. Borman, D. Ilgen, & R. Klimoski (Eds.), *Handbook of psychology: Industrial and organizational psychology* (Vol. 12, pp. 309–332). New York, NY: John Wiley & Sons.

Ballard, D. I., & Seibold, D. R. (2004). Organizational members' communication and temporal experience: Scale development and validation. *Communication Research, 31*, 135–172.

Barge, J. K. (2001). Creating healthy communities through affirmative conflict communication. *Conflict Resolution Quarterly, 19*, 89–102.

Barge, J. K. (2004). Reflexivity and managerial practice. *Communication Monographs, 71*, 70–96.

Barge, J. K., & Oliver, C. (2003). Working with appreciation in managerial practice. *Academy of Management Review, 28*, 124–142.

Barge, J. K., & Little, M. (2008). A discursive approach to skillful activity. *Communication Theory, 18*, 505–534.

Barker, J., & Cheney, G. (1994). The concept and practice of discipline in contemporary organizational life. *Communication Monographs, 61*, 19–43.

Barker, V. E., Abrams, J. R., Tiyaamornwong, V., Seibold, D. R., Duggan, A., Park, S. H., & Sebastian, M. (2000). New contexts for relational communication in groups. *Small Group Research, 31*, 470–503.

Bartunek, J. M., Austin, J. R., & Seo, M. G. (2008). Conceptual underpinnings of intervening in organizations. In T. G. Cummings (Ed.), *Handbook of organizational development* (pp. 151–166). Los Angeles, CA: SAGE Publications.

Beer, M. (1976). The technology of organization development. In M. D. Dunnette (Ed.), *Handbook of industrial and organizational psychology* (pp. 937–994). Chicago, IL: Rand-McNally.

Berteotti, C. R., & Seibold, D. R. (1994). Coordination and role-definition problems in health care teams: A hospice case study. In L. R. Frey (Ed.), *Group communication in context: Studies of natural groups* (pp. 107–131). Hillsdale, NJ: Lawrence Erlbaum.

Boss, R. W., & McConkie, M. L. (2008). Team building. In T. G. Cummings (Ed.), *Handbook of organizational development* (pp. 237–259). Los Angeles, CA: SAGE Publications.

Buller, P. F., & Bell, C. H. (1986). Effects of team building and goal setting on productivity: A field experiment. *Academy of Management Journal, 29*, 305–328.

Cohen, S. G., & Bailey, D. E. (1997). What makes teams work: Group effectiveness research from shop floor to the executive suite. *Journal of Management, 23*, 239–290.

Cooper, L. O., Seibold, D. R., & Suchner, R. (1997). Listening in organizations: An analysis of error structures in models of listening competency. *Communication Research Reports, 14*, 312–320.

Covey, S. R. (1989). *The 7 habits of highly effective people.* New York, NY: Simon & Schuster.

Cresswell, J. W. (2003). *Research design: Qualitative & quantitative approaches.* Thousand Oaks, CA: SAGE Publications.

Cummings, T. G., & Worley, G. (2005). *Organization development and change* (8th ed.). Cincinnati, OH: Southwestern.

Cunliffe, A. (2004). On becoming a critically reflexive practitioner. *Journal of Management Education, 28*, 407–426.

Deetz, S. (2001). Conceptual foundations. In F. M. Jablin & L. L. Putnam (Eds.), *The new handbook of organizational communication: Advances in theory, research, and methods* (2nd ed.) (pp. 3–46). Thousand Oaks, CA: SAGE Publications.

Dyer, W. G. (1995). *Team building: Current issues and new alternatives* (3rd ed.). Reading, MA: Addison-Wesley.

Festinger, L. (1954). A theory of social comparison processes. *Human Relations, 7*, 117–140.

Franken, L., & Seibold, D. R. (2010). Business process modeling at the Internal Funding Office: Structuring group interaction processes to structure business processes. In L. Black (Ed.), *Group communication: Cases for analysis, appreciation, and application* (pp. 17–24). Dubuque, IA: Kendall Hunt.

Gouran, D. S. (2003). Communication skills for group decision making. In J. O. Greene & B. R. Burleson (Eds.), *Handbook of communication and social interaction skills* (pp. 835–870). Mahwah, NJ: Lawrence Erlbaum Associates.

Greenbaum, H. H., & Query, J. L. (1999). Communication in organizational work groups: A review and analysis of natural work groups. In L. R. Frey, D. S. Gouran, & M. S. Poole (Eds.), *The handbook of group communication theory and research* (pp. 539–564). Thousand Oaks, CA: SAGE Publications.

Hackman, J. R. (1990). *Groups that work (and those that don't): Creating conditions for effective teamwork*. San Francisco, CA: Jossey-Bass.

Hackman, R. J. (2004, June). What makes for a great team? *APA Science Briefs, 18* Washington, DC: American Psychological Association.

Hackman, R. J., & Edmondson, A. C. (2008). Groups as agents of change. In T. G. Cummings (Ed.), *Handbook of organizational development* (pp. 167–186). Los Angeles, CA: Sage.

Hartwig, R. T., & Frey, L. R. (2007, November). *Facilitating team communication facilitation.* Paper presented at the annual meeting of the National Communication Association. Chicago, IL.

Holmes, P., Cockburn-Wootten, C., Motion, J., Zorn, T. E., & Roper, J. (2005). Critical reflexive practice in teaching management communication. *Business Communication Quarterly, 68*, 247–256.

Kozlowski, S. W. J., & Ilgen, D. R. (2006). Enhancing the effectiveness of work groups and teams. *Psychological Science in the Public Interest, 7*, 77–124.

Krikorian, D., Seibold, D. R., & Goode, P. L. (1997). Re-engineering at LAC: A case study of emergent network processes. In B. D. Sypher (Ed.), *Case studies in organizational communication* (2nd ed., pp. 129–144). New York, NY: Guilford.

LaFasto, F., & Larson, C. (2001). *When teams work best.* Thousand Oaks, CA: Sage.

Lawler, E. E. (1995). *Creating high-performance organizations.* San Francisco, CA: Jossey-Bass.

Lewis, L. K., & Seibold, D. R. (1993). Innovation modification during intra-organizational adoption. *Academy of Management Review, 18*, 322–354.

Lewis, L. K., & Seibold, D. R. (1996). Communication during intra-organizational innovation adoption: Predicting users' behavioral coping responses to innovations in organizations. *Communication Monographs, 63*, 131–157.

Lewis, L. K., & Seibold, D. R. (1998). Reconceptualizing organizational change implementation as a communication problem: A review of literature and research agenda. In M. E. Roloff (Ed.), *Communication yearbook 21* (pp. 93–151). Thousand Oaks, CA: SAGE Publications.

Mathieu, J., Maynard, M. T., Rapp, T, & Gilson. L. (2008). Team effectiveness 1997–2007: A review of recent advancements and a glimpse into the future. *Journal of Management, 34*, 410–476.

Myers, K. K., Seibold, D. S., & Park, H. S. (2011). Interpersonal communication in the workplace. In M. C. Knapp & J. A. Daly (Eds.), *The SAGE handbook of interpersonal communication* (4th ed.) (pp. 527–562). Thousand Oaks, CA: SAGE Publications.

O'Toole, J., & Lawler, E. E. III (2006). *The new American workplace.* New York, NY: Palgrave.

Pedlar, M. (2005). A general theory of human action. *Action Learning: Research and Practice, 2*, 127–132.

Poole, M. S. (1991). Procedures for managing meetings: Social and technological innovation. In R. A. Swenson & B. O. Knapp (Eds.), *Innovative meeting management* (pp. 53–109). Austin, TX: 3M Meeting Management Institute.

Rousseau, V., Aubé, C., & Savoie, A. (2006). Teamwork behaviors: A review and an integration of frameworks. *Small Group Research, 37*, 540–570.

Schein, E. H. (1988). *Process consultation: IT roles in organizational development* (2nd ed.). Upper Saddle River, NJ: Prentice-Hall.

Seibold, D. R. (1990). Management communication issues in family businesses: The case of Oak Ridge Trucking Company. In B. D. Sypher (Ed.), *Case studies in organizational communication* (pp. 163–176). New York, NY: Guilford.

Seibold, D. R. (1995). Developing the "team" in a team-managed organization: Group facilitation in a new plant design. In L. R. Frey (Ed.), *Innovations in group facilitation techniques: Case studies of applications in naturalistic settings* (pp. 282–298). Cresskill, NJ: Hampton.

Seibold, D. R. (1998). Groups and organizations: Premises and perspectives. In J. S. Trent (Ed.), *Communication: Views from the helm for the twenty-first century* (pp. 162–168). Needham Heights, MA: Allyn & Bacon.

Seibold, D. R. (2005). Bridging theory and practice in organizational communication. In J. L. Simpson & P. Shockley-Zalabak (Eds.), *Engaging communication, transforming organizations: Scholarship of engagement in action* (pp. 13–44). Cresskill, NJ: Hampton.

Seibold, D. R., Hollingshead, A. B., & Yoon, K. (2014). Embedded teams and embedding organizations. In L. L. Putnam & D. K. Mumby (Eds.), *The SAGE handbook of organizational communication: Advances in theory, research, and methods* (3rd ed., pp. 327–349). Thousand Oaks, CA: SAGE Publications.

Seibold, D. R., & Kang, P. (2008). Using critical praxis to understand and teach teamwork. *Business Communication Quarterly, 71*, 421–438.

Seibold, D. R., Kang, P., Gailliard, B. M., & Jahn, J. (2009). Communication that damages teamwork: The dark side of teams. In P. Lutgen-Sandvik & B. Davenport Sypher (Eds.), *Destructive organizational communication: Processes, consequences, and constructive ways of organizing* (pp. 267–289). New York, NY: Routledge/Taylor & Francis.

Seibold, D. R., Lemus, D. R., Ballard, D. I., & Myers, K. K. (2009). Organizational communication and applied communication research: Parallels, intersections, integration, and engagement. In L. R. Frey & K. N. Cissna (Eds.), *Routledge handbook of applied communication research* (pp. 331–354). New York, NY: Routledge/Taylor & Francis.

Seibold, D. R., & Meyers, R. A. (2007). Group argument: A structuration perspective and research program. *Small Group Research, 38*, 312–336.

Seibold, D. R., & Meyers, R. A. (2012). Interventions in groups: Methods for facilitating team development. In A. B. Hollingshead & M. S. Poole (Eds.), *Research methods for studying groups and teams: A guide to approaches, tools, and technologies* (pp. 418–441). New York, NY: Taylor & Francis/Routledge.

Seo, M., Putnam, L. L., & Bartunek, J. M. (2004). Dualities and tensions of planned organizational change. In M. S. Poole & A. H. Van de Ven (Eds.), *Handbook of organizational change and innovation* (pp. 73–107). New York, NY: Oxford University Press.

SunWolf, & Seibold, D. R. (1999). The impact of formal procedures on group processes, members, and task outcomes. In L. R. Frey (Ed.), *The handbook of group communication theory and research* (pp. 395–431). Thousand Oaks, CA: SAGE Publications.

Tompkins, P. K., & Cheney, G. (1985). Communication and unobtrusive control in contemporary organizations. In R. D. McPhee & P. K. Tompkins (Eds.), *Organizational communication: Traditional themes and new directions* (pp. 179–210). Newbury Park, CA: SAGE Publications.

Tracy, S. J., & Geist-Martin, P. (2014). Organizing ethnography and qualitative approaches. In L. L. Putnam & D. K. Mumby (Eds.), *The SAGE handbook of organizational communication: Advances in theory, research, and methods* (3rd ed., pp. 245–269). Thousand Oaks, CA: SAGE Publications.

CHAPTER TWELVE

Facilitating Training

When Organizational Members' Skills Need to Be Addressed

MARIAN HOUSER

Texas State University

> *Organizational change requires an instructional orientation because consultants act as teachers whenever they are involved in assessment and intervention with the goal of facilitating organizational change.* (Dallimore & Souza, 2002, p. 86)

Training, a specific type of consulting intervention, is aimed at developing organizational members' skills in target areas that can enhance organizational outcomes. Trainers impart knowledge, and promote the practice and implementation of critical skills. Communication is pivotal in the trainer's repertoire of skills. To be effective, one must understand the transactional nature of communication in training—the constant exchange of messages to achieve shared meaning and understanding (McCroskey & Richmond, 1996). This chapter offers a framework for viewing training as a communication event, and for designing it effectively. Further, it addresses trainers' skills, attitudes, and behaviors important to effective learning in organizational settings.

This chapter is framed by two important theoretical assumptions. The first is that of *andragogy*, a theory of adult learning that suggests that adults have unique characteristics important to consider in the design, delivery, and assessment of training. Training requires that the consultant develop and implement programs based on a consideration of what participants need; already know and are doing in their work; and will perceive as useful, purposeful, and relevant. The second critical assumption of this chapter is the *instructional communication perspective*. Acknowledging the value of communication in training and development, demonstrated through a breadth and depth of empirical research, will aid in an understanding of the important behaviors and concerns necessary for facilitating adults' learning and development.

WHAT IS INSTRUCTIONAL COMMUNICATION?

Instructional communication, an interest area within communication studies, is informed by three disciplines: *pedagogy/andragogy* (teaching), *educational psychology* (learning), and *communication*, which enables teaching and learning. Because the goal of training and development is to create lasting knowledge and skills, the successful trainer must rely on all three of these disciplines. In my work at Texas State University developing future educators and trainers, my objective is to establish communication as the foundation for learning. A trainer may teach a group how to use a software program, for example, but trainees learn how to use it only if their communication with the trainer is effective. In other words, it is not enough to know the subject matter; effective trainers know that "message sent ≠ message received." Competent trainers acknowledge the current skills, attitudes, behaviors, and needs of learners and meet them, through competent instructional communication, to build new knowledge and skills. What follows is a discussion of the three components of instructional communication.

What Is Andragogy?

The art, science, and strategy of teaching adults is known as **andragogy**. Specifically, adult professionals: (a) need to know why they should learn something, (b) prefer experiential learning, (c) approach learning as problem solving, and (d) learn best when the topic is of apparent value to them (Knowles, 1980). Trainers must begin by setting training objectives. The questions then become "How do I teach it?" and "How do I know my students/trainees/clients learned what I wanted them to learn?" This is where adults must be approached differently than children. In order to ensure understanding and learning, the trainer must specify instructional methods and an assessment plan that correlate to their objectives, with the principles of adult learning in mind. Shortly, we will explore a four-part process for designing, delivering, and assessing training that accounts for the unique nature of adult learners.

Educational Psychology and the Domains of Learning

Second, to develop effective training, consultants must have an understanding of *educational psychology*, or the general science of how people learn. Consider, "Why have I been hired? What does this group need to know and be able to do?" As important as the content of training might be, trainers must define learning goals for training first, and the science of educational psychology provides some insight for doing so. Specifically, there are three domains, or goals, of learning (Bloom, 1956) critical to trainers' work: (a) *cognitive* (trainees' ability to recall, comprehend, and apply training content; and analyze, synthesize, and evaluate what they are learning during training relative to existing knowledge frameworks); (b) *affective* (the formation of trainees' positive attitudes toward your content and the training experience); and (c) *behavioral* (related to trainee skill acquisition [e.g., presentational speaking, effective telephone or email use, how to perform a series of steps related to customer service, negotiating a conflict with a coworker, or implementing a process for dealing with a customer complaint]). Waldeck (2014) offers an in-depth exploration of the three domains of learning and how they intersect. For now, it is important to understand three things: (a) the distinctions among the three learning goals; (b) that they are empirically related to one another (e.g., affect is a precursor to cognitive gains and motivation to use recommended behaviors [Rodriguez, Plax, & Kearney, 1996]); and (c) trainers' actions relevant to instruction before, during, and after training have a powerful influence on trainee cognitive, affective, and behavioral development.

For example, Scott et al. (2008) reported on a project that involved the development of a worksite wellness program for ski resorts. Specifically, the consulting team's goal was to promote understanding (cognitive learning) and enthusiasm about sun safety (affective learning), and to teach skills (behavioral learning) relative to sun protection and skin cancer prevention. The cognitive goal of awareness about the dangers of unprotected sun exposure was just the first step; participants also needed to develop positive motivation to protect themselves, and to learn the behaviors and skills necessary for protection. The consulting team's own communication competence and ability to train, with the principles of effective instructional communication as a backdrop for their work, were essential for addressing all three learning goals.

Communication as a Key to Learning

In addition to andragogy and educational psychology, the third component that frames training is the communication among learners and trainers. As the trainer and his or her participants exchange verbal and nonverbal messages, they create understanding with important implications for trainees' learning and subsequent application of training content. More effective communication will result in more accurate understanding; less effective communication will yield misunderstandings. Important to effective communication in the training context are trainer communication skills and subject matter expertise. Additionally, research illuminates the impact of peer-to-peer communication on learning. Referred to as student-student connectedness or classroom connectedness (Dwyer, et al., 2004), numerous studies have revealed the value of learners working together for creating positive affect and enhancing learning (Frisby & Martin, 2010; Glaser & Bingham, 2009; Sollitto, Johnson, & Myers, 2013). In organizations, this connectedness can contribute to organizational assimilation and identification (Jablin, 1982; Jablin & Krone, 1987; Miller & Jablin, 1991)—positive, desirable outcomes. In other words, the trainer's communication is very important for creating understanding and facilitating the achievement of training objectives. However, to attain maximum immediate and long-term results, the trainer must also create conditions in which training participants collaborate.

INSTRUCTIONAL DESIGN PPPA: PLAN, PREPARE, PRESENT, AND ASSESS

No intervention will be successful and no cognitive, affective, or behavioral outcomes realized without a sound instructional communication design plan. Successful training involves designing content and instructional methods that allow participants to apply their new knowledge (Saks & Belcourt, 2006). Thus, trainers need instructional design skills. One useful and concise description of the process through which trainers might develop their training and bring concepts to life for learners is the *Plan, Prepare, Present, Assess* (PPPA) model (Beebe, Mottet, & Roach, 2013). Even if a consultant lacks extensive training in the science of instructional design, this framework will help him or her organize, develop, deliver, and evaluate instructional programs. Without a carefully developed PPPA, the consultant risks a haphazard training plan characterized by messages and activities that can block learning outcomes. What follows is a description of each of the four stages of instructional design included in the PPPA model.

Plan

The planning stage is critical for ensuring that trainer and client agree on the learning objectives of the program. Jorgensen (Chapter 5) and Waldeck, Plax, and Kearney (Chapter 7) discuss the conversations consultants must have with clients (and employees of the client organizations) to define appropriate, valid objectives. Training objectives must be specific enough to direct the planning of instructional activities, which will facilitate the transfer of knowledge from training to the worksite. Additionally, objectives must be measureable (Hutchins & Burke, 2007). For example, if a trainer asks participants to engage in a role-play activity to determine their understanding of conflict management skills, he or she must specify what constitutes good conflict management (e.g., a calm demeanor and control of negative nonverbal facial expressions), and then assess participants' ability to demonstrate those component behaviors. The results of assessment, then, will indicate the success of the program, serve as a measure of accomplishment for participants, and illustrate return on investment for clients (Phillips, 2003).

To accomplish measurability, trainers begin by creating a list of what trainees should know (cognitive objectives) and master (behavioral objectives), and attitudes they should develop (affective objectives) as a result of training. For each domain of learning, trainers may have multiple goals. To develop objectives, consider the following prompts: "Upon completing training, participants will:

(a) *understand...*;
(b) *be able to do...*: and
(c) *possess the following attitudes...about....*"

Reevaluate each item on the list to ensure its measurability, and consider, "Will I know it when I see it?" and "What tool will I use to determine success?"

Prepare

Preparation involves gathering necessary resources for meeting the predefined goals and objectives. More specifically, once the trainer has developed objectives, he or she must consider, "What do I need to communicate to participants, and how will I do this in order to facilitate their understanding?" and "What resources will assist me in garnering their participation and practice the skills the client and I have agreed should result from training?"

This phase requires you to (a) write the content of your session(s); (b) design or select participant activities; (c) obtain equipment (e.g., a microphone for public speaking practice, point-of-sale terminals for customer service practice, audience response systems/clickers for trainee participation); (d) develop or gather training materials (e.g., digital slides, handouts, images, charts, videos, audio, models); and (e) craft specific communication strategies within the training plan (e.g., planned nonverbal cues, specific examples, and humor).

Brown et al.'s (2010) case study of a training session designed to heighten patient-centered communication among oncology fellows illustrates the importance of preparation. The consultants spent a substantial amount of time preparing a training booklet (which included learning objectives, a review of literature, an outline, homework, and a reference list); digital slides to support instructional modules, a set of demonstration video clips, and role-play scenarios for participants to practice effective physician/patient communication. Trainers' attention to detail in the preparation phase, as illustrated in the example we just considered, is critical for ensuring the accomplishment of training objectives. The more specific and concrete a trainer's preparation, the more likely that facilitation/presentation will run smoothly and objectives will be accomplished.

Present

This stage involves the actual delivery of training. If a trainer is, for example, conducting a workshop with the overall objective of ensuring physicians can effectively communicate with their patients, the planning and preparation stages have already illuminated what knowledge must be taught, and through which methods. Now it is time to execute the behavioral and affective component of the plan.

The value of learning via experience highlighted by Knowles (1980) has long been understood. John Dewey's (1938/1997) assertion that "...there is an ultimate and necessary relation between the processes of actual experience and education" illustrates the timeless importance of experiential learning. What this means for trainers is the importance of creating an environment that allows participants to discuss how the content is relevant and applies to their work.

The E*D*I*T model of instructional design (Lundy, 1996; Myers & Myers, 1985) offers trainers a four-step approach to creating participant experiences during the delivery stage. Specifically, learning follows a structure that begins with a discussion of trainees' experiences in training and then illustrates how trainees can *transfer those experiences to their actual work*. If this does not occur, "chances are good that there will be failure" (Lundy, 1996, p. 91). *Transfer* refers to trainees' ability to generalize what they learned in training back to the work environment (Baldwin & Ford, 1988), and is a significant challenge for training professionals. Research indicates that training participants transfer a very small percentage of what they learn to their jobs and workplace activities (Fitzpatrick, 2001). Implementation of the E*D*I*T method holds promise for boosting transfer.

The four steps of E*D*I*T—Experience, Describe, Infer, and Transfer—are separated by symbolic asterisks, which serve as a reminder that participants must be involved in each step of the process during training in order for them to successfully transfer what they learned to their work (Myers & Myers, 1985). Each step is consistent with Bloom's hierarchical taxonomy of cognitive learning, where participants move from basic knowledge to synthesis and useful application.

Experience (E). Experience is the first step in the application of training knowledge. In order to determine whether trainees have actually learned important material and know how to enact the knowledge, behaviors, or attitudes recommended, engage them in a pre-planned training experience. Discussions and activities like case studies, role-plays, and simulations work well. For example, in training team members to manage conflict through active listening, the trainer may teach paraphrasing skills. After presenting a conceptual overview of paraphrasing and offering sufficient relevant examples, the trainer might engage learners in a role-play activity so they can demonstrate and experience the skill. The key is to create an experience with sufficient impact and significance such that participants really "get it." When trainers trigger engagement and involvement, participants have an experience that they can then describe and discuss—and the trainer has distinguished him or herself from those who merely transmit information as one who has a real impact on participants.

Describe (D). Here, the trainer's role is to guide participants in a description of what they saw, heard, thought, and felt during the experience stage. For this step to be effective, the trainer must establish ground rules for what is to be discussed in this step of the E*D*I*T process, and remind participants of the need for descriptive, concrete language in discussing their experiences. Participant descriptions must be limited to what is observed or observable. Participants should withhold inferences, judgments, and hypotheses about what they've learned and experienced until the next step of the session. Descriptive statements are those that can be verified by recalling or reviewing the experience without making evaluations or judgments.

Focusing only on the observed experience may be a difficult concept for participants—especially on subjects of personal importance. Even skilled trainers might be challenged to manage this phase of the process, because trainees are typically inclined to go beyond mere description and discuss why they did what they did, why they felt what they felt, or why the recommended behavior will or will not work for them. Trainees will likely leap to inferences, make generalizations, stereotype, or bring up their own biases about activities and people. Effective trainers gently confront participant comments that go beyond description. Myers and Myers (1985) recommended recording descriptions on a whiteboard or flipchart to keep participants focused on the goal of making objective, descriptive statements.

This part of the E*D*I*T sequence helps trainers guide participants in reviewing and reflecting on the actual experience of engaging in recommended behaviors. For example, trainers might ask what was said or done during a simulation of the visioning element of strategic planning. Ask probing questions (e.g., "What happened when Steve asked you to avoid discussing available resources and just brainstorm freely?" or "What did your teammates say/do when you proposed your idea?") to get them talking about what they experienced—what they experienced in being assertive in communicating ideas and brainstorming freely without negative, limited thinking about scarce resources. This step sets the stage for the last two steps of the E*D*I*T process.

Infer (I). In this step, participants infer general principles, concepts, or hypotheses that might be developed from their personal descriptions of their training experiences. Recall our earlier example of a conflict management role-play in which trainees learned and practiced paraphrasing skills. In the inference stage, the trainer should encourage participants to relate their experiences (e.g., from the conflict management role-play) back to the cognitive items or skills that were initially presented prior to the training activity (e.g., the importance of paraphrasing to manage understanding and control tensions during conflict). For example, Brown et al. (2010) discussed communication skills training aimed at clinicians

working with cancer patients. When participants observed video role-plays of simulated doctor-patient interactions, they inferred or interpreted all of their previous
descriptions of their own communication experiences through the lens of what
was recommended in the video. At this stage, the trainer asked questions such as
"What specific emotions does the doctor convey to the patient nonverbally? How
do you know this; what did you see? How does the patient react to this emotion?"

An essential question to ask participants in this step is: "What have you
learned from the experience?" Statements should come from the experience provided in training (e.g., the conflict management role-play or video simulations)
rather than from any prior or outside experiences. Trainers should limit inferences
to those issues that emerged in descriptions of that particular training experience. Additionally, insist that inferential comments be grounded in concepts presented during the workshop (e.g., elements of communication skills training and
patient-centered communication principles).

Transfer (T). This step of training delivery involves preparing learners to transfer training content to their everyday work experiences in useful ways. Effective
trainers find ways to explain how learners might use a particular aspect of training
content in other situations and guide participants in identifying opportunities for
transfer as well. The idea is to illustrate how the content applies to everyday life
within a particular context as well as to answer the "so what?" question for trainees
(and then guide them in discovering the answer). Useful questions to ask include,
"How would you put this to work for you?" and "How would you use the concepts/
strategies/methods you saw developing in this discussion?"

One of the most critical (and exciting) parts of the training process is when
learners use their new knowledge outside the training environment. Effective
trainers understand the value of encouraging participants to discuss the usefulness
of these concepts/skills/methods. They facilitate understanding of how trainees
might respond to different organizational events and demands with what they
learned in training. Transfer ensures that future behaviors can be improved with
the knowledge and skills acquired during training experiences.

Assess

The final stage of the PPPA is *assessment*. In order to determine the success of
training, the consultant must systematically assess whether the objectives developed at the outset of the plan have been realized. Assessment can be accomplished
by participant self-evaluation methods and testing strategies designed to assess
knowledge acquisition and skill performance. Great trainers don't wait to see how
participants perform on summative assessments; they engage learners in formative assessments during training, which helps them address lingering questions,
skill deficiencies, and/or knowledge gaps. Examples of self-evaluation techniques

include "muddiest thoughts," where the trainer takes a break between content modules and asks trainees to briefly and anonymously write about elements of the training that remain unclear, and "personal thought inventories," where participants reflect and write about, or share with others, their thoughts on how they might employ training content in actual work situations.

Formal, summative evaluations of trainee performance, administered after training, assess participant accomplishment of training objectives. Surveys, tests, or interviews can measure cognitive and affective outcomes. Demonstrations and observations can measure behavioral learning. Important to all evaluation are the criteria of reliability and validity (see Jorgensen, Chapter 5).

In addition to measuring immediate training outcomes, trainers and their clients should consider ways to measure long-term outcome indicators of the impact, benefits, or changes resulting from training (Waldeck, Kearney, & Plax, 2013). For example, the trainer may consider asking participants to set performance goals for specified future times, such as 30 days or 6 months after training, and design assessments that can be administered at that time. Trainers should also evaluate the role of third-party stakeholders, such as supervisors or clients/customers in assessing training participants. For instance, changes in client satisfaction survey data might represent one long-term indicator of customer service skills or problem resolution training effectiveness. Finally, Waldeck et al. suggest evaluating trainee perceptions of trainer effectiveness.

Although it may seem simple and intuitive to create an assessment of trainee learning, trainers should rely only on psychometrically sound, empirically tested instruments. The Mental Measurements Yearbook database produced by the Buros Center for Testing at the University of Nebraska contains over 3000 contemporary testing measures. Numerous valid and reliable instruments created by communication researchers enable trainers to measure participants' skills (e.g., to evaluate trainees in a conflict management workshop on their ability to manage contentious conversations, consider Burleson and Samter's [1990] Communication Functions Questionnaire). These are available in peer-reviewed journals and on scholars' personal websites. The late James C. McCroskey's website contains an extensive collection of communication skills measures (http://jamescmcroskey.com). As well, proprietary testing and consulting companies sell licenses to valid and reliable tests, and will provide computation and interpretation of trainee results on a number of outcomes.

DELIVERING TRAINING: WHAT EVERY TRAINER SHOULD KNOW

The predominant descriptive model of instructional communication suggests that educators, including trainers, have both *rhetorical* and *relational* goals (Mottet, Richmond, & McCroskey, 2006). According to this framework, when training, *rhetorically*, trainers communicate strategically to influence participants' thinking, feelings, and behaviors relative to their content. The goal is to persuade learners to understand and practice the concepts. *Relationally*, trainers communicate with learners to create the type of relationship that is critical to their learning. Trainers who encourage content mastery do so, in part, because they are able to establish a sense of closeness with trainees (Beebe, Mottet, & Roach, 2013; Rodriguez et al., 1996). That closeness seems to encourage their participation and engagement, positive attitude toward the content and learning process, and ultimately, mastery of specific skills and concepts (Frymier & Houser, 1999; Frymier & Houser, 2014; Rodriguez et al., 1996). Novice trainers often think that their content is the most important aspect of their work, and emphasize their rhetorical goals at the expense of developing critical learning relationships with participants. Effective trainers understand the importance of balancing these goals. In the next two sections, we will discuss the rhetorical and relational dimensions of training in greater depth.

The Rhetorical Dimension of Training

Rhetorical communication is receiver-centered. To ensure focus on participants and their training needs, trainers must implement several specific communication practices. These include audience adaptation; source credibility; and the vital message components of relevance, clarity, and humor.

Audience adaptation. Cheri was eager to conduct her first professional training workshop for the local sales team at Q&A International, a large presentationl software firm. She had created her slides, practiced all week, had a good night's sleep, and was ready to speak to the team about enhancing their communication during sales presentations. To open her presentation, she told a joke that concluded with the punchline, "BS may get you to the top, but it won't keep you there." Cheri looked at the 25 people staring back at her. Almost all of the men were either laughing or smiling, and *all* of the women were glaring at her. "Why do these women look so annoyed?" she thought to herself.

What Cheri had forgotten was the most basic rule of communication—know your audience! Cheri did not conduct a preliminary audience analysis and, therefore, did not know how the men and women she was working with would respond to a joke about "getting to the top" of an organization. Trainers must plan their rhetorical strategies carefully. Humor, in particular, is a subjective type of communication to which audience response can vary greatly (Wanzer, Frymier, Wojtaszczyk, & Smith, 2006). In another example, a college professor invited a trainer, Sheila, to give a workshop for women faculty about intergenerational communication in the university. Much to the faculty member's distress, Sheila did not address her audience as college professors; instead, she used irrelevant corporate examples of "managers" and "subordinates." She failed to include the more obvious and targeted examples of "older" and "younger" faculty, or even to discuss the age-related disconnections between faculty and young college students. The disappointed trainees evaluated the experience negatively and many left the workshop early.

Before conducting training, trainers must obtain preliminary information about participants, and then use that information effectively. Jorgensen (Chapter 5) makes a persuasive case for implementing formal needs assessments for any consulting or training engagement. The needs assessment process yields a range of data that can be helpful to your planning and facilitation of training. One of the most important things to understand about learners concerns their orientation and preferences relative to communication. After preliminary interviews with key organizational members, consider:

- Is this a receptive audience? Do they know why I am here and how my information relates to them and the work they do every day? Should I anticipate resistance?
- What does my audience's age, gender, and cultural makeup (Houser, 2013) suggest to me about its communication preferences? For instance, generational differences (Howe & Strauss, 2000) and cultural differences (Joy & Kolb, 2009) can contribute to an individual's preference for different types of evidence (e.g., statistical data or narrative examples), willingness to orally participate, and expectations for your delivery and facilitation style. We might expect, for example, that Millennials (those born after 1982) will be more responsive to and expectant of technology-aided training (e.g., computer-based simulations, digital gaming, or web-based learning modules) than Baby Boomers born between 1943 and 1960 (Howe & Strauss, 2000).
- How cohesive or similar to one another are these trainees? What areas of the organization and job functions do these people represent? (Houser, 2013)
- What is my audience's current performance or knowledge level relative to the issues I plan to address in training? (Houser, 2013)
- What is the group's overall attitude toward communication? Are they willing, open, and confident communicators? If they have a strong willingness to communicate (McCroskey, 1992), then a group discussion might be productive. If, however, pre-session research reveals that participants are apprehensive, the trainer will need to explore other methods that do not require as much oral participation. Be aware that oral participation is only a small part of learning engagement, and that many trainees may be "silently engaged." To encourage talk, trainers must establish safe climates where apprehensive participants feel reassured, and not judged or evaluated (McCroskey, 1982).

Being able to answer these questions in advance of training can make or break the training experience, and help trainers avoid Cheri's and Sheila's mistakes related to poor audience adaptation. The effective trainer recognizes where an audience is in terms of ability and willingness to engage in particular ways. Addressing the issues above through pre-session research, such as that discussed by Jorgensen (Chapter 5), will yield helpful information.

Once the trainer has some basic audience awareness, he or she can plan the delivery of training. Audience analysis will indicate how much time to spend on each objective and concept. Additionally, a nuanced understanding of the audience assists trainers in planning appropriate and effective language, examples, and instructional activities. Get started immediately by personalizing the introduction to the session with references to the audience; this sets the stage for connection, trust, and learner engagement (Anderson, 1965). Then, continue to seek learners' ideas and experiences during training. Avoid generic questions like "Does this make sense?" which are unlikely to feel personal or inviting to trainees. Instead, address people with questions like "Maria, how could you see yourself implementing this idea in your role as a front-line customer service representative?" Such strategies will help facilitate a learner-centered training session.

Source credibility. A trainer's credibility is critical in any consultation. The trainer arrives with some credibility established; after all, he or she had the credentials and experience to get the job. McCroskey and Teven (1999) described source credibility as reliability that is built and established through communication. It is composed of three dimensions: speaker competence (expertise or intelligence), character (trustworthiness or believability), and goodwill (caring about one's audience and its best interest). Behaviors associated with credibility include content organization, subject matter expertise, and communication competence.

One of the more difficult aspects of training is appearing credible in front of an unfamiliar audience, or one that actively resists training in general or training relative to your topic in particular. For example, trainers working with a group of engineers on the topic of client communication may recognize that they lack inherent value for the topic. Many of them may have entered their field with the expectation they could leave client interactions to others, and instead focus on behind-the-scenes technical aspects of work. The trainer must convince them of his or her reliable and useful experience, skills, and knowledge. Further, the trainer must express authentic concern for them and their experiences—a solid understanding of them and the challenges they face, and a desire to help them learn knowledge and behaviors to overcome those challenges. What follows is a discussion of several essential message variables that have been empirically demonstrated to have positive impact on others' perceptions of credibility.

Relevance. Expectancy Value Theory (Fishbein & Ajzen, 1975) frames our understanding of training content relevance. Specifically, individuals will be motivated to act if they (a) perceive self-efficacy relevant to the recommended behaviors and (b) believe the recommended behaviors will meet their personal needs/values. Interested in the value of these assumptions in learning contexts, Keller (1987) established that learners' motivation is a byproduct of their perceptions of content relevance—that is, their belief that they have the abilities relevant to performing the recommended behavior, as well as a perception that the content is personally relevant. Thus, effective trainers, based on their understanding of client objectives and formative assessments of their trainees, establish relevance to interest and motivate participants. They do so through the use of examples, language, and experiential methods particularly suited for their session. As well, they avoid "off-the-shelf" training methods, which may not be directly targeted (and relevant) to the particular organization's unique needs. Remember, training success is ultimately dependent on the consultant's ability to address what is important to the client and help the organization meet its particular needs. When trainers create perceptions of content relevance among trainees, learners experience motivation, feelings of self-efficacy, and positive attitudes toward the content and—important to the consulting goals of trust and relationship-building—the trainer (Frymier, 2002; Frymier & Shulman, 1995; Frymier, Shulman, & Houser, 1996).

Keller (1987) identified six relevance strategies for developing learner perceptions of relevance. They have implications in the training context and are presented here along with examples:

- *Present future usefulness of the material for the audience* (i.e., illustrate through training methods and participant engagement how they can apply the content in their work).
- *Present current worth of the information to the audience* (i.e., address issues of urgent present need during training. For example, perhaps your consulting role involves facilitating a planned change involving software; if participants need new skills to implement the new technology, plan to provide them with structured time for learning these skills).
- *Meet pre-established learner needs with content and instructional strategies* (i.e., perform a valid and reliable needs assessment; design appropriate training objectives based on the results; and provide information and plan activities that will facilitate accomplishment of those objectives).
- *Relate the content to learners' past experiences* (i.e., illustrate through your own examples how the training content synthesizes with what trainees already know and have already done; encourage them to do the same through the use of targeted questions and discussion).
- *Model recommended behaviors for learners* (i.e., when training participants perceive you as credible and see you engaging in the behaviors you are promoting with positive results, relevance is heightened [see Beebe, Chapter 8, for a discussion of influence strategies credible consultants can use]. Additionally, using demonstrations, videos, and/or conceptual discussion of others' best practices can accomplish this same modeling effect).

- *Offer participants alternative methods for accomplishing recommended outcomes* (because adult learning theory suggests that your trainees know that there is rarely one best way for everyone to attain the same goal).

When trainers successfully implement Keller's strategies, they show learners how training content relates to personal and organizational goals.

Clarity. Another variable important for trainers to master is that of clarity, or "the fidelity of instructional messages" (Powell & Harville, 1990, p. 372). Training content needs to ring true and make sense to listeners. Trainers achieve clarity by using clear language and presentational methods that enable audience understanding. Below are some suggestions for using the empirically documented strategies to enhance learner perceptions of clarity.

- Stress important aspects of the content by defining major concepts; giving clear guidelines for assignments or activities; using an appropriate pace; following an organized outline; and using transitions and signposts such as "next," or "the first of three key ideas is…". Organizational cues such as these strengthen cognitive learning in instructional settings (Titsworth, 2001).
- Explain the content through the use of sufficient, specific, and relevant examples (Chesebro & Wanzer, 2006).
- Attend to verbal and nonverbal cues that indicate lack of understanding (e.g., confused looks, questions, and statements indicating misunderstanding). Respond by repeating information, rephrasing ideas, offering alternative examples, clarifying the audience's understanding, asking questions, and answering their questions.

Humor. The careful use of humor can be effective in promoting trainee cognition and positive affect for training in general, the specific content, and the trainer (Wanzer, Frymier, & Irwin, 2010). Educators who use humor with adult audiences are better liked and generally viewed more positively than those who do not (Hackman & Barthel-Hackman, 1993). Goodboy, Booth-Butterfield, Bolkan, and Griffin's 2015 study of humor has implications for trainers: Carefully enacted humor can lead to an enhanced relationship with trainees, heightened motivation in the training room, and enhanced learning and transfer.

So what is "carefully enacted" humor? First, trainers must establish (through pre-session audience analysis and the interactions they have with trainees during training) how much and what type of humor participants will appreciate. Second, effective trainers should be aware of the research on humor. Specifically, excessive use of humor can work against training goals (Downs, Javidi, & Nussbaum, 1988); further, participants must find trainer humor appropriate (Wanzer et al., 2006). In terms of appropriateness, Wanzer et al. found that educational audiences tend to appreciate humorous examples, stories, or language that are *relevant to the topic.* Further, they accept stories or jokes that are *off-topic but not offensive* (e.g., a story about a current event or something funny that happened in your travels to the training). Third, audiences will generally find trainers' *self-deprecating humor* amusing—but be careful not to damage your credibility with too much of this humor or by being self-disparaging. You should always avoid offensive humor such as sexual, racist, sexist, or ethnocentric jokes; vulgar language; or vulgar nonverbal gestures. Never direct sarcasm at trainees or disparage them based on any personal characteristic (Kearney, Plax, Hays, & Ivey, 1991).

Furthermore, effective, appropriate humor is a useful skill to model in communication-focused training. Managers with a sense of humor are perceived as more effective and better liked by employees than managers who use less humor. Subordinates rate humorous managers as personable and relatable, and report strong feelings of cohesion in the workplace (Holmes & Marra, 2006). In another context, doctors who laughed with their patients and used humor were perceived as understanding and tended to elicit openness from their patients (Levinson et al., 1997). Thus, even trainers who aren't focusing on humor as a communication skill might benefit participants in a number of ways by incorporating humor effectively into their sessions.

The Relational Dimension of Training

Whereas a trainer's rhetorical goals are focused on the delivery of information, the relational component of training is concerned with the social interactions among trainer and trainees within the learning context. The relational dimension of interaction is critical: "[For] two (or more) people…to reach a shared perspective…Of paramount concern is the relationship between the two people and the perceived well-being of the 'other'" (McCroskey & Richmond, 1996, p. 234). The rhetorical dimension focuses on the message itself; the relational dimension focuses on the people involved, and the meaning that that they co-create through their communication. Specific to learning, Frymier and Houser (2000) found that positive teacher-student relationships "facilitate affective learning, which in turn enhances cognitive learning" (p. 208). Recall that affective learning is a pivotal component in training (Isen & Reeve, 2005); trainees who have positive affect toward the content of training will internalize and retain the information. Ultimately, this affect influences motivation (Ellis, 2000; 2004), which enhances the nature of training and its outcomes. *In this way, the rhetorical and relational dimensions do not exist in isolation of the other; they work in tandem* (Mottet & Beebe, 2006).

Rapport between trainers and trainees can create increased perceptions of facilitator credibility, as well as heighten participants' willingness to listen (Richmond, Lane, & McCroskey, 2006). Numerous studies have established the potency of positive teacher/student, mentor/protégé, superior/subordinate, and trainer/trainee relationships on learning (Faylor, Beebe, Houser, & Mottet, 2008;

Frymier & Houser, 2000; Waldeck, Orrego, Plax, & Kearney, 1997). The best way to establish this kind of positive, influential relationship with training participations appears to be through the use of a set of communication behaviors known as *immediacy cues* (Chesebro & McCroskey, 1998, 2000, 2001).

Verbal and nonverbal immediacy. To create closeness and minimize both physical and psychological distance from training participants, trainers should become comfortable employing both verbal (VI) and nonverbal immediacy behaviors (NVI). Immediacy is the perceived physical and psychological closeness between communicators; in consulting contexts, trainers should work to cultivate these perceptions with trainees to promote positive outcomes of the intervention. Mehrabian (1971) explains, "People are drawn toward persons and things they like, evaluate highly, and prefer; they avoid or move away from things they dislike, evaluate negatively, or do not prefer" (p. 1). Nearly 50 years of research has demonstrated that immediacy is associated with the results trainers seek: positive affect, increased cognitive learning, and positive evaluations of instructors (Faylor, et al., 2008; Richmond & McCroskey, 2000).

A meta-analysis conducted by Witt, Wheeless, and Allen (2004) examined more than 80 studies documenting the positive relationships between instructor NVI and VI and learning outcomes across learning settings. Specific to training, Faylor et al. (2008) reported consistent findings: "Participants had higher levels of self-reported affective learning when their trainers used higher levels of nonverbally immediate, verbally effective, and clear instructional behaviors. These results remind trainers that they have the ability to influence trainees' affective learning by increasing their use of these key instructional communication behaviors" (p. 156).

Table 1 illustrates a range of verbal and nonverbal immediacy trainers might adapt (Beebe, Beebe, & Ivey, 2013):

Table 1. Verbal and Nonverbal Immediacy Behaviors of Effective Trainers.

Nonverbal Immediacy Behaviors	Verbal Immediacy Behaviors
Move closer to trainees	Use personal examples
Gesture while talking	Talk about relevant experiences outside of training
Make eye contact	Use moderate amounts of appropriate humor
Maintain relaxed body position	Address participants by name
Move around the room during training	Engage in small talk during breaks and before and after workshop
Smile	Encourage participants to talk
Use a variety of vocal expressions	Use pronouns "we, us, our"
Use appropriate touch behaviors (e.g., touching someone on the arm in understanding)	Encourage trainees to refer to trainer by first name

Training in the global workplace can present challenges to facilitators wishing to be immediate. Many teachers and trainers I've worked with report uncertainty about whether participants from different backgrounds will respond positively to immediacy, and whether they will understand the meaning and intent of some messages—particularly subtle nonverbal ones. However, research over the past 30 years has revealed very few significant cultural differences in how immediacy is perceived across cultures (Powell & Harville, 1990; Sanders & Wiseman, 1990). Thus, although trainers should always assess their audiences to gauge the appropriateness of behaviors such as direct sustained eye contact, or standing close to a trainee, immediacy is, overall, a valuable enhancement within any training context.

The great news about immediacy, especially for trainers uncomfortable or unfamiliar with using this important skill, is that it is teachable. Richmond, McCroskey, Plax, & Kearney (1986) found that teachers trained in the use of verbal and nonverbal immediacy behaviors created high levels of affect among their students. Conversely, teachers untrained in immediacy skills used more negative influence techniques with learners, such as punishment and guilt, resulting in less liking and motivation among trainees. Thus, trainers uncomfortable or unskilled in using verbal or nonverbal immediacy skills should seek communication training themselves or engage in some systematic practice of the behaviors indicated in Table 1 and self-reflection. Research indicates that trainers can improve their performance as a result of education and practice of immediate communication.

Confirmation. Another relational component of effective training is *confirmation.* Confirmation behaviors indicate that the trainer recognizes, acknowledges, and even endorses participants (Sieburg, 1985). According to Ellis (2000), when instructors confirm learners, they are telling them they are valuable and they and their thoughts are important. In addition, confirmation has a significant, positive relationship with cognitive and affective learning and overall motivation to learn (Ellis, 2000). This is good news for any trainer hoping to generate interest and enthusiasm among participants.

Learners who feel confirmed by trainers and educators tend to evaluate them more positively and as more credible than less confirming educators (Schrodt, Turman, & Soliz, 2006). In an experimental study, learners in the most confirming condition were more motivated to communicate with their educator on a relational level and to learn; they excelled in learning and were more satisfied than those enrolled in less confirming learning conditions (Goodboy & Myers, 2008).

Confirming trainees can also have a positive effect on the overall training climate. In essence, by engaging in behaviors that create feelings of personal relevance and importance, trainers develop a sense of connectedness and community among participants. This sense of community will learners them engaged and positive about the training tools and concepts utilized (Edwards, Edwards, Torrens, & Beck, 2011). When learners feel connected to one another and to their instructor, they will become engaged both verbally and nonverbally (Rovai, 2002), leading to enhanced learning (Cross, 1998) and heightened participant feelings of self-efficacy (Freeman, Anderman, & Jensen, 2007).

When trainers attend to the relational dimension of their work, they usually observe a variety of improved outcomes. If immediacy and confirmation are new concepts for you, one way to evaluate their role in your work is to have participants rate your immediacy and confirmation in post-session evaluations (*instrumentation available at http://www.jamescmccroskey.com/measures/nis_o.htm and http://www. psychwiki.com/dms/other/labgroup/Measufsdfsdbger345resWeek1/Joel/Ellis_2000. pdf*). Immediacy behaviors are not easy for everyone; as you begin to consciously focus on them, select a few that are already comfortable and use those, and add others as you become more at ease with being an immediate communicator. Evaluation data can enhance your confidence for incorporating even more immediacy cues into sessions. Such data will also serve as evidence of training effectiveness for marketing purposes and enhancing credibility with clients. Data on your rapport with trainees add to your credibility and professionalism, and indicate you are well liked and easy to work with. Waldeck, Kearney, and Plax (Chapter 7) discuss evaluation of trainer effectiveness, including communication in Chapter 7.

CONCLUSION

This chapter has illuminated the dynamic interplay among trainer content expertise, instructional design skills, communication competence, and participant learning. Effective communication surrounding the training process—from assessing needs to delivering and evaluating training—will facilitate goal accomplishment. This chapter has laid out a framework for training that is informed by theories of adult learning, as well as instructional communication theory and research. When trainers accurately assess client needs and then approach their work with participants through the lens of adult learning principles, design their training appropriately, and facilitate sessions effectively using documented principles of instructional communication, participants experience positive cognitive, affective, and behavioral outcomes. In this chapter, we have overviewed a four-part model for designing, delivering, and assessing training (PPPA), explored a schema for delivery (E*D*I*T process), and discussed two critical components (rhetorical and relational goals and related behaviors) for effective training.

Learning and practicing the skills discussed in this chapter requires effort, practice, and careful consideration of all forms of feedback related to training. But the use of the principles covered here distinguishes adequate trainers from those who make a true impact with learners. Training is communicating, and communication is a transactional process—a give-and-take exchange among trainers and trainees that the very best trainers facilitate expertly.

REFERENCES

Anderson, N. H. (1965). Primacy effects in personality impression formation using a generalized order effect paradigm. *Journal of Personality and Social Psychology 2*, 1–9.

Baldwin, T., & Ford, J. K. (1988). Transfer of training: A review and directions for future research. *Personnel Psychology, 41*, 63–105.

Beebe, S. A., Beebe, S. J., & Ivy, D. K. (2013). *Communication: Principles for a lifetime* (5th ed.). Boston, MA: Pearson.

Beebe, S. A., Mottet, T. P., & Roach, K. D. (2013). *Training and development: communicating for success* (2nd ed.). Boston, MA: Pearson.

Bloom, B. S. (1956). *Taxonomy of educational objectives: Handbook I: Cognitive domain.* New York, NY: McGraw-Hill.

Brown, R. F., Bylund, C. L., Gueguen, J. A., Diamond, C., Eddington, J., & Kissane, D. (2010). Developing patient-centered communication skills training for oncologists: Describing the content and efficacy of training. *Communication Education, 59*, 235–248.

Burleson, B. R., & Samter, W. (1990). Effects of cognitive complexity on the perceived importance of communication skills in friends. *Communication Research, 17*, 165–182.

Chesebro, J. L., & McCroskey, J. C. (1998). The relationship of teacher clarity and teacher immediacy with students' experiences of state receiver apprehension when listening to teachers. *Communication Quarterly, 46*, 446–456.

Chesebro, J. L., & McCroskey, J. C. (2000). The relationship between students' reports of learning and their actual recall of lecture material: A validity test. *Communication Education, 49*, 297–301.

Chesebro, J. L., & McCroskey, J. C. (2001). The relationship of teacher clarity and immediacy with student state receiver apprehension and cognitive learning. *Communication Education, 50*, 59–68.

Chesebro, J. L., & Wanzer, M. B. (2006). Instructional message variables. In T. P. Mottet, V. P. Richmond, and J. C. McCroskey (Eds.), *Handbook of instructional communication: Rhetorical and relational perspectives* (pp. 89–116). Boston, MA: Allyn and Bacon.

Cross, K. P. (1998, July/August). Why learning communities? Why now? *About Campus*, 4–11.

Dallimore, E. J., & Souza, T. J. (2002). Consulting course design: Theoretical frameworks and pedagogical strategies. *Business Communication Quarterly, 65*, 86–113.

Dewey, J. (1938/1997). *Experience and education.* New York, NY: Simon and Schuster.

Downs, V. C., Javidi, M., & Nussbaum, J. F. (1988). An analysis of teachers' verbal communication within the college classroom: Use of humor, self-disclosure, and narratives. *Communication Education, 37*, 127–141.

Dwyer, K. K., Bingham, S. G., Carlson, R. E., Prisbell, M., Cruz, A. M., & Fuss, D. A. (2004). Communication and connectedness in the classroom: Development of the Connected Classroom Climate Inventory. *Communication Research Reports, 21*, 264–272.

Edwards, C., Edwards, A., Torrens, A., & Beck, A. (2011). Confirmation and community: The relationships between teacher confirmation, classroom community, student motivation, and learning. *Online Journal of Communication and Media Technology, 1*, 17–43.

Ellis, K. (2000). Perceive teacher confirmation: The development and validation of an instrument and two studies of the relationship to cognitive and affective learning. *Human Communication Research, 26*, 264–291.

Ellis, K. (2004). The impact of perceived teacher confirmation on receiver apprehension, motivation, and learning. *Communication Education, 53*, 1–20.

Faylor, N. R., Beebe, S. A., Houser, M. L., & Mottet, T. P. (2008). Perceived differences in instructional communication behaviors between effective and ineffective corporate trainers. *Human Communication, 11,* 149–160.

Fishbein, M., & Ajzen, I. (1975). *Belief, attitude, intention, and behavior: An introduction to theory and research.* Reading, MA: Addison-Wesley.

Fitzpatrick, R. (2001). The strange case of the transfer of training estimate. *Industrial-Organizational Psychologist, 39,* 18–19.

Freeman, T. M., Anderman, L. H., & Jensen, J. M. (2007). Sense of belongingness in college freshmen at the classroom and campus levels. *Journal of Experimental Education, 75,* 203–220.

Frisby, B. N., & Martin, M. M. (2010). Instructor-student and student-student rapport in the classroom. *Communication Education, 59,* 146–164.

Frymier, A. B. (2002). Making content relevant to students. In J. L. Chesebro and J. C. McCroskey (Eds.), *Communication for teachers* (pp. 93–103). Boston, MA: Allyn and Bacon.

Frymier, A. B., & Houser, M. L. (1999). The revised learning indicators scale. *Communication Studies, 50,* 1–12.

Frymier, A. B., & Houser, M. L. (2000). The teacher-student relationship as an interpersonal relationship. *Communication Education, 49,* 207–219.

Frymier, A. B., & Houser, M. L. (2014, November). The relationship of oral participation in student motivation and engagement. Paper presented at the Annual Meeting of the National Communication Association, Chicago, IL.

Frymier, A. B., & Shulman, G. M. (1995). "What's in it for me?": Increasing content relevance to enhance students' motivation. *Communication Education, 44,* 40–50.

Frymier, A. B., Shulman, G. M., & Houser, M. (1996). The development of a learner empowerment measure. *Communication Education, 45,* 181–199.

Glaser, H. F., & Bingham, S. G. (2009). Students' perceptions of their connectedness in the community college basic public speaking course. *Journal of the Scholarship of Teaching and Learning, 9,* 57–69.

Goodboy, A. K., Booth-Butterfield, M., Bolkan, S., & Griffin, D. J. (2015). The role of instructor humor and students' education orientations in student learning, extra effort, participation and out-of-class communication. *Communication Quarterly 63,* 44–61.

Goodboy, A. K., & Myers, S. A. (2008). The effect of teacher confirmation on student communication and learning outcomes. *Communication Education, 57,* 153–179.

Hackman, M. Z., & Barthel-Hackman, T. A. (1993). Communication apprehension, willingness to communicate, and sense of humor: United States and New Zealand perspectives. *Communication Quarterly, 41,* 282–29

Holmes, J., & Marra, M. (2006). Humor and leadership style. *Humor: International Journal of Humor Research, 19,* 119–138.

Houser, M. L. (2013). *Fundamentals of human communication 2013: COMM 1310 student guidebook.* San Marcos, TX: Department of Communication Studies.

Howe, N., & Strauss, W. (2000). *Millennials rising: The next great generation.* New York, NY: Vintage.

Hutchins, H. M., & Burke, L. A. (2007). Identifying trainers' knowledge of training transfer research findings: Closing the gap between research and practice. *International Journal of Training and Development, 11,* 236–264.

Isen, A. M., & Reeve, J. (2005). The influence of positive affect on intrinsic and extrinsic motivation: Facilitating enjoyment of play, responsible work behavior, and self-control. *Motivation and Emotion, 29,* 297–325.

Jablin, F. M. (1982). Organizational communication: An assimilation approach. In M. E. Roloff & C. R. Berger (Eds.), *Social cognition and communication* (pp. 255–286). Beverly Hills, CA: Sage.

Jablin, F. M., & Krone, K. J. (1987). Organizational assimilation. In C. R. Berger & S. H. Chaffee (Eds.), *Handbook of communication science* (pp. 711–746). Newbury Park, CA: Sage.

Joy, S., & Kolb, D. K. (2009). Are there cultural differences in learning style? *International Journal of Intercultural Relations, 33*, 60–85.

Kearney, P., Plax, T. G., Hays, E. R., & Ivey, M. J. (1991). College teacher misbehaviors: What students don't like about what teachers say and do. *Communication Quarterly, 39*, 309–324.

Keller, J. M. (1987). Strategies for stimulating the motivation to learn. *Performance and Instruction, 26*, 1–7.

Knowles, M. S. (1980). *The modern practice of adult education: From pedagogy to andragogy.* Englewood Cliffs, NJ: Prentice Hall.

Levinson, W., Rotter, D. L., Mullooly, J. P., Dull, V. T., & Frankel, R. M. (1997). Physician-patient communication: The relationship with malpractice claims among primary care physicians and surgeons. *The Journal of the American Medical Association, 227*, 553–559.

Lundy, J. C. (1996). General semantics and phenomenology on conducting classroom discussion: The E*D*I*T System. *The New Jersey Journal of Communication, 4*, 91–98.

McCroskey, J. C. (1982). *An introduction to rhetorical communication* (4th ed). Englewood Cliffs, NJ: Prentice Hall.

McCroskey, J. C. (1992). Reliability and validity of the willingness to communicate scale. *Communication Quarterly, 40*, 16–25.

McCroskey, J. C., & Richmond, V. P. (1996). Human communication theory and research: Traditions and models. In M. B. Salwen & D. W. Stacks (Eds.), *An integrated approach to communication theory and research* (pp. 233–242). Mahwah, NJ: Lawrence Erlbaum.

McCroskey, J. C., & Teven, J. J. (1999). Goodwill: A reexamination of the construct and its measurement. *Communication Monographs, 66*, 90–103.

Mehrabian, A. (1971). *Silent Messages.* Belmont, CA: Wadsworth.

Miller, V. D., & Jablin, F. M. (1991). Information seeking during organizational entry: Influences tactics, and a model of the process. *Academy of Management Review, 16*, 92–120.

Mottet, T. P., & Beebe, S. A. (2006). Foundations of instructional communication. In T. P. Mottet, V. P. Richmond, & J. C. McCroskey (Eds.), *Handbook of instructional communication: Rhetorical & relational perspectives* (pp. 3–32). Boston, MA: Pearson.

Mottet, T. P., Richmond, V. P., & McCroskey, J. C. (2006). *Handbook of instructional communication: Rhetorical & relational perspectives.* Boston, MA: Pearson.

Myers, G. E., & Myers, M. T. (1985). *Instructor's manual to accompany the dynamics of human communication: A laboratory approach* (4th ed.). New York, NY: McGraw-Hill.

Phillips, J. J. (2003). *Return on investment in training and development programs.* Burlington, MA: Elsevier Science.

Powell, R. G., & Harville, B. (1990). The effects of teacher immediacy and clarity on instructional outcomes: An intercultural assessment. *Communication Education, 39*, 369–379.

Richmond, V. P., Lane, D. R., & McCroskey, J. C. (2006). Teacher immediacy and the teacher-student relationship. In T. P. Mottet, V. P. Richmond, & J. C. McCroskey (Eds.), *Handbook of instructional communication: Rhetorical & relational perspectives* (pp. 167–193). Boston, MA: Pearson.

Richmond, V. P., & McCroskey, J. C. (2000). *Nonverbal behavior in interpersonal relationships.* Boston, MA: Allyn & Bacon.

Richmond, V. P., McCroskey, J. C., Plax, T. G, & Kearney, P. (1986). Teacher nonverbal immediacy training and student affect. *World Communication, 15,* 181–194.

Rodriguez, J. I., Plax, T. G., & Kearney, P. (1996). Clarifying the relationship between teacher nonverbal immediacy and student cognitive learning: Affective learning as the central causal mediator. *Communication Education, 45,* 293–305.

Rovai, A. P. (2002). Sense of community, perceived cognitive learning, and persistence in asynchronous learning networks. *Internet and Higher Education, 5,* 319–332.

Saks, A. M., & Belcourt, M. (2006). An investigation of training activities and transfer of training in organizations. *Human Resource Management, 54,* 629–648.

Sanders, J. A., & Wiseman, R. L. (1990). The effects of verbal and nonverbal teacher immediacy on perceived cognitive, affective, and behavioral learning in the multicultural classroom. *Communication Education, 39,* 341–353.

Schrodt, P., Turman, P. D., & Soliz, J. (2006). Perceived understanding as a mediator of perceived teacher confirmation and students' ratings of instruction. *Communication Education, 55,* 370–388.

Scott, M. D., Buller, D. B., Walkosz, B. J., Andersen, P. A., Cutter, G. R., & Dignan, M. B. (2008). Go sun smart. *Communication Education, 57,* 423–433.

Sieburg, E. (1985). *Family communication: An integrated systems approach.* New York, NY: Gardner Press.

Sollitto, M., Johnson, Z. D., & Myers, S. A. (2013). Students' perceptions of college classroom connectedness, assimilation, and peer relationships. *Communication Education, 62,* 318–331.

Titsworth, B. S. (2001). The effects of teacher immediacy, use of organizational lecture cues, and students' notetaking on cognitive learning. *Communication Education, 50,* 283–298.

Waldeck, J. H. (2014). Communication and learning. In J. Nussbaum (Ed.), *Handbook of life span communication* (pp. 135–156). New York, NY: Peter Lang.

Waldeck, J. H., Kearney, P., & Plax, T. G. (2013). *Business and professional communication in a digital age.* Boston, MA: Cengage.

Waldeck, J. H., Orrego, V. O., Plax, T. G., & Kearney, P. (1997). Graduate student/faculty mentoring relationships: Who gets mentored, how it happens, and to what end. *Communication Quarterly, 45,* 93–109.

Wanzer, M. B., Frymier, A. B., & Irwin, J. (2010). An explanation of the relationship between instructor humor and student learning: Instructional humor processing theory. *Communication Education, 59,* 1–18.

Wanzer, M. B., Frymier, A. B., Wojtaszczyk, A. M., & Smith, T. (2006). Appropriate and inappropriate uses of humor by teachers. *Communication Education, 55,* 178–196.

Witt, P. L., Wheeless, L. R., & Allen, M. (2004). A meta-analytical review of the relationship between teacher immediacy and student learning. *Communication Monographs, 71,* 184–207.

CHAPTER THIRTEEN

How & Why Technology Matters in Consulting & Coaching Interventions

KERI K. STEPHENS AND ERIC D. WATERS

University of Texas at Austin

Margaret Keys is watching a YouTube video of her client's latest presentation to help her prepare for her coaching call later this afternoon.

Celia Berk focuses on maintaining a "human touch" combined with shared platforms, email, and conference calls as she participates in an unprecedented global reorganization of the IT infrastructure taking place across her parent company WPP.

Ignacio Cruz just finished a Google Hangout discussing the implementation of a nonprofit social media platform, and one client who missed the meeting sent a GroupMe text asking for a quick recap.

Consulting in contemporary organizations typically requires consultants to use technology as a central part of their client communication strategy. Margaret, Celia, and Ignacio are real people actively engaged in different types of consulting, but what they have in common is the central role that technology plays as they communicate with their clients. In this chapter, we treat consulting as activities that advise and guide organizational members on how to implement and maintain positive change(s) within the organization, thereby improving the effectiveness of the organization or specific individuals therein (March, 1991). Consultants are most commonly thought of as people external to an organization, but there are also people within organizations who function as consultants, especially in large organizations undergoing major change initiatives (see Keyton, Chapter 3, for an overview of the various types of consultants). Since consulting often includes working one-on-one with individual clients in addition to working with teams, in this chapter we incorporate examples of how technology is changing consulting in general, and coaching practices, in particular.

Throughout this chapter, we feature our own consulting experiences, discuss the research literature, and provide extended examples of Margaret, Celia, and Ignacio's diverse experiences. Both authors have experience working in industry as well as consulting with private clients. Their organizational change interventions have shaped the directions of companies, and their training programs have helped corporate, nonprofit, and government clients become better communicators. In addition, they have consulted with clients on website design and the incorporation of technology into their communication practices. All three of these professionals have coached people in a variety of industries. The authors of this chapter have extensive experience working with groups and teams, and privately coaching students in MBA and Executive MBA programs. Together, their experiences, along with the extended examples, demonstrate the range of technologies used in consulting and coaching today. Collectively, the ideas and information presented in this chapter provide a glimpse into the future of consulting.

THE RISING USE OF TECHNOLOGY IN CONSULTING ACTIVITIES

Whether consulting as an insider to an organization or working as an external consultant our work has changed in a number of ways over the past decade. The most obvious changes have been created through the use of information and communication technologies (ICTs). Specifically, ICTs influenced consulting by changing communication activities, speeding up feedback, increasing accessibility, and improving efficiency (Ahrend, Diamond, & Webber, 2010; Otte, Bangerter, Britsch, & Wüthrich, 2014; Rossett & Marino, 2005). For example, consulting and coaching most commonly occur over an extended period of time and many functions that consultants perform today can happen at a distance. Clients and consultants no longer need to be co-located. Furthermore, as technology use in consulting and coaching practices has expanded, consultants and their clients are using mobile devices to connect on an interpersonal level. Mobile devices provide a different type of accessibility because calls, text messages, and Internet access can happen 24 hours a day, regardless of where people are located. Both clients and consultants have many ICTs available to them, yet with these ICT options, there are new challenges in finding tools that all parties understand, have available, and use in productive ways.

Therefore, in this chapter, we call the mix of ICTs and face-to-face (FtF) communication, *combinatorial ICT use* (Stephens, 2007; Stephens, Sørnes, Rice, Browning, & Sætre, 2008). Before we elaborate on the combinatorial ICTs used in consulting practices, let us discuss the backgrounds of our three professionals in more detail, as their work serves to illustrate many of our premises about combinatorial ICTs and consutling.

Margaret Keys is the owner of a top-tier speaking consulting company (see MargaretKeys.com), and she has a perspective on using technology to coach and consult based on 30 years of experience. She was training Dell executives when PowerPoint became the standard in giving presentations. She has coached clients on how to effectively use most types of technology presentation tools, speak on television and video, and negotiate their own career advances. She also uses technology and face-to-face communication to work with her global client base.

Celia Berk is the Chief Talent Officer at Young & Rubicam Group, one of the largest agency holding companies within WPP (a British multinational advertising and public relations firm). She has held several executive positions within her firm over the past two decades and currently works in close partnership with its leaders to attract, develop and retain the best talent, and to promote collaboration across a global network comprised of some of the most powerful brands in marketing communications. She recently participated in a global IT restructuring that will enable WPP to better serve its clients and strengthen its competitive position.

Twenty-one-year-old Ignacio Cruz is already sitting on the board of a national nonprofit organization, Advocates for Youth. He consults with them on how to use social media to help mobilize youth make informed and responsible decisions about reproductive and sexual health. Although few 21-year-olds have the kind of expertise necessary to consult, Ignacio has knowledge and experience that few people of any age have. He understands the issues on the minds of young people, and he knows they like to text, tweet, and have access to information faster than anyone else. He does his consulting work while attending The University of Texas at Austin, where he is a McNair Scholar and on the Dean's List.

These three consulting professionals have varied proficiencies that provide a reality check on how ICTs are used in global organizations today, and that augment the authors' consulting experience. We have found that mobile devices allow us to connect with clients in personal and continuous ways. Quickly sending a text message of encouragement and being available outside of typical business hours allows us to provide a new level of customer service that expands our reach and impact. Margaret, Celia, and Ignacio use combinations of ICTs organically, in direct response to their clients' needs. Their stories and and our own experiences support, explain, and sometimes contradict the research findings we also present in this chapter.

USING COMBINATIONS OF ICTS TO ENGAGE CLIENTS AND DRIVE RETENTION

Organizations hire and utilize consultants to change their employees' behavior and to have those changes be sustained over time (Block, 2011; March, 1991). ICTs can support the consulting process by enabling clients to take an active role in their own interventions—increasing the likelihood of successful, lasting change. Now clients can leverage their preferences for communication media, the pace of an intervention, and their access to external resources—thus allowing for a more personalized engagement than one without new, interactive technologies. ICTs also support the consulting process by providing consultants a means of conducting preliminary research and needs assessments (see Jorgensen, Chapter 5) to ensure a more effective and expeditious engagement. Finally, the variety of ICTs keeps tardy or absent clients connected to important conversations while allowing for effortless post-meeting follow-up. We begin our discussion of how ICTs enhance client engagement and retention by examining how ICT use fosters interactivity in consulting interventions.

Combinatorial ICTs Better Facilitate Interactivity

Interactivity—the active engagement in dialogue to achieve goals—is essential in technology-mediated consulting interventions because it facilitates important client involvement. (See Waldeck, Plax, & Kearney, Chapter 7, for more on the importance of getting and keeping clients actively involved in the consulting process). From a physical or structural perspective, interactivity refers to the affordances, features, or characteristics of technologies that create an collaborative environment (Ramirez & Burgoon, 2004). From a perceptual and behavioral view, interactivity refers to an individual's cognitive, perceptual and behavioral abilities and limitations when using technology (Ramirez & Burgoon, 2004). In the context of combinatorial ICT media use, interactivity often occurs through sequential, repetitive exchanges of interrelated messages between clients and consultants. Combinatorial ICTs empower clients to initiate and self-regulate their learning, co-create a communal learning experience, and choose the technologies that work best for their needs. Having clients engaged in the consulting environment is desirable since interactivity helps clients receive advice that is relevant, timely and opportune (Warner, 2012).

There are myriad ways to make consulting interventions interactive and inclusive of clients, and many include technology (Bouchal et al., 2012). ICTs allow clients to control the pace of an intervention by promoting a generative approach to learning. Generative learning situates the consultant as more of a peripheral guide than a central figure, while encouraging the client to actively create and apply new ideas (London & Hall, 2011). As such, a client can use ICTs not only to glean prescribed information, but also to link new ideas with existing knowledge, making discoveries in the process. Furthermore, self-regulation positively affects learning over time, even during the initial stages when learners experience higher cognitive load (Sitzmann, Bell, Kraiger & Kanar, 2009). The interactive affordances of many contemporary ICTs allow the client to socially construct a temporally personalized intervention (London & Hall, 2011). Essentially, ICTs help consulting interventions meet client needs.

When consultants use a combination of ICTs, clients have flexibility and choice in how interventions are administered. Not every client will exhibit the same level of comfort or expertise with every ICT. What overwhelms some clients will bore others (Waldeck, 2008). Research suggests that many clients prefer using a combination of video and audio in their conversations and that a multi-modal approach is particularly effective (Marshall & Rossett, 2011; Rossett & Marino, 2005). An interactive graphic interface can often highlight the specific details needed for an intervention (London & Hall, 2011). Consultants and clients can work together to revise documents online and use chat applications to discuss additional ideas (Davis, 2012). Document sharing systems can facilitate a type of interaction that is less likely in an FtF environment (Davis, 2012; London & Hall, 2011). Many consultants, including the authors of this chapter, integrate videoconferencing to add a sense of direct involvement, and use VoIP (voice over Internet protocol) and audio recorders to summarize complex concepts into digestible sound bites (London & Hall, 2011). When provided the right combination of ICTs, clients are likely to perceive the intervention as interactively stimulating (Warner, 2012).

ICTs also enhance interactivity in consulting interventions because they grant clients access to learning and development resources beyond the consultant. While working directly with clients, a consultant can pull up a YouTube video on a mobile device and show the clients a clear example of what he or she is recommending. Consultants can refer clients to white papers that can provide additional support for a particular action path. These interactive, technology-mediated interventions work because they encourage communal learning and collaboration through online tools like message boards, access to shared files and media, virtual office hours with industry experts, and access to private industry networks (London & Hall, 2011; Waldeck, 2008). Organizations and their members report high levels of satisfaction with these types of interactive environments (Waldeck, 2008) because socially mediated discovery, buy-in, and positive change often result (London & Hall, 2011).

Using ICTs Sequentially to Prepare and Reinforce Interventions

When using combinations of ICTs, it is important to view consulting interventions as processes that occur over time; one conversation leads to the next conversation. But before these conversations even begin, consultants prepare for their first meetings by learning about their clients. Communication scholars view this preparation as information-seeking behavior, and one particular theoretical model considers how people use ICTs to learn social information about others before they meet (Ramirez, Walther, Burgoon, & Sunnafrank, 2002). These scholars claim that "communicators begin by gathering information passively, evaluate said information, and begin formulating impressions of others, which serves as the basis for determining whether or not to proceed interactively" (pp. 224–225). The Ramirez et al. model is situated in interpersonal interaction, something very relevant for consulting and coaching interventions, which constitute a type of interpersonal relationship. However, considering how easy it is to search the Internet for information about people and organizations today, there are many ways consultants seek information before engaging a client.

Take Margaret, for example. She uses a combination of technologies to help her prepare for meetings with new and existing clients. "YouTube is one of the most helpful technology tools to help me prepare to meet a client," says Margaret. Many of her clients have presentations available on YouTube, one or more TedTalks, and/or corporate websites. She uses these to preview their strengths and weaknesses before she meets with them. Margaret's use of online resources to augment conversations with her clients during the pre-consultation needs assessment saves her clients time and money, and allows Margaret to see how they really perform in an actual high-stress situation.

Thus, using ICTs to prepare for initial client interactions can enhance the overall effectiveness and efficiency of consulting interventions. Consultants can generate a set of potential solutions with the client's needs and resources before they meet with clients (Rossett & Marino, 2005). Consultants can also use ICTs to personalize messages and materials that better address the clients' problems (Marshall & Rossett, 2011). For example, consultants often conduct a needs assessment early in the consulting encounter. By employing ICTs to locate and document pertinent information before—as opposed to during client meetings—consultants can be better prepared, reach their objectives swiftly, and potentially end the engagement sooner (Averweg, 2010).

ICTs also help consultants consultants work effectively with clients who are late or miss consulting update meetings. For example, Ignacio explains that in his consulting meetings, one of his clients may miss at least part of the meeting. The clients who miss the meeting want to get up to speed quickly so they send a GroupMe message (GroupMe is a group text messaging application where group members can chat in real time together) to Ignacio and his team, and almost immediately get a two-sentence summary of what took people an hour to discuss. Sometimes that is enough content, but other times, the situation requires a direct conversation to keep the group moving forward. "Waiting for meeting minutes can take a day or more and GroupMe is so immediate," explains Ignacio. Ignacio's example demonstrates that ICTs, like GroupMe, and other team-based tools can expand communication options during the consulting process in meaningful ways.

Celia and Margaret also believe that ICTs play an important role in following up on meeting outcomes. Specifically, ICTs help them summarize and focus messages around specific agreed-upon tasks. Even when all clients are present at meetings, both of these experienced professionals use a mix of email and other ICTs to reinforce their conversations. Margaret explains that a quick text message reminder to her client, who has perhaps flown to India for an important meeting, reinforces content and provides a level of support and encouragement needed to sustain their business relationship. People are busy today, and re-focusing and reminding clients of the key actions needed for progress are vital for successful coaching and consulting progress.

GROWTH IN SPECIFIC INFORMATION COMMUNICATION TECHNOLOGIES

To this point, we have referred to ICTs in aggregate as a general designation for the technology consultants may employ in interventions. Next, we will highlight the individual ICTs paramount in the consultant's repertoire. In this section, we discuss how highly interactive media such as video and webconferencing enable consultants to coach clients from a distance. We also examine why FtF is often still the go-to medium to initiate engagements, build trust, and cultivate relationships. But first, we explain why the constant connectivity afforded by email makes this ICT vital to the consulting process.

Email Is Still Important

Even though email is not a new ICT, and for personal communication some people prefer to use text messaging and social media, it still plays a prominent role in how consulting messages are communicated and shared. Two reasons for the continued use of email include, first, the ease with which it can be accessed on mobile devices, and, second, the digital "paper trail" that it affords. Unlike instant messages, email can be easily archived and retrieved. Celia explains that she "can't see any other communication tool taking its place." As her team was planning their global restructuring, emails allowed members to share information on a 24/7 basis. Celia explains that when working on deadlines, her team is on email "all day, all night, and all weekend." To maintain work-life balance, she has to take to define the end of her day, because the global and time-sensitive conversations never stop. Furthermore, constant connections to people and global and time-sensitive conversations are vital and her team expects all members to return email messages promptly.

Celia has a clear opinion on how email became the primary business communication tool in her organization and her explanation begins with the tragedy of 9/11. Celia lives and works in Manhattan, and she vividly remembers how everyone instinctively reached for email to establish and maintain contact in the wake of the tragic events that occurred on September 11, 2001. "Companies had already starting giving us devices to carry around so we would never break our connection with them. Then [after 9/11] we became addicted to the connection. This is a double-edged sword," says Celia. Researchers have summarized this double-edged sword by saying, "we have introduced a type of mobile logic into our interactions…and there is an emerging norm of connectedness, an assumption that all of us are available via a mobile phone." (Ling & Donner, 2013, p. 135). Celia's comments highlight the challenges that consultants face when they must set boundaries between communicating with clients and having a personal life.

Video and Webconferences

In addition to using email as a core consulting tool, video and webconferencing are important tools for personalizing communication and providing interactive opportunities for clients. Video includes traditional videoconferencing as well as desktop and mobile video tools and apps. Webconferencing is a blended platform best described as an audio-bridge or VoIP (voice over Internet protocol) combined with a web-based tool that allows people to share slides, jointly edit on whiteboards, or chat. Webconferencing offers a mixture of interactive tools that are not available on stand-alone video platforms (Stephens & Mottet, 2008).

Videoconferencing and webconferencing use has increased considerably in the past decade, especially for coaching interventions. Sherpa, a professional coaching firm, surveyed over 21,000 internal and external organizational coaches from 50 countries in 2014 and found that nearly 40% of coaching is being delivered with webcams—quadruple the amount reported four years ago. As high-definition video-conferencing continues to improve, some people speculate that we might see this trend shift (Sherpa, 2014).

Ignacio explains that in between FtF meetings with clients, he has monthly meetings where "we do the Google Hangout or Go-to-Meeting; it depends on who manages the meeting." Both Google Hangout and Go-to-Meeting are online tools that support online group meetings. Cruz prefers Google Hangout because it enables a live video feed broadcast to all 10 team members, which tends to keep participants focused and accountable. He calls it, "making us meet FtF online." Ignacio describes Go-to-Meeting as a traditional webconference with an audio feed and slides. He says that these meetings relying on this particular medium are longer, less interactive, and result in less member accountability than meetings with a video component. Accountability is vitally important in consulting because clients are paying for outcomes. Consultants must find ICTs that create accountability among members to encourage progress and to avoid becoming scapegoats when progress is slow. Ignacio's example shows how switching the meeting mode to include more interactive and visual cues can subtly pressure clients to engage and participate.

E-Coaching and New Terms Involving Combinations of ICTs

The extensive use of videoconferencing, webconferencing, and other distance ICTs for consulting and coaching has led to the development of new practices and terms to describe them. For example, the term *e-coaching* can mean online coaching, virtual coaching, distance coaching, or video coaching. Geissler, Hasenbein, Kanatouri, and Wegener (2014) describe e-coaching as "coaching mediated through modern media" (p. 166). Geissler et al. also acknowledge that e-coaching can be combined with face-to-face communication but, and refer to that combination as blended coaching. Essentially the coaching literature has a similar problem to the workplace technology use literature (e.g., Stephens, 2007; Stephens et al., 2008); *defining* how ICTs and face-to-face conversations work together to help people achieve their objectives is difficult. Yet it is more common for consultants to use a combination of ICTs than rely on a single device or communication medium.

FtF Still Matters

Even though most consultants use a mix of ICTs in their daily work, many of them insist that the relationships they create through in-person meetings are unparalleled. Quite often, consultants will insist on meeting face-to-face for kickoff meetings and for important milestones throughout engagements. Margaret says that trust is best built in person, and that if she is going to make significant breakthroughs with clients that result in lasting change, she needs to see them in person. Ignacio explains that his client, Advocates for Youth, values FtF meetings so much that they insist that everyone meet face-to-face in Washington, DC two times a year. Ignacio says that this FtF time is spent on strategic issues like decision making and conducting leadership training. Celia believes that consulting must include a "human touch" achievable only through some degree of face-to-face communication, even when it means flying people around the globe to meet in person. These in-person meetings allow people to discuss important topics and build trusting relationships that help them weather difficult situations that arise in the future.

ADVANTAGES OF DISTANCE CONSULTING & COACHING

Using ICTs to guide remote interventions has several benefits. Technology-mediated distance consulting and coaching can be less expensive than traditional FtF consulting, more convenient, and optimized to meet the needs of the particular client and consulting engagement. In this section, we specifically address how distance consulting and coaching adds economic value, enhances focus on the intervention, creates tighter feedback loops between consultants and their clients, and promotes accessibility to more employees. We begin by explaining how a technology-mediated intervention can be an efficient option.

Efficiency and Convenience

Consulting fees are often heavily laden with travel costs that can inhibit a client's willingness to engage necessary actions in collaboration wit the consultant. Distance consulting and coaching, on the other hand, often reduce travel costs and create benefits similar to FtF coaching—including motivation, focus and information exchange (Rossett & Marino, 2005). Imagine being a consultant in California and having a client in New York. Update meetings might only need to last two hours, but the time it takes for the consultant to travel to New York, have the meeting, and return home will take at least one to two days and the consulting fee will reflect that travel time. In contrast, administering consulting expertise via ICTs removes some of the traditional monetary barriers and provides many organizations a lower cost option that still affords them many of the positive attributes of in-person interventions (Ahrend et al., 2010). Thus, cost containment is a major reason organizations consider using distance coaching and consulting (Warner, 2012).

Distance interventions can be more convenient for both the consultant and the client. An employee in the field does not have to take time away from day-to-day work to take part in meetings or training. And, the consultant need not travel to the client's office to conduct a meeting or training session. In fact, ICTs allow consultants to be in multiple places at the same time (Rossett & Marino, 2005), allowing for a virtual connection with geographically dispersed parties to an engagement. In line with the global operating environment of contemporary organizations, distance coaching and consulting are convenient for foreign employees and non-native English speakers. A meditated interaction allows these individuals more time to check their grammar and word choice than an FtF meeting (Davis, 2012).

While not all consulting interventions can thrive relying on ICTs, these tools can open doors for new forms of participation. Ignacio says that communicating online is a challenge, but has many advantages as well. When traveling in Ghana, he still attended the monthly online meeting to check in with his client. Ignacio claims that meeting regularly online actually makes FtF meetings more comfortable. He feels like he knows people's life stories because he "sees them once a month online. I know them better than people I see physically once every two weeks in my FtF meetings." Once again, we see an important potential advantage of technology and the combinatorial use of ICTs for maintaining client relationships.

Documentation and Focus

The mediated nature of distance coaching and consulting also allows consultants to document and archive their interventions with clients. Email and chat discussion threads become valuable corpora of text that many employees and consultants may save and analyze for recurring themes (Rosset & Marino, 2005). Employees may also record textual, audio and/or video content to share progress and ideas with other individuals or groups within the organization (Averweg, 2010). Emerging leaders in the organization may use these saved virtual exchanges to assess the intervention's effectiveness (Backus, Keegan, Gluck, and Gulick, 2010). Consultants may track themes derived from archived coaching sessions to scale their intervention between an individual employee and the larger organization (Rossett & Marino, 2005).

Many mediated ICTs reduce the number of social cues available during an intervention; thus the intervention changes and can occur more quickly. While this can be a disadvantage, as we will discuss later in this chapter, it also can allow consultants and their clients an opportunity to focus on the task at hand. For example, in voice and text-based media, distractions such as visual indicators of class, race, or gender are filtered out, allowing for singular focus and faster progress (Davis, 2012). Also, in some cases, it takes less time for users to comprehend content presented electronically than in FtF exchanges (Warner, 2012). These are some of the reasons that distance coaching and consulting can be more time efficient while still accomplishing the intervention goals in fewer meetings than a conventional in-person arrangement (Averweg, 2010).

Immediate and Brief Feedback Is a Key Advantage of Mobile Devices

One of the biggest reasons to incorporate ICTs into consultatations for to facilitating conversations with clients is that almost all knowledge workers—indeed, almost all members of contemporary organizations—have access to personal communication technologies like mobile phones. These multifunctional devices can serve as audio and video-recorders in addition the more obvious communication tasks they support, such as talking and texting.

The constant connection that people have with their mobile devices allows for quick, sometimes instantaneous, just-in-time communication and feedback. Margaret often coaches corporate executives who deliver presentations in private situations where she cannot directly observe them and recording is prohibited. The closest thing she has to being physically present is being connected through mobile ICTs. Her clients can update her or ask for advice using text messaging, and she can give near-real-time feedback. The brief messages are often exactly what her clients need in the moment and limited content is all they have time to read and digest.

ICTs Extend Involvement to Multiple Organizational Levels

There was a time when consulting interventions were limited to high-level engagements with organizational leadership. While that is still the case in many consulting engagements today, ICTs have enabled nearly all organizational members to be included in of consulting situations. One particular situation where ICTs have allowed more widespread involvement is in coaching (Backus et al., 2010; Rossett & Marino, 2005; Warner, 2012). Even non-management employees now have access to qualified experts through search engines or databases (Rossett & Marino, 2005). Users can exercise control over their learning experience by selecting coaches from different backgrounds and locations with varying levels of knowledge and experience (Backus et al., 2010).

In addition to the enhanced precision in distance coaching, there is a greater degree of accessibility. A consultant can easily provide resources, solutions, and motivating conversations to staff at multiple organizational levels in any geographic location and at convenient times (Rossett & Marino, 2005). Additionally, distance interventions allow coaches to respond to employees' queries at times convenient to the client (Marshall & Rossett, 2011). Essentially, through distance coaching and consulting, staff at many levels have the flexibility to receive the practical expertise they need, when they need it, and can then implement the advice quickly (Ahrend et al., 2010; Warner, 2012).

CHALLENGES OF DISTANCE COACHING AND CONSULTING

While benefits such as low cost and the affordances of archiving or rapid feedback make distance coaching and consulting appear advantageous, there are some key drawbacks worth noting. This section delves into some of the challenges presented by distance coaching and consulting. We will examine how ICTs encourage an expectancy of accessibility on the part of clients, regardless of time or space. We will also explore the necessity of the "human touch" and the functional limitations of ICTs in a consultative context. Additionally, we address the equivocal role generational difference may play in distance coaching and consulting moving forward. First, we examine trends in multitasking and how that might affect consulting interactions.

Multitasking and Multicommunicating

Being distracted when pretending to be focused is a problem for telephone distance coaching and consulting. Both the consultant and the people being coached need to understand how to pay close attention to verbal conversations. Margaret is a master at listening closely and she explains that when she uses mediated channels, she sometimes listens with her eyes closed to give her undivided attention to her client. But multitasking, or doing multiple things at once, is tempting when others cannot see what you are doing. Furthermore, Celia explains that "everyone is multitasking during conference calls." She explains that people "half listen to a number of things" because that is the efficient thing to do. In other studies conducted by the first author of this chapter, consultants have confessed, "I've put clients on mute so I could order through a drive-through during our hour-long phone conversation." Another consultant described how she scheduled some clients during her morning commute because she needed to work around their schedules on a European time zone. These honest comments describe the working reality of global consultants and the types of task-interweaving that mobility affords.

While many people think they can multitask, well-established and recent research challenges those assumptions (e.g., Ophir, Nass, & Wagner, 2009; Rogers & Monsell, 1995). Stroop (1935), a psychologist, is often credited with initially documenting how the brain cannot process multiple simultaneous tasks because they interfere with one another. Since that time, the field of psychology has shown that cognitive multitasking almost always leads to decreased performance (e.g., Rogers & Monsell, 1995). Although some scholars believe that people performing repetitive tasks might become more practiced (e.g., Ophir et al., 2009), cognitive processes, like consulting conversations, will likely suffer when people switch tasks.

But when others cannot see your behaviors, it is easy to check email, send a text message, or drift off momentarily. And sometimes, the reality of working life means that you will have to—even when engaged in some other task. *Multicommunicating*, then, is the practice of engaging in two or more overlapping conversations facilitated by the use of synchronous and near-synchronous media such as face-to-face conversation, phone, videoconferencing, email, and chat (Reinsch, Turner & Tinsley, 2008). In organizations, multicommunicating may occur during mediated conversations as well as FtF encounters, like meetings (Stephens & Davis, 2009). Sometimes people need to multicommunicate during a consulting conversation, and research suggests that people believe they have done so successfully when they satisfactorily minimize communication errors and simulate active listening (Turner & Reinsch, 2010).The status of the communication partners can influence how and when people multicommunicate (Turner & Reinsch, 2007). For example, some of our clients find it stressful when their managers expect immediate responses, even when they are attending important meetings. These employees have to read the room to see multicommunicating is normative (Stephens & Davis, 2009), and may decide to conceal their behavior.

Researchers have found copious evidence of multicommunicating when organizational members use instant messaging, email, text messaging, and audio calling (e.g., Stephens, 2012; Stephens & Davis, 2009). These overlapping interactions sometimes help team members get a jump on the action items emerging from a conversation, or even to exchange ideas and reactions with a colleague. Celia confirms that many of these side conversations are necessary to help her global team make decisions as quickly as they need to. "People are emailing colleagues sitting across the table and colleagues sitting across the world from them, because they need to better understand the issues. Waiting until after a meeting will simply slow down the process," explains Celia.

Temptation to Be Always On

Jarvenpaa and Lang (2005) provide a thorough description of how mobile ICTs can both enslave and empower individuals, a core paradox in how people use ICTs in consulting interventions. The same useful mobile devices can also be the demon that allows others to text in the middle of the night and awaken our sleep. Indeed, several researchers have uncovered mobile device paradoxes created by this near-constant connection (Jarvenpaa & Lang, 2005; Mazmanian, 2012; Mazmanian, Orlikowski, & Yates, 2013). Mazmanian (2012) examined two different occupational contexts in the same organization and found that it is a combination of the norms that groups enact and individual practices that influence peoples' mobile device habits and their views toward newer technologies.

For example, Celia's group expects accessibility around the clock. Even though Celia functions as an internal organizational advisor and executive, the issues of expected accessibility are similar for external consultants. Margaret coaches many clients who need to perform under intense pressure. During these pressure situations, Margaret's clients expect her to be accessible. This is one of the many reasons that Margaret relies extensively on her mobile phone.

Sometimes Limited Technology Is Most Beneficial

All three of our experienced professionals cited throughout this chapter mentioned that they are sometimes inhibited from achieving their goals by combinatorial ICT use. Celia explains that her organization began the IT restructuring project by getting all the companies in a specific region of the world to think about their own needs in addition to the needs of their global company. This required talking openly about concerns, spending days in the field meeting with key people, and getting them together to meet face-to-face. With such a major organizational change, Celia says, "technology does not take the place of the relationship. Start with the human touch." She wanted to have people in each region build bridges to help one another through such a major change.

Margaret is quick to say that the greatest gift she gives her clients is her ability to "listen deeply," and that can be damaged with too much technology (see Beebe, Chapter 8, for a discussion of consultants' listening skills). Whether meeting in person or coaching on the phone, Margaret believes that listening is a gift consultants must give their clients. She says that Skype and video feedback can be distracting in many of her coaching situations because they mislead her into thinking that she has a deeper understanding of her client than she actually does. Margaret reminds us that technology can be helpful, but nothing can substitute for being face-to-face and finding that true connection with another person. During close in-person work, people are often willing to take the biggest risks and trust their coach or consultant.

Challenges Encountered When Using ICTs as Part of Consulting Interventions

Although ICTs can help consultants interact with clients, they can present some challenges. For example, ICTs do not always work. Meetings can be delayed and clients and consultants can spend considerable time troubleshooting Internet and telephone connections. In addition, consulting interventions can be challenging to facilitate when people misunderstand time zone differences and interrupt conference calls after they begin. Participants on global teams and in multicultural consulting work may experience confusion due to limited contextual cues when comments are put in writing. Celia explains that people need to consider translation differences and take the time to truly understand the meaning of specific words. This issue is heightened in a fast-paced communication environment where people skim multiple replies to long email trails. Consultants must be aware of these technology use challenges and cultural differences and realize that ICTs can heighten problems in some situations.

Another challenge of using ICTs is that, because they are becoming so advanced in the ways they simulate interpersonal communication, they might one day replace some of the current consulting and coaching functions currently provided by humans. Recently, there has been growth in an area called automated e-coaching, and although these platforms are still in the early phases of implementation, they hold some promise for certain consulting interventions. Automated e-coaching systems provide performance coaching through an asynchronous, non-human, computer-mediated interface (Warner, 2012). These autonomous systems represent a contemporary iteration of decision support systems, designed to guide and promote individual self-improvement (Kamphorst & Kalis, 2015; Warner, 2012). To this end, e-coaching systems incorporate e-learning technologies to generate interactive, adaptively derived responses to user inputs (Paramythis & Loidl-Reisinger, 2004; Warner, 2012). As users interact with the system more frequently over time, the system enhances their learning by understanding the users' patterns and needs. This trend is something to watch, because while these systems need considerable work to make them viable (and it might be odd to have a robot as a consultant), these systems could offer advantages to clients and further expand coaching and consulting accessibility.

COACHING AND CONSULTING FUTURE GENERATIONS

Although the research literature on aging cautions us to interpret generational differences in the workplace with care and to avoid generalizing, there are some differences worthy of discussion here. First, millennials are growing up with more mobile ICTs than any generation before. While these tools are also available to workers in all generations, younger people use a mix of ICTs and often report greater comfort with these devices than older workers (Myers & Sadaghiani, 2010). Further, Myers and Sadaghiani claim that millennials want a work environment focused on teamwork and opportunities to feel like an integral part of their organizations. Celia has noticed some variance in communication preferences among members of different age groups when she trains and coaches, and has paid particular attention to the young talent in her organization. Her observations, combined with the current research provide some basis for speculating how consulting interventions might change in the future.

One possibility is that distance consulting become as credible as traditional consultant for establishing trust. For example, in Celia's role as Chief Talent Officer, she has the opportunity to help hire and train recent college graduates. She gets to observe quite a few young people who enter through internship programs and she says there is a significant shift in how these young new hires view collaboration and build trust easily when using ICTs to interaction. She recounts how one company recently brought a group of digitally savvy summer interns together in a room to brainstorm a business problem. As the company's HR Director watched the group, she noticed that the team members immediately opened up their mobile devices and starting collaborating silently. In fact, they seemed almost perplexed by the need to be together physically. They were working at a distance while in the same room. The HR Director was struck by what she observed, and felt certain that she was seeing a glimpse into the future of working relationships. The work they produced was good. The HR Director could see that some quieter interns could more easily be "heard" in a digital collaboration space. Celia considers this anecdote a clue about the formation of digital working relationships, and while it is too early to tell if this is a trend, she is watching it closely. Perhaps trust is built differently in these digital relationships than in more traditional ones; here, the value of the information you find and share with the group determines the quality of your relationship.

While the three experienced professionals we interviewed to provide our extended examples valued face-to-face communication, consulting practices could change as a younger generation brings their communication preferences into consulting interventions. It is too early to tell if this will change consulting in the future, because even twenty-one-year old Ignacio still values FtF connections. What we may be seeing is a generation that realizes that global conversations necessitate extensive ICT use because FtF is an often cost-prohibitive luxury. Furthermore, younger workers will benefit from the increased accessibility and decreased cost of electronic and distance coaching opportunities. They may accept virtual coaching, consulting, and communication practices as the norm, and not expect FtF contact. Research suggests that communicating at a distance can still build close relationships over time, but relationship-building processes that occur exclusively using ICTs take longer to reach the level of satisfaction and benefits of the relationships found with FtF communication (Walther, 1992).

SUMMARY

In this chapter, we have examined the role of ICTs in consulting interventions by juxtaposing real-world examples from actual consultants with relevant contemporary research from a variety of disciplines. We have discussed how combinatorial ICT use helps consultants prepare for client meetings, promote interactivity during interventions, and reinforce the commitments reached. We have offered reasons why distance coaching and consulting can be advantageous as well as identified some of the risks that come with this practice. Finally, we look to the future of ICT use in consulting, noting the rise of automated e-coaching and forecasting how millennials may further incorporate technology into consulting interventions as baby boomers age out of the workforce.

Organizations operate in environments that change continuously. This state of flux often necessitates the use of consultants to help clients adapt and improve. As ICTs become more diverse and ubiquitous, it will be important to watch consultants integrate them into their charge of moving organizations and individuals forward.

REFERENCES

Ahrend, G., Diamond, F., & Webber, P. G. (2010). Virtual coaching: Using technology to boost performance. *Chief Learning Officer, 9*(7), 44–47. Retrieved from: http://ww.w.cedma-europe. org/newsletter%20articles/Clomedia/Virtual%20Coaching%20-%20Using%20Technology%20 to%20Boost%20Performance%20(Jul%2010).pdf

Averweg, U. R. (2010). Enabling role of an intranet to augment e-coaching. *Industrial and Commercial Training, 42*, 47–52.

Backus, C., Keegan, K., Gluck, C., & Gulick, L. (2010). Accelerating leadership development via immersive learning and cognitive apprenticeship. *International Journal of Training and Development, 14*, 144–148.

Block, P. (2011). *Flawless consulting: A guide to getting your expertise used.* New York, NY: John Wiley & Sons.

Bouchal, M. C., Fahs, M., Frei, S., Martin, J., Patton, G., & Stephens, K. K. (2012, November). *100 Ideas for increasing interactivity in training and teaching.* Paper presented at the National Communication Association Meeting, Orlando, FL.

Davis, A. (2012). The implementation of computer mediated communication in communication centers. In E. L. Yook & W. Atkins-Sayre (Eds.) *Communication centers and oral communication programs in higher education: Advantages, challenges, and new directions* (pp. 217–230). Lanham, MD: Lexington Books.

Geissler, H., Hasenbein, M., Kanatouri, S., & Wegener, R. (2014). E-coaching: Conceptual and empirical findings of a virtual coaching programme. *International Journal of Evidence Based Coaching & Mentoring, 12*, 165–187. Retrieved from: http://ezproxy.lib.utexas.edu/login?url=http://search. ebscohost.com/login.aspx?direct=true&db=bth&AN=98490637&site=ehost-live

Jarvenpaa, S. L., & Lang, K. R. (2005). Managing the paradoxes of mobile technology. *Information Systems Management, 22*, 7–23.

Kamphorst, B., & Kalis, A. (2014). Why option generation matters for the design of autonomous e-coaching systems. *AI & Society, 29*, 1–12. doi:10.1007/s00146-013-0532-5.

Ling, R., & Donner, J. (2013). Mobile phones and mobile communication. Malden, MA: Polity Press.

London, M., & Hall, M. J. (2011). Unlocking the value of Web 2.0 technologies for training and development: The shift from instructor-controlled, adaptive learning to learner-driven, generative learning. *Human Resource Management, 50*, 757–775.

Marshall, J., & Rossett, A. (2011). Mapping the e-learning terrain. *International Journal on E-Learning, 10*, 169–198. Retrieved from: http://www.editlib.org/p/33089/ Ling, R., & Donner, J. (2013). *Mobile phones and mobile communication.* Hoboken, NJ: Wiley.

March, J. G. (1991). Organizational consultants and organizational research. *Journal of Applied Communication Research, 19*, 20–31.

Mazmanian, M. (2012). Avoiding the trap of constant connectivity: When congruent frames allow for heterogeneous practices. *Academy of Management Journal, 56,* 1225–1250.

Mazmanian, M., Orlikowski, W. J., & Yates, J. (2013). The autonomy paradox: The implications of mobile email devices for knowledge professionals. *Organization Science, 24,* 1337–1357.

Myers, K. K., & Sadaghiani, K. (2010). Millennials in the workplace: A communication perspective on Millennials' organizational relationships and performance. *Journal of Business Psychology, 25,* 225–238.

Ophir, E., Nass, C., & Wagner, A. D. (2009). Cognitive control in media multitaskers, *Proceedings National Academy of Science, 106,* 15583–15587.

Otte, S., Bangerter, A., Britsch, M., & Wüthrich, U. (2014). Attitudes of coaches towards the use of computer-based technology in coaching. *Consulting Psychology Journal: Practice and Research, 66,* 38–52.

Paramythis, A., & Loidl-Reisinger, S. (2004). Adaptive learning environments and e-learning standards. *Electronic Journal on e-Learning, 2,* 181–194. Retrieved from: http://www.ask4research. info/Uploads/Files/Citations/issue1-art11-paramythis.pdf

Ramirez, A., & Burgoon, J. K. (2004). The effect of interactivity on initial interactions: The influence of information valence and modality and information richness on computer-mediated interaction. *Communication Monographs, 71,* 422–447.

Ramirez, A., Walther, J. B., Burgoon, J. K., & Sunnafrank, M. (2002). Information-seeking strategies, uncertainty, and computer-mediated communication: Toward a conceptual model. *Human Communication Research, 28,* 213–228.

Reinsch, N. L., Turner, J. W., & Tinsley, C. H. (2008). Multicommunicating: A practice whose time has come? *Academy of Management Review, 33,* 391–403.

Rogers R. D., & Monsell S. (1995). Costs of a predictable switch between simple cognitive tasks. *Journal of Experimental Psychology, 124,* 207–231.

Rossett, A., & Marino, G. (2005). If coaching is good, then e-coaching is. *Talent Development, 59,* 46–49. Retrieved from: http://www.vickistasch.com/files/DMS/coaching_article.pdf

Sherpa Coaching (2014). *Executive coaching survey '14: Evidence & interaction.* Retrieved on November, 11, 2011 from http://www.sherpacoaching.com/pdf%20files/2014%20Executive%20 Coaching%20Survey%20-%20Public%20report.pdf.

Sitzmann, T., Bell, B. S., Kraiger, K., & Kanar, A. M. (2009). A multilevel analysis of the effect of prompting self-regulation in technology-delivered instruction. *Personnel Psychology, 62,* 697–734.

Stephens, K. K. (2007). The successive use of information and communication technologies at work. *Communication Theory, 17,* 486–509.

Stephens, K. K. (2012). Multiple conversations during organizational meetings: Development of the multicommunicating scale. *Management Communication Quarterly, 26,* 195–223.

Stephens, K. K., & Davis, J. D. (2009). The social influences on electronic multitasking in organizational meetings. *Management Communication Quarterly, 23,* 63–83.

Stephens, K. K., & Mottet, T. M. (2008). Interactivity in a web conferencing training context: Effects on trainers & trainees. *Communication Education, 57,* 88–104.

Stephens, K. K., Sørnes, J. O, Rice, R. E., Browning, L. D., & Sætre, A. S. (2008). Discrete, sequential, and follow-up use of information and communication technology by managerial knowledge workers. *Management Communication Quarterly, 22,* 197–231.

Stroop, J. R. (1935). Studies of interference in serial verbal reactions. *Journal of Experimental Psychology, 18,* 643–662.

Turner, J. W., & Reinsch, N. L. (2007). The business communicator as presence allocator: Multicommunicating, equivocality, and status at work. *Journal of Business Communication, 44*(1), 36–58.

Turner, J. W., & Reinsch, N. L. (2010). Successful and unsuccessful multicommunication episodes: Engaging in dialogue or juggling messages? *Information Systems Frontiers, 12*, 277–285.

Waldeck, J. H. (2008). The development of an industry-specific online learning center: Consulting lessons learned. *Communication Education, 57*, 452–463.

Walther, J. B. (1992). Interpersonal effects in computer-mediated interaction: A relational perspective. *Communication Research, 19*, 52–90.

Warner, T. (2012). E-coaching systems: Convenient, anytime, anywhere, and nonhuman. *Performance Improvement, 51*, 22–28.

CHAPTER FOURTEEN

Providing Research Services for Clients

FRANKLIN J. BOSTER

Michigan State University

"Serious academics write journal articles, not books. Serious academics write data-based papers, not essays…" And so the conversation would go as Nick Henry and I sat together chuckling over lunch. I was a young assistant professor at Arizona State University (ASU), and Nick was the Dean of our college, the College of Public Programs. The fact that both Nick and I grew up in and around St. Louis, Missouri meant, among other things, that we rooted for the same baseball team, knew or knew about some of the same people, could argue whether Phil the Gorilla or Blondie the Python was a bigger attraction at the St. Louis Zoo, and could voice reasoned opinions on the merits and limitations of restaurants located in the Central West End. That explained why a Dean would have lunch with a lowly assistant professor. The game developed from these lunches, and we played it almost every time that we lunched together. The goal was to generate a new statement that characterized the stereotypical view of what was considered a "serious academic" at that time. Had we both stayed at ASU, and had we continued the game, one of the statements might have been "Serious academics do NOT consult." Of course, we were being facetious. Nick wrote books, and good ones. I wrote some essays. Back then, however, I would have agreed with "Serious academics do NOT consult." Given that I am writing this chapter, it is obvious that a change occurred.

The change might not at first blush be thought of as obvious, however. I still have similar ideas as to what serious academics do, although admittedly my views have broadened a bit. What has changed substantially, though, is my view of what consultants do. What I came to realize is that the skill set that I use when working with my clients involves the same skills I employ in my laboratory work. Indeed, in the main, my consulting experience has centered around performing applied communication research.

My consulting experience started out innocently enough. One of my ASU colleagues, who would likely prefer to remain anonymous, called one day soliciting my interest in a project. A manager in the check processing department of a bank had a problem that he characterized as a communication problem, and knowing that my colleague was a faculty member in the Department of Communication he asked for his help. Because a solution might involve knowledge of social influence and group dynamics, matters in which I specialized, he asked if I would accompany him and I agreed to do so.

The problem was hardly a communication problem. To curry favor with his supervisors, the manager had cut the piece rate formula of those working in the check processing room. The best employees immediately applied for jobs at a competing bank, and they were hired almost as soon as they finished their applications. Now that more errors were being made, and it was taking significantly longer to complete the task, and because the manager anticipated that more of his skilled work force would be leaving soon, he asked us to convince them to remain on the job. We declined, suggesting that he restore the previous rate, the same rate that his competitor was offering.

Suffice to say that the experience was far from what I had expected. Trying to make sense of the experience I reflected on the differences between what it was that I thought consultants did and what I had just done. My view of consultants invoked people with complex, highly specific skills being asked by perplexed high-level public sector or private sector leaders to solve very specifically identified and perplexing problems. My mental image was of W. Edwards Deming, the great management consultant. My expectations were violated in at least three ways: (1) the person asking us to solve his "problem" was not a high-level leader, (2) the problem was not perplexing, and (3) the problem identified by the client was not the problem as we viewed it. My stereotypical view of what consultants do had been challenged. My view is more nuanced today than what it was then, but I continue to be amazed at the consulting experiences of others as well as my own.

HAVE COMMUNICATION PH.D., WILL CONSULT

Since that rather unfulfilling and less than highly compensating event, numerous other consulting opportunities have presented themselves. I use the phrase "presented themselves" because I have not marketed my consulting services. Rather, a few clients have come calling. In some cases it has been a telephone call, in others email messages, in one case a personal visit to my office, and in another a personal visit to my home.

These opportunities have been varied, but they fit neatly somewhere within a framework familiar to many of us. Each of them has involved employing some or all of the skills that are acquired when, in the course of one's graduate training, one learns how to conduct a study and communicate the results of that study in a research report. Put simply, I found that the skills that I acquired getting my Ph.D. were very marketable. Some of my clients knew that I possessed these skills because of word of mouth; they spoke to others who knew me. In other cases, I was surprised to learn that people in the private and public sectors were familiar with some of my research. They had actually spent time reading the communication literature, had come across some of my papers, and had been impressed sufficiently by what I had written to pursue a working relationship with me. In yet other cases, their reasons for contacting me remain mysterious.

A Range of Research-Focused Consulting Experiences

In this section I shall discuss the broad categories of consulting research in which I have engaged. They will sound very familiar to those engaged in scholarly communication inquiry. I have reviewed literatures, developed measuring instruments, designed and executed experiments, and analyzed data. In the process of engaging in these activities it has been necessary to make ample use of my communication skills and project coordination skills in order to produce a product acceptable to my clients. Several examples will be provided, and major challenges that had to be confronted will be described.

Conducting literature reviews. The range of my consulting experiences parallels the sections of the traditional social scientific research report. So, for instance, one law firm with which I have worked asked me to report on particular areas of research relevant to cases pertaining to their clients. These tasks involved identifying the relevant literatures, reading them critically so that general conclusions could be drawn from them, trying to understand these conclusions theoretically, and communicating these conclusions to the firm. You will, no doubt, recognize these tasks as work that we do when writing the introduction section of a research paper.

Because of helpful databases, such as PsychINFO, the Social Science Citation Index, and others, identifying a relevant literature is less challenging than it once was. But, reading it critically remains as challenging, or more, than it has ever been. One reason is that literatures are ever growing, so that mastering them requires reading and processing vast amounts of information. Progress in quantitative literature review techniques, aka meta-analysis, is helpful in this regard. This technique has had the beneficial effect of producing less biased, more rigorous, more precise, and more accurate literature summaries. On the other hand, it also requires acquiring what for many might be a new skill, or set of skills, namely learning some things about meta-analysis. And, some literatures are not particularly amenable to meta-analysis. For example, the manner in which results are reported in some areas of health communication and public health render it difficult to extract the bivariate effect sizes needed to perform meta-analyses. Finally, not infrequently, there are multiple meta-analyses on a given subject and they do not always reach the same conclusion.

In the absence of available meta-analyses, reading critically requires applying those methodological and analytic skills in which we are trained. The adequacy of samples for allowing investigators to assess their hypotheses or research questions; evidence pertaining to the validity and reliability of measures; features of experimental designs that limit the external, internal, and ecological validity of experiments; and features of procedures that might produce confounds in experiments all inform how confidently the conclusions that investigators draw from their research are embraced. And, these considerations factor into the advice communicated to our clients.

The application of theory was especially important in consulting with my law firm clients. Although relatively few cases come to trial, law firms must anticipate cases coming to trial and be prepared for them. Trial attorneys are constantly looking for effective ways to present their case, or, put differently, tell their story. Lucid theories provide those stories. Because many of the literatures you will be called upon to review are very much applied, and because in such areas investigators often give only a cursory nod to matters theoretical, providing useful advice to law firms often requires being familiar with many theoretical frameworks so as to be better equipped to make sense of any empirical regularities that you might observe.

So, for example, when trying to explain why peers and family members might influence a plaintiff's behavior more than advertisements, it has been useful to refer to the subjective norm component embedded in the Theory of Reasoned Action and the Theory of Planned Behavior. When explaining the matter to attorneys, Fishbein and Ajzen's (1975) narrative provides an articulate way to express the point. Similarly, to explain why the credibility of the source of a message would be effective under certain conditions, and not others, I have found that cognitive response theories (e.g., Chaiken, 1980) provide an understandable narrative for attorneys.

After reaching some conclusions about a literature and finding a theory or theories that allows them to be presented in an understandable way to audiences such as juries, CEOs, or school principals, these conclusions must, at some point, be presented to the client, e.g., the law firm. Once again, this process is informed by the manner in which we typically write literature reviews, but it highlights ways in which our reviews might be improved. Jurors, CEOs, and school principals tend to understand cogent arguments. Communication scholars understand how to construct arguments. Being audience-oriented allows us to do something that is both natural to us and is effective; namely, present any written or oral product as an argument. The simple structure of an argument, premises which entail a conclusion, allows us to present empirical generalizations as the premises and draw a conclusion(s) from them. The empirical studies or the meta-analyses provide the evidence which leads the audience to embrace the premises. All of this information can be produced in a concise manner for an audience that already has much too much to read.

Lest I paint too rosy a picture, there are formidable challenges involved in such work. One is that there is never enough time. Studies are being conducted and published at a rate that render reading all relevant research impossible, particularly with topics that might lead to litigation. Couple this social force with client deadlines, and one realizes quickly that being thorough will be problematic. But, then again, this state of affairs is nothing new to us. It characterizes the spheres in which we do research as well. Just as the conclusions of any and all literature reviews are unable to anticipate what future studies might find, so too our reports to our clients have the same limitation. The best that we can do is conduct a broad and *unbiased* search for relevant, well-conducted studies that will inform the client.

The unbiased part of the last sentence is particularly important. I have been blessed with legal clients who want to know the truth about some proposition. Others in my acquaintance have not. To provide an example of the kind of client that I have in mind, allow me to share one such interaction. From 1973–1977 my major professor, Gerald R. Miller, had two large NSF grants the focus of which was the study of videotape in the law—a project to which his students referred as Videotape in the Legal Environment, or VILE for short. One of the requirements (or perks, depending on how you view it) of these grants was that each year we had to present the results of our research conducted during that year to the legal community of some large city of our choosing. One member of the legal community at one of these workshops (as we referred to them) was a judge who had been using videotape in his courts for some time. At this time this practice was very controversial, Miller's research being instrumental in it becoming the common practice that it is today. This judge loved our research and raved about it. The reason was simple: we found no evidence that videotaped trials or inserting segments of videotape testimony into otherwise live trials had any substantial effect on trial outcomes. It confirmed his bias and his practice at the time. At dinner one night, one of our more mischievous research team members asked him what he would think of our research if we had found that videotaped trials and live trials produced very different trial outcomes. He responded rapidly and vehemently that he would disregard it and characterize it as invalid.

It is important to note that this gentleman was not lacking in intelligence, nor was he evil. Rather, his own personal experience convinced him that our conclusions were correct because they were consistent with his own. The possibilities that his experience might be unusual or that he might have misinterpreted it did not occur to him. Consequently, he used scientifically generated evidence in much the same way that the town drunk used the lamppost—more for support than illumination. Such clients pose special challenges for the consultant, and there are times when one simply has to dissolve the relationship due to a client's unwillingness to acknowledge alternative perspectives.

Overcoming methodological challenges. The methodological skills obtained while pursuing the Ph.D. are pivotal to becoming a productive scholar. But, as witnessed by the number of communication Ph.D.s working outside of the academic environment, they also have tremendous value both in the private and public sectors. This point was mentioned earlier in the chapter in the context of conducting a critical review of a literature, but it applies in two other ways as well. First, some consulting projects are methodological projects. Second, some consulting projects involve conducting original research, and similar methodological principles apply in both these projects as well as in academic research.

As an example of the former I was once hired by a utility to perform a challenging measurement task. In many states, if not all of them, those managing construction projects are required to contact a state-sponsored facility announcing their intention to dig or work overhead at a particular location. The state-sponsored facility then contacts relevant units such as cable companies, those in municipalities in charge of maintaining sewer lines and water lines, those utilities with gas lines in the area, and others. These units are then charged with marking where in that area their cable lines, water and sewer lines, gas lines, etc. are located. In that way, they may be avoided by those performing the construction work so that people can avoid losing cable service, municipalities can avoid suffering water or sewer lines breaks, and gas line explosions can be avoided. Likely you have seen small colored coded flags stuck in the ground around construction sites or chalk (or paint) on the pavement of your street where construction is about to take place. Gas companies refer to this marking activity as staking, and the stakes in marking in a timely and accurate fashion are high. If failure to mark in a timely manner results in a contractor's crew beginning to dig under the assumption that there are no gas lines in the area, or if inaccurate staking results in a contractor's crew hitting a gas line, death and substantial destruction of property is likely to ensue.

Working under the assumption that it is impossible to assess how well their team of stakers was performing without being able to measure it, representatives of a utility once asked me to develop measures of the timeliness and accuracy of their stakers. This task was to be accomplished by a team composed of stakers, dispatchers, representatives of management, and me. Although initially I thought that this task would be an easy one, far more challenges arose than I anticipated. Additionally, I found that one of the more esoteric bits of knowledge that I had about measurement was surprisingly useful.

The primary challenge was a lack of trust between labor and management, with the consultant stuck between the two camps. Stakers and dispatchers were convinced that management wanted to eliminate some of their jobs. Management was convinced that the stakers and dispatchers wanted to avoid being evaluated. And, both groups were suspicious of me! It likely was not personal, but rather was a suspicion of academics in general.

So, to be able to work effectively with them I had to use the listening skills that I taught in my classes (see Beebe, Chapter 8). I had to understand their jargon while explaining myself using a minimum of my own jargon (see Plax, Waldeck, & Kearney, Ch. 6). I had to spend time separately with each group so that I could better understand their jobs—to the extent that I rode with stakers as they went about their jobs (see Pettegrew, Chapters 4 & 18). I had to be very careful to present my credentials, both as someone who knew something about measurement and as someone who could understand their position. Fortunately, I had done a reasonable amount of physical labor, such as working in steel mills, brass mills, dairies, and concrete block plants. Sharing these experiences with the stakers and dispatchers in casual conversation contributed to building relationships with these team members, as studies investigating the effect of source similarity on source trust have shown (e.g., Racherla, Mandviwalla, & Connolly, 2012), and as Plax et al. advocate in Chapter 6 of this volume. Also, fortunately, I had done other consulting work with Fortune 500 companies, and sharing some of these experiences with the managers on the team contributed to building relationships with these team members. One important conclusion that I drew from this experience was that it may be impossible to separate the politics of organizational life from the process of doing research in an organization (Waldeck, Plax, & Kearney, Chapter 7), and when such circumstances arose it was necessary to use the communication skills at one's disposal to do research effectively.

Specialized knowledge of measurement was important as well. One of those specialized pieces of knowledge involved the Spearman-Brown Prophecy Formula. Near the turn of the 19th to the 20th century both Spearman and Brown derived and published an identical psychometric result. They demonstrated that all things being equal (i.e., all measures being of the same quality), the more indicators one employed to measure a construct the more reliable would be the construct. By explaining this principle in a non-technical way, and without using the phrase, *the Spearman-Brown Prophecy Formula*, I was able to get all sides of the controversy to accept certain measures of which they were suspicious and so to develop a multiple indicator indices of timeliness and accuracy. Parenthetically, a phrase that I used to help make this principle very concrete to the team was one taken from the world of sailing, although it would be readily understood by those doing many types of physical labor. It was "if you cannot tie good (as in perfect) knots, tie a lot of them." This experience demonstrated the importance of being able to translate the skills you employ as a researcher for people more interested in outcomes than in measurement theory.

A second set of examples of the usefulness of methodological skills arose from projects in which I agreed to evaluate products and services for those who produced them. Primarily, these studies were experiments conducted for firms which design and market products and materials for K–12 classrooms. To provide some context, the pressure placed on schools to increase students' standardized test scores expanded the market for products and services that promised to meet this need. Consequently, a spate of educational products were developed, particularly numerous products that involved technological innovations (e.g., Smart Boards, Discovery Streaming, and others). School officials soon began to suspect (and correctly so) that not all of these costly products were effective, and began demanding to see evidence of product effectiveness prior to purchase.

As a result, a need arose for firms to have their products evaluated, and because performing these evaluations themselves was deemed to be a conflict of interest, they sought outside consultants to do this task. Surprisingly, early on, faculty in Colleges of Education did not pursue these opportunities as often as most of us would expect. Because many of these products (interventions) were communication related—communication technology particularly—an opportunity arose for communication consults to engage in this type of work.

Knowledge of sampling, design, and measurement were crucial to conducting these experiments. For example, one complicating factor in these experiments was that stakeholders were wary of results produced outside of the context of actual classrooms. They demanded field experiments. Furthermore, because their products often produced only small effects in the time available for evaluation, and because stakeholders used simple decisions rules, such as "statistically significant = it works, not statistically significant = it does not work" (despite my advice or vehement objections or both) the experiments also demanded large sample sizes if the null hypothesis was to be rejected.

The composition of the sample was also of considerable concern to the educational product development firms. Marketing a product to a California school district by presenting the results of an evaluation conducted in Virginia proved to be a remarkably tough sale. A number of California districts argued that their districts were unique, and that only an evaluation performed on their students would be acceptable. My clients soon learned that California was not the only state in which they heard this argument. The result was that multiple evaluations had to be conducted, and the districts in which these evaluation experiments were conducted needed to be diverse in terms of performance of the district(s), racial composition of the district, size of the district, and other characteristics.

In some ways, designing the evaluations was easy. Minimally, they needed to compare a group that received the intervention with one that did not. But, numerous complications arose. For example, as we were taught in our methods courses, the highest standard is the randomized trial, randomly assigning students to the control or experimental condition in this case. Because the assignment of students to classes was not a task that schools were willing to delegate for the purposes of research, however, this strategy proved impossible. Instead, classes were typically assigned randomly to conditions, requiring that the extent of dependence in the data be assessed.

A second, related challenge, was whether or not to make assignment to conditions within or between buildings. Again, to provide some context, suppose that the intervention is targeted at 4th graders, and that a school district has eight elementary schools with each of these eight schools having two 4th grade classrooms. One way to assign classrooms to conditions is to assign randomly each of the sixteen 4th grade classes to either the control or experimental condition, usually with the constraint of equal cell size (eight in the control group and eight in the experimental group). An alternative procedure is to assign randomly four of the schools to the control condition and four of the schools to the experimental condition, so that there are eight classrooms of students in the control group and eight in the experimental group.

There are other options, but each option has some less than optimal features. For example, in the former case the consultant must worry about "bleeding." There is the concern that students in the same school, some of whom might be in the control condition, and others who might be in the experimental condition, will talk to each other about what they are doing in class. There might even be some loss in the fidelity of the intervention if teachers share educational materials or strategy. Such circumstances provide a serious challenge to the internal validity of the experimental results.

Alternatively, randomly assigning schools to conditions raises the question of whether the control schools and the experimental schools are comparable. Even within district there tend to be non-trivial differences in the performance of students, teachers, and principals. Once again, these differences, if not controlled or measured, provide a challenge to the internal validity of the experimental results.

In addition to principles of sound scientific experimental design, important ethical issues that affected the quality of the experiment arose in the design of these experiments. Frequently, school administrators were loath to assign students to the control condition. Despite a lack of evidence that the educational intervention was effective, they tended to presume that it was, and they wanted the best for their students. Generally, a compromise was reached, and that compromise was that the intervention would take place only over a relatively short time after which the intervention would then be made available to control condition students. One implication of this compromise was that the effect of the intervention on high stakes tests, or "long tests," such as those administered by every state to assess achievement were rarely affected because the intervention was of insufficient duration to distinguish control and experimental students' scores. Thus, the less than optimal strategy of conducting "short tests," examinations testing the material covered in perhaps a month's duration, had to be constructed to evaluate the intervention. The short test criterion measures were generally of lower reliability and unknown validity relative to the "long tests." Moreover, from the standpoint of educational decision makers, finding differences between control group performance and experimental group performance on short tests was less persuasive than differences on long tests when reaching conclusions regarding the efficacy of the intervention.

From experiences like these, and others, I have concluded that the methodological principles that I have learned have wide applicability both in the private sector and in the public sector. On the other hand, the consultant often has to supplement these principles with other skills. Specifically, communication skills are crucial to explain to clients why an experiment will be better received by their target audience if designed in a particular way, to describe certain trade-offs so that they can make an informed choice in matters such as how to assign students or classes to experimental conditions, or to build the trust required to execute a project effectively. It must be anticipated that clients and those who become the focus of study will raise issues that demand pragmatic solutions to problems unique to each research setting. The combination of research and communication skills that communication scholars possess prepare us, perhaps uniquely, to solve such problems.

Analyzing primary data. For those of us who conduct academic research, the data analysis task that follows data collection is a natural part of the craft. Nevertheless, as a consultant conducting an educational product evaluation, for example, you may find yourself placed in difficult and sometimes uncomfortable situations. One reason is that not infrequently, clients think dichotomously rather than quantitatively about matters that are decidedly quantitative. So, for example, the question they tend to ask is, "Did my product (intervention) work?" The question that they do not ask (and should) is, "How well did my product work?" These questions are not the same. Suppose that in an evaluation experiment examining Product A there are 1,200 participants, and the experimental group outperforms the control group by approximately 0.12 standard deviations, i.e., $d = 0.12$. Contrast this result with an evaluation experiment examining Product B in which there are also 1,200 participants, but the experimental group outperforms the control group by 1.15 standard deviations. Both results are statistically significant. Yet, the latter is of such a magnitude that the product evinced strong evidence of effectiveness. Put differently, one could predict students' scores from knowing whether they were in the control group or the experimental group with relatively high accuracy. The former effect, on the other hand, indicates little evidence of effectiveness. The magnitude of this effect, corresponding to a correlation of .06 between the condition to which the student was assigned and dependent variable score, informs us that knowing the condition to which students were assigned has little ability to predict their score on the dependent variable. Furthermore, comparing the effects produces statistical evidence indicating that Product B is more effective than Product A.

Communicating this fact to clients who have developed Product A is difficult, but, as discussed subsequently, it is manageable. Nevertheless, one must keep in mind that it is not what they will want to hear. They will want to focus on a simple narrative: "the experimental group outperformed the control group, the effective was statistically significant, and therefore my product works." They will tend to resist any mention of the meager size of the effect. They will wish to edit any discussion of the effect of their product relative to others.

Their narrative is fueled by two factors. First, the stakes of these evaluations are high. Often, relatively small firms must spend a substantial amount of their operating budget to have an evaluation conducted. To find no evidence, or weak evidence, of effectiveness places their business in a difficult position. They have spent scarce resources that cannot help the firm immediately, and for small firms that fact looms large. Moreover, they run the risk that the results might become known to their competitors.

Second, the simple heuristic that is the null hypothesis statistical significance test is a contributing factor. It presents a clear and simple bar for clients to reach. It may also affect the design and conduct of evaluation research. Given the pressure to produce statistically significant results, clients might demand that the sample size be extraordinarily high or that more data be collected if initial results are not statistically significant. The pressure that they bring to bear might result in consultants employing unwarranted one-tailed tests rather than warranted two-tailed tests.

A second message that is difficult to present to the client occurs when unwanted (by the client) effects emerge. Although I have experienced this problem, the most interesting example of it arose with one of my students. A consultant had obtained a contract to examine some of the factors that impact physical aggression in schools, and he had employed my student to perform the data analyses for him. In her analyses, she found that a strong predictor was marijuana use, but that the correlation was negative. That is, those students who reported using marijuana were less aggressive than were those who reported not using marijuana. This news would be expected by anyone who had ever used marijuana, but it was clearly not what the funding agency wanted to hear. The student wrote up the results, and the consultant edited out that part of her report.

Once again, I have found that our communication skills are very useful in such circumstances. And, the place that they need to be introduced is prior to signing a contract with the client (see Waldeck, Plax, & Kearney, Chapter 7). It must be made clear to the client, in writing if necessary, that the results that they would prefer cannot be guaranteed. If the client is reluctant to agree to this principle, then walking away from the contract is the best course of action.

Moreover, insofar as it is possible, it is useful to provide a template of the analyses that will be conducted, and of the conclusions that might be drawn. For example, pointing out that one will perform a t-test to compare mean test scores on the Michigan Educational Assessment Program test in the control group and experimental group, that effect sizes will be calculated, and that effect sizes will be used in the Discussion Section of the report to draw conclusions about the effectiveness of the intervention, forms a useful foundation from which to start a conversation about the analyses. Generally, you will have to explain statistics such as d, but that task is accomplished easily. Often clients will suggest additional analyses that they would like conducted. For example, they might want the effects of the intervention to be broken down by racial affiliation of the student. The consultant might have to point out that such an analysis, although certainly desirable, might be impossible due to the small numbers of certain racial groups. Making that point may lead the client to rethink the venue that they have proposed for the study, or might lead them to seek entry into additional districts so as to increase the diversity of the sample.

Program or product evaluation research. It is also useful to discuss matters of product improvement based on data that you have collected. That is, raise the issue of whether the evaluation needs to include a component that will allow specific weaknesses in the product to be identified if they exist. For me, raising this question has produced some interesting results and a stronger client relationship. In an experiment evaluating a video streaming product, the question was raised as to the effectiveness of all sections of the firm's video library. This discussion led to including an evaluation of multiple parts of the library (e.g., science, social studies, mathematics). The subsequent results indicated deficiencies in certain parts of the library that resulted in the company purchasing new and better content in the deficient area. In a subsequent evaluation, exposure to this content resulted in experimental students outperforming control students by a substantial margin.

A question to raise prior to conducting an evaluation experiment is "who owns the data?" In my experience, the client will be reluctant to cede control, and that is likely reasonable. They may even insist that the consultant not discuss the existence of the experiment or the results of the experiment without their permission. Although this position conflicts with values that most academics endorse, in proprietary research situations, it is understandable, and may be a deal breaker should you not agree to it. When I accept such terms I comfort myself with the thought that if the product failed to produce evidence of effectiveness in my experiment, it is likely to produce similar results for others. Consequently, the client is unlikely to be able to amass the quantity of evidence necessary to satisfy those to whom they are trying to market the product. Alternatively, if subsequent evaluations do produce evidence of effectiveness, then there might have been a flaw in my experiment (or the client had improved the product).

A similar issue that might be raised is one of publication. If the results indicate effectiveness, then you might want to be able to publish them. It is important to discuss this possibility with the client, as well as trying to ascertain their expectations. For example, I have had, after the fact, clients who urged me to publish the results of evaluations. For reasons that are no doubt clear from the preceding paragraphs, I have found that these conversations are much more productive before conducting the experiment, as opposed to explaining to the client after the fact why you are unable to answer certain questions that interest them.

Analyzing secondary data. Because of the data analytic skills acquired in communication Ph.D. programs, many communication scholars are well equipped to serve as statistical consultants. In my experience, that type of work has involved analyzing data already collected by marketing research firms. Analyzing secondary or archival data raises many of the same issues discussed in the previous section, but there are some unique challenges that arise from being brought in after the data are collected. The chief challenge is that the consultant must frequently deal with data inadequate to answer the questions the marketing research firm, as well as their clients, want answered.

One way in which these data may be inadequate involves measurement. In the world of marketing, research questions and measurement scales or tools are viewed as profit generating mechanisms. In the arena of syndicated business, clients can create, and pay for, unique questions placed on surveys. Alternatively, or additionally, they may pay for access to answers to certain questions. Hence, it is profitable for marketing research firms to try to measure as many different constructs as possible. And, because of natural limitations to the length of surveys, this goal is best accomplished by measuring each construct with one item. In some cases the firms simply ask items the answers to which will interest prospective clients with no thought to the construct being measured. Put differently, they have no measurement model.

Unfortunately, we know that all things equal, the more items employed to measure a construct, the more reliable will be the resulting index, i.e., the sum or mean of responses to those items. It follows that measuring a construct with only one item is likely to result in a very unreliable measurement. Furthermore, it is also well known that unreliability has the systematic effect of attenuating estimates of association, such as correlation coefficients. The result of these two psychometric facts is that it is often difficult to find strong associations among constructs in the marketing research world even when they exist, because they are attenuated due to large errors of measurement. The lesson here is that if you, as a data analytic consultant, are able to contribute to constructing the questionnaire, it is in your best interest (as well as the project's) to do so. Trying to get at least two indicators of pivotal constructs will serve you well in their subsequent analyses of the data.

A second data analytic challenge that characterizes much of the marketing research world is that data collection is cross-sectional, or static, and clients may want to draw causal conclusions. Two caveats are necessary at this juncture. First, some marketing research projects involve description only. Means or percentages are all that is required. Marketing research firms can do such work in house, however, so that data analytic consultants are not required. Second, some marketing research is longitudinal in the sense that the same questions are asked annually, or at other time intervals. Rarely, however, do they track the same people over time so that actual change can be observed and so that better causal inferences can be drawn.

But the mainstay of the industry, the cross-sectional survey, puts the data analytic consultant in an unenviable position. All of us learned in our undergraduate methods course, if not before, that it is dangerous to infer causal relations from cross-sectional association; the relationship might be spurious, or the causal order the opposite of what we suppose. Once again, without input into the design of the project, there is little the data analytic consultant can do other than resist drawing the unwarranted causal inferences.

I have observed marketing research firms advising their clients in ways that are unwarranted given their data, and perhaps their analysts' recommendations. Sometimes the unwarranted advice stems from premature causal claims; in other cases it may be something quite different. Consider one example that I have encountered.

A client in the fast food industry approached a marketing research firm for which I did occasional work and raised an interesting question. They knew that their offerings were not particularly tasty and that they were certainly not very nutritious. They also knew that they could improve substantially on both criteria, but that to do so would require a substantial financial investment in the form of revamping their kitchens. They were willing to make the investment if it would be cost effective, but not otherwise. So, they asked the marketing research firm in question to propose a study to answer their question. The CEO did so. The fast food company, however, thought the price of the project excessive. They mentioned that they had hired another marketing research firm to collect data for another purpose and that they thought these data would be relevant to answering the focal question. They went on to suggest that these data could be reanalyzed, and offered the marketing research firm for which I did occasional work a smaller contract to perform and write up the results of these reanalyses. These reanalyses involved some statistical techniques with which the marketing research firm's personnel lacked the skills to answer, and I was offered the job.

After extensive examination of the data set two things became clear. First, the data were not adequate to answer the question. But, second, they were not even adequate to answer the questions that they were designed to answer. Dismayed, I called the CEO of the marketing research firm and reported my findings. Expecting him to be equally dismayed, I was shocked when he said, "Great! Write it up and send it to me." I did, and sent in my bill.

Less than a week later he called and said that two vice-presidents wanted to meet with us to discuss the report, and asked me to accompany him. The meeting raised suspicion. Instead of meeting at corporate headquarters they wanted to meet us at a room in the local airport. It might be a tad of a hyperbole to say that the meeting was Kafkaesque, but not by much. Although it lasted longer than 90 minutes, the bottom line was pretty simple. The two vice-presidents had hired the other marketing research firm to collect data for a particular purpose, our report said that their data did not accomplish that purpose, and the combination of those two facts would have serious negative consequences for their careers. So, they informed the CEO that if we "softened" our report, his marketing firm would be given the original contract they had pitched.

When we walked out of the room and headed toward our gates to make our respective flights, the CEO asked if I knew what had happened. I essentially repeated the previous paragraph. He said that I was right, and then we made eye contact—prolonged eye contact—before I said, "I am not doing it." His reply was "no problem, I will." I supposed that I had unwittingly aided and abetted a CEO in giving bad advice to one of his clients. The best that I could do at that point, however, was simply to disassociate myself from the project, which I soon did. One conclusion that I drew from this experience is that if one engages in this type of work, one must be aware that situations such as this one may arise and that one is relatively powerless to change the outcome. You do not own the data; you do not communicate directly with the marketing research firm's client. The best you may be able to do is remove your name from any report and divorce yourself from the project.

THE REPORT

Regardless of the type of research project on which I have served as a consultant—reviewing a literature, developing measures, conducting experiments, performing secondary data analyses—at the end of the project the results of the work must be communicated to the client. The structure of the report varies depending upon the nature of the project. The literature review is structured as a white paper, or gray literature. Measures that have been developed can be described in memo form using bullet points. The results of experiments and secondary data analyses can be presented in the academic four-section report format with the necessary addition of an executive summary. Independent of format, however, two principles have served me well in communicating accurately the results of my work to my clients. Both would be considered hackneyed by many academics. But, when communicating with clients I have found them to be effective. Stated simply, they are to keep things simple and to use both pictures and examples liberally. Those who read my reports are always pressed for time. Anything that can be done to make it easier for them to get through the report and understand the gist of it is valued. Experience has led me to the conclusions that simplicity, visual summaries, and examples accomplish that goal.

First, I have argued for the importance of simplicity. To keep reports simple, I eliminate jargon whenever possible, favor simple declarative sentences or compound sentences over more complex sentence forms, use sub-headings liberally, and minimize length. Especially, I have sought to find words or phrases that are sticky (note subsequent reference to the Heath brothers). So when answering the inevitable question from clients who have asked me to conduct an experiment to evaluate their product, "How big does the sample have to be?" I tend to respond, "The bigger the better, God rewards those with big samples." Or, when in a literature review I want to convey the sense of the literature that jurors might be overwhelmed by the complexity of certain arguments that attorneys might desire to present, I might point out that people tend to act as "cognitive misers." Or, when responding to a criticism that a particular measure might not be perfect, I might respond "That's OK, if we cannot tie perfect knots, then we will tie a lot of them."

I have also found it helpful to read people who write effectively about technical issues for a general audience as a way of picking up techniques for conveying ideas. Particularly, I have found James Surowiecki (*The Wisdom of Crowds* and his *New Yorker* columns), Malcolm Gladwell (*The Tipping Point, Outliers, Blink*, and his *New Yorker* columns), Robert Cialdini (*Influence*), and Chip and Dan Heath (*Made to Stick*, particular note to the SUCCES principle) useful for this purpose. These people, among others, have studied thoroughly how to convey the complex to audiences who may have ample intelligence, but who lack domain-specific knowledge and who are unfamiliar with the jargon of academic specialties.

The second principle relevant to effective reports is that "a picture is worth a lot of words" (perhaps a thousand plus or minus a few hundred). Included in the meaning of the term "picture" in the preceding sentence is examples and stories because these modes of transmitting information create valuable mental pictures. So, when writing a literature review in which meta-analyses are unavailable, tables and graphs summarizing results are very useful to and appreciated by clients (see Tufte, 2001). And, when there are multiple meta-analyses, a table summarizing them serves the same ends. When presenting measures, working through some very specific calculations in a step-by-step progression enhances understanding, and may contribute to useful critiques (either negative or positive, sometimes both) of the measures. When performing experiments or secondary data analyses, tables and figures summarizing results serve the same function, and generally are the focus of the post-report discussion with the client.

Readers may notice that to this point I have said nothing about the report being actionable. The reasons are simple. First, I cannot recall ever having a client who wanted me to tell them what I thought that they should do. Attorneys want me to summarize literatures; they will apply the findings (or not) to the cases that they litigate. Utilities want me to suggest to them ways in which they can measure the effectiveness of performance for processes that are pivotal to their operation; they will decide what measures (if any) to employ. Educational product firms want me to tell them something about the effectiveness of their product; they will decide whether or not to use that information to market or improve (or both) their product. Marketing research firms want me to make sense of their data as they pertain to very specific questions; they will decide how (or if) to convey that information to their clients. All of them expect my report to inform their decisions, and by being specific about the nature of the work to be performed prior to starting the project and by carrying it out honestly and competently, my reports have had that potential. What remains is up to the client.

SOME CONCLUDING THOUGHTS

Shortly after my first consulting experience in the check processing department of the Arizona bank, I spent some time thinking about consulting. Some of my thinking about the issues I considered at that time has changed. What has not is that consultants have two superordinate assets. The first is their skill set. The second is their integrity. The former must be upgraded consistently. Clearly keeping up with the literature in communication and related disciplines is necessary. Although the fields of methodology and statistics sometimes seem to change at glacial pace, they do change. If one thinks of oneself as a corporation (and it is a good idea to incorporate), then consider applying the principles of continuous quality improvement to your corporation. For reasons that are no doubt obvious the second asset, integrity, must not be compromised. Do not "soften" reports.

I shall conclude by returning to a comment made near the beginning of this essay. From discussions with colleagues who consult and from my own experiences I continue to be amazed by what it is communication consultants do and how well they do it. It has long amused me when people, particularly academics, employ the phrase "the real world." Generally, what they have in mind is contrasting academia with life outside of academia. Of course things are different within and outside of academia. But, what is more interesting is that what academics know, and what they have the skills to find out, is very much coveted outside of the academy. Our communication Ph.D.s are very employable in both the private the public sectors. Communication professors' expertise is solicited extensively by both the public and private sectors. Knowledge and skills that we often take as commonplace are often lacking and needed in both the private and public sectors. That fact never ceases to surprise me. Even better, it is a pleasant surprise.

REFERENCES

Chaiken, S. (1980). Heuristic versus systematic information processing and the use of source versus message cues in persuasion. *Journal of Personality and Social Psychology, 39*, 752–766.

Cialdini, R. B. (1984). *Influence: How and why people agree to things.* New York, NY: William Morrow and Company, Inc.

Fishbein, M., & Ajzen, I. (1975). *Belief, attitude, intention, and behavior: An introduction to theory and research.* Reading, MA: Addison-Wesley.

Gladwell, M. (2002). *The tipping point: How little things can make a big difference.* New York, NY: Little, Brown and Company.

Gladwell, M. (2005). *Blink: The power of thinking without thinking.* New York, NY: Little, Brown and Company.

Gladwell, M. (2008). *Outliers: The story of success.* New York, NY: Little, Brown and Company.

Heath, C., & Heath, D. (2008). *Made to stick: Why some ideas survive and others die.* New York, NY: Random House.

Racherla, P., Mandviwalla, M., & Connolly, D. J. (2012). Factors affecting consumers' trust in online product reviews. *Journal of Consumer Behavior, 11*, 94–104.

Surowiecki, J. (2004). *The wisdom of crowds: Why the many are smarter than the few and how collective wisdom shapes business, economies, societies, and nations.* New York, NY: Doubleday.

Tufte, E. (2001). *The visual display of quantitative information* (2nd ed.). Cheshire, CT: Graphics Press.

PART FOUR

Briefs and Case Studies in Consulting That Matters

CHAPTER FIFTEEN

Consulting in the Healthcare Context

A Case Study of the Community Liaison Project

GARY L. KREPS
George Mason University

HEALTH COMMUNICATION CONSULTING

Communication consulting within the health context demands unique expertise in communication research and theory, coupled with a deep understanding of and appreciation for the complex communication processes performed within the modern health system. Consultants offer healthcare practitioners and organizations specialized expertise, assisting with designing and evaluating health promotion campaigns, gathering health data, promoting cooperation between health system participants, and informing health decision making. This consulting work helps to promote quality of care and achievement of important health outcomes, including preserving life. The health communication consultant must be credible, experienced, and able to adapt to unique constraints within the health system.

Health communication consultants serve as advisors to major government agencies (such as the CDC and the NIH), local government agencies (such as public health departments), as well as for government contractors, healthcare delivery centers, and health corporations (such as pharmaceutical firms). They work with a broad range of nonprofit organizations (such as social service agencies, advocacy groups, and foundations), as well as with institutions of higher education (particularly medical, nursing, pharmacy, public health, and communication schools) on health communication projects.

My own communication consulting work within the healthcare system has focused primarily on health communication research and training. I help to conduct important research projects, provide expertise for designing and delivering health education programs, evaluate health programs, and translate research results into evidence-based health programs and policies. The educational programs I offer (through workshops, seminars, in-service training courses, and presentations) for healthcare providers, healthcare consumers, health educators, and public health officials are delivered through specially designed communication campaigns, media, and technologies. In this case I worked with a national nonprofit organization on a federally funded research and intervention project to improve prevention of HIV/AIDS. And in this particular project, I collaborated with a national nonprofit organization to design, implement, and evaluate a health education project to promote participation in HIV/AIDS vaccine clinical trials.

CONSULTING ON THE COMMUNITY LIAISON PROJECT

Early in 2009 I was invited by the Program Director for the Technical Assistance, Training, and Treatment Division of the National Minority AIDS Council (NMAC) to help with a pilot program (funded with an NIH grant) to increase minority group participation in HIV/AIDS vaccine clinical trial research in the US. NMAC is a national nonprofit organization headquartered in Washington, DC, founded in 1987 to address the growing national HIV/AIDS epidemic in communities of color. NMAC represents over 3,000 community- and faith-based organizations nationwide, providing these organizations with a variety of capacity building assistance programs, online and classroom-based trainings, printed and electronic resources, grassroots organization, and political advocacy. These activities help deliver HIV/AIDS services efficiently and effectively to mitigate the impact of HIV/AIDS in minority communities across the US.

The Consulting Problem

Minority (particularly African American) populations in the US have been disproportionately harmed by HIV/AIDS. The Centers for Disease Control (CDC) (2010) estimates that while African Americans/Blacks represent approximately 14% of the US population, they account for almost half of new HIV infections nationally. One of the best hopes for the prevention of this disease may be on the horizon with HIV/AIDS vaccines. While clinical trials for these vaccines have shown promise for infection prevention, there has been very low minority representation in HIV vaccine clinical trials (Frew et al., 2010). Sullivan et al. (2007) found that a major reason for low minority participation in vaccine studies was due to limited information and support for the research. Traditional approaches to disseminating information about HIV/AIDS vaccine research programs from official sources often fell on deaf ears within minority communities due to lack of trust for these information sources. This health-education intervention was designed to overcome these problems with HIV/AIDS education in minority communities.

The Intervention

As a communication consultant, I helped NMAC design a unique community-based intervention strategy for disseminating HIV/AIDS information. This program was grounded in community-participative research, the diffusion of innovations model, and social network theory. I assisted with collecting and interpreting relevant audience analysis data to guide design of culturally sensitive messaging for educational materials. I also helped NMAC design, collect, and analyze formative and summative evaluate research data for refining the educational program and assessing how effective it was in achieving its goals.

NMAC's innovative community-based approach. This project used a community participatory approach, where members of minority communities were actively engaged in disseminating HIV/AIDS information (Kelley, Hannans, Kreps, & Johnson, 2012). The project invited trusted members of minority communities (community liaisons) to disseminate culturally sensitive information about HIV vaccine research within their own personal social networks, demonstrating that social-networking programs can be cost-effective and assessible across minority communities. This approach builds on previous research showing that health messages shared within social networks, especially among those with similar race and/or ethnicity, are generally well-received (Kreps & Sparks, 2008).

This pilot program trained seven community liaisons in five US states to deliver culturally sensitive HIV-vaccine messages for members of their personal social networks using participatory engagement. The purpose of this initiative approach was to promote awareness of HIV-vaccine research to minority populations, to encourage participatory engagement concerning HIV/AIDS within minority communities, and to enlist community members in adapting and disseminating an HIV/AIDS message across their social networks. The community liaisons not only disseminated information to members of their social networks, but also invited members of their social networks to also disseminate HIV/AIDS health information to their social networks in an iterative, evolving process of information diffusion through social networks (Valente, 2010).

Disseminating culturally sensitive messages about HIV/AIDS vaccine research was the core of the program. The program used community liaisons to infuse the message of HIV-vaccine research through meetings with members of their social networks. This participatory engagement allowed members of each network to provide feedback about the messages, and then recommend the most appropriate channels of dissemination (interpersonal, print, etc.), given the culture of their network. The liaisons used information provided with printed materials and online in their group discussions. The printed materials were given to all participants, providing them with the opportunity for later reference of the messages.

Recruitment and selection of liaisons. The pilot program recruited volunteer liaisons with diverse backgrounds, races and/or ethnicities, and geographic locations. The most salient requirement for participation was a commitment to the purpose of this pilot program, and a willingness to dedicate the necessary time to the program activities, such as HIV communication plan development, self-reporting, and program evaluation. We recruited liaisons at major HIV/AIDS events sponsored by NMAC at the United States Conference on AIDS (USCA), the largest AIDS-related gathering in the US. This conference brings together over 3,000 people from various parts of the country who are interested in HIV/AIDS. The conference is a forum for building or reconnecting with networks, and for exchanging the latest information and cutting-edge tools to address the challenges of HIV/AIDS. Seven persons committed to being part of the first cohort of liaisons.

The seven volunteer liaisons who participated in the program were affiliated with various organizations, such as community- and faith-based organizations, clinics, AIDS-service organizations, and colleges or universities. The majority of the liaisons were African American females between 41 and 60 years of age who lived in primarily urban areas. There was one Latina and one Caucasian male liaison, both of whom made specific outreach to Latino communities. The liaisons were located in five states—Texas, Pennsylvania, Oklahoma, North Carolina, and Georgia. While all liaisons were not from states that had ongoing vaccine-research programs, nor were they representative of the entire nation, the funder, NIAID, was most interested in garnering support and debunking the myths among African Americans and Latinos through this volunteer pilot project. With more education and awareness, the hope was that more HIV-vaccine research trials could be conducted in other areas to accommodate growing support.

Program implementation timeline. During the first four months of liaison recruitment, a great deal of time and attention was devoted to refining the design of the training component for the liaisons and initiating the development of the training materials. This was done to make sure we recruited community members who were well-positioned and committed to serve as liaisons, as well as to develop training materials that would help them succeed in this important role. The time put into recruitment, planning, and training were essential elements in the success of this initiative. Then, during the next four months, an advisory committee was recruited, composed of experts in health communication, program development, evaluation, and clinical research, with experience in fieldwork in communities of color. The liaisons worked individually with the program manager to craft plans for how they would integrate HIV-vaccine research education into their existing activities. They were also required to view two online, introductory tutorials about HIV/AIDS and HIV-vaccine research. In addition, background research assisted in the development of culturally sensitive and informative health messages about the benefits of HIV/AIDS-vaccine research and the importance of community support relevant to the targeted audiences.

The training program included a series of three audio conference calls with all the liaisons. The first conference call was an orientation session which included an in-depth review of the logic model developed for the training program. This session also provided the liaisons with an opportunity to introduce themselves to each other, and to share information about their individual networks and the strategies they planned to utilize to inform the members of their networks about HIV-vaccine research. The second conference call was devoted to reviewing the materials the liaisons would use to conduct focus groups to test the different variations of the message they would use to build community awareness and support for HIV-vaccine research, and conduct a process-and-outcome evaluation of their individual health communication campaigns.

The focus group (see Plax, Waldeck, & Kearney, Chapter 6) sessions served dual purposes to engage members of their network in discussing the effectiveness of the culturally sensitive message for use with their networks, and discuss the most appropriate message channels for further dissemination into their social communities. The use of focus groups also provided the liaisons with a snapshot of baseline information about the level of HIV knowledge and awareness that existed within their communities. The third and final conference call took place at the end of the pilot program. After reviewing the data collected from the program, the liaisons shared their views about the pilot program and what they had gained from the experience.

My graduate research assistant and I conducted an exhaustive literature review during the second four-month period of the project focused on the use of culturally sensitive materials with targeted audience members. We incorporated this information into the discussions of participatory engagement held with the liaisons about communicating within their networks. Previous research suggested that most successful interventions in HIV/AIDS prevention among African American communities were grounded in theory, provided skills training, and were culturally sensitive to the needs of the community, particularly African Americans (Beatty, Wheeler, & Gaiter, 2004; Jemmott, Jemmott, & Hutchinson, 2001). Prior research suggested that use of messages that stressed gains/benefits (gain-framed) or losses/ costs (loss-framed) could influence the persuasiveness of the HIV/AIDS messages for minority audiences (Apanovitch, McCarthy, & Salovey, 2003). For example, a gain-framed message might be: "if you use condoms you are lowering your risk of getting a sexually transmitted disease." A loss-framed message might be, "If you don't use condoms, you are at greater risk of sexually transmitted diseases." We tested the influences of message framing in this project.

Developing the health communication message. During the training, each liaison received individual instruction about the fundamentals of planning and delivering their messages. They were instructed that information provided should be credible, messages should be compatible with the community norms and vernacular, messages should consider key cultural factors, and messages should incorporate aspects of the culture into the discussion.

After the training, the liaisons had seven weeks to deliver the messages to their communities. They were given a high level of autonomy over the exact numbers of times that they should present their messages and the channels they should use to engage with their communities. This autonomy was central to the pilot program design, which was that the HIV/AIDS-vaccine message be integrated into existing service-delivery processes.

Next, the liaisons were given two weeks to reflect on the effectiveness of their work in disseminating the message to their community, and report the results of the data they collected from their message-dissemination efforts. These data included the ages and gender of those who received the messages, how many of those reached increased their awareness of HIV-vaccine research, and how many were willing to share the messages with others.

Program Evaluation and Outcomes

Key to the success of this project, the consulting team implemented continuous process monitoring of the liaisons. Following the focus-group activity, all liaisons submitted reports on the participant responses to the nine focus-group questions that the program team and liaisons had developed. The reports described participants' summaries of the main messages provided, as well as their evaluations of the clarity, believability, usefulness, and trustworthiness of the messages. They were also asked to identify the features of the messages that they liked best and least, whether the gain-frames or loss-framed messages were most effective, and what message changes, if any, they suggested.

These reports were analyzed by the program team using a manual content analysis technique that enabled us to note trends in the focus-group information. Results suggested that the loss-framed message would be most effective when used with our target audiences on printed pocket cards to be disseminated, and that gain-framed messages would be most effective when diffused through interpersonal communication. Following this, the liaisons were interviewed to determine how well their focus group discussions went and how they might be improved for the future.

The evaluation research provided consistent data from the liaisons that their focus group information sessions worked well. The liaisons reported that they were assisting their community by sharing information about HIV/AIDS and helping to give voice to their communities. Further outcome findings revealed a significant increase in self-reported HIV awareness. Also, many of the network members became early adopters of the HIV-vaccine message and were willing to share that information with others. The most provocative finding was the rapid and extensive reach of the liaisons into their networks. The seven liaisons were able to reach 644 community members and 343 participants said that they would be willing to serve as community liaisons to share the HIV/AIDS messages with others. This demonstrated the utility of this community-based social networking intervention strategy for disseminating relevant health information within at-risk minority populations.

Lessons Learned About Effective Health Communication

We learned many things about effective health communication with at-risk populations from this study. For example, we found that it was vitally important to get a full understanding of the strongly held cultural beliefs and values of members of these groups to design health promotion programs that would resonate with them. It was also important to select sources for providing information to members of these groups who could speak the groups' language, understand the needs of the groups, and be perceived as trustworthy and credible by group members. Further, we found that by using influential members of the at-risk groups as spokesperson, and encouraging them to recruit members of their personal social networks to also serve as spokespersons, we could disseminate relevant health information widely and effectively. This strategy also reduced resistance to health promotion messages and was very cost-effective. The social network–based health communication strategies employed in this project have the potential to be effectively used in many health promotion projects designed for vulnerable and at-risk populations.

REFERENCES

Apanovitch, A. M., McCarthy, D., & Salovey, P. (2003). Using message framing to motivate HIV testing among low-income, ethnic minority women. *Health Psychology, 22*, 60–67.

Beatty, L. A., Wheeler, D., & Gaiter J. (2004). HIV prevention research for African Americans: Current and future directions. *Journal of Black Psychology, 30*, 40–58.

Centers for Disease Control and Prevention. (2010). HIV incidence. (Available at: http://www.cdc.gov/hiv/statistics/surveillance/incidence/index.html, accessed 12/28/2014).

Frew, P. M., Hou, S. I., Davis, M., Chan, K., Horton, T., Shuster, J., Hixson, B., & del Rio, C. (2010). The likelihood of participation in clinical trials can be measured: the Clinical Research Involvement Scales. *Journal of Clinical Epidemiology*, 63(10), 1110–1117.

Jemmott, L. S., Jemmott, J. B., & Hutchinson, M. K. (2001). HIV/AIDS. In R. Braithwaite, & S, Taylor, (Eds.). *Health Issues in the Black Community*, 2nd Ed. San Francisco: Jossey-Bass, 309–346.

Kelley, R., Hannans, A., Kreps, G. L., & Johnson, K. (2012). The Community Liaison Program: A health education pilot program to increase minority awareness of HIV and acceptance of HIV vaccine trials. *Health Education Research*, 27, 746–754.

Kreps, G. L., & Sparks L. (2008). Meeting the health literacy needs of vulnerable populations. *Patient Education and Counseling*, 71, 328–32.

Sullivan, P. S., McNaghten, A. D., Begley, E., Hutchinson, A., & Cargill, V. A. (2007). Enrollment of racial/ethnic minorities and women with HIV in clinical research studies of HIV medicines. *Journal of the National Medical Association*, 99, 242–50.

Valente, T. W. (2010). *Social Networks and Health*. Oxford, UK: Oxford University Press.

CHAPTER SIXTEEN

Reaching for Big Data

Using Analytics to Address Organizational Challenges

JOSHUA B. BARBOUR
Texas A&M University

SHIRLEY J. FAUGHN AND ROBERT L. HUSBAND
University of Illinois & The Aslan Group

The allure of "big data" is insight. Its advocates seek to create new knowledge and enrich decision making by drawing on massive stores of data and harnessing advances in computing power, automation, and analysis (Bisel, Barge, Dougherty, Lucas, & Tracy, 2014; Puschmann & Burgess, 2014). The move toward data-intensive knowledge creation is reflected in advances in computational social science (Lazer et al., 2009), the push for evidence-based practice (Pfeffer & Sutton, 2006), and organizational efforts to derive competitive advantage by understanding their data with increasingly sophisticated analyses (Davenport & Harris, 2007).

The following narrative explores our experiences working with data. The case follows the creation of a 360-degree (or multipoint) leadership development tool. The trajectory of our 360-degree and the datasets it created demonstrate the multiple ways in which consultants may work with data. From the start, we created data-rich systems informed by organizational and communication science, and embedded systematic analysis of data into the reporting to clients. We describe too our efforts to use the data produced by the 360-degree instrument in the aggregate to generate insight for teams of leaders. We conclude with our efforts to link the data we created through this project with other data sets to inform executive decision making. The case highlights the technical and social challenges of working with data inside organizations.

Data-driven decision making was very important at Multiline Communications (MC), a Fortune 500 firm. Their focus on data paralleled waves of high-profile analytics-focused books (Ayres, 2007; Davenport & Harris, 2007) and analytics success stories (Lewis, 2003; Silver, 2012; Zaillian, Sorkin, Chervin, & Lewis, 2011). For MC, analytics meant using more readily available computing power to derive insight from existing organizational data that might provide an advantage to the business. Mining big data typically involves the quest for predictive accuracy (e.g., will a customer default on their credit card?) over traditional social scientific explanation (Bisel et al., 2014; Foster & Stine, 2004; Friedman, 2001; Hand, Blunt, Kelly, & Adams, 2000). At MC, the promise of analytics and predictive tools in leadership development were gaining traction just as our consulting group, The Aslan Group, was developing and implementing a company-wide system for conducting 360-degree or multipoint assessments (Antoniono, 1996; DeNisi & Kluger, 2000; Salam, Cox, & Sims, 1997) to support leadership development at MC.

Founded in 1985, The Aslan Group conceives of itself as a small community of consultants focused primarily on executive coaching, leadership development, and communication process design. The Aslan Group relies on consultants from business and academics, many with research backgrounds. Aslan often designs data-intensive research projects to address clients' problems. Aslan's core strengths include applying organizational communication theory and methods to address pressing business problems. Aslan also creates and facilitates communication processes that help organizations achieve desired outcomes, and coaches leaders in team settings and one-on-one to make them more effective.

DEVELOPING DATA-RICH TOOLS

Aslan first began negotiations with MC for the development of a 360-degree instrument to assess leadership behaviors in the late 1990s. MC had previously crafted the MC Leadership Model (MCLM) focusing on the specific components of leadership they believed led to success in their organization. They wanted to create a suite of development tools grounded in the MCLM. Aslan had often worked with the Learning Academy, a division of MC focused on leadership development and other learning functions. Bob had been involved in the development of the MCLM, and the Learning Academy asked him to assist with the development of the 360-instrument and process. We gathered a project team led by Bob, Shirley, and Josh. Over a few weeks, Bob met with the Learning Academy and negotiated a fixed fee and a per-participant price for the development of (a) an assessment tool and (b) an online system for administering the 360s.

Approaching the problem like a research project, we drafted items for the assessment derived from the MCLM. The MCLM was comprehensive, encompassing eighteen specific areas (e.g., communication, teamwork, vision). It was also developmental, in that specific skills and behaviors were articulated for each area at differing levels of leadership (e.g., manager, director, executive). We drew out key behaviors from each area and translated them into items. We verified the items by gathering test data and then refined them using factor analysis. We were left with a 60-item assessment, (2–3 items per area) including 4 overarching dependent variables (e.g., "This person is an effective leader").

We worked with multiple programmers to design and implement an online system that would collect and collate assessment data, generate individualized reports for participants, give MC access for monitoring participant progress, and manage invoicing for the per-participant cost. We worked side-by-side with the programmers translating the measurement and reporting functions needed into the application over several months. MC had over 50,000 employees, and no fewer than sixty individuals in the company's Learning Academy would have access to the system for entering participants' contact information and monitoring their progress. We created a separate support function to handle technical problems and recorded a support video demonstrating step-by-step instructions. After a soft start to allow for fixing technical problems, we launched the system to the entire company, and MC used it for the next 10 years.

The 360 data set eventually contained approximately 4,500 participants and 30,000 evaluations of those participants. The system included functionality for drawing on this large repository of data for benchmarking. Participants were able to see how their scores compared to other leaders at MC, and the reporting function guided participants through an analysis of their own results weighted by priorities set by participants and their supervisors. In this way, simple analytics were incorporated into the reporting of the results automated for participants.

SMALL DATA: USING THE 360 FOR LEADERSHIP DEVELOPMENT

A year into the implementation, Bob reached out to Shirley and Josh with news. MC wanted to use the 360 specifically with a group of top performing individuals (TPIs) who had been identified for development as part of MC's succession planning. The Aslan team discussed a strategy for the identification, implementation, and analysis as the TPIs completed the assessment. Once the TPIs completed the 360, their data would be analyzed and presented in a workshop setting.

By this time, the size of MC's participation in the 360 had grown to about one thousand participants involving about six thousand evaluations. The 360 data offered a useful analytical tool for generating insight informed by the MCLM. We were able to identify the behaviors that those completing the 360 viewed as most closely associated with leadership effectiveness. We were able to use the entire data set for benchmarking while focusing analyses on specific groups within the company.

We ran models looking specifically at the top performers comparing them to MC as a whole. The TPIs performed better on all but two behaviors in the assessment. More specifically, the TPIs were seen as distinctive in their focus on prioritizing the development of others. Indeed, across the data sets, the behaviors associated with leadership effectiveness in general were other-focused. Most importantly, though, using the data, the team could discern the TPIs from the rest of the organization with a great deal of accuracy, which meant the data might be useful as a tool for predicting future leadership success.

Word spread throughout MC after Aslan presented the results to the first group of TPIs. Other units clamored to complete 360s, compare their scores to the TPIs, and look for insights about their units' leadership. For a couple of years, the Aslan team booked many such projects and presented the results in workshop settings. These analyses were small projects in the sense that they were focused on particular teams, yet they drew on extensive data—the 360 data captured across the whole company and more specifically the 360 data for the TPIs.

INTEGRATED DATA: CONNECTING THE 360 TO EXISTING DATA AT MC

At the end of one of these workshops in which we shared 360 results, the Vice President in charge of the Learning Academy, Ben, approached Bob. The Academy was dedicated to training and development throughout the organization, but was particularly interested in making their mark in executive leadership development. He wanted to take the 360 data and the promise of the insights it might generate to the top executives in the company. The organization was increasingly looking for ways to draw competitive advantage by mining their large databases. Until now, the Academy had never had an opportunity to contribute to MC's competitive advantage through the use of data and analytics. Now, through an aggregation of the 360 data, the Academy could speak to leadership behaviors that most directly contributed to leadership effectiveness at MC.

Ben scheduled meetings with other key executives for Aslan to present its findings. For example, Bob and Ben were asked to visit privately with the Senior Executive Vice Presidents of Operations and Human Services to share their findings regarding the Leadership Model, its validity, and its relevance to leadership development within the company. The executives expressed concern because the data seemed, on the surface, to be contrary to the CEO's upcoming public announcements about getting results as a leadership focus for MC. The leaders had zeroed in on a pair of nonsignificant but negative correlations between goal attainment and leadership effectiveness. Bob explained the results and highlighted other aspects of getting results (e.g., teamwork, influence, and courage) embedded in the MCLM. By creating a more nuanced understanding of the findings, Bob helped alleviate their fears and give strategies for presenting the information to the CEO (See Boster, Chapter 14).

On another occasion, Bob and Josh went to the organization's headquarters to join Ben in meeting with Evan, the Senior Executive Vice President (VP) of Sales and Marketing. Josh felt nervous, having never visited the executive floor. Bob had visited with this executive many times and put Josh at ease. When Evan arrived, Ben opened the discussion explaining that he felt they had data, specific to the company, they could use to derive a competitive advantage. He commented on how excited he was that the Learning Academy had developed its own data and garnered insight from it. Bob and Josh described how they hoped to integrate the 360 data with existing, internal company data to make the leadership modeling more robust. We explained how the data integration might more effectively let MC predict leadership in sales and marketing.

We knew that the data they were hoping to integrate existed in many different places throughout the company. To make matters worse, several of the units felt protective of their data—a common challenge to consultants attempting to build support for programs across large, complex organizational systems. For example, People Systems, the company's human resources unit, held most of the data and believed they owned leadership development. Another unit in the company, Tactical Research, which focused on research and development, believed it was solely responsible for marshaling data into competitive advantage insights. Other units also saw themselves as co-owning leadership development with the Learning Academy and/or saw their control of data-driven insights threatened by Aslan.

Analysis was difficult, too, because the data were not connected. Connecting them meant not only solving difficult data problems (i.e., connecting complex databases containing hundreds of thousands of data points) but also organizational ones. Getting data connected meant working across divisions. People at MC tended to be reluctant to share data without passing the request up through the hierarchy. Making those connections might also create problems. For example, linking sensitive employee data and providing that to an external contractor meant exposing the data. At MC, data were tightly controlled.

Evan asked a few questions about the model and what we had learned. He seemed noncommittal but interested. The meeting finished without a specific action plan. Bob explained to Josh in private that Evan got million-dollar pitches every day and to be patient.

A few weeks later, we received our data challenge. We were given a list of a dozen names. The list, compiled by Henry, who worked in People Systems, contained a randomly selected group of individuals identified as TPIs. The challenge was to distinguish the truly top performers. Generating a new discriminant analysis in combination with existing data, Josh developed a model to identify the "best of the best" performers. A meeting was set with Henry and his team, and Hazel, a representative from Tactical Research, to share the results of Josh's analysis.

Hazel asked questions about the modeling and the quality of the data. She challenged, "The relationships between these variables are so high. Aren't these results just a by-product of multicollinearity?" Josh noticed that the questions puzzled the rest of the people in the meeting. He explained the problem of multicollinearity to the group as a whole: "The danger with measuring these phenomena is that you might end up measuring the same thing. So, it can be hard to know if the predictive power you have is meaningful or just echoes." At the same time, Josh had to respond to the interrogation in terms that Hazel would buy. He explained, "We use diagnostics to look for that sort of problem." Josh walked through concepts like tolerance and variance inflation factors. He then explained that the we had looked for those problems and not found any. The meeting continued with Henry and Hazel challenging the results.

As Bob and Josh left the meeting, the future 360 data integration initiative was unclear. Bob called the meeting a success; Josh had doubts. The team had been able to respond to all the challenges; and Bob pointed out that what made the interaction most effective was that we had been able to translate and explain the data to everyone at the table while still responding to Hazel's concerns.

DISCUSSION

This case offers at least three examples common to the use of data in consulting: problem-focused research projects, analysis for problem solving relying on data for benchmarking, and integrating data across the organization to inform executive decision making. As a research project, the development of the 360-degree assessment and the means by which data were delivered drew on expertise in measurement, analysis, and data reporting. Working with particular units, we could draw on the larger body of 360 data to frame unit-specific analyses. Using data to assist executives in decision making depended on understanding leadership and communication theory, organizational theory, and research design and analytics.

These examples also make clear the challenges involved. In Josh's work with organizations, he had a refrain, "People with an agenda hate data." Like most consulting work, developing and using data interacts with organizational politics. Working with data involved negotiating internal and external boundaries across units and expertise differences. MC had hoped to make use of data to drive decision making, and they relied on expertise outside of the organization as well as from multiple units within. Aslan's engagement in this case depended on a long-term relationship with the company, as well as a deep understanding of analytics *and* the particular issues facing MC. For Aslan, navigating those boundaries required careful relationship management, technical skill, and mentoring within the community of consultants. Acting as data translators, Aslan had to explain the results to experts, fluent in the latest techniques, and general audiences with little knowledge of or interest in them.

REFERENCES

Antoniono, D. (1996). Designing an effective 360-degree appraisal feedback process. *Organizational Dynamics, 25*, 24–38.

Ayres, I. (2007). *Super crunchers: Why thinking-by-numbers is the new way to be smart.* New York, NY: Bantam.

Bisel, R. S., Barge, J. K., Dougherty, D. J., Lucas, K., & Tracy, S. J. (2014). A round-table discussion of "Big" data in qualitative organizational communication research. *Management Communication Quarterly, 28*, 625–649.

Davenport, T. H., & Harris, J. G. (2007). *Competing on analytics: The new science of winning.* Boston, MA: Harvard Business School Press.

DeNisi, A. S., & Kluger, A. N. (2000). Feedback effectiveness: Can 360-degree appraisals be improved?. *Academy of Management Executive, 14*, 129–139.

Foster, D. P., & Stine, R. A. (2004). Variable selection in data mining: Building a predictive model for bankruptcy. *Journal of the American Statistical Association, 99*, 303–313.

Friedman, J. (2001). The role of statistics in the data revolution. *International Statistics Review, 69*, 5–10.

Hand, D. J., Blunt, G., Kelly, M. G., & Adams, N. M. (2000). Data mining for fun and profit. *Statistical Science, 15*, 111–131.

Lazer, D., Pentland, A., Adamic, L., Aral, S., Barabasi, A.-L., Brewer, D.,... Van Alstyne, M. (2009). Computational social science. *Science, 323*, 721–723.

Lewis, M. (2003). *Moneyball.* New York, NY: W. W. Norton and Company.

Pfeffer, J., & Sutton, R. I. (2006). *Hard facts, dangerous half-truths, and total nonsense: Profiting from evidence-based management.* Boston, MA: Harvard Business School Press.

Puschmann, C., & Burgess, J. (2014). Metaphors of big data. *International Journal of Communication, 8*, 1690–1709.

Salam, S., Cox, J. F., & Sims, H. P., Jr. (1997). In the eye of the beholder: How leadership relates to 360-degree performance ratings. *Group & Organization Management, 22*, 185–209.

Silver, N. (2012). *Signal and the Noise: Why some many predictions fail.* New York, NY: Penguin Press.

Zaillian, S., Sorkin, A., Chervin, S., & Lewis, M. (Writers) & B. Miller (Director). (2011). Moneyball. In S. Zaillian (Producer): Sony Studios.

CHAPTER SEVENTEEN

Championing
NOV Ventures

Consulting in Competitive, Corporate Contexts

JOHN DALY[1]

University of Texas at Austin

PREFACE: SPECIAL CONSIDERATIONS FOR ACADEMICS CONSULTING IN COMPETITIVE, CORPORATE CONTEXTS

This case is an illustration of the role of consulting and training in a corporate environment. What is unique in this setting is a strong orientation to bottom-line results. Leaders who sponsor programs in corporate settings want to make sure the firm will get a significant return on their investment. Further, in these firms there is a strong competitive streak—we want to do better than our competitors. The challenges one faces working in these environments including being able to provide proof of contribution, as well as a deep understanding of the marketplace. There is also a strong emphasis on time constraints. Corporate clients will insist on no wasted time since anytime employees are attending a session they are not doing what the company needs them to be doing—contributing to the income of the firm. Corporate employees have far less patience with long exercises, extended discussions of academic work (but they love the application of the work), and the sorts of advice you would offer college students. They want substantive answers to problems they are facing. You often have to sacrifice the complexities you would discuss in a class, being very careful of saying "it depends."

NOV VENTURES

The sky was a brilliant blue in Stavanger, Norway one late August day in 2014. Trey Mebane looked at the pristine harbor filled with small ships and reflected on the start of a fifth year of "NOV Ventures," a program he had created and now led. The entering class this year, composed of about 45 high-potential employees, would bring the total number of participants to more than two hundred.

NOV (National Oilwell Varco), a company a history extending more than 150 years, designs, manufactures, and sells equipment and components used in oil and gas drilling and production. As a result of numerous mergers and acquisitions, it currently employs 64,000 people throughout the world.

NOV Ventures is an internal program that teaches some of NOV's best engineers how to bring interesting, and potentially lucrative, technologies to market. Over one year, while working full-time in their jobs, teams of participants identify a technology that might be commercialized, assess its feasibility and possible financial return, develop a business plan, and advocate it to senior leaders in the company. Since its start, the program has launched a number of new technologies with impressive returns. Participants attend four one-week sessions held in Stavanger, Houston, Amsterdam, and Austin. These sessions are led by university faculty members as well as NOV leaders.

My role in NOV Ventures began years ago when I taught the Advocacy and Innovation graduate course in a program Trey attended at the University of Texas. I work with many different global companies every year as a consultant (e.g., Roche, Astra-Zeneca, Essilor, Samsung, LG, Siemens, Hines, Goldman Sachs, Credit Suisse) and Trey found my experiences fascinating given how many of the examples I used applied to his firm. In addition, I have spent many years working with global energy firms (e.g., ExxonMobil, Petrobas, Shell, AGIP, SINOPEC, Petrochina, CNOOC, Imperial, EcoPetrol, Total, Chevron). So, in class, I often used energy examples that again intrigued Trey. Consulting teaches you a lot about companies, industries, and cultures— and a good consultant knows how to leverage that knowledge when working with other firms. Currently, I work with NOV Ventures helping participants hone their advocacy skills along with leadership, teamwork, and change management competencies.

NOV Ventures is Trey's brainchild. After completing a master's degree program on the commercialization of technology (MSTC) at the University of Texas at Austin, Trey, who at that point was a senior engineer, convinced his company to send some other engineers through the degree program. Then, when the economy got bad, Trey opted to replicate, internally, much of the MSTC degree as a non-degree program. It wasn't an easy sell, and throughout the process of getting buy-in, Trey faced many obstacles.

How It Began

When Trey was considering enrolling in an advanced degree program, he discovered that NOV typically sent their best employees through MBA programs to hone their business skills. In Trey's mind, not every engineer (including himself) needed, or desired, an MBA. Instead, many wanted to enhance their skills in ways directly related to their technical roles. They wanted to have impact through developing and sponsoring new technologies, to capitalize on their natural drive and desire to innovate.

Trey saw the MSTC program as a potential avenue for giving engineers, like himself, a way to learn how to bring new product ideas to market. After extensive discussions with his bosses, Trey prevailed and got NOV to sponsor him in the degree program. He loved the program and saw its potential for his company. He thought many of his peer engineers would want to participate. And although Trey is a creative person who has a contagious enthusiasm, he understood that it would take more than his personal passion to get his company to send others through the degree program. He had to successfully advocate his notion.

Selling the Degree

Trey was, formally, five or six levels below the top executives. That meant he needed a champion at the top of the company if he wanted to successfully advocate the legitimacy of the MSTC degree. He built an influence map—identifying people who were part of the decision tree when it came to technical leadership. And then he had to figure the catalysts that would make people in the network buy into his proposal. The truth is that it is hard for someone far below the executive level to create corporate-wide change. You need someone who is in the firm's leadership to make the case for you. Senior people who buy into your idea can advocate for you in meetings to which you would never be invited. They can also coach and mentor you about the best ways to pitch a proposal, the appropriate timing of your proposal, and the roadblocks you will need to overcome. Change is hard in any organization, but many of the challenges are amplified in a large multinational. Minimally, it is about coordination. It is also about making everyone see that your brainstorm applies to their industry sector. And, it's about inclusion. At NOV, to be successful, one needs to include leaders from throughout the world and from very different parts of the firm in a decision.

Bob Bloom came to mind at once. Bob was the Chief Technology Officer at NOV. Because of his position and reputation, he had access to, and influence with, the leadership of NOV. Trey, who knew Bob, felt he would be a great sponsor for his initiative. Trey reasoned that Bob, who was quickly approaching retirement, would want a legacy of his time in the company. The MSTC program might be just that thing. Bob would have the opportunity, by supporting Trey's initiative, to help shape the culture of NOV in terms of intrapreneurship for decades. Plus, Bob had written a letter of recommendation for Trey's admission into the Texas program. He had already shown some commitment.

Bob agreed to open doors for Trey, telling him, "I'll introduce you to anybody." At a company-wide meeting of the engineering leadership designed to showcase new products, Bob invited Trey to propose his idea. In that presentation, Trey discussed the challenges he faced as an engineering director. For instance, it was hard to get the right products at the right time to the right markets. NOV's engineering leaders needed to tackle not just the technical aspects of their projects, but also the market concerns—time to market, hitting the right markets with what was needed. To do that, NOV needed to equip its people to think differently not only about engineering issues, but also market issues. The MSTC degree would give NOV a way to groom tomorrow's leaders. After all, if the business is made up of people, and you want the business to improve, then you have to equip your best people to improve.

Trey faced push-back. For instance, some senior leaders felt that on-the-job training—the way they had learned—was more important than anything else. Trey parried this by saying that the company couldn't wait the 30 years it takes to teach all the lessons that on-the-job training would deliver. NOV needed to build the next level of leadership in much faster ways. Plus, NOV had to quickly enter new markets. NOV's earnings before taxes, interest, and amortization (EBITA) is lower than many of its competitors partly because the company is seen as a manufacturing and tool company while some of competitors (e.g., Schlumberger) are seen as faster moving, more technology-driven companies. In essence, Trey put the decision-makers in a difficult position. "We could wait 30 years, but why? All you are doing is handing an advantage over to the competition by waiting."

After the meeting, Trey received the leadership's commitment to send more than a dozen select NOV engineers through the MSTC program. During their coursework, they worked as part of small teams on specific concepts that might have value to NOV. Trey regularly asked participants questions like "Do you understand the need to apply this? What are you learning? How can we bring this into the company?" He wanted these engineers to become evangelists for the degree. A crucial moment came when one of the NOV teams came up with an innovative land rig design—a spread rig—that was featured in a prominent trade magazine. NOV loves bragging rights and this was a perfect case. After seeing the public impact of the rig idea, one team member, a very distinguished engineer, became a convert. He got the religion and started proselytizing the degree to his peers. The next year , the company sent more people through the program. As a result, they ended up commercializing a vertical drilling tool (VDT) that was a market success. Graduates started bringing others into the program. The MSTC was proving its value and Trey was gaining allies. Trey was no longer a lone advocate. Others were joining in to pitch the program.

Changing the Focus

The MSTC became a popular degree for NOV engineers. In 2009, though, the energy market softened and NOV couldn't afford to send bevies of people through an entire degree program. Leaders were telling Trey, "Great program, great things coming through, but we just don't have the pocketbook. We need to curb expenses." Messages like this told Trey that his brainchild was viewed as an expense, and not an investment. "I was winning with the people who were going through the program, but I still had a number of things to prove to the leadership."

So Trey pulled the NOV graduates of the MSTC degree together to talk for a day about how, from the grass-roots, they could build commitment to the program. Every graduate felt the MSTC degree was an extremely important for NOV. As the conversation progressed, people started saying things like, "We need to touch more people" and "We need to evaluate more ideas because ideas can translate into dollars." As Trey listened, it occurred to him that the discussion was leading to what was, essentially, a requirements document. Even as the meeting continued, Trey started to think that maybe a formal degree program for NOV's high potential technical people wasn't necessary. What if we were to reinvent the MSTC and make it our own? Could NOV design an internal program that would allow the firm to get the best from the degree program as well as customize it to the company's specific needs and interests? What components of the MSTC program were crucial to what NOV needed?

After the meeting, Trey authored an extensive prospectus laying out the rationale for a program, the syllabus, the requirements, the professors, and the NOV experts who could contribute. Luckily, there was a precedent for what Trey was outlining. NOV already had a sales leadership program associated with Purdue University. Trey's question was simple: "Is NOV saying that they (sales leaders) are more worthy of an investment than we are? If NOV spends this kind of money on sales teams why don't we spend an equivalent amount on technology folks?

Trey lacked access to the CEO to pitch his proposal. But he did have access to Bob Bloom's replacement, Hege Kverneland, who had taken over as Chief Technology Officer for NOV in June of 2009. Hege was a very smart, energetic, and well-respected engineer based in Norway (in 2014 she was recognized as one of the 50 most powerful women in the energy world). When Trey first met with her, she said two of her goals were to knock down silos and ensure the company didn't reinvent the wheel in different places. Trey saw his proposal helping her do both. The program was not simply going to be a training exercise; it was also going to offer incredible opportunities for networking among many of the company's brightest people.

Hege was non-committal at first about Trey's idea. She wasn't familiar with the MSTC degree. No one from Norway had participated. She was, however, willing to pass Trey's prospectus about the program to the company's CEO, Pete Miller. During Miller's term, NOV had grown immensely through acquisitions. Trey's cover letter asked the CEO, "Are you consolidating the market to harvest or are you consolidating to innovate? If you are consolidating to innovate, then you need this program." The CEO (a proud West Point graduate) had always talked about the vital importance of people. Trey asked, "What do you want your legacy to be? Are you willing to actually put into action what you have longed talked about?"

Trey knew it would take more than inspirational words to get buy-in for his program. NOV leaders would need to be confident that their decision to support the program wouldn't make them look bad. That meant they had to see all the detailed homework behind the decision. They had to realize the idea had been thoroughly thought through. The curriculum needed to be specific and well-reasoned. NOV leaders needed to see how the program would work and how it would resolve some pains the company was experiencing. They also needed to see how it would eventually create meaningful benefits for NOV. This was all part of Trey's prospectus.

The CEO approved Trey's proposal and Hege immediately encouraged Trey to start the program. With her experience and stature she was able to help Trey recruit some of the best NOV employees from throughout the world as the first NOV Ventures class. Hege quickly became one the program's biggest champions. (She has attended every session over the past five years).

Fighting Obstacles and Proving the Case

All of this was happening while Trey still had a full-time job in NOV working on instrumentation and monitoring technologies. "I still had my day job," he said. Some people in his division felt he ought to invest all of his time on his division's projects. "Quit advocating for the Ventures program," they said. "We want 100% here." Trey thought he was contributing everything he could to his current position since he was doing his work on NOV Ventures mostly on weekends and evenings. Plus, he was being a good corporate citizen—thinking not only about his unit, but the entire company. What could be wrong about that? At one point, his manager was so highly critical of what Trey was doing that the word on the street was that Trey might lose his job.

Hege heard about Trey's troubles and rescued him. "Do you want to join me?" she asked in a phone call. Trey responded, "Done." The decision ended his career in his division. "I had over 13 years invested in building up the division and I was out. I had a lot of emotional investment that I had to move away from." But it was important, both personally and professionally, for him to move. Trey moved from Austin to Houston and joined the CTO's office three years after the Ventures program had started. Close to 120 top engineers had graduated from the program by then. Business cases emerging from the Ventures program were transitioning into business units for execution.

At the Amsterdam session each year, there is a contest among the teams enrolled in that year's program. After months of work, each team presents a business case for their product to a panel of top executives. At the close of one business case contest in Amsterdam, the president of one division (the floating production systems) said to the room, "I need to say something. You don't understand how important, how valuable, how significant this program is. These business cases are gold to me. I'll be using them to help me guide the business into the future. These ideas are is the foundation we need." At last, the leadership was telling Trey and the company that the deliverables emerging from NOV Ventures mattered. And there was empirical proof as well. One team took a product that helped NOV's customers maintain their rigs more effectively and turned it into something that aided NOV's manufacturing people better manage their business. Overall, the transfer rate of innovations was around 60%. The influence rate was much higher. Trey measured influence in an interesting way. When an NOV Ventures team developed a product concept, it often spurred people within a unit to move forward on related technologies they were already working on. For instance, one NOV Ventures team came up with an innovative technique for slop water treatment. After the team presented their technology, the unit responsible for slop water technology in NOV felt pressured to actually solve the problem—something they had not done previously.

For a program that has a budget of only about $1.2 million a year, the total opportunity (financial) potential of all the products that have come out of NOV Ventures is a little over $9 billion in terms of a 5-year forecast. Given how much the program has influenced and seeded the organization with articulate plans for taking concepts to market (where the potential payoff is in the billions), one could actually argue that the Ventures program is underfunded. Indeed, people in NOV are talking about creating an internal venture fund to speed up the commercialization of many of the ideas created by participants in NOV Ventures.

NOV Ventures has done more than create commercial value for the firm. It has also fostered a network of enthusiastic, bright, engineers. In a global company it's hard to get people to meet and work with each other. NOV Ventures systematically creates teams representing different units in the company and composed of people from various parts of the world. More than one participant has said that a major payoff of the program was that it put him within five minutes reach of anyone he needed to know in the company. Equally important, many of these very gifted technical people enrolled in the program learned a lot about political savvy through the years. They learned that having a brilliant idea is never enough. Like Trey, they also must craft, and then sell, a business case for it.

From my perspective as someone who has worked with NOV Ventures since the start as both a consultant and teacher, there are some important lessons that can be learned from NOV Ventures.

First, consulting work can be extraordinarily generative. I started with one session on how innovators advocate their ideas as part of Master's program on technology commercialization (or how people sell their ideas) and a few years later I am working with hundreds of people in a program that is, to some degree, based on that one session.

Second, consulting within a corporate setting requires behavioral and cognitive flexibility from academics. Many academic people who were initially involved in the program as consultants or teachers are no longer part of the initiative. In truth, many academics have a hard time working within corporate firms. They are, in the lines of one person, "too academic." They aren't willing to take the risks that giving advice demands. When you are working with companies, your recommendations have meaningful consequences on people and even the future of the firm. You need to be confident enough of your base of knowledge to answer questions and offer advice even when there are no clear academic answers (see Waldeck, Plax, & Kearney, Chapter 7, for more on the importance of self-confidence in consulting).

Third, NOV Ventures is a multicultural initiative, and working in such an environment can pose challenges. In a typical program, you will have people both from, and working in, multiple continents. I have been lucky enough to work for many multinational firms as a consultant. I have learned some important cultural differences that affect how one works across cultures. The obvious issue of language barriers can pose numerous difficulties. For instance, accents—yours and theirs—can be a problem (one suggestion based on my experience: have more details on slides. People tend to read English better than they understand accented speech). Additionally, when it comes to language differences, translation is critical. There are multiple forms of English and a word may mean different things in different parts of the world. When working with people who don't have a good understanding of English, make sure your translator is extraordinary. Nothing matters more. And, don't use someone inside the company because people will wonder about the translator's agenda.

Also important to keep in mind when working on a corporate multicultural initiative:

- *Hierarchy is more important in some cultures than others.* In some cultures, the only person who matters is the decision-maker; in other cultures, anyone in the firm can talk.

- *People want to know that you know what's happening in their part of the world.* They want examples of companies that are local and familiar to them; they want you to know the names of national leaders; they want you to have some knowledge of their nation's history as well as some experience in their culture (one thing I do to prepare read local newspapers for a few weeks before traveling). They don't care that much about the U.S. and they often find annoying the tendency of U.S consultants to push the U.S. method of doing things.
- *Participation styles differ across cultures.* Some cultures are more direct and argumentative (e.g., the Dutch) than others (e.g., Indonesians). I have worked with Japanese companies a number of times, and to this day I have little idea of how effective I was. There is seldom any feedback. But, at the same time, when dealing with managers in global companies, there are more commonalities than differences. With few exceptions the language of business is English, and that is a blessing for people with English as a first language.

NOTE

1. Disclosure: Working through the University of Texas, the author has been compensated for teaching in NOV Ventures since its inception.

A Delicate Balance

When the Researcher Is Also an Interventionist in Healthcare Settings

LOYD S. PETTEGREW

University of South Florida

INTRODUCTION

This essay presents two case studies involving research and intervention in two very different healthcare settings. The first is from the five years I spent as an assistant director of the Office of Communication Research (OCR) at University Medical Center[1]. The second is from the 29 months I spent as a paid researcher and volunteer concierge/patient advocate at a for-profit radiation cancer treatment center. I performed both quantitative and qualitative research in both settings and also had responsibility to improve internal communication among patients and healthcare professionals. My dual responsibility was to the centers' senior executives as well as to employees and patients. These were very different sets of masters, requiring that I balance the conflicts delicately.

Using research data to improve conditions in healthcare organizations carries with it risk. First, the people providing the feedback data can be scapegoated by top-level managers for making them and their change efforts look less than stellar. Second, if this happens, the consultant who interprets and reports the results may alienate employees, thus making it difficult to gain their future confidence and support. Third, if these two consequences happen, it is likely to disrupt the organization more than had the consulting not been undertaken and the consultant's reputation becomes sullied. By minimizing such risk, the consultant seeks to make a difference *through*, as opposed to *from* the research (Frey, 2009, pp. 209–210).

Witteborn, Milburn, and Ho (2013, p. 189) refer to this approach as, "Examining research through participants' perspectives and privileging their ends." As such, I was a reflexive researcher and a participant in the organizational life I was studying (Hartwig, 2014).

My Reflexivity GPS

Michael Polanyi (1958) chided the hard sciences because personal knowledge is essential and contextualizes the knower with what is being known; the two cannot be separated. In these case studies, I continuously point to my reflexive stance on organizational knowledge, relying on key informant input, interviews with line employees and management, and quantitative survey data that were then vetted and challenged by all members of my research team (see Cunliffe, 2003).

Much of the work on reflexivity focuses on philosophical issues, while the bulk of my reflexive stance is aimed at actual research practice and how to better understand both my social experience and the data collected in these two research sites (Cunliffe, 2003). Alvesson (2003) treats qualitative organizational interviews as reflexive opportunities that stimulate a critical interplay between producing interpretations of an organization and its actors, and challenging them. "Reflexivity emphasizes that the researcher is part of the social world that is studied, and this calls for exploration and self-examination" (Alvesson, 2003, p. 24).

Reflexivity is thus a property of a relationship, not of individuals, where an awareness of *how* those constructing activities that we attempt to understand are mirrored by our own constructing activities in research (Steier, 1995). Lynch (2000, p. 43) warns "there is no particular advantage to 'being' reflexive, or 'doing' reflexive analysis, unless something provocative, interesting or revealing comes from it." Such outcomes are the coin of the realm of successful practitioners. While an author, focused primarily on scholarship and publication, may try to achieve similar outcomes, most of us know that an author's personal conviction is hardly a criterion of success (Lynch, 2000).

WHY SETTING MATTERS

Each case study details my dual responsibility for conducting research to improve the effectiveness of the organization, and the productivity and working lives of employees treating patients. As a secondary gain, these case studies underlie my belief that different settings within the healthcare context involve very different communication dynamics and the generalizability of findings across healthcare settings is problematic. In Chapter 4 of this book, I elaborate on this particular concern.

Elsewhere I have argued that setting is a much overlooked and little researched area of applied communication research (Pettegrew, 1988, 2015). I attribute this to scholars' desire to generalize their findings as widely as possible, without a concomitant effort to specify site limitations or idiosyncrasies. This, in turn, may limit the consultant's ability to use business and organizational communication research findings with maximum effectiveness across a range of applied settings. For example, do findings from a study of staff communication in a large academic cancer research/treatment center (see Ellingson, 2003, 2005) generalize to those of a private, for- profit cardiac catheterization center (see Morgan & Krone, 2001)? By exclusion, the field is left believing that research findings from such disparate settings must somehow cohere, but I present data (Pettegrew, 2015) to the contrary. Waldeck, Seibold and Flanagin's (2004) research on the impact of advanced communication and information technologies on organizational assimilation across four different organizations is an important exception. They actually tested for differences between these settings. Their work is notable because while most academic research is confined to one site, they tested the generalizability of their findings across these different settings. On the other hand, differences in health settings are most detectable through the kind of "thick description" advocated by Nussbaum (1989). This means that the researcher/consultant adopts an ethnographic mantle which is to understand the situated rationality of the healthcare setting within which people's actions make sense (Parker, 2007).

THE CONFLICTED ROLE OF CONSULTANT

My role as communication consultant is fourfold. First, I must be able to read the particular setting in which the work is to be done. I try to suppress my implicit assumptions about a new setting from past experience and force myself to quickly become an expert on the culture, history, market niche, personnel and leadership that are characteristic of that organization. This takes time, energy and is inherently ethnographic (see Hartwig, 2014; Sprain & Boromisza-Habashi, 2013; Witteborn et al., 2013). My approach is outlined by Maletz and Nohria (2001) describing a group from McKinsey & Company investigating white space (all the informal enterprise in a company that falls outside of formal budgeting, planning and management). The team was comprised of a dozen ethnographers who performed consulting research in twelve diverse companies, spending several months in each company learning its unique culture, strategy, structure and business drivers. The authors conclude that this work provides "a rich body of data on the possibilities and pitfalls associated with working in the whitespace" (Maletz & Nohria, 2001, p. 105).

Second, I bring theoretical and methodological preferences to the consultancy that have worked well elsewhere and that are consistent with my own values and paradigms as a researcher (see Keyton, Chapter 3). Ludwig Wittgenstein decimated the foundation of logical positivism by insisting that there could be no theory-free language. There also is no theory-free consulting; we are all driven by explicit and/or implicit human and organizational theories (see the Craig & Tracy, 2014 review of practical theory; also Ellis, 1991; Fairhurst & Putnam, 2004; Keyton, Chapter 3; Plax, 1991; Ruben, 2005). Even though consultants operate from well-defined theoretical paradigms and methodological approaches/assumptions, they must maintain some degree of flexibility because different settings, even in the same context, demand unique treatment. The real and underappreciated challenge is assessing how generalizable the consultant's tools are across these different settings and being able to adapt when necessary.

Third, I must grasp quickly the underlying communication exigency—what actually needs attention and change, often in spite of top executives' beliefs. Frequently, there is a disconnect between the various levels of management and employees about what the real problems are (see Jorgensen, Chapter 5). The consultant must divine this reflexively from observation and discussion with people at various levels and revise or reframe the communication exigency as (s)he learns more.

Finally, I must assess quickly and accurately these first three issues and develop an action plan that has the optimal chance of improving the conditions that brought me to the organization. This latter step is often what distinguishes consulting from academic research (March, 1991). As opposed to successfully collecting data and returning to the academy, consultants have an obligation to improve conditions or offer the organization a plan for doing so. Consultants must prioritize these four challenges because they often compete for the scarce consultant resources: time, personal energy, and a commitment to doing the right thing even when it produces conflict with and tests one's personal credibility with management and employees.

UNIVERSITY MEDICAL CENTER

My years at University Medical Center (UMC) began in the theoretical shadows of the University of Michigan's Institute for Social Research (ISR) where I had trained. When I first arrived, I used ISR's "Survey of Organizations" (Bowers, 1973; Taylor & Bowers, 1972) as my guide. Dan Costello, the OCR director, and I privileged UMC's goals over our scholarly research goals (c.f., Costello & Pettegrew, 1979; Witteborn et al., 2013). UMC aspired to become one of the top five academic medical centers in the nation by updating its physical plant with state-of-the-art facilities, patient care equipment and a medical information system, all of which were a decade ahead of their time. OCR's mission was to facilitate this human, medical and information systems upgrade, making sure everyone knew how to use the new upgrades while minimizing human turnover in the transition.

I was fortunate to have brought on Rick Thomas, an early communication ethnographer who, during the first survey administration, saw two serious drawbacks. First, the literacy of many employees in housekeeping, dietary services and facilities maintenance was very low. Many could not read the questionnaire, written by academics presuming a high reading level. Subsequently, we had members of the OCR team read the questions to employee groups with literacy issues. Second, this survey did not match the reality many employees were facing. Rick came back and said, "We are asking employees the wrong questions because they don't pertain to anything these folks are experiencing and tell us nothing helpful. They are under a huge amount of stress and UMC is like a powder keg ready to explode."

UMC was transitioning from a 1930s style physical plant and culture to a brand-new physical plant, medical education facility, and learning resource center that were driven by an entirely automated medical information system (MIS). With one flick of a power switch, employees' lives would change forever. I immediately began looking at two new foundations. The first was the job-related stress literature. I returned theoretically to the work of one of my ISR mentors, Bob Kahn (c.f., Kahn et. al., 1964), creating an updated job-related stress model and measuring instrument (Pettegrew et al., 1980) with a palpable connection to employee experiences documented through interviews. The second was resistance to change. The recognition came about as we attempted to train staff and physicians on how to use the new MIS.

Computers would fail unexpectedly; we found that employees were sticking bobby pins in the machines or in other ways sabotaging them. We discovered a concerted effort at all levels to resist forced technological change. The job-related stress feedback surveys gave us a clear indication of the problem. Levels of role ambiguity (not having enough information to do one's job effectively) and role conflict (a difference in the way employees thought their jobs should be performed and the way management thought it should be done) were very high. Based on this information, our training coordinators redoubled their efforts to assure employees that technology would not replace them. It worked slowly and our efforts were painstaking, but the resistance began to evaporate. For the few pockets of continued resistance, we met with the employee and her/his supervisor to explain the advantages of learning this technology. The supervisor provided a complementary stick (job security) to our carrot.

Physicians were a more difficult challenge. They responded to technology passive-aggressively. We would invite 20 physicians to come for training and 2 would show up. The physicians always had plausible deniability—they had emergency cases or were too busy with patients. The OCR team assembled one day and Dan Costello pointed to this glaring failure, soliciting fixes. Most of the ideas were heavy-handed—"make their specialty chiefs demand the doctors come."

From my interviews with the chiefs of surgery, medicine, anesthesiology, etc., I believed that physician compliance was *our* problem, not theirs, and that we would have to solve it. Hearing no ideas that I thought would work, I suggested we reframe the situation, drawing on the work from *Change: Problem Formation and Problem Resolution* (Watzlawick, Weakland, & Fisch, 1974). Rick Thomas and I had discussed this possibility a week before. I was familiar with the basic elements of mini-computer programming and knew a programmer who would cobble together a medical diagnosis game (crude by today's gaming standards) on a small budget. The game would present a set of medical symptoms and the user would have to discern the correct diagnosis. A month later it was ready for testing. We had the Medical School dean invite the 14 chief residents to a training program where they would learn how to use the new medical diagnosis game, and by default, the MIS. When the Dean called, the chief residents reported, all 14 of them.

During these sessions, chief residents would actively tell us how to improve the diagnosis game and become active enablers in our reframing strategy. With this accomplished, we put new computers (terminal and keyboard) in the physician lounges. We hoped the chief residents would train other residents on how to log onto the MIS so they could play the diagnosis game. Within two months, 70% of the medical residents knew how to use the medical information system. More importantly, attending physicians would come into the lounges and see a chief resident absorbed with the computer and ask what was so interesting. It was, of course, the diagnosis game, and the implicit challenge was whether the attending physician could better the chief resident's accuracy score. In 90 days, most of the attending physicians were up to speed and they, in turn, seduced other physicians to learn the system through playing the game. Our goal of training 90% of the physicians to use the medical information system was reached four months ahead of schedule. Employee turnover dropped to a 5-year low and nursing unit and medical record efficiency climbed to historically highs.

SUNCOAST CANCER RADIATION CENTER

Suncoast Cancer Radiation Center (SCRC) is a private, physician-owned cancer radiation treatment center in a metropolitan area in the southeastern U.S. It is a concierge-type facility[2] with wonderful amenities and state-of-the-art radiation equipment. A 12' by 12' water wall greeted people when they came in the front entrance and there was an outdoor Zen garden with a fountain and harmonic wind chimes. Large flat-screen TVs that played Blu-Ray DVDs (of the world's most beautiful places) were stationed in the front and clinic waiting rooms and had very comfortable chairs for the patients and their companions. Two workstations were placed in the front waiting room for patient/companion use. There was a snack bar serving gourmet coffee and tea, healthy snacks and double-filtered water. With its amenities and open access, the SCRC physical setting was nothing like that at UMC. My first consulting role at SCRC was as a paid researcher, recruited by the physician-owners to discover how and by whom patients were referred to SCRC for a consultation and potential treatment, and to gain patient feedback on their experience at SCRC after completing treatment. The instruments included both quantitative and qualitative questions; I coded and recorded them and reported back the data anonymously to the SCRC owners, executive director and staff tri-yearly.

Sprain and Boromisza-Habashi (2013) discuss how ethnographic methods can open new possibilities and realities through immersion in the cultural practices of an organization. The reverse happened at SCRC. My researcher role thrust me into a series of planning meetings several months before SCRC opened. At one meeting, one of the doctor-owners enthused, "We're going to deliver concierge radiation oncology to our patients!" The head nurse turned and said, "But then we'll need a concierge." It grew quiet and everyone in the room looked directly at me. I agreed to become the volunteer SCRC concierge/patient advocate for 29 months. Unlike the researcher, I would have to define and develop this new role. As concierge/patient advocate, I had dual responsibilities—to patients and their companions/families, and to the SCRC doctors, executive director and employees. I accepted the position with the approval of the physician managing partner that I could collect data and write an ethnography of my experience.

SCRC couldn't have been a more different healthcare setting than UMC. The campus was comparatively small, both in physical size and in personnel. UMC was an old medical facility, dark, serious and uninviting—a total institution (Goffman, 1961). It was hierarchically organized from the vice president of medical affairs down the chain of command. Because of its size and structure, it was an easy place for people to avoid one another. SCRC was brand new, well lit and appointed, and employees were purposively available to patients and one another. It was privately owned, not part of a hospital-based organization, unlike UMC or the cancer care setting described by Ellingson (2002; 2003; 2005). There was little backstage behavior at SCRC because the doctors intended for everyone to be accessible to each other and patients. On any given day, patients might interact with ten or more staff and physicians. SCRC was characterized by a flat, rather than hierarchical structure; as a result, it was a communication-rich environment.

The physician-owners believed, from their extensive experience at hospital-based treatment centers, that SCRC needed to take a different approach to communication among staff and patients and their companions. To help this healing mission, I partnered with the physician managing partner to create an institutional humor-orientation, both with patients and among employees as a way to counter the deadly seriousness of cancer (du Pré, 1998; Lockwood, & Yoshimura, 2013; Wanzer, Booth-Butterfield, & Booth-Butterfield, 2005). The research literature, coupled with my own experience at UMC, supported the idea that institutionalized humor, while very needed, is unlikely in large hospital-based centers.

THE DELICATE BALANCE OF RESEARCHER AND CONSULTANT: LESSONS LEARNED FROM PERFORMING DUAL ROLES

My dual roles as researcher and interventionist at both UMC and SCRC required I delicately balance intervention, conflict and ambiguity (Argyris, Putnam, & Smith, 1985). Research gave me entre, and allowed me to experience and diagnose organizational problems. It informed my interventionist consulting role, giving me an action agenda. However, significant trust and relationship problems can arise when you assume both roles. The following examples illustrate this.

At UMC, I provided research results to executives personally and to employees and supervisors through the OCR training coordinators. We always solicited feedback from those we presented data to test its operational validity. One example of helpful feedback occurred when the UMC executive director mentioned that the operating room (OR) had a 200% RN turnover rate. I promised to check our job-related feedback survey to see what might be leading to this high turnover, and discovered that we had no OR data since we began the process. My training coordinator and I visited the OR head nurse and were told that her nurses were too busy to take the survey. I responded that the data could help her diagnose why there was such high turnover in her unit. She promised to have the surveys completed and returned if we gave them to her again.

Two weeks later they still hadn't been returned, so our training coordinator interviewed several of the OR nurses after their shifts and was told that the OR head nurse had thrown the surveys in the trash the day they arrived. The nurses said their boss's Marine drill sergeant style (requiring all nurses to arrive 15 minutes early without pay, line-up for a military inspection of their uniforms—clean, starched and shoes polished, make-up checked) made the OR an intolerable place to work. As a result, many nurses quit, easily finding work at less prestigious local hospitals. I took this information to the UMC nursing director, setting in motion a contentious process with the chief of surgery leading to the OR head nurse's retirement. I later found that the reason she stayed on for 25 years was because she and the chief of surgery were close friends; she was quite adept at camouflaging her mistakes and he was willing to overlook any negative reports about her. In the following year, OR nurse turnover dropped to 37%, a five-fold reduction. When someone loses their job as a direct result of your research and intervention tactics, it can be a disquieting situation for a consultant. Looking back, I believe the organization benefitted by saving the disruption and expense of OR nurse turnover, and surgery patients were undoubtedly safer with a more committed and less stressed nursing staff.

At SCRC, the role balance was even more delicate. I reported the research data I collected to the executive director, the doctors and employees. I assessed all aspects of patients' experience at SCRC on a 4-point Likert scale, from strongly agree to strongly disagree. There were also several qualitative questions at the end where patients could tell us how we could have improved their experience and what issues needed our greatest attention. Two themes emerged from patient experiences: (1) excessive wait times for treatment, and (2) excessive wait times during their weekly visit with their doctor.

The Tomotherapy machine was a technological marvel, but notoriously delicate and would break down every few weeks. We were using it at its highest capacity range (40 treatments per day). Sometimes it could be fixed quickly; other times a new part would have to be flown in and the machine would be down for 1–2 days. Reporting the first results to the head radiation therapist (RT) was difficult. I told him that patients were bothered by being delayed or missing a treatment entirely (we would make up the missed treatments and we often open SCRC on the weekends). He responded defensively that he couldn't make a finicky machine more reliable. Rather than drive home the point, I suggested *we* be more proactive. If the machine went down, the RTs should immediately tell me, and I would inform the patients in the waiting room about the delay. The RTs would call the rest of the patients scheduled on that machine and tell them of the delay and that they would be kept apprised. If the machine was seriously broken, I would tell the patients in the waiting room and the radiation therapists would call the rest of the scheduled patients, and inform them of the problem and the anticipated time/day it would be back on-line. During the next survey period, patient responses improved appreciably. The simple fix, though first resisted, was to *share* responsibility for apprising patients of delays across the care team.

Habitually, the worst performance factor at SCRC was patients' experiencing excessive wait times to see their doctor. This was a particular problem for one of the doctors who was habitually late for everything at SCRC. He would stand patients up for 40 minutes while working on something inconsequential! The nurses in the clinic would grow more frustrated as the wait time grew longer; sometimes patients would leave in disgust. Neither the executive director nor the nurses were comfortable "bugging" this doctor when patients were waiting excessively. After all, he was one of the owners. I had known the doctor socially for a number of years before I came to SCRC and had a rapport with him that others did not have. When I reported the data to the SCRC executive director, she shook her head in frustration and said she would talk to him. The data were worse in the second trimester and the executive director told me that this doctor had blamed the bad results on the other doctors. In the next survey I added a question about which doctor the patient saw. In the third trimester of the first year, the executive director now had statistically significant evidence of the doctor's now unequivocal contribution to the problem.

I intervened in two ways. First, I presented the results at the next owners' meeting and confronted his objections with statistical significance. He was not pleased. Second, because we were friends, I told the nurses to tell me when the doctor made a patient wait for more than 15 minutes. At that point, I would go to his office or track him down since he seldom responded to paging, and tell him directly that the clinic was backing up and patients were growing restless waiting so long. He began calling me his nanny, but his performance improved only slightly in the following patient survey. Second, this doctor also saw many fewer patients than his colleagues, largely because he wouldn't make himself available for new patient consults. At owner meetings, the other doctors confronted him about this issue. He responded to their criticism by saying that he was seeing as many patients, but at another facility they partially owned. This contentiousness continued for months until I offered to build a spreadsheet for the executive director to track all the patients each doctor saw across several facilities. The data clearly showed that he saw at least 40% fewer total patients across the different facilities. His two partners confronted him with the survey data, but his behavior never changed. My efforts estranged our social relationship somewhat, and even though change was not dramatic because of his ownership position at SCRC, others felt less victimized by his behavior and patients received the benefit of the work-around I provided. Data are not all-powerful!

CONCLUSIONS

In this essay I have described my two consulting roles as both researcher and interventionist. It requires leveraging information to direct organizational change and packaging and presenting it to all organizational members. Doing so effectively demands a delicate balance of the power of information and the possibilities of intervention. I have also tried to provide a secondary gain—that consulting gives one a much clearer understanding of how setting makes a difference in communication behavior, limiting the scholarly assumption of generalizability across different settings in the same context.

I would be remiss if I didn't provide a brief personal contextualization. As our field has known since *Pragmatics of Communication* (Watzlawick, Beavin and Jackson, 1967), what we say is conditioned by how we say things. My communication behavior can be characterized as strong and persuasive (see Ng & Bradac, 1993, Chapter 6). More specifically, my communicator style is attentive, dominant, open, dramatic (see Norton, 1978). As such, I evoke both support and resistance from people in organizations with whom I consult. Top-level administrators are encouraged by the confidence I display and are not threatened because they have brought me into the organization to get things done. On the other hand, middle management tends to be threatened because my style challenges their sense of power and control. At the level of line employees, my style offers confidence that what they say will be forcefully communicated to the top. Dealing reflexively with this tripartite effect on the organization also necessitates a delicate balance that over the years I have learned to control more effectively.

NOTES

1. Both UMC and SCRC are fictitious names.
2. Concierge medicine is largely a product of the new millennium, begun by Internal Medicine (IM) doctors to counter the pressure by Medicare and health insurance companies to churn patients (as many as 60 patients per day), giving them more time with each patient (Wieczner, 2013). Unlike IM concierge care, SCRC didn't charge extra fees, but accepted all forms of payment, were available 24-hours/day and would see emergencies the next business day. For a discussion of concierge care and patient-centered medical homes see Majette (2009).

REFERENCES

Alvesson, M. (2003). Beyond neopositivists, romantics, and localists: A reflexive approach to interviews in organizational research. *Academy of Management Review, 29*(1), 13–33.

Argyris, C., Putnam, R. & Smith, D. (1985). *Action science: Concepts, methods, and skills for research and intervention.* San Francisco, CA: Jossey-Bass.

Bowers, D. G. (1973). OD techniques and their results in 23 organizations: The Michigan ICL study. *The Journal of Applied Behavioral Science, 9* 21–43.

Ng, S. H., & Bradac, J. J. (1993). *Power in language: Verbal communication and social influence.* Beverly Hills, CA: Sage Publications, Inc.

Costello, D. E., & Pettegrew, L. S. (1979). Health communication theory and research: An overview of health organizations. In D. Nimmo (Ed.), *Communication Yearbook III.* (606–624). New Brunswick, NJ: Transaction.

Craig, R. T., & Tracy, K. (2014). Building grounded practical theory in applied communication research: Introduction to the special issue. *Journal of Applied Communication Research, 42,* 229–243.

Cunliffe, A. L. (2003). Reflexive inquiry in organizational research: Questions and possibilities. *Human Relations,56*, 983–1003.

du Pré, A. (1998). *Humor and the healing arts: A multidimensional analysis of humor use in health care.* Mahwah, NJ: Lawrence Erlbaum Associates.

Ellingson, L. (2002). The role of companions in the geriatric oncology patient multidisciplinary health care provider interaction. *Journal of Aging Studies, 16*, 361–382.

Ellingson, L. (2003). Interdisciplinary health care teamwork in the clinic backstage." *Journal of Applied Communication Research, 31*, 93–117.

Ellingson, L. (2005). *Communicating in the clinic: Negotiating frontstage and backstage teamwork.* Cresskill, NJ: Hampton Press.

Ellis, D. G. (1991). The openness of opposites: Applied communication and theory. *Journal of Applied Communication Research,19*, 110–122.

Fairhurst, G. T. & Putnam, L. L. (2004). Organizations as discursive constructions. *Communication Theory, 14*, 5–26.

Frey, L. R. (2009). What a difference more difference-making communication scholarship might make: Making a difference from and through research. *Journal of Applied Communication Research, 37*, 205–214.

Goffman, E. (1961). *Asylums: Essays on the social situation of mental patients and other inmates.* London, UK: Pelican Books.

Hartwig, R. T. (2014). Ethnographic facilitation as a complementary methodology for conducting applied communication scholarship. *Journal of Applied Communication Research, 42*, 60–64.

Kahn, R. L., Wolfe, D. M., Quinn, R. P., Snoek, J. D., & Rosenthal, R. A. (1964). *Organizational stress: Studies in role conflict and ambiguity.* New York, NY: Wiley.

Lockwood, N. L. & Yoshimura, S. M. (2013). The heart of the matter: The effects of humor on well-being during recovery from cardiovascular disease. *Health Communication, 28*, 410–420. doi =10.1080/10410236.2012.762748

Lynch, M. (2000). Against reflexivity as an academic virtue and source of privileged knowledge. *Theory, Culture & Society, 17*, 26–54.

Majette, G. (2009). From concierge medicine to patient-centered medical homes: International lessons & the search for a better way to deliver primary health care in the US. *American Journal of Law & Medicine, 35*, 585–619.

Maletz, M. C., & Nohria, N. (2001). Managing in the whitespace. *Harvard Business Review, 79*, 102–111.

March, J. G. (1991). Organizational consultants and organizational research. *Journal of Applied Communication Research, 19*, 20–31.

Morgan, J., & Krone, K. (2001). Bending the rules of "professional" display: Emotional improvisation in caregiver performances. *Journal of Applied Communication Research, 29*, 317–340.

Norton, R. W. (1978). Foundation of a communicator style construct. *Human Communication Research, 4*, 99–112.

Nussbaum, J. F. (1989). Directions for research within health communication. *Health Communication, 1*, 35–40.

Parker, M. (2007). Ethnography/ethics. *Social Science & Medicine, 65*, 2248–2259.

Pettegrew, L. S. (1988). The importance of context in applied communication research. *Southern Speech Communication Journal, 53*, 331–338.

Pettegrew, L. S. (2015). Time spent with cancer: An ethnography of humor, ritual and defiance in a cancer care setting. Unpublished manuscript, Department of Communication, University of South Florida.

Pettegrew, L. S., Thomas, R. C. Costello, D. E., Wolf, G. E., Lennox, L., & Thomas, S. (1980). Job-related stress in a medical center organization: Management/communication issues. In D. Nimmo (Ed.) Communication Yearbook IV. New Brunswick, NJ: Transaction.

Plax, T. G. (1991). Understanding applied communication inquiry: Researcher as organizational consultant. *Journal of Applied Communication Research, 16*, 39–43.

Polanyi, M. (1958). *Personal knowledge: Toward a postcritical philosophy.* Chicago, IL: University of Chicago Press.

Ruben, B. D. (2005). Linking communication scholarship and professional practice in colleges and universities. *Journal of Applied Communication Research, 33*, 294–304.

Sprain, L. & Boromisza-Habashi, D. (2013). The ethnographer of communication at the table: Building cultural competence, designing strategic action. *Journal of Applied Communication Research, 41*, 181–187.

Steier, F. (1995). Reflexivity, interpersonal communication, and interpersonal communication research." In W. Leeds-Hurwitz (Ed.), *Social approaches to communication*, (pp.63–87). New York, NY: Guilford Press.

Taylor, J. & Bowers, D. (1972). *The survey of organizations: A machine-scored, standardized questionnaire instrument.* Ann Arbor, MI: Institute for Social Research.

Wanzer, M., Booth-Butterfield, M., Booth-Butterfield, S. (2005). "If we did not use humor, we'd cry:" Humorous coping communication in health care settings. *Journal of Health Communication, 10*, 105–125.

Waldeck, J., Seibold, D. & Flanagin, A. (2004). Organizational assimilation and communication technology use. *Communication Monographs, 71*, 161–183.

Watzlawick, P., Beavin, J. H. & Jackson, D. D. (1967). *Pragmatics of human communication. A study of interactional patterns, pathologies, and paradoxes.* New York, NY: W. W. Norton.

Watzlawick, P., Weakland, J. & Fisch, R. (1974). *Change: Principles of problem formation and problem resolution.* New York, NY: W. W. Norton.

Wieczner, J. (2013, November 11). The pros and cons of concierge medicine. *Wall Street Journal*, p. R8.

Witteborn, S., Milburn, T. & Ho, E. Y. (2013). The ethnography of communication as applied methodology: Insights from three case studies. *Journal of Applied Communication Research, 41*, 188–194.

CHAPTER NINETEEN

White Shirts, Blue Shirts

A Case Study of Leadership Development Consulting for Law Enforcement

SEAN ROSS
Professional Consulting Associates

JENNIFER H. WALDECK
Chapman University

BACKGROUND

Professional Consulting Associates (PCA) LLC, founded in 1998 by Robert Ross, is focused on building communication, leadership, and intercultural/intergroup competencies within organizations. The group specializes in providing customized consultative leadership development programs for public service environments, and it has developed a particular niche within the law enforcement sector. The first author of this case, Sean Ross, is the company's Chief Operating Officer and Chief Learning Officer; Waldeck functions an external contract consultant for PCA, providing curriculum development and instructional design, original research services, and occasional training facilitation.

PCA's programs focus on *system-wide leadership at all levels, leadership competency development, enhanced management and communication effectiveness, competent intercultural communication within diverse systems, conflict resolution, talent development, and internal and external customer services.* The group's assumption is that these assets provide a platform for transformational change within organizations, and the results of their numerous engagements over the years support that assumption. The consulting team accomplishes its work through training programs, coaching, facilitated conversations and exercises, online learning and discussion, and relationships with clients. PCA has developed several evidence-based proprietary models for pre-consultation research, facilitation, and program evaluation, as well. Overarching all the team's interactions and interventions is the mission to encourage commitment to leadership and communication competence from all levels of the client organization—from the "top brass" to the most recent hire.

In 2010, PCA launched a program known as the Public Service Leadership Institute (PSLI), dedicated to helping members of public service organizations to "inspire, serve, and lead" (PSLI's guiding catchphrase and website address). Over time, we have observed and collected data which suggest that this program offers deep value to its participants and their organizations. For example, many of our graduates have moved into significant leadership roles within their organizations. Further, clients report cost savings associated with the negative outcomes averted by practicing the principles and engaging in the behaviors recommended by our programs.

On a subjective level, because we have a lengthy history with many of our clients and are deeply embedded within their organizations through ongoing relationships and return engagements, we have had the opportunity to observe many positive impacts. They reflect the *servant leadership theoretical model*[1] our graduates use to frame their work, and they positively change the lives of individuals, both inside the organizations and within the communities our public servant clients serve. Even more specifically, participants from rank and file officers to department chiefs report in summative evaluations that "this kind of leadership training is sorely lacking in law enforcement. [This program] teaches each officer that is chosen, 'you are accountable for your actions'"; "...a staple for our command people...prepares officers for real leadership through more effective communication, a more open mind...teaches them about planning, resource allocation, dealing with media, and recognizing people and leading them"; "[This program] pushes us into areas we don't always consider or think about until it is too late...every officer should go through this training" (Public Service Leadership Institute, 2015). As readers of this chapter are undoubtedly aware, the U.S. news media has featured a number of high profile cases involving poor police/community relations in recent years. The most recognizable example is the officer-involved shooting of Michael Brown in Ferguson, Missouri in 2014. Our team has seen an increased interest among law enforcement departments in the PSLI programs for their potential to shape more effective communication and leadership behaviors at all levels of police departments. The case we profile in this chapter illustrates the need to create internal cultural changes as a basis for improved internal and external relationships.

THE CASE

The primary purpose of this case study is to share the challenges and opportunities inherent in building a scalable leadership development program that can be facilitated effectively within a diverse range of organizations and sectors. In this particular case, the client, a law enforcement agency, came to us with a general need to assess and improve organizational systems and structures it viewed as critical to its effectiveness, including hiring and, training, and evaluating personnel, and police management practices and policies. Our responsibility, then, was to adapt our leadership, management, and organizational development programs to this agency's unique needs, challenges, and opportunities. In doing so, we sought to provide the agency with its own model and relevant skills to apply routinely to a variety of issues.

The Client

Like the genesis of many consulting engagements, this one began when we were contacted by a leader he within this agency, who had a general sense that the organization needed to improve performance on some key variables and believed that some training would help. But as is almost always the case in consulting work, the client's initial representation of the department's needs and challenges was fairly general and limited. We quickly discovered in initial conversations with our contacts and other organizational members that this police department's needs were unique and deeper than what could be solved with a few simple workshops (see Jorgensen, Chapter 5; Plax, Waldeck, & Kearney, Chapter 6, and Waldeck, Plax, & Kearney, Chapter 7).

The department is situated in an affluent section of a suburban Midwestern city in a predominately politically conservative state. Like many suburban police departments across the country, it has experienced the impacts of urban sprawl since the beginning of the new millennium, including changing demographics and more people to serve with what most stakeholders perceive as inadequate, stretched resources. However, with a strong tax base, a good mix of commercial and residential developments, and insightful city planning, the city remains one of the most desirable cities to live in the country, and its police department is a highly sought after place to work.

This agency is a historically high-performing department with a highly educated sworn and civilian workforce. The officers are predominately white males, consistent with research revealing that in the United States, police forces are often as much as 50–60% less racially diverse than the communities they service (Ashkenas & Park, 2015). The median wage for this department is higher than the national average (US Department of Labor, Bureau of Labor Statistics, 2015), often contributing to a larger than average, highly qualified applicant pool.

Culturally, police departments are notorious for a strict hierarchical structure and a "do as I say" message communicated by higher-ranking officers with internal power to those with less. Structure, order, rank, and control are viewed as critical values for keeping officers and communities safe. This client was no exception. As in many of our other engagements, we encountered officers here who saw transformative change, collaborative leadership, communication, and improved relationships as relatively "soft" topics compared to their "exciting" ventures into tactical training on weapons, hand-to-hand combat, and SWAT. With our foot in the door, we had the opportunity to strategically acknowledge the importance of tactical training for good police work. This helped to create a baseline of understanding that we related to the agency's goals and values. Confirming what the department was already doing well and focusing its resources on (instead of diminishing the importance of its strengths relative to what we had to offer), we were able to demonstrate an appreciation of the day-to-day work faced by the profession. (In Chapter 6, Plax et al. discuss the importance of building this kind of credibility, trust, and understanding by learning the language that your clients use, and confirming what is important to them).

However, over the course of the engagement, we needed to communicate that police officers' tactical work is a necessary but insufficient condition for effective policing. Tactical training, for instance, does not provide officers the skills and strategies they need to interact effectively with one another or with members of the community during tense situations. As our relationship with the client deepened, we were able to illuminate and illustrate the relationship between strategies and tactics in order to enhance the value of our work for all members of this organization. Without a strategy, tactics become a matter of rote memorization and practice. With a strategy, officers can use their critical thinking and decision making abilities to evaluate available alternatives and make effective, impactful choices in the field and in the department.

In an organization like this particular one, steeped in traditions and hierarchy, the decision to hire a consultant is a significant one. When a client gives us access to their organization, they are signaling a commitment to change that may, initially, be weak. The client understands that there is something problematic with the status quo, but typically wants an easy fix from the consultant. But as we reinforce and strengthen their commitment to doing things differently through our interactions with organizational members, we build motivation and momentum toward changes that really matter and that go beyond a simple fix that we can provide. Our goal is to empower organizational members to become involved in identifying the full range of problematic conditions, and become participants in transforming those conditions. One way we did that in this case was to acknowledge what the client was already doing "right" (e.g., strong tactical training and presence), and make the case for how our program would build on what they already did well and enjoyed doing for even greater results. As a result, in any consultation, we maximize the potential of our impact because we are taking steps to move client organizations from a consultant-dependent position to one in which they are adaptive, nimble, and decisively independent.

Digging Deeper

The PSLI consulting team implements a series of steps designed to arrive at a customized program appropriate for each client's needs and critical concerns. Pre-intervention consultation involves research, targeted content development, and needs analysis. Figure 1 illustrates this process. Each phase is focused on learning about individual, unit, and organization-wide performance on critical metrics, and each level's perceptions about leadership and communication within the system (internal to the department) and across system boundaries (with the community).

Through the process defined in Figure 1, the first thing we learned was that this particular consulting engagement was going to be especially sensitive and potentially challenging. The department was dealing with the fallout from a recent politically motivated leak of confidential survey data meant for internal use. The leak and its aftermath had negatively affected morale, trust, and communication within the agency. We needed to establish trust quickly to ensure that the officers participating in our program would not breach any confidential information exchanged during the consultation. Further (and not uncommon to all of our work but more pronounced in this instance), we were held to strict agreements that survey and interview data were strictly for internal use and only to be used for purposes of the training and development process. Recognizing department members' apprehension about taking another survey and talking with outside consultants so soon after their trust had been violated, we worked diligently to create trust and maintain a strong communication network among sworn and civilian personnel in the department.

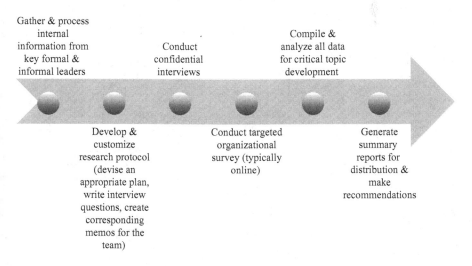

Figure 1. Intervention Design.

After many years of consulting in politically charged, resistant environments, we have come to understand that there is no perfect situation for a consultant to enter; we have to accept what we are confronted with and use it to build something better. In this case, we knew we needed to demonstrate that we not only belonged, but could actually help. It took about a month of meetings, interviews, and consistent communication to establish this trust and credibility, but once we were able to capture officers' buy-in, we knew (based on years of experience working with similar organizations) that the transformative change process would begin for this department. Once we broke through the barriers related to trust, we were able to begin the real work of analyzing this department's culture. The theoretical constructs of *power, organizational culture, psychological reactance, social influence,* and *cultural transformation* and corresponding research directed most of our efforts in this engagement. So, what did we find?

"Staunch, traditional, stale, underperforming, mediocre"—such conditions of highly stable, entrenched cultures often result in low expectations, missed opportunities, and ultimately, underperformance. Police departments in the United States are characterized by a strong culture of tradition, hierarchy, and power, and their strict adherence to these ideals can take them dangerously close to the edge of those negative outcomes we just mentioned. Within these paramilitary organizations, rank-based command and control are prioritized and considered essential elements for success. As leadership development researchers and practitioners, we are often struck by the stale, conforming, traditional, stifling nature of these organizations' policies, processes, and interactions. Rarely, we see a notable exception to these cultural tendencies, such as an instance of a new patrol officer taking an idea to the chief of police without first going through the chain of command. But in general, through extensive experience with numerous departments, we find that traditions are one of the primary obstacles to change, development, and innovation. For this department to co-create and execute a transformative, impactful change process, members needed to confront some deeply entrenched cultural traditions.

Specifically, we found a particular tradition dating back to the beginning of the department that was inhibiting change. Although it seemed simple and innocuous on the surface, its implications ran deep and resulted in a set of unproductive, unhealthy attitudes and behaviors. In fact, officers at every level of the agency used it as a justification for resisting our leadership development initiative with a "that's just the way it is," "that's the way it's always been" attitude. This tradition had survived several leadership transitions and was viewed as an homage to heroes no longer part of the department. Our task involved, first, defining the tradition and exposing it as an obstacle to change.

The Problem: White Shirts/Blue Shirts

The specific cultural tradition that we identified as a key challenge in this agency's development was a problem related to participation and power, which we dubbed *white shirts/blue shirts*. During our early interviews and focus groups with the mid-level ranks, officers asked our team if we had noticed the color of the shirts worn by the upper-level ranks. Indeed, we had noticed the color discrepancy they were referencing. The upper-level ranks wore white shirts, and everyone else wore blue shirts. Bringing this seemingly simple issue to the surface was a powerful moment in the engagement, because in that instant we saw a pivotal opportunity to turn from the unnecessary to the necessary. The white shirt/blue shirt issue provided a backdrop for cultural change and a starting point for motivating this group to make some changes in how power was viewed and used within the department—and how examining internal structures would help improve the department's ability to serve its community.

The issue was of much greater consequence than the simple color of the shirts that officers wore. Instead, the issue had everything to do with the internal culture of power within this department. Rookie and midlevel rank officers felt powerless and excluded from leadership and decision making. One of the questions we pose in early conversations during a leadership development consultation is "Do you feel like you are a part of the leadership team?" In this organization, the overwhelming response from the rank and file ("blue shirts") was "absolutely not!" In other words, the more highly ranked officers (from lieutenants on up), the "white shirts," had all of the power and control to the detriment of empowerment at other levels of the organization. For example, officers reported immediately shifting into a subordinate role when white shirts entered the room, abdicating decision making, accountability, and self-confidence.

The lack of empowerment was a particularly frustrating and stifling condition for this highly educated force. However, owing to tradition and culture, everyone in this system accepted his or her place within the hierarchy and behaved accordingly. "Empowered regardless of rank" was a phrase from a foreign language for people in this organization. Power was for the white shirts. Blue shirts didn't make decisions; they followed white shirts' orders. So, when we launched our work with this group, designed to empower *everyone* to think and act as strategic leaders, both the blue shirts and the white shirts resisted out of lack of understanding and experience. As Lewis (2011) explained, people often resist organizational change even when they stand to benefit from it.

We had tapped a critical issue that, if unpacked and resolved, would open the possibilities for transformative change. But, if the concerns about power and leadership that we had discovered were not addressed, we knew they would remain potentially insurmountable barriers to the positive change we were hoping to facilitate.

The Objectives

Our guiding objectives were to create a measurable sense of empowerment and to improve leadership across levels of the organization, thereby diminishing the inhibiting impacts of the rigid, hierarchical power structure that had characterized this organizational culture for many years—and that was common to policing nationwide. We recognized that a shift in thinking about power and hierarchy in the policing context would take time. Change would be gradual. To confidently empower all of the officers within this department, we needed to develop a leadership development framework that was (a) suitable for the nature of policing work; and (b) would improve the communication structures that, at this point, were blocked by a disempowering hierarchy.

We knew that we were not going to eliminate or radically change the formal structure of this organization. Nor did we want to. There are rational, evidence-based reasons for a chain of command in policing. But we needed to relieve the stranglehold that this structure had on its members—to empower the middle (and enhance its accountability), without diminishing the power at the top. The changes that this organization and our team sought were related to attitudes and behaviors about individual empowerment that would lead to strong leadership, collaboration, and unit synergy. We needed to guide the members of this department to think differently about power roles, and to communicate more effectively across lines within the defined hierarchy. And, we needed to help this department develop and utilize its human capital—talent, ideas, and abilities—regardless of where it lay within the formal power structure.

Establishing Commonality

As we moved through the process of needs assessment and intervention design, we established the platform upon which our training and coaching sessions with this client would be based. We applied our proprietary "Five Keys" Model of Leadership Effectiveness as a lens with which to examine, diagnose, and motivate change at the individual, team, and organizational levels of this agency. The first key, *awareness,* was addressed when the blue shirts/white shirts issue came to light. Like many of our clients, this agency knew there was an "elephant in the living room," but lacked awareness of its impact on the organization as a whole. In this particular setting, creating a shared perspective on politically charged, difficult issues and pushing people to raise their awareness about topics they are accustomed to sweeping under the rug can be challenging. Police officers' values and behavioral styles tend to be consistent with the organizational culture we described earlier: resistant to change, dogmatic about the status quo, and traditional. Changing the color of the shirts as a starting point to shifting the culture of power to one of widespread empowerment was initially anathema to them. However, it was imperative for us to move past simple awareness of the issue to the second stage, *commitment*, without bruising too many egos.

Through formal and informal conversations, interviews, and focus group discussions, the officers and our consulting team gradually raised the individual and collective level of awareness about power issues in the department. At that point, we were poised to examine the organization's readiness for *commitment* to change based on new awareness of gaps, problems, oversights, and other problem situations (and their concomitant decision to "walk the walk" rather than simply "talk the talk" of organizational change and development). Through training, coaching, and facilitated discussions, we needed to move this agency to the point where they would commit to wearing the same color shirts. The symbolic commitment relative to shirt color was a challenging one to build, but it proved easier the commitment to the real issue of importance: *new ways of viewing (and enacting) power and power relationships within the department.*

Toward that end, we facilitated officers' *participation* in a series of activities designed to give each leader/participant the opportunity to experientially try out a new way of acting and organizing. These included training, facilitated communication strategy sessions, leadership development and teambuilding exercises, and some restructuring of the system and its policies to empower a wider range of officers in substantial ways. And, yes, we needed to symbolically empower the members of this department by getting them to start wearing the same color shirts.

Fundamental to our approach was our role of liaison between the top brass and rank and file. Recognizing that change would not occur without widespread organizational buy-in, we worked with both groups to build a *support* base for empowerment and leadership development across all levels within the department. Pointing to heightened awareness, demonstrated commitment, and observed results of officer participation in training experiences, we mediated gradual, phased change that was acceptable to all stakeholder groups. Building such widespread support requires a working knowledge of social influence theories that suggest guiding *incremental* change and avoiding asking for too much, all at once, or too soon.

Finally, we worked to build *accountability*, which involved each relevant member of the organization adopting and implementing recommended changes in their everyday work, and taking responsibility for the outcomes of their personal experience with the changes. Because we were asking officers to be accountable for attitude and behavioral changes they did not initially understand or have a workable heuristic for, we created resources to help them align with the new direction.

Accountability is a critical aspect of the changes we help our clients create; when individuals and teams are accountable for implementing new ways of working and being, they become part of the change (instead of shifting responsibility for the change to the consultant or someone else higher up on the organizational ladder).

In this case, to encourage accountability, we created short- and long-term evaluation systems for all of our interventions, along with an online performance management system. Further, we supported the client in developing communication channels for disseminating official information about the leadership initiative, and for officers to interact about the changes as they were proposed and implemented. For this client, opportunities to communicate involved training sessions, a website, and social media platforms. By developing evaluation processes that encouraged personal accountability for change, and creating methods to support sensemaking (Weick, 1995) and transparency about the change, we worked with the agency to heighten accountability at all levels.

The next several months were productive and meaningful. Evaluation data indicated that the department was well on its way to redefining an important aspect of its culture. At the individual and group levels, the agency was showing readiness for increased empowerment through its performance in leadership development activities. For example, we gathered tangible evidence of heightened cohesiveness within units, and increased communication competence, trust, and both job and relationship satisfaction at the individual, group, and organizational levels. Organizational members reported clearer expectations and greater amounts and frequency of communication; additionally, interactions became more efficient and of heightened quality. Roll call meetings were characterized by greater clarity, less conflict, and more productive interactions across hierarchical lines. Officers reported more feedback, a greater sense of certainty and information adequacy, and more productive feedback loops. Overall, members of the police department were utilizing better internal conflict resolution solutions and demonstrating empowered leadership internally and in the field. The sense of self-efficacy and self-confidence among members of this department measurably improved. The achievements relative to extinguishing negative, limiting practices and perceptions about power were felt throughout the department and noticed by community members. Even the city's mayor formally recognized the department for being willing and determined to redefine unhealthy aspects of its culture.

The willingness and determination emanated from a commitment that lay dormant among loyal, intelligent, tactically skilled police officers. Through competent, strategic consulting practices, we were able to engender and motivate the desire for and actions associated with transformation. Members at all levels of this organization shifted their thinking from rigid frameworks that gave all of the power and accountability to the white shirts to a more flexible, contemporary view that enabled all members to exercise leadership, decision making, and problem solving strategies within a given formal organizational structure. These were not people who had intentionally behaved in ways counterproductive to their goals or job performance. They simply didn't know any other way due to the traditional views their culture held about power and leadership. Through carefully constructed consulting plans, we co-created and guided them through a process designed to shift limiting views and accomplish dramatic improvements in their organizational experiences. We got them thinking and behaving differently when it came to power roles, leadership, and individual empowerment.

This case revealed several learning lessons that are important (and scalable) for any consultant and his/her work. First, we began by building trust, credibility, and an affable communication relationship at all levels of the organization. We established common ground when we confirmed what this organization was doing "right." Second, although our contacts had given us a vague sense of the problems the unit was experiencing, we listened carefully to everyone we met within the organization. Through the data we collected, we discovered a simple theme (shirt colors); but, importantly, we recognized that the shirt color issue was merely symbolic and symptomatic of a larger set of undesirable conditions. Then, we created a plan for change that was appropriate for this client and its long, strong traditions. Our plan was guided by the theory and research on resistance to organizational change, organizational culture, and transformation. These literatures suggested to us that only with widespread buy-in would we be able to create change. Thus, we created conditions that enabled people in this department to gradually, incrementally, try out behaviors they were uncomfortable with, but that our theoretically-informed consulting framework suggested were important. And then we helped them assess the results of their experiences in order to build their motivation and positive attitudes toward the changes.

Over the years, we have learned that the mere belief that positive transformation can happen is often enough to keep organizational members motivated. One of our primary responsibilities is to create and sustain that motivation. We do not have all the answers and do not solve problems for our clients. Instead, we work collaboratively with them to generate conditions that are in alignment with their needs and those of their members. The white shirt/blue shirt case illustrates this well. Additionally, this case illustrates what happens when members decide to conceptualize themselves as a real team—a collective unit—and then, operationally, engage in the kinds of communication and collaboration that results in the synergy of strong teamwork. Our consulting role, then, involved creating a plan and leveraging activities designed to temper egos yet enhance individual team members' performance to create a system in which "the whole is greater than the sum of its parts."

Today, all members of this police department, including the Chief, wear blue shirts.

NOTE

1. *Servant leadership* refers to a perspective on leadership first developed by Greenleaf in his 1970 publication *The Servant as Leader*, which emphasizes leadership behaviors that promote the growth, satisfaction, empowerment, and well-being of all organizational members and the communities in which organizations exist.

REFERENCES

Ashkenas, J., & Park, H. (2015, April 8). The race gap in America's police departments. *The New York Times*. Retrieved from http://www.nytimes.com/interactive/2014/09/03/us/the-race-gap-in-americas-police-departments.html?_r=1

Greenleaf, R.K. (1970/2008). The servant as leader. Atlanta, GA: The Greenleaf Center for Servant Leadership.

Lewis, L. K. (2011). *Organizational change: Creating change through strategic communication*. Malden, MA: Wiley.

Public Service Leadership Institute. (2015). Impact. Retrieved from https://www.inspireservelead.com/pca-impact/.

US Department of Labor, Bureau of Labor Statistics. (2015). Police and detectives. *Occupational Outlook Handbook, 2014–2015 Edition*. Retrieved from http://www.bls.gov/ooh/protective-service/police-and-detectives.htm

Weick, K. E. (1995). *Sensemaking in organizations*. Thousand Oaks, CA: Sage.

CHAPTER TWENTY

Consulting in the Educational Context

Serving as an External Program Reviewer

MICHAEL J. CODY

Annenberg School for Communication and Journalism
University of Southern California

INTRODUCTION

The "external review" is a unique, yet common, form of consulting occurring in an educational context. Every several years academic units, like a department of psychology, communication, or history, will be reviewed by external reviewers. External reviews are conducted for a variety of purposes, such as accreditation, improving a program's national ranking, or to obtain independent assessment of a program's quality in order to allocate resources. The external reviewers are typically two senior faculty members from "comparable" or "sister" institutions selected by top administrators at the institution being reviewed. The decision to select the external reviewers is often made with input from and coordinated through institutional review groups internal to the university and composed of faculty from other departments and professional staff members (analysts, program evaluation specialists). "Comparable universities" are typically ones that offer the same types of programs (Ph.D., MA, and BA; or MA and only BA), or are similar in national rankings. Reviewers may be selected from a short list of local leading institutions. The two external reviewers are typically selected because they have some perceived credibility about current and future trends in the discipline, and can provide objective and unbiased insights about how to strengthen existing programs. The recommendations for strengthening an existing program can vary tremendously from one institution to another, and can include strategies for improving curriculum; increasing visibility; securing external funding; redistributing workload; and making units increasingly competitive and contemporary through hiring, funding, and programming.

If the reviewers prove to be successful consultants, the report they write will be read widely and can have a significant impact on the direction of the academic unit. The university (including its students) and the program's discipline can benefit by improving curriculum, securing resources to improve instructional delivery and attainment of pedagogical goals, expanding the number of faculty or teaching lines, and engaging students in more diverse leadership roles. An effective program review advances the profile of the unit and the relevance of its discipline across levels at the university and among alumni.

THE CONSULTING EVENT

The goal of the review is to have experts in the field visit the University and meet with upper administration (deans, vice presidents/chancellors/provosts), the chair, full professors, associate professors, assistant professors, graduate students, undergraduate students (usually leaders of student clubs and organizations) and staff (secretaries, advisers, recruiters) to discuss the current and future status of the academic unit. Prior to the campus visit, the Vice President of Academic Affairs (or, at some institutions, the Provost's office) and the Chair of the program being reviewed provide the two external reviewers a considerable amount of documentation about the academic unit. The external reviewers are provided a copy of the previous external review document, the university's five-year strategic plan, the mission statement of the school, faculty bios, and any other materials that may be deemed relevant for providing an unbiased but informed review of the academic unit. These might include evidence of collaboration with other academic units and assessment data regarding attainment of educational objectives within the unit. Finally, reviewers are provided a schedule for their visit.

It is important for each external reviewer to study the documents provided immediately as these will guide them in facilitating a successful review. Although most may be inclined to focus on what they view as the more substantive documents, and look at the schedule as a last-minute afterthought, the schedule should be studied carefully. Do not underestimate the importance of how meetings with various stakeholders have been structured. For example, the classic literature on self-disclosure indicates that communicators are more likely to disclose and reveal personal information when trust is high and when they do not feel vulnerable (Altman & Taylor, 1973; Derlega, Metts, Petronio

& Marguilis, 1993; Petronio, 2002; Rawlins, 1983), so the individuals with less power (students and untenured faculty) should be guaranteed their own forum separate from others with more power (administration, full and associate professors).

Second, in considering the larger portfolio provided, one should study the documents in order to see if there is a common narrative or theme in the materials about the program's history, role in the university, perceived acclaim and reputation, and if it is credited with helping fulfill the university's goals or five-year plan. Themes assist the reviewer in drafting questions about how the university wants to allocate resources to improve the program, and what type of growth is most beneficial to the universities, its undergraduates and graduates. Is it beneficial to hire a more senior faculty member who can provide assistance in writing grants? Or, is it beneficial to hire younger faculty with more practical experience in new technology?

Unfortunately, there may be a discrepancy between the perceptions of the administration and what the school views as its strength. Alternatively, administration and the program may agree that the school has underachieved in some ways. If either of the situations surfaces, the reviewer should explore possible causes and solutions and perhaps request additional materials. Following the review of documentation, the two external reviewers may need to talk prior to the visit to discuss potential problems, causes and solutions—and to strategize their approach for the campus visit.

For example, one common problem that may surface in documentation review is retention of younger faculty. Every program views a new hire as breathing new life into a program, replacing retired faculty who taught core courses, and expanding or updating the program's offerings. But if professors leave in a few years, a program fails to grow and develop. Reviewers will want to know the cause of the problem and assess the university's attempts to resolve any systemic or underlying problem. Some faculty may leave because they are teaching too many classes, have too many students, are assigned time-consuming classes, or serve on too many committees. On the other hand, some untenured assistant professors may feel that the faculty (who will vote on their merit and promotion) do not support them sufficiently to risk staying five years before being considered for tenure. These conditions should prompt the reviewers to explore what mechanisms the program (or university) has in place to support, protect, and develop its pre-tenure faculty. A reviewer needs to use the documents provided to plan a successful review—to find out what works, what needs improvement, and how improvements might be implemented.

The external reviewers usually visit the campus for two or three days—and often spend at least one full day in meetings with specific groups. It is an intense series of experiences in communication reflecting fundamental principles of self-disclosure, listening, discovery (decoding meanings behind phrases and non-verbal behaviors) and self-presentation. The first meeting is with the individual who organized the visit and an administrator (the dean, vice president, or department chair). The following day, the two reviewers will typically visit with these administrators again early in the day. These meetings are devoted to talking about the history of the university and the academic unit, actions that have been taken since the last external review, the academic unit's role within the university, the administration's general perspective of the strengths of the program and what it offers students, and services the unit provides to the university (e.g., general education courses) in addition to the program's connections to the community or alumni groups. Finally, the dean or vice president emphasize their interest in advice and recommendations that would strengthen the program and its reputation on and off campus.

The external reviewers then embark on a series of meetings with specific groups: full professors, associate professors, assistant professors, adjunct or clinical faculty, graduate teaching assistants, graduate students, undergraduate students and leaders of students clubs and associations, staff, and advisers/recruiters. Sometimes the external reviewers conduct meetings with all undergraduate groups together, but there are times due to logistics that the external reviewers will meet separately with some groups.

The different groups reviewers meet with will differ in their strategic self-presentation. One of the basic principles of self-presentation is to present a positive view of the self, and those with seniority are likely to portray a view of the academic unit as one that has been largely successful, in part because they can claim to have made good strategic choices in building the program over the last five to 20 years. They may defend and justify choices made over the years, and they may resist the changes sought by new, younger scholars. On the other hand, younger scholars are more likely to disclose their ideas for making an academic unit more contemporary and competitive. The candor of these meetings is dependent on my earlier advice that reviewers be sure that the schedule allows them to meet with people in their cohort groups.

In each session, the external reviewers talk alone with the individuals of a cohort group, who are asked to provide frank opinions about the academic unit's role in the university, its mission, strengths that could be built upon, weaknesses and problems that can be rectified and resolved, and what resources they need to achieve their career goals. The reviewers may only have an hour or two with each specific group, and the goal is to prompt honest and candid opinions during every meeting. Thus, as the discussion leaders in the group meetings, the external reviewers need to promote a climate of openness and candor by listening attentively, engaging in competent questioning and feedback, and fosteing a dialogue among all participants (as opposed to having each individual talk in a series of monologues). Of each cohort group, typically the student groups and the assistant professor groups are the most engaged, talkative, inquisitive and energetic, followed by the associate professor and full professor groups.

Competent external reviewers not only need to work on promoting a climate of openness and candor, but also need to facilitate the entire group's communication. Plax, Waldeck, and Kearney (Chapter 6), provide advice for focus group facilitators which applies here—including managing dominant members, noticing tension, seeking input from quiet people, and observing nonverbal behavior. External reviewers will never know all the dynamics that are in play among the members of these groups, but one should view the group discussions as valuable sources of information and observe everything closely.

One of the most important observations to be made deals with how unified the various groups are in identifying the mission of the school, its role in the university at large, strengths and weaknesses, and its future goals. There is usually consensus on the mission and strengths of the school, and on a few weaknesses (which are often fairly obvious to everyone). When asked questions about improving the school or needed resources (e.g., "What improvements or changes do you wish to see to make the school better?" "What resources are needed in order to improve the school?" "What can be done to help you achieve your goals?"), the assistant professors, associate professors, and graduate students provide many constructive and diverse ideas, followed by comments made by the chair. Meetings with the secretaries, staff and advisers are useful because they can share their insights on a sense of climate in the organization and they can provide some meaningful technical ideas for improving efficiency. Student groups ask the most questions, because they are interested in what occurs at other universities and the often are motivated to seek leadership roles (which will facilitate entrance to professional schools and jobs). They became majors and leaders in a particular academic unit in part because of the strengths of the unit, and they often recommend more resources to broaden and expand on existing strengths. On occasion, student leaders may be aware of new programs or developments at other universities, and recommend launching similar programs at their home institution.

Listening Skills and Discovery

One of the most important skills that the reviewer-as-consultant brings to the engagement is listening (see Beebe, Chapter 8); additionally, the reviewer should be attuned to whether members of the interviewed cohort groups are listening to one another. They must be willing, attentive listeners. An effective external review consultant can show attentiveness by their engagement with others are talking, providing "backchannel" verbalizations like "uh huh," "yes," "oh," and "ummmm," and by nodding agreement or using empathic facial expressions (cf. Canary,

Cody, & Manusov, 2008 Halone, Cunconan, Coakley, & Wolvin, 1998; Halone & Pecchion, 2001; Halone, Wolvin, & Coakley, 1997). Good listeners ask questions and make eye contact. They manage conversations competently through the use of turn-taking and turn-yielding cues, do not interrupt, and do not shift topics inappropriately. They acknowledge and appreciate input. Appropriate listening skills signal to others in the meeting that the external reviewer is in fact attending to what is said and values their input. These skills are critical for prompting open discussions among colleagues and the reviewers.

One communication competency that can help reviewers effectively acknowledge participants is the ability to confirm others during conversation (Sieburg, 1976). Confirming messages recognize another person's existence as a unique individual, acknowledge his/her significance, show acceptance of another person's way of experiencing life, and/or expresses a willingness to become involved with or engage the person more fully or again in the future. Disconfirming messages show indifference, imperviousness or disqualification—meaning the listener ignores the speaker, provides minimal responses, or even switches topics. Ideally, the external reviewer will be cognizant of the fact that confirming each person's presence, identity and contribution at the meeting is a preferred communication strategy (see Plax et al., Chapter 6).

Although the majority of my reviewer colleagues have been engaged, focused, and confirming listeners, I recall a case in which an external reviewer I worked with had done two reviews in one week and was determined to fly home as early as possible. This reviewer had completed many department reviews in the past, had already made certain decisions about the school being reviewed, and was going to be paid no matter the outcome. The faculty noticed this individual's demeanor, and were clearly disappointed that their voice and opinions may not be heard. So, I decided to spend more time on the emotional/supportive aspects of our sessions to ensure they knew we were listening and that their input was valued. I did so because a successful external review is one in which members can express their thoughts and feelings, and I saw no way to prompt the rushed reviewer to engage more actively; I could only exert control over my own behavior and responsibilities to the review process.

External reviewers should engage in listening competence, but they also need to analyze participants' listening skills as each group answers questions and discusses needs and the future of the school. When camaraderie is high and there is a climate of trust, honesty, transparency and support, individuals are likely to freely exchange opinions, listen to one another, and build on another's comments. This obviously makes the external reviewer's work easier. However, one needs to have all participants share their thoughts and opinions, and encourage critical listening. Encourage and explore disagreements whenever they arise. Guard against any groupthink that results in all participants agreeing to vent about certain problems or all agreeing on one future course for the school.

Group members who are not actively engaged in the conversation should be a matter of special concern for the reviewer. In any dyadic encounter or group setting, one individual may experience listener anxiety, communication apprehension, or shyness. Still, it is unusual for a professional working in an academic unit like a communication program to attend one meeting and fail to communicate freely. The reviewer should attempt to determine whether the reluctant participant lacks trust and thus conceals rather than reveals, or if he or she may be withholding useful information. Such exploration by a consultant requires a sophisticated set of advanced observational, facilitation, interviewing, and conversational skills.

Finally, we know that listening is fundamental to social support, which should occur to some extent among members of the same cohort group discussing their careers and the future of their program at the university. An external reviewer can easily tell if and when coworkers show social support verbally and nonverbally to certain colleagues (or to all), and when they fail to do so. Lack of support for one another or distracted, passive, habitual listening among groups should be closely evaluated along with other observations from the visit about group dynamics and collegiality.

After each session, the external reviewers meet alone and compare their perceptions of what was communicated—drawing parallels and commonalities with comments made in other groups, and noting new, innovative ideas. The reviewers should discuss their perceptions of participants' honesty and candor, which may be discussed later with the chair in a general way (without mentioning names). Such observations should never be reported higher than the chair, because administration might not have enough knowledge of individuals within a unit to interpret your perceptions accurately.

Norms and Principles of Self-Presentation

Today we live in a world of "self-presentation," in which people monitor their self-presentational tactics in order to groom a specific image at work, online, on dating sites, and far more (cf. Sandberg, 2013). Modern-day work on the presentation of self dates to Goffman (1959; 1967) (cf. Canary et al., 2008) who examined how individuals create and maintain a desired presentation of the "self" to the public in different contexts. The basic argument is that all members of a society grow up to learn rules and norms for behaving in a civil manner (cf. Leary, 1996). It is also assumed that individuals are motivated to portray a public image of the "self" as competent, responsible, successful, attractive, skilled, and more. Communication scholars have devoted considerable attention to self-presentation at work, during employment interviews and, most recently, online (DeAndrea, Tong, Liang, Levine, & Walther, 2012; Gibbs, Ellison, & Heino, 2006; Hall, Park, Song, & Cody, 2010; Hancock & Toma, 2009), where findings largely confirm the operation of certain norms and principles of self-presentation. External review discussions are no exception.

Leary (1996) provides a thorough discussion of the norms and principles of self-presentation that guide communication and proposes three principles of self-presentation. The first principle focuses on settings and roles, the second on values and preferences, and the third focuses on self-enhancing presentations. These are summarized in Table 1.

Table 1. Leary's (1996) Norms and Principles of Self-Presentation

---

Principle of settings and roles:
The **decorum norm:** People are expected to present themselves in ways that conform to standards for proper polite behavior, manners, etiquette, dress and appearance.

The **modesty norm:** People are expected to present themselves as modest individuals and avoid public portrayals of superiority—at least during the early stages of an interaction. Many people who want to be liked by others begin by being modest, and then "match" the level of achievements and accomplishments of other participants (self-promotional statements).

The **self-presentational positive norm:** People should present themselves as being as positive as everyone else in the encounter, matching "liking," praise, humor and more during the encounter.

The **depth of self-disclosure norm:** People will reciprocate and match personal self-disclosures.

The **self-presentational consistency norm:** People should present a consistent public image.

Principle of Values and Preferences:
The **principle of values and preferences** is the most strategic of all the principles of self-presentation, and states that self-presentations are tailored to the perceived values and preferences of the target.

Principle of Self-Enhancing Presentations:
People present themselves in **a self-enhancing way** unless they think that others have (or are likely to obtain) information that would contract or discredit excessively or overly positive self-presentations.

Applying Self-presentational Principles to Consulting

Each session external reviewers facilitate will feature key elements of self-presentation. Your work will be aided by your understanding the dynamics of self-presentation and your ability to find ways to move parties beyond self-presentation tactics (which champion the individual) to discussion of more communal and substantive issues relative to improving the academic unit. As noted earlier, external reviewers may only have one hour to talk with each group, so although they must allow for some inevitable strategic self-presentation, they must also maintain focus on issues relevant to the program.

The first set of principles focus on the norms relevant to the setting and roles (scholars, teachers, mentors, etc.). The *decorum norm* states that individuals will behave politely and will dress appropriately (in this case, professionally). In my experience, over 90% of all faculty, staff, advisers and students are polite and courteous, and are motivated to help ensure that a positive and helpful review is written and circulated. They are almost always *positive* (the principle of self-enhancing presentation), because in theory, everyone shares the overarching goal of a positive review that may help strengthen the school by increasing resources or proposing other needed changes. In only one case have I witnessed an individual show annoyance, if not hostility, about certain other faculty members (not present) over a spousal hire issue. This is a clear violation of expectations, and word spread through the school to the chair and the dean by that evening. The external reviewers heard public apologies throughout the rest of the visit. [This faculty member left and went to a different university a few years later].

It is also almost always the case that the group discussions begin with each person introducing themselves *modestly* (the second norm listed) but as time goes on, some individuals will begin to self-promote by referring to their latest 5-year grant, their book award, their teaching award, etc. People are modest first, and then they typically like to self-promote or appear as *self-enhancing* as possible, and if not handled appropriately, more and more of the participants will be motivated to self-promote by matching achievements. These self-promoting signs of competence, expertise, and skills are typically already listed for the reviewer in pre-visit materials. But it is important to allow individuals to engage in a limited amount of self-promotion in order to publicly acknowledge them and confirm their identity as a "teacher," "mentor," or "researcher." So, external reviewers say, "Oh, yes. I read that in your bio and in the school's newsletter. That is quite an accomplishment. Only a few individuals win 'top book' award." External reviewers should also write down these facts in their notes (even if already known); and include some of the achievements in their report.

However, the external reviewers also need to control time during each session. So, one can politely nudge the conversation back to the whole group, by saying "Yes, I just bought that book. We should talk about it when we have the chance" or "I also had a grant on tobacco control, maybe tonight you can fill me in on your five-year grant at dinner." The reviewer needs everyone to present certain highlights and then move on with the agenda—saving time to address the substantive issues of ways to improve, and needed resources.

The principle of values and preferences states that sometimes communicators are motivated to present a public image that is adapted to a specific audience, or strategically communicate a "self" to others that may be less than completely honest. For example, women may think that men prefer females who are young, attractive, and physically fit and work to cultivate this image. Men may think that females value males with power, high incomes and social status who are tall, handsome, athletic and witty; similarly they present such an imagine (see DeAndrea et al., 2012; Gibbs et al., 2006; Hall et al., 2010; Hancock & Toma, 2009). The principle of values and preferences apply to many contexts, including job interviews where workers can emphasis skills they believe the interviewer is seeking or is listed in the job description (a conscientious, dedicated worker vs. a sociable people person, vs. efficient work skills, etc.).

The astute external reviewer might easily recognize self-enhancing or self-promoting presentations and respond appropriately. However, this principle operates in more complex ways during the review. For example, some individuals may present a position or express a preference for a change at the school largely because they want to court approval from others, or to bandwagon on a popular idea. Possibly, some individuals will support a proposal because the chair and/or some senior faculty support it. Perhaps the individual thinks that advocating a position and voting in favor of it will facilitate a positive vote for promotion? This is a motivation that external reviewers should keep in mind, although ultimately there is usually plenty of material to draw upon when writing a final report. The idea is to look for themes and consistencies within groups, and to some extent, across them.

THE REPORT: SUGGESTING OUTCOMES

In most external review contexts, university administration provides a suggested outline for a report. Plax et al. (Chapter 6) point out that consulting reports are sensitive, political documents; and external review reports are no exception. They have long-term implications for academic units and should be written strategically. The reviewers usually take sections and write the original material on the strengths of the program, strengths of the faculty, comment on the focus on the school (public speaking, mass media, interpersonal, etc.), and comment on the number of students and quality of the students. The most important sections focus on the strengths of the school, shortcomings or limitations, and recommendations for the near future. The reviewers are often provided space, coffee and a catered lunch for creating a draft. The visit ends with by meeting with one or more key administrators and chair, where the reviewers make a verbal report on recommendations and obtain some feedback. Then, the reviewers go home and produce a final written report over a weekend.

Program evaluation work is challenging, but often results in meaningful outcomes. It requires organizational skills for designing the review process, the ability to review documents with an eye for what is "between the lines," and strong interviewing, observational, and facilitation skills for the campus visit. Effective program review work is framed by an understanding of the theories and research concerning self-disclosure, self-presentation, listening, and persuasion. Finally, the competent external reviewer is prepared, based on his or her insights about the information gathered, to write a compelling report. In that report, the reviewer makes well-reasoned recommendations designed to enhance the program. In many cases, institutions I have reviewed have made specific changes and experienced growth and improvement as a result of the review team's visit. For instance:

- We advised one school to reduce the work load of the doctoral students, who were offered plenty of opportunities to teach stand-alone classes, in addition to serving as teaching assistants. Many of those doctoral students, as a result of this teaching experience and skill, accepted jobs in regional colleges and universities that required a continuation of the heavy teaching load. They quickly suffered burnout as assistant professors. Far too few of the students were publishing in top-tier journals during and immediately after securing their doctorate degrees, and as a result, they weren't building the type of national reputation that would ultimately position them to be hired in nationally ranked universities and that would reflect strongly on their doctoral institution. In response to our recommendations, this program reduced the teaching loads for graduate students, and created a mentoring program in an effort to prepare students for a greater diversity of employment opportunities.
- We advised one school to encourage faculty to collaborate more fully with parallel programs (psychology, sociology, social work, public health, etc.) on an important university-wide initiative on the concerns of military families. The communication faculty members were visibly absent, despite the fact that some faculty were experts in family communication and health communication. As a result of our recommendations, the program hired an assistant professor researching health issues; this individual and a number of the doctoral students became involved with the initiative.
- We advised one school to hire at least one visible and successful grant writer with the idea that such a person would mentor associate and assistant professors in the practice of writing grants. This university hired a person, but this person was recruited back to his/her former school three years later. Nonetheless, some of the faculty had submitted grants during those years and continue to do so. So, the hire probably did have some positive influence on this aspect of the unit's culture.

- We praised one school for successfully hiring talented and highly successful assistant professors. This was a school where full professors received excellent teaching ratings and there were very few associate professors. The school had grown in popularity over several years, and consequently class sizes were large. We advised and wrote a justification for new hires to teach undergraduates, build the MA program, and activate a student honors' society and other student clubs. We specifically recommended hires with national or international visibility. To build on their existing strengths and better serve their students, this program took many of these recommendations.

REFERENCES

Altman, I. & Taylor, D. A. (1973). *Social penetration: The development of interpersonal relationships.* Austin, TX: Holt, Rinehart & Winston.

Canary, D. J, Cody, M. J., & Manusov, V. L. (2008). *Interpersonal communication: A goals-based approach* (4th ed.). Boston, MA: Bedford/St. Martin's.

DeAndrea, D. C., Tong, S. T., Liang, J. Y., Levine, T. R., & Walther, J. B. (2012). When do people misrepresent themselves to others? The effects of social desirability, ground truth, and accountability on deceptive self-presentations. *Journal of Communication, 62,* 400–416.

Derlega, V. J., Metts, S., Petronio, S., & Marguilis, S. T. (1993). *Self-disclosure.* Thousand Oaks, CA: Sage.

Gibbs, J. L., Ellison, N. B., Heino, R. D. (2006). Self-presentation in online personals: The role of anticipated future interaction, self-disclosure, and perceived success in internet dating. *Communication Research, 33,* 152–176.

Goffman, E. (1959). *The presentation of self in everyday life.* Garden City, NY: Doubleday.

Goffman, E. (1967). *Interaction ritual: Essays on face-to-face behavior.* New York, NY: Pantheon.

Halone, K. K., Cunconan, T. M., Coakley, C. G., & Wolvin, A. D. (1998). Toward the establishment of general dimensions underlying the listening process. *International Journal of Listening, 12,* 12–38.

Halone, K. K., & Pecchioni, L. L. (2001). Relational listening: A grounded theoretical model. *Communication Reports, 14,* 59–71.

Halone, K. K., Wolvin, A. D., & Coakley, C. G. (1997). Accounts of effective listening across the life-span: Expectations and experiences associated with competent listening practices. *International Journal of Listening, 11,* 15–38.

Hall, J. A., Park, N., Song, H., & Cody, M. J. (2010). Strategic misrepresentation in online dating: The effects of gender, self-monitoring, and personality traits. *Journal of Social and Personal Relationships, 27,* 117–135.

Hancock, J. T. & Toma, C. L. (2009). Putting your best face forward: The accuracy of online dating photographs. *Journal of Communication, 59,* 367–386.

Leary, M. R. (1996). *Self-presentation: Impression management and interpersonal behavior.* Boulder, CO: Westview Press.

Petronio, S. (2002). *Boundaries of privacy: Dialectics of disclosure.* Albany, NY: State University of New York Press.

Rawlins, W. K. (1983). Openness as problematic in ongoing friendships: Two conversational dilemmas. *Communication Monographs, 50,* 1–13.

Sandberg, S. (2013). *Lean in: Women, work, and the will to lead.* New York, NY: Random House.

Sieburg, E. (1976). Confirming and disconfirming organizational communication. In J. L. Owens, P. A. Page, & G. I. Zimmerman (Eds.), *Communication in organizations* (pp. 129–149). St. Paul, MN: West.

CHAPTER TWENTY ONE

The Graying
of the Organization

Intergenerational Communication Consulting

ROBERT M. MCCANN
*Anderson School of Management,
University of California, Los Angeles*

A PROLOGUE

Between 2000 and 2050, the proportion of the world's population over 60 years will double from about 11% to 22%, with the number of people aged 60 years and above expected to reach 2 billion by 2050 (from close to 700 million today). In other words, it is projected that approximately 1 in 5 people around the world will be 60 years or above within 35 years (World Health Organization, 2014).

In much of the world, tomorrow's workplace will become—perhaps even more so than it is today—a focal point for intergenerational interaction. As we consider how the workplace of ten, twenty, or even thirty years from now will look, we can predict with near certainty that older workers will be prominent in the workplace; technological advances will continue at blazing speed; teams and work groups will become increasingly virtual; new modes of organizational leadership and influence will emerge; and the generations will interact in ways that are new, exciting, and unforeseen. But one thing remains certain as we consider these changes—that *communication*, whether mediated, face-to-face, or other, will remain at the heart of how we relate to and interact with those of different ages. The more that we can understand about how people of different generations communicate (and perceive their communication) with each other, the better poised we are to craft solutions for the intergenerational workplace opportunities and challenges of now and of the future. It is in the crafting of these solutions where the age diversity (and sometimes communication) consultant enters the picture.

Theoretical Frameworks for of Workplace Ageism

As we consider the role of the consultant in the graying workplace, it is useful to step back and examine some of the theories—in this case, intergroup theories - that explain workplace ageism. Two prominent theories underpin much of my consulting work in the aging domain—*social identity theory* and *communication accommodation theory*. These two theories, which highlight the *intergroup* nature of age-influenced behavior in organizations, provide the workplace age diversity consultant with invaluable guidance and structure as s/he creates assessments, develops training materials, and generally tries to make sense of the role of age in the organization.

Organizations are inherently intergroup in nature. Sometimes these groups are formally mandated within the bounds of an organization (e.g., rank/position); at other times workers bring their various group identities along with them simply by the nature of their biological makeup (e.g., race, gender, age) or upbringing (e.g., university attended, where raised). As social identity theory (Tajfel & Turner, 1986) informs us, the existence of these groups inevitably leads to "us versus them" comparisons along group lines. Across group boundaries, individuals often focus on differences rather than similarities, mistrust "the other," and are biased in favor of one's own group. These differences are particularly salient in organizations, where negative stereotypical evaluations are frequently cited as an outgrowth of intergroup comparisons.

In line with this in/out-group-driven favoritism (or lack thereof), a wide range of research points to robust findings that people of different generations communicate in ways that are biased in favor of their own age group and not the other age group. This research is driven by communication accommodation theory (CAT; e.g., Giles, Coupland, & Coupland, 1991), which examines the ways in which individuals use language in intergroup encounters. For example, older adults (i.e., aged 65 and above) have been found to display an in-group bias in favor of communicating with their peer age group, while younger adults (i.e., aged 17–29 years) have described a similar preference toward communicating with their peers. Younger adults report that older people communicate with them in patronizing ways, which, in turn, make them feel alienated and discourage them from initiating intergenerational contact (for a review of this literature, see McCann, 2012).

Impacts of Workplace Ageism

Age stereotypes. In general, older and younger workers are stereotypically perceived differentially, with older worker stereotypes typically having negative overtones and younger worker stereotypes tending to be comparatively more positive (e.g., young workers as physically and mentally more prepared to take on the demands of today's workplace). That said, there are exceptions to these findings (e.g., older workers as more loyal to the organization). Age workplace stereotype perceptions have also been found to vary by age of the rater, type of the profession of the worker being rated, and if the job in question is perceived to be a "young person's job" or an "older person's job. Generally speaking, "stereotype types" of older and younger workers include (for review, see Posthuma & Campion, 2009):

- Memory and ability to learn (i.e., older workers have poorer memory skills, make more mental mistakes)
- Technology (i.e., older workers are more fearful of new technology, are slower to adapt to new technology)
- Physical (i.e., older workers are physically weaker, are absent more)
- Productivity/performance (i.e., older workers are less productive, work slower)
- Flexibility (i.e., older workers are less flexible, are more cautious in work)
- Loyalty (i.e., older workers are more loyal, have a better attitude toward work, and have a higher level of commitment to work)

Ageist communication & age discrimination. In the domain of workplace aging and communication, stereotypical expectations by management and staff can serve as powerful harbingers to a wide range of behavioral outcomes including discriminatory practices toward older (and in some cases, younger) workers, ageist language and hostile discourse at work, decisions about (early) retirement, age influenced work termination, reduced or lost training opportunities, age graded hiring, and reduced intentions among young people to take up careers involving older people.

Ageist behaviors (including communication) are often at the heart of discriminatory practices toward older (and very occasionally younger) workers. To understand the breadth of the age discrimination problem, let us consider just a few of the headlines from major news outlets involving age discrimination lawsuits that have recently been settled or resolved in the USA:

- *Minneapolis StarTribune:* 3M will pay $3 million to settle age-bias suit (Crosby, 2011)
- *Business Management Daily:* Allstate pays $4.5 million to settle age bias suit (Brown, 2009)
- *Business Insurance:* The Ruby Tuesday Inc. restaurant chain pays $575,000 to settle a class action age discrimination lawsuit (Greenwald, 2013)
- *Los Angeles Times:* Hollywood writers' age-discrimination case settled (Verrier, 2010)

A content analysis that Dr. Howard Giles and I conducted on age discrimination lawsuits over a two decade period revealed that ageist communication played (and continues to play) a central role in a significant percentage of the ADEA cases brought before the courts (McCann & Giles, 2006).

THE ROLE OF THE CONSULTANT

Looking back only five to ten years ago, the "age diversity consultant" was typically brought into organizations for *reactive* requests. These requests frequently centered around compliance (e.g., a company needed to comply with age discrimination laws) or some type of age related dysfunction within the organization (e.g., skews in company age demographics, communication problems between workers of different ages, older worker difficulties with new technology, etc.). While compliance and dysfunction still apply to many of the requests that age diversity consultants receive, the consulting landscape has unquestionably shifted to more *proactive* requests. As I think about the requests that have landed on my desk in recent years, many (though certainly not all) have been proactive in nature. For example, smaller companies have reached out for advice regarding company-wide age diversity strategies as they prepare for growth, while more established companies (with broad age diversity strategies in place) are interested in issues such as older worker recruitment, customer service, technology (and other) training, workplace modification and design, and a wide range of "corporate culture" issues that revolve around intergenerational interaction.

While the range of tasks for age diversity consultants is thus very broad, it is safe to say that most consulting efforts fall into the following four categories (see AARP annual survey of the *Best Employers for Workers Over 50*, AARP, 2013). These categories are: (a) recruiting; (b) workplace culture and continued opportunities; (c) benefits (health, financial, alternative work arrangements); and (d) retiree opportunities. Although the communication specialist often finds himself or herself in the "workplace age culture" domain, a wide variety of other specialists (e.g., finance, compensation, health, legal) also fill the graying workforce consulting space.[1] The remainder of this chapter will focus on the workplace culture sphere, as this is where the communication consultant often works.

Age Inclusion Strategy

Workplace "age culture" consulting generally revolves around the goal of creating a supportive workplace that promotes worker satisfaction and motivation for workers of all ages. At the organizational strategy level, in some cases consultants find that there is no guiding strategy for age diversity in a given organization.

In other instances, an age diversity strategy may be in place, but poorly defined. For many organizations, the reality is that age diversity initiatives at a company-wide level often come after other diversity strategy initiatives. In the words of Philomena Morrissey Satre, Vice President of Diversity & Inclusion, Wells Fargo (Roundtree, 2011):

> *The first areas of diversity we focused on as a company were gender and representation of women in the workplace. The next major focus areas were culture, ethnicity and sexual orientation. Recently, we expanded beyond the traditional approach to focus on diversity and inclusion and this is where age comes in.* (p. 9)

Most qualified age diversity consultants will begin by asking company leadership and/or HR about the organization's age diversity strategy, and query whether age is a "diversity imperative" at the organization. For example, not long ago, HR representatives from a major defense industry company approached me to speak to their staff about workforce ageism. Such requests from the defense industry are not uncommon due to the graying of the industry (the average age for aerospace and defense workers is 45–47 for an aeronautical engineer—versus the median age of 42 for all American workers; Hedden, 2013). Upon speaking with representatives of the company, it became clear that the company (in their words) "had a problem on its hands" and was just beginning to formulate strategy in the area. Although I was ultimately asked to create a presentation that addressed some smaller, more micro-level initiatives (e.g., cross generational teams), it was quite helpful for me to understand how the management of this organization viewed the role of age in its overall diversity efforts, and see how far along they were in these efforts.

Intergenerational Contact Programs

Cross-generational mentoring, age-sensitive job rotation strategies, and inter-generational team formation represent a staple of many successful age diversi-fied companies. The general idea behind these programs is that increased con-tact—in a targeted and (ideally) age-aware manner—between the generations can help alleviate some of the embedded age stereotype and ageist communication issues highlighted earlier. To this end, Glaxo Smith Kline promotes *intergenera-tional mentoring* throughout its organization and internally stresses the "value of mentoring someone different" (Roundtree, 2011), and the University of Central Lancashire in England has won praise (AARP award in 2010—as a part of its annual *Best Employers for Workers Over 50* awards) for its "Fresh Step" program where employees age 50 and above mentor younger employees. Communication consultants are regularly tasked to find ways to facilitate the professional and per-sonal collaborations and relations at work for older employees, and mentoring programs are one often used method. Indeed, mentoring plays a key role in areas including planning for succession, facilitating knowledge transfer, adjusting newer employees to an organizational culture, engaging older workers, and retaining employees through meaningful relationships.

Consultants may also focus on "generational engagement" activities that might co-exist alongside mentoring programs. For example, the consultant might encourage clients to implement age-inclusive social events (and avoid those that might disadvantage older workers) and cross-generational training programs (e.g., younger employees train older employees in technology while older employees train younger employees in finance or other skills appropriate to a given industry) may be held in conjunction with mentoring efforts. I have seen some of the positive effects (e.g., skill transfer, increase in age awareness) of cross-generational teams firsthand, and these effects can be quite profound at both the individual and organizational levels, as well.

Job Rotation Programs

Job rotation programs, particularly with employees of different ages placed alongside each other, represent another common consulting recommendation to increase cross-generational inclusion in organizations. For example, at CheapCaribbean. com (AARP 2013 winner), older employees rotate through temporary assignments in other departments and on age diversified team projects, whereas at the National Institutes of Health (another AARP 2013 winner), older employees develop new skills by working on temporary assignments in other departments and on team projects. Consultants may profitably recommend the creation of generational training advisory boards, which consider the age diversity of learners in a given company and select training and rotation assignments accordingly.

Cross-Generational Teams

Consultants may also recommend and facilitate the formation of age diversified teams represents another common organizational age diversity strategy. While training can be conducted around simulated (fictitious) projects, many consultants work with organizations to create intergenerational interaction around "live" team projects. At Deutsche Bank AG in Germany, for instance, age-diversified projects teams were intentionally created to bridge intergenerational divides. At S&T Bank in Indiana, Pennsylvania, older employees have opportunities to gain new experiences by working on team projects with those of different ages and on temporary assignments in other departments. Other companies specifically address the issue of cross-generational *conflict* in the organization (which can plague teams and numerous other areas of intergenerational interaction) via workshops and other targeted training methods. At the University of Pittsburgh, a "Please Respect My Generation" training program incorporates methods for bridging the gap between generations as participants are trained how to avoid conflict and increase productivity in their generationally diverse workplaces.

Symbols of Worker Achievements

Research indicates that older workers' aspirations can be positively influenced—or "boosted"—by the communication of positive information of older worker abilities and achievements (Gaillard & Desmette, 2010). In other words, when an organization promotes its achievements (or those of their similarly aged colleagues), older workers tend to be motivated, productive, and satisfied. Whether these positive messages are conveyed interpersonally (e.g., from boss to worker), in small groups (e.g., in meetings), or via widespread distribution throughout the organization (e.g., via blogs and ceremonies), such positive communication can help debunk common ageist stereotypes and may lead to greater morale and even productivity among the older workforce. Many consultants use this reasoning as a rationale for their age diversity training. For example, at both Scripps Health in San Diego and Michelin North America in South Carolina, long-standing service anniversaries are celebrated with special announcements, parties and awards. But there is also something extra special at Michelin for long-standing employees—you guessed it—free tires!

Age Discrimination Training

Communication, age diversity, and legal consultants (sometimes as a team and sometimes individually) may be called upon to advise organizations in the area of age discrimination. For the intergroup-trained consultant, the overarching objective of a given training program would most likely be to foster employee awareness of how intergroup ageist stereotypes and biases impact older individuals. The communication specialist would typically add to this by highlighting the key role that language plays in intergroup interaction. Common consulting methods to achieve these objectives include workplace ageism lectures, seminars, and online and video training modules.

Employees at all levels of the organization may require specific, *preventive* age discrimination training with specialized pre- and post-intervention assessment of participants. While the range of available instruments in this area is still limited, the vast pool of United States Equal Employment Opportunity Commission (EEOC) age discrimination legal cases provides the communication consultant with ample material to create his or her own "language and discrimination instrument" (for a detailed analysis of age discrimination lawsuits and the role of language in them, see McCann, 2012). The AARP website also has some basic quizzes and assessments. Age discrimination training is best done alongside a discrimination legal system expert due to the topic's sensitivity and specificity.

AN EPILOGUE

In closing, whether it be at a functional level (e.g., revising hiring and screening procedures, re-writing retirement and benefits policies, creating age friendly structures for evaluating job candidates) or a broader strategy level, the age diversity consultant has a tremendous opportunity to positively influence the organizations who call upon him or her. With the assistance of a well-trained and well-prepared consultant, the (perhaps poorly named) "graying" organization of today and tomorrow can move toward the goal of being a supportive and inclusive organization for employees of all ages.

NOTE

1. Age diversity consultants go by many monikers (inclusion consultant, diversity consultant, generational consultant, workforce effectiveness consultant, ageism consultant, etc.) and often are found via web searches with these terms. The age diversity space is largely dominated by boutique firms (sole proprietorships, etc.) who typically offer a range of diversity and generational training programs. Academics also operate in the age diversity consulting space, and are commonly identified by companies due to their research in the area (for example, I study the subject) or via their institutions. Boston College's Center on Aging & Work is one such well-known entity, and is also an excellent source of materials on the subject of workplace ageism. They disseminate practice case reports, research studies and executive case reports, and there is also a useful Innovative Practices Database on their web site. The USC Davis School of Gerontology, founded in 1975, is the oldest and largest school of gerontology in the world. The National Institute on Aging, SHRM and AARP are common entry portals for organizations seeking age diversity information. Many large organizations have *in-house* diversity and inclusion specialists (e.g., Deloitte's Chief Inclusion Officer) who handle age diversity along with other aspects of inclusion such as gender and race. Other organizations (e.g., Marriott International, Inc.) utilize a "Workforce Effectiveness and Diversity Department" who consider the generations in the workplace from a productivity standpoint, and specifically address the issue of how to engage and involve all the generations at work. Said differently, Marriott has moved from an "aging workforce strategy" to a "generational workforce strategy."

REFERENCES

AARP (2013, June). *Best Employers for Workers Over 50 Winners.* Retrieved from: http://www.aarp. org/work/on-the-job/info-06-2013/aarp-best-employers-winners-2013.html

Brown, N. (2009. September 14). Allstate to Pay $4.5M to Settle EEOC Age Bias Suit. Law360.com. Retrieved from http://www.law360.com/articles/121884/allstate-to-pay-4-5m-to-settle-eeoc-age-bias-suit

Crosby, J. (2011, August 22). 3M will pay $3 million to settle age-bias suit. *Star Tribune.* Retrieved from http://www.startribune.com/business/128179578.html

Gaillard, M., & Desmette, D. (2010). (In)validating stereotypes about older workers influences their intentions to retire early and to learn and develop. *Basic and Applied Social Psychology, 32,* 86–95.

Giles, H., Coupland, N., & Coupland, J. (Eds.) (1991). *Context of accommodation: Development of applied linguistics.* Cambridge, UK: Cambridge University Press.

Greenwald, J. (2013, December 10). Ruby Tuesday to settle EEOC class action age discrimination lawsuit. Business Insurance. Retrieved from http://www.businessinsurance.com/article/20131210/NEWS07/131219984

Hedden, R. (2013, August 26). *Aviation Week 2013 Workforce Study.* Retrieved from: http://awin.aviationweek.com/portals/aweek/pdf/awst_2013_workforceissue.pdf

McCann, R. M. (2012). *Ageism at work: The role of communication in a changing workplace.* Girona, Spain: Editorial Aresta.

McCann, R. M. & Giles, H. (2002). Ageism and the workplace: A communication perspective. In T. D. Nelson (Ed.) *Ageism* (pp. 163–199). Cambridge, MA: MIT Press.

McCann, R. M. & Giles, H. (2006). Communication with people of different ages in the workplace: Thai and American data. *Human Communication Research, 32,* 74–108.

Posthuma, R. A., & Campion, M. A. (2009). Age stereotypes in the workplace: Common stereotypes, moderators, and future research directions. *Journal of Management, 35,* 158–188.

Roundtree, L. (2011). *Executive Case Report No. 4. Age: A 21st Century Diversity Imperative.* Chestnut Hill, MA: Boston College, The Sloan Center on Aging & Work.

Tajfel, H., & Turner, J. C. (1986). The social identity theory of intergroup behavior. In S. Worchel & W. G. Austin (Eds.), *Psychology of intergroup relations* (pp. 7–17). Chicago, IL: Nelson-Hall.

Verrier, R. (2010, January 23). Hollywood writers' age-discrimination case settled. *Los Angeles Times.* Retrieved from http://articles.latimes.com/2010/jan/23/business/la-fi-ct-writers23-2010jan23

World Health Organization (2014, October). *10 facts on ageing and the life course.* Retrieved from: http://www.who.int/features/factfiles/ageing/en/

Contributor Bios

Jennifer H. Waldeck (Ph.D., University of California, Santa Barbara) is Associate Professor of Communication Studies at Chapman University, where she also teaches in the M.S. program in Health and Strategic Communication. Her research in the areas of organizational and instructional communication and new technology has appeared in such journals as *Communication Monographs; Communication Education; The Journal of Applied Communication Research; Journal of Business Communication; Learning, Media, and Technology;* and *Journal of Education for Business.* She is author of a number of book chapters, co-author of *Business and Professional Communication in a Digital Age* and author of *Communication Competence: Goals & Contexts.* For several years, she worked full-time in the consulting and performance improvement industry for Scher Group, based in Cleveland, OH. Over the past 20 years, she has provided consulting services in the automotive, education, healthcare, real estate, financial services, public service and safety, and industrial sectors. Her roles have involved curriculum design, training and speaking, program evaluation, research design and data analysis, teambuilding and conflict facilitation, strategic planning leadership, and process and task analysis.

David R. Seibold (Ph.D., Michigan State University) is Professor and Vice Chair of Technology Management (College of Engineering), Professor of

Communication by courtesy (Division of Social Sciences), and Director of the Graduate Program in Management Practice, at the University of California, Santa Barbara. His research and teaching center on managing innovation, technology teams, group decision making and interpersonal influence, management communication and organizational change, and theory-practice issues. He is a former editor of the *Journal of Applied Communication Research*. Author of more than 140 books, articles and chapters, he is a Fellow of the International Communication Association and a Distinguished Scholar of the National Communication Association. He has consulted widely for nearly forty years, and with corporations, new ventures, healthcare systems, and nonprofit organizations. Working with more than 75 organizations in the technology, energy, financial, hospitality, entertainment, health, and human services sectors, he has consulted with talent from nearly every area and at all organizational levels from front-line teams and first-level supervisors through C-suite executives. His roles have included executive coach, strategic planning consultant, facilitator, technical advisor, program evaluator, trainer, curriculum designer, process consultant, and featured speaker.

Joshua B. Barbour (Ph.D., University of Illinois at Urbana-Champaign) is an assistant professor of Communication Studies in the Moody College of Communication at the University of Texas at Austin and a senior consultant at The Aslan Group. Dr. Barbour has worked as a consultant in areas of communication process design, analytics, and leadership for 15 years. His past projects have focused on collaborative, engaged scholarship in organizations including a toxic waste storage facility; nuclear power plants; organizations involved in disaster preparation, response and recovery; and healthcare organizations. His work has appeared in Communication Monographs, Management Communication Quarterly, Communication Theory, the Journal of Applied Communication Research, the Journal of Health Communication, and the Journal of Communication.

Steven A. Beebe (Ph.D. University of Missouri-Columbia) is Regents' and University Distinguished Professor of Communication Studies at Texas State University where his research and teaching focus on communication training and development, group communication, instructional communication, and communication skill development. He has been a communication consultant, trainer, and conference speaker for more than 40 years with numerous clients including IBM, 3M, Motorola, American Express,

Side by Side Consulting, Prentice-Hall, Pearson, the Governor of Texas Executive Development Program, the U.S. Departments of Education and Defense. He is author and co-author of 12 books, and over 50 articles and book chapters. He is the senior author of *Training and Development: Enhancing Communication and Leadership Skills* and *Business and Professional Communication: Principles and Skills for Leadership*. He is past president of the National Communication Association.

Franklin J. Boster (Ph.D., Michigan State University) is Professor of Communication at Michigan State University where he teaches classes and conducts research in social influence, methods, and statistics. He also holds appointments as Adjunct Professor at the Michigan State University College of Law, as a Research Fellow of the Trial Practice Institute at the Michigan State University College of Law, and as an Adjunct Professor in the School of Community and Behavioral Health at the University of Iowa. He is the recipient of the Distinguished Faculty Award at Michigan State University (2003), the Faculty Impact Award from the College of Communication Arts and Sciences (2009), the Outstanding Achievement Award for Teaching (Arizona State University, College of Public Programs, 1981), the Charles H. Woolbert Award for Scholarship of Exceptional Originality and Influence (National Communication Association, 1989), the B. Aubrey Fisher Mentorship Award (International Communication Association, 2005), and the John E. Hunter Meta-Analysis Award (International Communication Association, 1998). He has consulted with numerous organizations, particularly marketing research firms and educational research firms.

Michael J. Cody (Ph.D., Michigan State University) is Professor at the Annenberg School for Communication, at the University of Southern California, where he has worked since 1982. He has served as the Associate Director of the School of Communication and as the Director of Doctoral Studies. He served as Editor-in-Chief of the Journal of Communication and Communication Theory. He published many original research articles, co-authored two textbooks, and co-edited five books on interpersonal communication and social influence processes. Additionally, Dr. Cody has served on the Advisory Board of the Office of Hollywood Health and Society (housed in the Norman Lear Center at USC) and the Board of Directors for Population Media Center (in Vermont). He has engaged in extensive legal consulting in the cities of Long Beach, Los Angeles and Palm Springs (CA), typically on causes of fraud, deception and misrepresentation.

John Daly (Ph.D., Purdue University) is the Liddell Professor in the Moody College of Communication, the Texas Commerce Bancshares Professor in the McCombs School of Business, and Regents Distinguished Teaching Professor at the University of Texas. He has published more than 120 scholarly articles, and nine books. He has served as President of the National Communication Association, Chair of the Council of Communication Associations, and on the Board of Directors of both the International Customer Service Association and the International Communication Association. He is a National Communication Association Distinguished Scholar and a Fellow of the International Communication Association. His work has been cited in many popular outlets including the *Wall Street Journal,* *the Washington Post, Investors Business Daily,* and *The New York Times.* He has worked with more than 300 organizations, public and private, in more than 20 countries including Goldman Sachs, JP MorganChase, Amgen, Merck, Pfizer, USAA, State Farm, Union Pacific, LG, Kraft, Apple, HP, IBM, PetroChina, Shell, ExxonMobil, CB&I, Halliburton, AT&T, Home Depot, Texas Instruments, UPS, McCarthy, American Airlines, United Airlines, 3M, Frito-Lay, Dell, and Samsung. In the governmental arena he has worked with a variety of local, state, and federal agencies throughout the U.S. including the White House.

Shirley J. Faughn (Ph.D., University of Illinois at Urbana-Champaign) is the co-founder of The Aslan Group, a leadership consulting firm in Champaign, IL and a retired faculty member in the Department of Communication, University of Illinois. She has instructed university courses in Communication for Business Leaders in the M.B.A. Program and Organizational Communication courses in the Department of Communication at the University of Illinois-Urbana-Champaign. She has 35 years of supervisory, training, group facilitation, and executive coaching experience in a wide variety of organizations across all fields and all levels. She serves as a process consultant, facilitator, and executive coach in areas of leadership and communication, specifically on listening, change management, conflict resolution, dialogue, transformational leadership, team building, speech writing, presentation, and issues of concern for women leaders.

Joseph P. Folger (Ph.D., University of Wisconsin) is Professor of Adult and Organizational Development at Temple University. He is a co-founder and fellow of the Institute for the Study of Conflict Transformation (www. transformativemediation.org). His work at the Institute included assisting with the design and delivery of the United States Postal Service REDRESS mediation program, as well as conducting assessment and benchmarking research for numerous organizations and mediation agencies. He has worked extensively as a consultant in organizational, community, court and small group disputes. He has acted as an executive coach and team development specialist in over 50 organizations. Folger has published extensively in the areas of communication and conflict, mediation, and third-party intervention processes. He has authored, coauthored, or edited four award-winning books on the topics of conflict and mediation, and delivered numerous keynote addresses on this issue. Most recently, he coedited *Transformative Mediation: A Sourcebook — Resources for Conflict Intervention Practitioners and Programs.*

Marian Houser (Ph.D., University of Tennessee, Knoxville) is Professor of Communication Studies and Associate Dean of Research and Faculty Development for the College of Fine Arts and Communication at Texas State University. She is an expert in the field of instructional communication, with a special emphasis on student learning, instructional training and development methods, student engagement, and the student-teacher relationship. She won the University President's Award for Research and was a recent recipient of the University Mariel M. Muir Excellence in Mentoring Award. Dr. Houser currently serves as editor of *Communication Teacher,* a National Communication Association journal. She has published over 35 research studies in national, international, and regional journals; three book chapters; and is the coauthor of an interpersonal communication textbook. She developed and published the widely-used and cited *Learner Empowerment, Learning Indicators,* and *Classroom Engagement scales.* Her work has been featured in *Men's Health Magazine* and *Psychology Today.* Over the past 10 years she has provided workshops and consulting around the country on presentational speaking, assessment, leader/instructor training, course and program design, and program evaluation.

Robert L. Husband (Ph.D., University of Illinois at Urbana-Champaign) is a retired faculty member and Director of Applied Communication Students in the Department of Communication at the University of Illinois at Urbana-Champaign. He has published or presented more than thirty-five papers and articles on a variety of communication related topics. His work has appeared in *Small Group Communication, Vocational and Technical Education Monographs, Quarterly Journal of Speech, Simulations & Games,* and *International Journal of Listening.* As co-founder and senior partner of The Aslan Group, he has served as a consultant to some fifty corporations, organizations, and institutions. Recognized nationally for his work in organizational leadership and management training, he consults primarily in the areas of executive development, leadership training, executive dialogue, strategic planning, team building, and conflict management. He also has had extensive experience evaluating communication structures of healthcare organizations, businesses, and administrative units in universities and small colleges.

Peter F. Jorgensen (Ph.D., University of Arizona) is Professor and Chair of the Department of Communication at Western Illinois University. He primarily teaches graduate and undergraduate courses in the communication department's organizational communication sequence. He is a former chair of the National Communication Association's Training and Development Division, and has presented a number of professional papers to national and international communication associations. He has published several disciplinary and interdisciplinary articles and book chapters. He has consulted for a number of regional, national and international organizations over the past thirty years, including Commonwealth Edison, Boise-Cascade, William C. Brown Publishing, MidAmerica National Bank, Caterpillar Inc., the Illinois Farm Bureau, Southwest Airlines, the Illinois Area Health Education Center, Gardner-Denver Manufacturing Products Group, and Roquette-America. His roles have included serving as a strategic planning consultant, facilitator, trainer, curriculum designer, program evaluator, and process consultant.

Patricia Kearney (Ed.D., West Virginia University) is Distinguished Professor of Communication at California State University, Long Beach. Her research and teaching, both theoretical and applied, focus on instructional communication, organizational training and development. The former editor of *Communication Education,* Kearney has written a variety of textbooks and industrial training packages, and she has published more than 150 research articles, chapters, and commissioned research reports and instructional modules. She is listed among the 100 most published scholars and among the top 15 published female scholars in her discipline. Kearney is the education director for Ross.Campbell, a Sacramento-based marketing and media production firm specializing in cause-related, social, and environmental issues.

Joann Keyton (Ph.D., Ohio State University) is Professor of Communication at North Carolina State University. She specializes in group communication and organizational communication in applied settings. Her current research examines the collaborative processes and relational aspects of interdisciplinary teams, participants' use of language in team meetings, the multiplicity of cultures in organizations, and how messages are manipulated in sexual harassment. She is the editor of *Small Group Research*, and a former Editor of the *Journal of Applied Communication Research*. Her research is field focused and she was honored with the 2011 Gerald Phillips Award for Distinguished Applied Communication Scholarship by the National Communication Association. Dr. Keyton has consulted with profit and nonprofit organizations, and served as an expert witness in litigation. As a consultant, she has been invited to consult on legal and policy issues; develop and deliver training on teamwork, collaboration, and sexual harassment; and facilitate interactions among stakeholders.

Gary L. Kreps (Ph.D., U of Southern California) is University Distinguished Professor and Director of the Center for Health and Risk Communication at George Mason University. He conducts research on health and risk communication, with a major focus on reducing health inequities, and has published in more than 420 articles, books, and chapters. He coordinates the Fairfax County Health Literacy Initiative community collaborative that develops culturally-sensitive health information programs for at-risk populations and co-directs the Global Advocacy Leadership Academy (GALA) for promoting effective consumer health advocacy. He served as the founding Chief of the Health Communication and Informatics Research Branch at the National Cancer Institute (NIH), where he planned national research programs for promoting cancer prevention and control. Gary has served as an organizational consultant for many years, in the areas of advertising, marketing, public relations, and organizational research. He currently offers applied research and training consultation services, primarily in the healthcare sector, for hospitals, clinics, government agencies (such as the FDA, VHA, CDC, and NIH), public health departments, foreign governments, research firms, and health promotion organizations.

Robert M. (Bob) McCann (Ph.D., University of California, Santa Barbara) is Associate Dean for Global Initiatives at the UCLA Anderson School of Management, where he is also on the School's Management & Organization faculty. In addition to his roles at UCLA, Dr. McCann is the President of the McCann Group, Incorporated, a consulting firm that specializes in the training of executives and professionals in workplace age diversity, persuasion, leadership, and all aspects of the strategic use of communication in business settings. He has over twenty years of experience working with Boards of Directors, C-Suite executives and management teams at major corporations both in the USA and across Asia. He has been published in several major refereed communication journals and has won research awards. He serves on the executive editorial board of the Journal of Asian Pacific Communication. His latest (2012) book is entitled Ageism at Work: The Role of Communication in a Changing Workplace.

Loyd S. Pettegrew (Ph.D., University of Michigan) is Professor of Marketing & Health Communication and former director of the Center for Organizational Communication in the Department of Communication at the University of South Florida. He also spent a year as a senior vice president for Louis Harris & Associates, the international public opinion research firm and was a member of the Board of Trustees for the Arthur W. Page Society, an association of Fortune 200 company chief communications officers. His research and teaching center on healthcare organizations, marketing communications and organizational change. He has one book and 38 articles in top communication and business journals. Over his 40 year career, he has consulted widely for companies like Yamaha USA & Yamaha Canada, Media General, AT&T, New York Yankees, Verizon, Outback Steakhouse Incorporated, CIGNA Insurance, Brighthouse Networks, along with a variety of hospitals, healthcare practices and nonprofit organizations. His work includes training program design and delivery, executive strategy, communication audits, product design and introduction strategies, customer feedback research, and corporate core competency analysis.

Timothy G. Plax (Ph.D, University of Southern California) is Distinguished Professor of Communication Studies. His research and teaching focus on social influence and interpersonal and organizational communication, but he is best known for his research in communication in instruction. His professional experiences include six years as a member of the Executive Staff at The Rockwell International Corporation and 35 years as a consultant in corporate, governmental, and instructional arenas. He has published over 150 manuscripts including textbooks, chapters, research articles, and commissioned research reports. He is listed among the 20 most published scholars in his discipline. He is a recipient of a number awards including the CSULB Distinguished Alumnus Award, the CSULB Distinguished Faculty Research and Creative Activity Award, the CSULB Associated Students Presidential Award, and both the "Triad of Excellence" Engineering Award and the Distinguished Research Award from the Space Shuttle Orbiter Division of The Rockwell International Corporation.

Sean Ross (Ph.D., Capella University) is Chief Operating Officer of Professional Consulting Associates, LLC, a Columbus, OH-based firm specializing communication and leadership training for public service organizations, where he is responsible for daily operations oversight, project management, leadership initiatives, program performance, and client growth. He is a former award-winning teacher, coach, and Dean of Students in the Columbus (OH) City School District. Additionally, he was Director of Diversity and Equity in the Dublin (OH) school district, where his responsibilities included program evaluation, community engagement initiatives, professional development, and training. He has a master's degree in Educational Administration and a doctorate in Leadership and Educational Administration.

Jesse Sostrin (Ph.D., Fielding Graduate University) is an internationally recognized author and thought leader whose innovative ideas on leadership and the changing world of work have been featured in a variety of media outlets, including MSNBC, Fox Business, NPR, *Entreprenur, Inc., FastCompany,* and *The Washington Post.* As a leadership coach and organizational consultant, Sostrin is known for translating complex ideas about the workplace into simple language and useful tools. He has worked with Fortune 500 companies as well as education, government, and nonprofit sector organizations including University of Arizona, InfoGard Laboratories, PR Newswire, Hyatt, MillerCoors, Walmart, ConAgra, Microsoft, and Allstate. Sostrin is also an experienced academic, serving as an adjunct faculty member at the Orfalea College of Business at California Polytechnic State University, and delivering lectures at The University of Arizona, and the University of California at Davis, among others. He has a Ph.D. in Human and Organizational Systems, and an M.A. in Organization Management & Development. He is the author of *The Manager's Dilemma, Beyond the Job Description,* and *Re-Making Communication at Work.* Learn more at www.jessesostrin.com.

Keri K. Stephens (Ph.D., The University of Texas at Austin) is Associate Professor and the Associate Director for Partnerships in the Center for Health Communication in the Moody College of Communication at The University of Texas at Austin. Her research on how people use technology in corporations and organizations has been published in over 50 articles, book chapters, and encyclopedia entries, and a co-authored. She is an Associate Editor of *Management Communication Quarterly,* the Secretary of the Organizational Communication Division of the International Communication Association, and past Chair of the Training and Development Division of the National Communication Association. Before she pursued an academic career, she worked as an analytical chemist, a field engineer, and in sales, marketing, project management, and corporate training. Over the past 20 years she has consulted, coached, trained, and facilitated projects with clients in industries such as biotechnology, computer storage services, oil and gas, public relations, and government.

Eric D. Waters (M.B.A., The University of Texas at Arlington) is a doctoral candidate in the Moody College of Communication at the University of Texas at Austin. His research investigates the use of information and communication technologies (ICTs) in organizations. He has co-authored a book chapter, edited another, and received a top paper award. Before entering the academy, he worked for over 10 years in the automotive industry with a primary responsibility of recommending and implementing process improvements at multiple organizational levels. He currently coaches M.B.A. students in the McCombs School of Business at the University of Texas at Austin on various aspects of business communication such as presentation, personal branding, and networking. His other roles have included trainer, facilitator, and strategic advisor.

Index